DIALOGUE ON GRIEF AND CONSOLATION

VIBS

Volume 208

Robert Ginsberg
Founding Editor

Leonidas Donskis
Executive Editor

Associate Editors

G. John M. Abbarno
George Allan
Gerhold K. Becker
Raymond Angelo Belliotti
Kenneth A. Bryson
C. Stephen Byrum
Harvey Cormier
Robert A. Delfino
Rem B. Edwards
Malcolm D. Evans
Daniel B. Gallagher
Andrew Fitz-Gibbon
Francesc Forn i Argimon
William Gay
Dane R. Gordon
J. Everet Green
Heta Aleksandra Gylling

Matti Häyry
Steven V. Hicks
Richard T. Hull
Michael Krausz
Mark Letteri
Vincent L. Luizzi
Adrianne McEvoy
Peter A. Redpath
Arleen L. F. Salles
John R. Shook
Eddy Souffrant
Tuija Takala
Emil Višňovský
Anne Waters
James R. Watson
John R. Welch
Thomas Woods

a volume in
Lived Values, Valued Lives
LVVL
Richard T. Hull, Editor

DIALOGUE ON GRIEF AND CONSOLATION

Terence O'Connell

Amsterdam - New York, NY 2009

Cover Design: Studio Pollmann

The paper on which this book is printed meets the requirements of "ISO 9706:1994, Information and documentation - Paper for documents - Requirements for permanence".

ISBN: 978-90-420-2627-8
E-Book ISBN: 978-90-420-2628-5
© Editions Rodopi B.V., Amsterdam - New York, NY 2009
Printed in the Netherlands

**Lived Values Valued Lives
(LVVL)**

Richard T. Hull
Editor

Other titles in LVVL

Dixie Lee Harris:
Encounters in My Travels:
Thoughts Along the Way.
2006. VIBS 174

Craig Clifford:
Learned Ignorance in the Medicine Bow Mountains:
A Reflection on Intellectual Prejudice.
2008. VIBS 199

To My Family
Past, Present, and Future

CONTENTS

EDITORIAL FOREWORD RICHARD T. HULL		xi
PREFACE		xiii
INTRODUCTION		1
ONE	Grief and Anger	7
TWO	"She's No Longer Suffering"	13
THREE	"She Had a Good Life"	23
FOUR	Types of Grief and Comfort Strategies	29
FIVE	The Annihilation Consolation	41
SIX	Death as a Deprivation	49
SEVEN	Would Immortality Be Good?	67
EIGHT	Life as a Work of Art	91
NINE	Death's Impact on Survivors	109
TEN	Is Constant Change Consoling?	127
ELEVEN	Is Present Existence Better than Past Existence?	161
TWELVE	Grief and Death's Inevitability	179
THIRTEEN	The Cycle of Life and the Importance of Emotions	191
FOURTEEN	Benefits and Harms of Grief	211
FIFTEEN	Grief as a Way of Knowing	233
SIXTEEN	Conclusion	257

ENDNOTES	265
BIBLIOGRAPHY	269
FOR FURTHER READING	271
ABOUT THE AUTHOR	281
INDEX	283

EDITORIAL FOREWORD

The Lived Values, Valued Lives Series is comprised of biographies, loosely defined, that express and explore how values appear in and shape human lives. The series aims at provoking readers to engage in reflective exploration of the values expressed in the decisions, actions, and thoughts of philosophically reflective individuals. From one another's narratives we can learn much and come to consider possibilities that might otherwise never occur to us.

The series aims at readers of all ages looking for inspiration not only for course papers but also for their lives. The value of thoughtful reflection, not conversion, is the goal. Terry O'Connell's *Dialogue on Grief and Consolation* is the third and notably valuable offering in this series.

Few events evoke such dramatic and sustained negative emotions as the death of a loved one. Philosophers throughout history have sought to provide reflective consolations for us as we cope with the finality of death in lives we have come to value. As friends of grieving ones, we feel awkward and inadequate to provide consoling remarks.

In this volume, Terry O'Connell, himself struggling with the deep feelings of loss of his mother, has examined thoroughly and eloquently the kinds of things we say to one another in the context of consoling. His masterful command of the history of philosophical and religious literature on consolation of individuals grieving loved ones' loss has provided him the widest scope in which to examine consolations that fail in one way or another to satisfy.

Written in the form of dialogue among close friends, O'Connell's characters capture philosophical discourse at its finest.

This book may make readers uncomfortable. Many of our consoling remarks are couched in cliché-ridden language. The effect of seeing that language analyzed and dissected may be unsettling. Yet, the possibility of meaningful, satisfactory, genuinely consoling behavior toward the grieving is a worthy objective that humanizes us and gives us alternatives to mindless or unsatisfying communication.

O'Connell's work earned him a PhD and the praise of those of his examining committee. Now, for the first time, he is making this brilliant work available to all readers. This work should be required reading for any professional dealing with the emotions caused by the loss of departed family and friends. Those of us who suffer those emotions need it even more.

Richard T. Hull, Editor
Lived Values Valued Lives Special Series
Tallahassee, Florida

PREFACE

As the structure of this book is unusual, an overview of its structure might be helpful to the reader. The dialogue form for presenting philosophical ideas is well suited to the topic of consolation because the goal of consolation is not simply to defend a thesis but to help a grieving person. Accordingly, the main body of this work is a dialogue—sixteen chapters in all. Three main characters, all close friends, participate in the dialogue. One grieves for the death of a parent; the other two try to comfort him. They try to comfort him in different ways, but the most obvious way—because the most verbal—is that they try to comfort him by offering reasons why he should not grieve (so much). Reasons not to grieve (so much) are what I mean by "consolations" in this work. Many of the consolations I consider can be found (scattered) in others' work; consolation was a common theme in classical literature. Other consolations come from contemporary conversations between grievers and those who would comfort them.

Most of the dialogue takes place at a Hard Rock Café—an apparently informal venue for such a serious conversation. I use songs in the background to underscore the idea then under consideration. These songs also demonstrate that some of the examined ideas find expression in popular culture.

Each chapter is followed by discussion topics. In addition, thirteen chapters are followed by summaries of the argument within the chapter. Though I attempt to provide a comprehensive review of consolations, no consolation drawn from a belief in the afterlife is used in this book, partly because I am quite skeptical of them, but largely because that topic alone requires a whole series of books.

For those who want "to read more about it," the suggestions for further reading could keep a diligent reader busy for years. The suggestions for further reading direct the reader to a wealth of literature, ancient, modern and contemporary, philosophical and psychological, which forms the basis of many of the ideas found in the dialogue. My comments accompanying those suggestions are designed to integrate the dialogue's discussion with these literary classics.

The discussion topics and many of the references are provided either to assist the reader attain an even more thorough understanding of grief than that squeezed between these covers or to acknowledge that we need to consider more. Perhaps the dialogue in this book will be part of a larger "dialogue" within the reader; a dialogue between this book and the reader's understanding of the discussion topics and other referenced works.

My emphasis is on the insights on grief to be obtained from philosophical analysis. Within this emphasis, I have deliberately omitted little because, again, the purpose is not to examine a thesis, but to illuminate a crisis.

Still, we can find illumination other than that which comes from philosophy. Philosophical insights on grief are not independent of psychological studies of grief. Indeed, I argue that the two disciplines complement each other on this subject. Partly because philosophy is sometimes done carelessly, it is understandable that psychologists have little acknowledged the relevance of philosophy to their study of grief. But they neglect careful philosophy to the detriment of a greater understanding of it.

Thoughts in general and evaluations in particular, and consequently emotions, have causes and effects, so are properly studied in psychology; but thoughts and evaluations have truth conditions and logical implications as well. Hence, these are properly studied by philosophical analysis. In addition, emotions are significant objects of study because they have value, and consequently are again of philosophical interest. In any case, as grief is so personal, powerful, and complex, I have not attempted to supplant other disciplines or other observations.

I wrote this book in response to my mother's death and the (I believe) frequently clumsy things that were said to console me. But as much as I disliked and even resented ill-conceived consolations, I did not want to be just "left alone" with my grief. I wanted a friend or two (if only imaginary) to gently "press" me and make me articulate the ideas (reasonable or unreasonable) that grief presupposes.

Fortunately, not all my friends are imaginary. If it weren't for Richard T. Hull, you would not be reading this book. Elizabeth D. Boepple provided great assistance in formatting and proofreading; David Danielson also assisted in proofreading.

Thanks to my wife, Barbara, for her patience on beautiful days I spent working on the manuscript, and for keeping this technophobe sane when things went awry.

Thanks especially to my daughter, Sara Beth, who gave up playtime so that I could finish the manuscript.

I also owe thanks to three old friends: James Nelson, for his assistance at a very early stage in preparation of the manuscript; Michael Schmid, who was my model for the character "Phil" in the dialogue; and Thomas Fumarelli, who dined with me at the Hard Rock Café the summer my mom died and who tried to console me by stating that my mom was no longer suffering.

INTRODUCTION

Is Grief Amenable to Reason?

Have you lost a loved one? The loss is inestimable and the grief excruciating. *What* helped you? Did anyone say anything comforting? On the other hand, did anyone offer a consolation you resented? Have you ever tried to comfort someone with a terminal illness or someone else who has lost a loved one? Knowing how to help, or what to *say* that it is not trite, insincere, or superficial is difficult. The point of view of a grieving person is very different from that of those who would want to offer comfort. In a multicultural society such as ours, it is even more difficult to anticipate the beliefs of the grieving person.

This book explores the perspective of a grieving person. It considers the merit and potential harm of alternative comfort strategies. As a philosophical analysis of grief, it emphasizes understanding beliefs that underlie grief and the usefulness (or dangers) of emotions. Because grief is so complex and sensitive, a narrow approach runs the risk of alienating the grieving person.

The ideas in this book unfold as a dialogue among three characters; their discussion is broad and fundamental. Two close friends try to persuade a third to lessen, or even stop grieving. They give him reasons such as, "She's no longer suffering," in an attempt to alter his feelings. In the present work, "consolation" means an argument or reason that one should not grieve (so much). Readers will discover that the grieving character resists his friends' consolations. The eventual consensus of the discussion is that many consolations are unconvincing.

Many take the view that emotions are not amenable to reasoning, that reasons cannot dissuade emotions in general or grief in particular. Others object that trying to use arguments or reasons to dissuade grief "disrespects" the griever's feelings. I hold that it is not feelings, but the grieving *persons* themselves who need our respect. In general, we respect others by reasoning with them, but only if we attempt to engage their presuppositions. Consolers disrespect grievers, not by reasoning on such an emotional subject, but by failing to engage the beliefs of the grieving person.

The question of reason's control over emotions such as grief has two aspects: How can or should we mentally prepare for losses before they occur, and perhaps even long before they occur? Mental preparation for death, especially long before its occurrence, would be of limited value were we incapable of believing that death will occur. Some authors have argued that people do not believe in their mortality. One reason for this phenomenon might be that people do not plan on dying; most of our plans presuppose our continued existence. Healthy persons are not "ready for" death; they have other plans.

The situation considered in the dialogue is one in which the loved one has already died. This brings us to the second aspect to be considered: What can persuasion do *after* the loss has occurred to limit the negative emotion? That grief is amenable to reasoning is a fundamental assumption of the dialogue, though only marginally discussed by the characters.

The consolations examined in the dialogue have two sources. One is the contemporary conversation between grievers and those who would console them, for example when consolers offer "She had a full life" or "She wouldn't want you to grieve." The other source for consolations considered is literature dealing with grief, a quite common theme in ancient western literature, for example.

In contrast to many ancient consolers, contemporary psychologists who have studied grief take a dimmer view of the ability of arguments to alleviate grief. Often, contemporary psychologists insist that grief is useful (or inevitable) as a phase, assisting the bereaved to adjust to the loss. Sometimes they also argue that some attempts to alleviate grief obstruct adjustment and so do not benefit the grieving person.

However, ancient consolers were not completely unaware of the psychological difficulties confronting consolers. Nevertheless, they also claimed that some of the bereaved maintained their grief even after the natural impulse to it was gone. Consolatory literature often took the form of epistles addressed to a mourner. In one such epistle, the philosopher Seneca wrote that the bereaved mother required consolation since she was now grieving out of habit, and she was ashamed to end an already long and passionate grief which had become a substitute for her son.[1] Despite these being Seneca's reasons for thinking his correspondent needed consolation, his consolations went beyond pointing out that habit is not by itself a sufficient reason to do anything; or that if something is wrong, it does not make it better to stubbornly abide by it; or that sorrow and inhibition are poor substitutes for a loveable son, even for the desperate. Instead, he offered many consolations that argued that death is not terrible. We cannot know whether the futility of Seneca's consolations only caused the forlorn mother to defiantly persist in her grief.

Contemporary Views on the Amenability of Grief to Reason

Moral judgments about grief, prevalent in contemporary psychological literature, hold that while we should limit grief, moderate grief should not be criticized. Grief should be "worked through," not "suppressed" because grief is inevitable and necessary for physical and psychological health. It fosters adjustment to a person's changed circumstances. While we should not criticize moderate grief, grief is *not* "warranted" in the same way as a conclusion is warranted based on evidence. Indeed, some psychologists do offer consolations to the bereaved. However, some contradictions might hold between the view that moderate grief should not be criticized and the view that offering consolations to persons with moderate grief is beneficial.

Introduction 3

The best known author on the subject of grief, Elizabeth Kübler-Ross, has offered several consolations, mostly directed against the claim that death is a terrible evil for the dead. A single example of her *many* unconvincing consolations is that she thinks that the fear of death is largely due to modern, technological society. People no longer die in familiar, loving, comfortable surroundings, but in antiseptic, impersonal hospitals. She believes that we fear death because it is associated with the evils of dying in the modern way.[2] Whatever the benefits or harms which might come of dying the modern way, Kübler-Ross's explanation is belied by the ancient need for consolation exemplified by classical consolers.

Despite the consolations she has offered, Kübler-Ross does not think that we should criticize moderate grief. I think that her most promising reason for the belief that moderate grief should not be criticized, despite all the criticisms she made of it, is that grief is a process which must be completed before grieving can end. To understand that process, I turn to the work of Collin Murray Parkes and Robert S. Weiss.

Psychological literature on grief is surfeit with comments that the bereaved must express their feelings to get over them. We might suspect that this conclusion is the result of nothing more than taking a physical metaphor or picture of the emotions too literally. We picture the emotions as something like a body of water behind a dam, and which, when full, must be sluiced off else the dam burst.

Some studies suggest that "dammed up" stress is harmful. But does the bereaved have no (intellectually honest) alternative between damming up or suppressing grief on the one hand and grieving on the other? Is ending grieving possible, not through suppression but through consolation?

Without relying on any metaphor, Parkes and sometime collaborator Weiss give an account of grief that might explain the process of (reactive) grief, and why it must complete itself. According to Parkes, the survivor searches for the dead intimate, even while acknowledging that the search is futile.[3] Because their dead loves ones were a part of many experiences, similar situations cause the survivors to mentally search for their dead intimates. The searching response is easily elicited because a person searching for an object that is difficult to find has heightened attention for that object or anything associated with it.[4] Of course, many things remind us of loved ones.

Sorrow pangs are (partly) the result of the frustration of this search.[5] Furthermore, one part of searching is keeping in mind the sought for object.[6] As the survivor knows that the person is dead, the survivor thinks about that death in addition to that person's life. The survivor might become obsessed with the lost person and with that person's death. Thinking about that person's death would "bring back" the feelings the survivor had when first learning of it.

This obsessive thinking and searching contribute to survivors' "retraining" themselves.[7] By searching for the lost object and reviewing the death of that person, survivors are finally able to stop responding in the same old way to stimuli that formerly elicited a response requiring the person who has died. For example, if dinner reminds the bereaved of the deceased family member, after a period of painful and obsessive thinking, the bereaved will stop thinking about the dead loved one at dinnertime.

Parkes is aware that this adjustment is a slow process, as it involves many different habits. For example, the bereaved needs to switch from using "we" to using "I" as in, "We/I had dinner last night." The transition is also slow because the bereaved does not desire to make those changes (without ambivalence).

The length and the course of the adjustment depend upon the attitude of the survivor. For example, desired transitions in life occur more quickly than those required of the bereaved.[8]

Parkes's account of the course of grief and its working itself out, as plausible as it is, is not a complete account of grief. The attitude of the survivor is a significant additional factor. If attitudes can be influenced by reasons, then it should be theoretically possible to modify grief through the presentation of evidence. But *if* it is the case that the length of grief is partly determined by the survivor's attitudes, *and if* these attitudes are subject to rational appraisal, then how could it be sensible to offer consolations *and* to maintain that grief has a course (of fairly great length) which it needs to run, as Kübler-Ross argues?

Grief is subject to rational control insofar as it is a response to *events* which, if the grieving person were to become convinced those events had never actually occurred, would more or less be stopped "in its tracks." So, the question concerning the rational control of grief is in part whether the survivor's *attitudes* that "underlie" the emotion are subject to rational control.

The survivor's attitudes towards the loved one's death are largely characterized by the belief that death is a terrible evil for the deceased and for those who love the deceased. I hold that these beliefs are as subject to rational appraisal as any other beliefs. The inefficacy of many consolations per se does not disprove the rational amenability of the survivor's attitudes. Instead, many consolations are largely inefficacious because they are generally poor arguments. Grief does not "close" the person's mind to sound consolations.

However, while resistance to retraining and consequent sorrow is partly due to the bereaved one's attitudes, still, retraining takes time even in the best of circumstances. Grief persists not only because the bereaved are ambivalent about the required retraining, but also because *any* extensive retraining takes time. Perhaps one reason for the anguish we feel during the first round of holidays following the death of a loved one (even if the holiday comes many months after the loss) is that the bereaved need to be retrained (to some extent) for each occasion.

My point is that we can maintain that grief must run its course and that this affect, or the *evaluations* upon which it is based, is rational in the sense of its being based upon evidence.

The "big picture" underlying this dialogue is first, as human psychology has its laws, under some conditions, grief is inevitable. Second, attitudes are still capable of rational assessment and assessment of attitudes can be one factor in human psychology. If we let it, the evidence for or against an attitude can influence corresponding emotions. Therefore, I conclude that emotions can be influenced by reasoning.

We can honestly assess feelings *and still* respect the person who has them. Emotions, including grief, can be stubborn or misdirected, and emotions can be painful in themselves, *especially* grief. Emotions can have harmful consequences. Regardless, they are amenable to reasoning, contrary to the detractors of emotion, who hold that emotions are irrational and should be reeled in, and contrary to the "protectors" of emotion, who hold that emotions are "nonrational"—neither right nor wrong—and therefore above (or below) criticism. Fortunately, emotions do not operate completely independently from judgment.

No analysis of grief and consolation is helpful if its results are merely superficial consolations. So, good philosophical analysis is useful even if only as a check to poor analysis of grief and death. As stated above, some think that it is disrespectful to criticize feelings. The view that feelings are neither right nor wrong and should not be examined critically is patronizing; but I suppose that view is as useful as attempting to discourage desperate or disingenuous consolations.

Philosophical analysis has a useful role in the alleviation of grief because grievers and consolers do not always try to understand grief. In their anguish, grievers might grasp at many unsound consolations. In contrast, I argue that *few* consolations are convincing; I offer to a grieving person only "strong medicine."

Many crises in life have practical solutions (we can prevent or mitigate the harm); we just need to find and implement them. Philosophy is often criticized as offering no practical solutions—being of no use in preventing or mitigating evils. When a loved one dies, the problem (prolonging life) is beyond practical solution. When there is no practical solution the desperate often turn to philosophy, as many turn to religion. But comforting words based on poor philosophical analysis run the risk of obstructing grief. *Rather than obstruct grief, careful philosophical analysis can aid adjustment, despite rejection of "easy answers," by supplying a better understanding of grief.*

One

GRIEF AND ANGER

On his way to meet two friends for dinner Jeff crossed the intersection at Fifth Avenue and Fifty-Seventh Street. He had passed there hundreds of times before, usually admiring the architecture, or spoiling his pleasure by grumbling about the misused wealth. Sometimes he would try to make the experience poignant by reminding himself that it was near this intersection that *Gentleman's Agreement*, one of his favorite novels, began. But this day, and for the previous six weeks, he was obsessed with one problem and had no concern for beauty or social ideals.

Jeff and Connie

Jeff entered the Solow Building and rode the elevator to Connie's forty-fifth floor office overlooking Central Park. As it was early in the evening the fading sunlight softly illuminated the park. In the distance, but seemingly near, the lights of Yankee Stadium shone brightly in preparation for a game. Alone in the company offices, Connie worked as the radio played "Ac-cent-chu-ate the Positive" by Johnny Mercer with Paul Weston's Orchestra. Connie buzzed in Jeff.

"Hi, Connie."

"Hello, Jeff, I'm glad you could make it. How are you?" Jeff shrugged and evasively returned the question. "Busy!" Connie answered. "I'll be through in a couple minutes. Oh! you know a little French, can you translate this memo?" Connie handed the memo to Jeff.

"I only know a few words and then only if it's about love, ice cream or philosophy, not finances," Jeff replied.

"Some scholar!" Connie teased.

While Connie organized for the following Monday, Jeff envied the view, and the radio played "Deep Purple" sung by Bea Wain with Larry Clinton and his Orchestra.

Connie rose and hugged Jeff. He half-heartedly returned her hug, but held it a moment longer than she. Stepping back Connie looked into Jeff's eyes and opened the subject most on his mind. "Like I said on the phone, I'm deeply sorry I was out of the country and couldn't be with you when your mom died."

"You didn't know. And if you had, there was nothing you could have done," Jeff said.

"I just meant that 'I wish I could have been with you,'" Connie said.

"Now neither one of us has our parents," Jeff said.

"What can you say?" Connie sighed.

Jeff said, "I don't know whether I've forgotten how long the grieving lasted when my dad died. I do remember feeling very bad on the first anniversary of his death, but this time the grief seems even more terrible and inescapable."

"It's worse with one's mother, they say," Connie said.

Jeff said, "In your case, your mother died *before* your father. I don't know, but I think that the sequence has a lot to do with the severity of the loss. It does seem more dreadful this time because it was the death of my remaining parent."

"How long ago did your dad die?" Connie asked.

"I was fourteen. Fifteen years ago," Jeff answered.

"Perhaps the time which has passed has made you forget just how bad it was then. Fresh pain almost always seems worse," Connie suggested.

Jeff replied, "I think that the passage of time not only makes the second loss *seem* worse, it also *makes* it worse. Of course, the loss of the remaining parent is worse because you don't have a parent upon which to rely. Having mom around every day helped so much when dad died. And she was strong."

"She had a son to care for. Perhaps your needs helped her," Connie added.

"Another result of these fifteen years is that I got to know my mom much better than I knew my dad. I'm reminded of her almost everywhere; my first thought about so many things is 'She liked this. She disliked that.' She was seldom indifferent!" Jeff said.

"Another thing. Not only did I know her longer and better, but there were more occasions for regrets," Jeff said.

"But you cared for her while she was sick. How long?" Connie asked.

"Four years. I took care *of* her, but sometimes it made me care *for* her less. But even prior to that there was ambivalence in my feelings toward her. As a boy I loved her as children love their mothers, and she always loved me; but I never adjusted comfortably to the kind of love we expect an older child to have. It created tension. Whenever we were apart, she wanted me to miss her and now I've waited until her death to miss her. I feel like a fool!" Jeff confided.

"There are always things to regret," Connie said.

"Therefore we shouldn't regret them?" Jeff replied.

"I'm not saying that. It's surprising when people say they have no regrets," Connie said.

"Maybe there are 'no regrets' kind of people, whatever that means. Or maybe they're lying to themselves to comfort themselves," Jeff said.

Connie said, "Maybe when people say they have no regrets what they mean is that, upon the whole, they have no regrets. And wouldn't you say that about your relationship with your mom?"

"Yes, I would. But anyway, I regret that it could only be said that upon the whole the relationship was good," Jeff said.

"Why regret the bad parts of a thing as long as it was good upon the whole?" Connie asked.

Rather than respond Jeff said, "I loved her but my ambivalence toward our relationship might have even resulted in her death being premature."

"What! How could you say that?! Didn't she die from an incurable cancer?" Connie asked eyes wide.

Jeff explained, "Presumably. One might think that, because of her diagnosis, at least her family would be spared doubts about the cause of her death, but that's not so. She had the disease for a long time and with a lot of pain and occasional complications but she had not, as far as outward appearances went, significantly declined since the diagnosis made four years earlier. Therefore, despite the specter of an incurable cancer, we were 'unprepared' and totally surprised by her death. We thought that the cancer had made no progress, until a couple months before her death, and even then I was told that it had grown only slightly. I projected that rate of increase into the future and ignorantly supposed that she had much longer to live. So not only were we surprised, we're still not completely sure of the cause of her death."

"What about an autopsy?" Connie asked.

"We didn't ask for one. I hated the idea but probably would have requested it except that I knew that my sisters would oppose it. At the time it was easy to bury my doubts about the cause of her death by revulsion at the idea of an autopsy and the anticipation of resistance. Recently my sisters expressed a wish that we had had an autopsy. I thought, 'Now you tell me!' But I think that that wish is a 'second thought' rather than a conviction upon which we would act if given the choice again. In any case, one thing that angers me about these events is that so little time and so little guidance, apart from ritual, is given for decisions about life and which will affect us the rest of our lives. Education doesn't prepare us for life's traumas."

"What could be done to prepare us for great losses? But, getting back to my earlier question: assuming the most likely cause, which is cancer, why do you partly blame yourself?" Connie asked.

Jeff said, "Not only are lessons sometimes learnt too late, which is a familiar lament, lessons also might be applied too late. I trusted the medical professionals. I trusted them with my mother's life. Even if, in fact, they were conscientious and my mother could not have lived longer, *I* was not conscientious enough. I realize that now because there are questions I now have about the treatment that I didn't have, though I should have had, when she was alive. Even if the doctors can satisfactorily answer these questions, the fact is that I'm only now asking them, after her death. And why wasn't I asking these questions before? Was it because I was less than totally committed to my mother's living? I know that many times people don't ask obvious questions because they don't really care about the truth."

Connie replied, "You're being *way* too hard on yourself! You're asking these questions now because previously you trusted the patient, your mother, to ask any obvious questions. She was a medical professional herself and an intelligent woman. But now that she's gone, you're left asking the questions.

It wasn't that you didn't care, it's because she did care and you relied on her. You didn't just trust the doctors!"

Jeff said, "Mom was intelligent and a nurse but these weren't good enough reasons to leave these things to her and I knew it, or should have known it. When it came to things she feared, and of course she feared cancer, she trusted too easily and questioned far too little, especially when she was given optimistic reports. And this horrible experience has taught me how little it can matter to have professional knowledge. I know so well, as a philosophy teacher, not to trust authority. I know this, you might say it's my business to know it, and yet I so easily trusted the doctors. Where was all my professional skepticism when it might have counted? In the classroom and the margins of my books."

"You raise a couple good points, but I think they can be used to forgive you, if you're willing to forgive yourself" Connie said.

"Yes?" Jeff asked, in a mixture of suspicion and hope.

"Fear made her too trusting and made her not apply her expertise. I think that fear did that to you, too. You were afraid of her death and so you didn't look too closely at her disease, its prognosis, or its treatment. Your mistakes, if you made any, were due to your love, not, as you say, because you weren't totally committed to her living," Connie said.

"Maybe you're right, but I regret other things as well. Things I didn't do for myself that I can't do now that she's dead," Jeff said.

"Such as?" Connie asked.

"That I've never married, never had a real career. A vocation, yes, but not one that has given me financial security. When dad died I was fourteen. I didn't think at that time that I should have accomplished more," Jeff explained.

"I understand," Connie said softly.

Jeff continued, "Suppose I do marry and have kids, there won't be any continuity in my life. So, not only do I feel bad that mom did not have the satisfaction of seeing my family, I feel bad because these two parts of my life will be separate. I won't have the satisfaction of seeing my mom and family together. A life should be more than the sum of its parts."

"I understand, and when you begin a family the experience will be tinged with pain, but you mustn't forego a family to avoid this bitterness," Connie said firmly.

"So I have less to which to look forward, as well as feeling guilty for having done this to myself," Jeff said.

Connie replied, "Having also grieved, I've read about the so-called phases of grief. Anger is one of them. I think that you're feeling anger, and without an obvious target for that feeling, you've directed it against *yourself*. You're not openly angry with the doctors because you don't know that their medical care was insufficient; you're not angry with God because you're an agnostic; and you're not angry with your mom. So, you're left with anger toward yourself—and maybe just a little toward your sisters. Your misdirected anger comes out as guilt. You're magnifying every flaw in your feelings toward your mom and ignoring the flaw in your anger—that it has no suitable object."

Connie tried to make a joke of her chastisement. "And where has your agnosticism gotten you? You're as hard on yourself as a stereotypical monk horrified by his every desire!"

Connie put her hand on the middle of Jeff's back and suggested, "Come on, let's head to the restaurant. Phil might be there already."

She added, "If you like, we can talk about this on the way." So saying, Connie switched off the radio, which was about to play George Gershwin's *Rhapsody in Blue*.

As they walked to the elevator Jeff continued, "As I said before, I miss her. I can't cook or eat the meals we used to share, nor can I watch the television shows we used to enjoy together. These remind me not only of my loss, but of hers as well, for she enjoyed these things. Even things I didn't like, but which she did, make me feel unwell because I think of what she's missing."

The elevator arrived and the ride interrupted their conversation. Connie and Jeff listened to a Muzak version of Simon and Garfunkel's "The Sounds of Silence." As she often does, Connie sang along under her breath, but stopped just prior to the line "Silence like a cancer grows."

Study Questions

(1) *Can* we prepare for either a loved one's death or our own death?
- Why or why not?
- If we can prepare, *should* we? (At the end of the book you might want to ask whether *this* book can help a person prepare for these events.)

(2) What *can* we do *after* a loved one's death to cope?

(3) Grief has been analyzed into the following phases or stages: denial, bargaining, anger, depression, and acceptance or resignation.
- Are acceptance and resignation the same?
- Do all these "phases" belong to both preparatory grief (grief before the loss) and reactive grief (grief after the loss)?

Two

"SHE'S NO LONGER SUFFERING"

Jeff and Connie resumed their conversation as they exited the elevator.

Connie began, "The only thing I can say, as some small consolation, is that she's no longer in pain. Four years is a terribly long time to be in pain. And as your mom was a very outgoing person and vigorous before the disease hit her, I'm sure it must have been very upsetting to her that she couldn't get around much anymore."

Jeff said, "Connie, many people have even gone so far as to say that she is better off that she's not suffering, but I don't understand how that can be much of a consolation."

Connie asked, "Why do you object to the consolation 'She's better off that she's not suffering?' After all, it's bad to suffer."

Jeff began, "True, and if death is annihilation, it's also true that mom is neither in physical pain nor is she suffering from frustration or in any other way. But if death is annihilation, as you and I think . . ."

"Yes."

"Then death not only ends suffering, it ends enjoyment as well. It isn't the end of her suffering that makes me grieve for her, nor am I grieving in the belief that she continues suffering pain or frustration. But I do believe that her death harmed her, for instance, by depriving her of the goods in her life. And that there were fewer goods in her life during the last part of her life doesn't give me reason to be cheered up."

Jeff continued, "You're not disingenuous, Connie, and that's one reason why it's good to talk with you at a time like this. I know it's tough to know what to say to a grieving person. Undoubtedly different grievers would like to hear different things. I'd like to hear the truth, and not be manipulated."

"Everyone thinks that's what they want," Connie said.

Jeff replied, "Otherwise they couldn't be manipulated! Well, let *us* try to rely on the truth. I sympathize with *you*. It's uncomfortable trying to help a grieving person."

"Especially you! But I'll try. Maybe because you're a challenge!" Connie said.

Jeff continued, "I feel better talking with you. Let's get back to the consolation that 'She's no longer suffering.' It's an *arbitrary* consolation. What I mean by calling it arbitrary is that it selects a truth which is comforting *because* it is comforting: while ignoring equally conspicuous truths that are grieving. Continuing with this example let me explain: 'She's not suffering' is comforting, but it is consistent with 'She's not enjoying' which is grieving.

I grieve, in part, because she's not enjoying. Unless one denies this or denies that it is something to grieve over, one is missing the point."

Connie said, "I agree with the objections you've made, but I think you've misinterpreted the point of the remark 'She's no longer suffering.' I agree that were it intended to prove that one should not grieve for a dead loved one, then it would not be a convincing argument, and for the reason you give. That is, it ignores the reasons why the person is grieving. And these reasons are right under the consoler's nose, so to speak."

"It's an unconvincing argument because it overlooks a countervailing truth, and because that truth, that she's no longer enjoying, *is* conspicuous, the consoler appears to be disingenuous," said Jeff.

"We agree that such an argument that one should not grieve would be unconvincing. We agree because we think that your mom's also not enjoying anything anymore. But maybe people who offer this consolation believe in an afterlife, specifically one in which the dead person is enjoying but not suffering. In that case, they weren't disingenuous in offering the consolation, 'She's no longer suffering,'" said Connie.

"What you say is probably true of some consolers. But what about you? You believe 'She's not enjoying,' yet you offered the consolation 'She's not suffering,'" Jeff replied.

"But I didn't intend to prove that you shouldn't grieve at all. Frankly, I'm not sure what I meant! Perhaps I meant that you should not grieve *so* much," Connie said.

"Granted, I should not grieve over her no longer suffering. But I wasn't grieving over that. I was grieving over *why* she is no longer suffering, if you would like to put it that way, that is, because she no longer experiences anything, and more specifically, that she can no longer enjoy anything," Jeff said.

"It Could Be Worse"

"I guess the point is that it could be worse, even that death isn't totally bad for the dead person," Connie said.

Jeff replied, "People do say 'It could have been worse' or 'It could be worse.' But I *don't* suppose that my mom's death is the worst thing that could *ever* happen, or even perhaps that it's the worst thing we could *conceive* of happening to *her*. Perhaps it would be worse were she still conscious but only experiencing bad things. People disagree about whether that's worse than annihilation, but I'll agree that it is. Arguably it could *be* worse for her: if she was still alive but suffering so much that it would be better that she didn't exist. Also, it could have *been* worse: suppose she had died earlier or lived with even greater suffering than she had. But my grieving supposes only that her death is a terrible thing for her, not that it is the conceivably most terrible thing for her, nor that it is the most terrible thing that's ever, or could, happen to her or anyone else," Jeff said.

"But don't grievers act *as though* the death of their loved one is the worst thing that has ever happened?" Connie asked.

"Do we?" Jeff asked. The train of their conversation was interrupted as they waited to cross the street.

Grievers and Consolers

Connie continued with a third interpretation of the remark that the dead person is no longer suffering. "Often consolers don't know what the bereaved believes. It's true, I knew that you believed that your mom was no longer in pain, but some people who said 'She's no longer suffering' to you might not have known that. So, perhaps they're reassuring you that your loved one is not suffering in death. A difficulty for consolers, probably especially in our society, is that they don't usually know just what the griever believes. This leads to awkwardness, clumsy attempts to comfort, and unwillingness to engage the grieving person's perspective."[1]

"Indeed!" said Jeff, "Consolers and grievers should try to understand one another. In order to understand and evaluate consolations we need to understand what grief presupposes and what it doesn't presuppose. In other words, we must find out what must be true in order that grief 'makes sense.' And unless a consolation addresses itself to that which must be true in order that grief makes sense, that consolation will miss the mark. It will be a challenge to determine what, if anything, grief presupposes. But I think that's necessary if we're to understand trying to console a grieving person.

"Can you think of any *other* interpretations of 'She's not suffering'?" Jeff asked.

Connie offered, "There's a version you mentioned earlier, 'She's better off that she's not suffering.' That goes further than what I was suggesting, which was merely that the end of her suffering *mitigates* or lessens the evil of her death. This new interpretation implies that death was *good* for her."

"But," replied Jeff, "good only in comparison with the final part of her life. . . . That is, arguing that her death is good for her because of the suffering in the final part of her life could at most show that her death was good in comparison. And that is consistent with its being a great evil for her. Furthermore, this supposedly comforting remark is really dreary. For it tries to lessen the evil of death, or even turn it into a good, by emphasizing the bad things in her life."

Connie said, "If the final years of her life were more suffering than enjoyment, then it would not be arbitrary to bring attention to the end of her suffering. That is, in an earlier interpretation of this consolation you complained that it was arbitrary because it ignored the fact that she is no longer enjoying. But if the final years of her life were more suffering than enjoyment, then it's not arbitrary emphasizing the fact that she's no longer suffering."

"Yes, that wouldn't be arbitrary, but it avoids arbitrariness only by being dreary, by implying that my mom's final years were so very bad for her," Jeff responded.

"Some truths are dreary," Connie noted.

"Yes, unfortunately, but dreary truths aren't comforting. Anyway, I don't think that it was true that, over an extended period of time, my mom had more suffering than enjoyment. Maybe that's easy for me to say. I admit that I can't begin to realize how much pain and aggravation she had to live through. But she wanted to live, and although I know that's not conclusive proof that her life was still good for her, I don't know of any better indication. So, in sum, this most recent interpretation of our supposedly comforting remark, that she is better off since she's no longer suffering, is dreary, false, and wouldn't show that death wasn't a great evil for her, anyway. Otherwise it was a perfect consolation!" stated Jeff.

"Do you want me to keep trying?" Connie asked.

"Definitely."

And so Connie resumed, "I'll still try to make sense of our latest version of this consolation which claims that her death is better than her life. Granted, this does not show that her death is good for her; it only claims that her death is comparatively good. But if only this much were true, wouldn't that show that there was something peculiar about grief?"

"It's not true that her death was better, but go on," Jeff said.

Connie explained, "As is common, you're grieving over her death. Yet, according to this consolation, her death was better for her than her life. Even if her death were bad for her, as long as it was not as bad as, or better than, her life, it would seem to make more sense to feel sorrow over her life. Yet grievers show more sorrow over the death. Does it make sense to show more sorrow over something less bad?"

Jeff said, "I think it will take us all evening to begin to get clear on this, but, for starters, I'd like to respond with the following points: first, even if sorrow should be in some sense proportioned to the evil, and her life was worse for her than her death, it wouldn't follow that I should grieve less over her death than I am grieving. Perhaps I should have felt *more* distress at her *life* than I felt."

"That's because it's a dreary consolation," Connie conceded.

"Yes. Second, had I believed that her life was worse for her than death I *would* have felt greater sorrow than I felt at the time. However, I'd agree that it probably would not have equaled the sorrow I feel at her death. That's partly because some of the sorrow I feel at her death is sorrow for myself. But I suspect that there are other reasons as well.

"One who would console me by saying 'She's not suffering' must be made aware that I do not think that that is sufficient to alleviate my grief. By examining different versions of this consolation we're getting a better understanding of what such a consoler might believe, and what a recalcitrant griever such as me might believe. But I agree that we shall have to try to settle these differences.

"There's something else I'd like to say about the suggestion that she's better off dead. Is it sincere? Would anyone who suggests this have advocated euthanasia for my mom? Maybe euthanasia is sometimes right, but my mom's case was never that bad. Consolers who imply that she is better off dead than sick might as well try to comfort me by saying 'Too bad she didn't die four years ago!'"

"Death Prevented Greater Suffering"

Connie said, "There is a similar point which consolers make which isn't as outlandish as to imply that she should have died earlier. Namely, to point out that the likely alternative course of the disease would have eventually led to even greater pain and frustration and fear. That is, if the disease hadn't killed her now, it would have only killed her after intensifying her suffering. So that while perhaps her life remained worth living until the end it would not have continued so."

Jeff recalled, "In fact, several people have said that to me. And it applies to my mom's case. Her cancer was multiple myeloma and it killed her, as far as we know, by causing kidney failure. Some victims of this type of cancer suffer broken bone after broken bone until they die. My mom had several compression fractures in her spine during the first year she had the disease but no fractures thereafter. So, I'll agree, it could have been worse. But grief does not presuppose that the worst conceivable thing happened."

Connie continued, "But the argument now says more than 'It could have been worse.' It says that death *prevented* that which could have been worse. You think that death deprived her of her future enjoyments, even the limited enjoyments she had since she had the disease, and so, her death makes you feel anguish. But in fact, her disease had *already* deprived her of future enjoyments so that death's only effect on her was to spare her further misery."

Jeff commented, "This also is dreary. The only alternatives were death and greater suffering."

Connie went on, "I agree that that's dreary. But that these were the only alternatives brings me back to a point I tried to argue earlier. In a case where the only realistic alternative is greater suffering, it's peculiar to grieve over that which prevents it, in this case, death."

"So? What follows? I should not grieve for her that she died, but I should grieve for her that she could only avoid greater suffering by dying? So what has this consolation accomplished?" Jeff asked. "And *why* is it dreary that a person can only avoid suffering by being dead? Because being dead is so terrible. Her death is so terrible for her because it means that she will never again enjoy anything. This is terrible even though the only way for her to have avoided greater suffering was by not being conscious at all, not even conscious of good things. What I'm saying is that I grieve for her over her death because it means she'll never have good things, and this is not altered by the fact that her death also spared her bad things."

"No, Jeff. You say that her death 'means' that she no longer enjoys anything. But, in this case, that's a mistake. It's not her death which meant this, it was her terminal cancer which would have progressed to the point that she no longer enjoyed anything," Connie replied.

Jeff asked again, "Then my grief for her, because of the facts of her case, should be directed, not towards her death, but towards the *cause* of her death? Then where has this gotten us? Still, *something* terrible has happened to my mom. Perhaps that terrible thing is only elliptically expressed as 'Her death is a terrible evil to her.' Perhaps I should grieve over the cause of her death.

"I grieve for her because she'll never enjoy anything again and 'the only realistic alternative' scenarios, no matter how grim, don't change that! I still grieve over the fact that she'll never enjoy anything again even though that is correlated with the fact that she won't suffer any more or any worse."

Revisionism

"It's tempting," Jeff continued, "to think about what could have been, especially when there's nothing you can do to change what you don't like. But what's the point? We can always imagine something worse and we can always imagine something better, as well. But neither changes the intrinsic goodness or badness of what is. The fact that we can imagine something worse doesn't make what is, intrinsically better than it is, just as the fact that we can imagine something better doesn't make what is, intrinsically worse than it is. Something can be terrible even though there are worse things. And it won't do to say that we should bring attention to the worse scenario, greater suffering, as consolers do, rather than the better scenario, continued enjoyment of life, because the worse scenario was the more realistic alternative to the actual outcome."

"I question the purpose, after the fact, of speculating on 'the most realistic alternative' to her death. After all, at this point there is no alternative to her death. It's not as though we could undo her death, though I don't know what I wouldn't do if I could. And if I could, I would have to know exactly what to undo in order to avoid unintended bad consequences. And so, in this case, it would be important to cure her cancer, for it would be regrettable to only prevent it from attacking her kidney if instead it tortured her. But alas, none of these things are in my power. I cannot bring her back, cancer—free or not. So what does it matter, 'the most realistic alternative?' When we deliberate we consider different alternatives. But I'm not deliberating about whether to bring her back. I can't bring her back.

"There is a conversational game called 'historical revisionism.' In this game, players speculate on how history would have turned out differently had some initial conditions been different. For example, what would have happened to US foreign and domestic policy had Oswald missed? Now, one of the rules of the game is that one should imagine alternative initial conditions as close to those which actually prevailed while still rendering an important divergence from actual history. When one departs too much from the actual initial conditions the game becomes silly, as it sometimes does when the game is played by children. 'What would have happened if the ancient Romans had the atomic bomb?' or 'What if dinosaurs were alive?' or as *Saturday Night Live* once humorously speculated, 'What if Superman had been raised in Nazi Germany?'

"A consequence of the rule that one should imagine slight alterations in the initial conditions is that one usually should imagine as recent as possible an alteration in the initial conditions. This is a consequence because the earlier the imagined alteration the more likely it is that the initial conditions would have been quite different from the actual conditions.

"Now, grievers would like to alter a lot, at least when the loved one died from an illness, and to do so they would have to go further back in time. For example, a griever wishes not only that the loved one still lives, but also that the loved one hadn't developed a terminal illness. But a consoler such as we imagine, indeed, such as we encounter, points out that the griever's wishes require a major revision of the actual events. The consoler, on the other hand, who maintains that longer life would have increased suffering, does not think about a possible world in which the dead person never contracted the illness, but thinks about a possible world in which the dead person lingers with illness. Thus, the possible world which the consoler considers comes closer to the actual initial conditions. The alteration that the consoler considers is an alteration of a more recent condition, the particular 'direction' the illness took, than the alteration wished by the griever, that the loved one never got cancer or that it had been cured. However, such a consoler more closely following the rules of historical revisionism has nothing to do with the evaluations made by the griever; grief is based on these evaluations.

"In sum, grievers and consolers are not deliberating about how we should tinker with the past, nor are we playing historical revisionism. We're *evaluating* what has happened. Has a consoler who emphasizes 'the most realistic alternative' confused the context of deliberation or the game of historical revisionism, on the one hand, with the context of evaluation, on the other? I think so."

The two resumed their walk, and though their destination was near, their conversation had only just begun.

"But I'll go further," Jeff said. "What irks me about the attempt to lessen the evil of death by referring to the death's 'only realistic alternative' is that such a consolation violates the rules of 'wishing revisionism.' 'Wishing revisionism' is different from historical revisionism. Wishing revisionism is a fantasy wherein we imagine a different set of initial conditions because they would have had a better outcome. Like historical revisionism, wishing revisionism has a rule that the imagined alteration in initial conditions should not depart greatly from those which were actual. So, for example, it would violate this rule were I to imagine that I was an oncologist who found a cure for myeloma, or were I to imagine that there was no such thing as myeloma.

"However, unlike historical revisionism, wishing revisionism has a rule that the imagined alteration in initial conditions be sufficient to provide a *better* outcome. So, a griever who plays wishing revisionism would not only wish that the loved one had not died but that the loved one hadn't gotten the cancer which caused the death, which means that the loved one would not have suffered from it as well.

"Thus, when a consoler imagines an alternative in which something *worse* occurs he or she is not playing the game of wishing revisionism at all. So, the consoler and the griever are not engaged in the same revisionist game. Once again, we see a failure of a consoler to 'engage the perspective of the griever,' as you put it.

"However, I must remember that the fact that a revisionist consoler makes this error does not alter the evaluation which should be made about the death of a loved one. The death is not worse because a consoler has blundered."

Distractions

Connie added, "I have a final thought on the remark, 'She's no longer suffering.' All along we've been assuming that it is an *argument* intended to lessen your grief, by showing in some way that your grief is too strong. Maybe this assumption is wrong! The consoler knows, or assumes, that the griever is obsessing over unpleasant thoughts. So, the consoler's just trying to throw a less unpleasant thought into the mix. It *is* intended to lessen grief, but maybe not as an argument that the grief is too strong. Maybe the purpose is to take the griever's mind off the evil of death and onto suffering in life."

Jeff replied, "I think the fact that the remark can be construed as an argument in the several ways we've examined suggests very strongly that it is intended as an argument. Also, if the consoler is just trying to mix in a less unpleasant thought, then the consoler must think that the grieving person *should* be grieving less. If they think that, why wouldn't they *argue* for it, perhaps in a concealed way?"

Connie said, "Because they might think that an argument would be insensitive or that grief is unresponsive to reasoning."

"Besides," Jeff continued without immediately addressing Connie's remark, "if one wishes to lessen grief by distracting the griever, there are much better ways to do it. It's a peculiar distraction which reminds me of her suffering, even if it's to remind me that it's over. The remark 'Think of the good times' would be more on the right track, even though it has as much a chance at aggravating, as it has at alleviating, grief. That 'there were good times' is a counterproductive argument against grief. For the more good times there were, that's all the more that death has deprived us. As a distraction, however, it might fare better than the bleak 'She's no longer suffering.'

"In any case, I prefer other distractions. Hopefully, dinner and music tonight will provide some distraction. And strangely, talking about grief is a distraction from grief, or perhaps I should say that talking about grief is a part of grief which distracts me from other parts of grief, such as the fits of horror, desperation, whatever you call it."

"Yes," said Connie softly. "Maybe you think that the more you talk about grief the longer you can put off those fits."

Jeff laughed at himself. "Yeah, I just have to keep *talking* about grief for the rest of my life so that I won't ever have to *feel* it again! A moment ago you said that maybe consolers or comforters think that grief is unresponsive to reasoning or arguments. Maybe we should put that to the test tonight. Let's see whether grief is unresponsive to arguments."

Then Jeff said, "My dad died of a heart attack a long time ago. Your dad died two years ago from a heart attack whereas your mom died many years ago from lupus. So she suffered, but your more recent loss was sudden. I think it's interesting that the one consolation you've offered me, 'She's no longer suffering,' would *not* have been offered to you recently. Instead, you probably got a lot of 'At least he didn't suffer' consolations when your dad died two years ago."

"Yes, I believe I did," Connie reflected.

"It seems like there's 'a consolation for every occasion,'" Jeff sneered.

"And it seems you find that suspicious?" Connie asked.

"Yes, I do!" said Jeff, emphatically. "Things can't be good *no matter what* happens."

The pair finally arrived at the restaurant, the Hard Rock Café. Their friend Phil had not yet arrived, and they had to wait for a table, anyway, so Jeff and Connie waited at the bar.

Summary of the Conversation

The conventional and supposedly comforting remarks "She is no longer suffering," "She is better off," "It could be worse," and "It could have been worse" were considered. They are interpreted as enthymemes with the purpose of showing that there is something wrong with grief. These arguments are either aimed at overturning or mitigating the evaluation that the loved one's death is evil for the loved one, or aimed at criticizing grief as too "strong."

Consolations (reviewed in this chapter) that grief is too strong are based on the facts that grief is (often) the strongest affect (in terms of intensity, frequency, and duration), yet there are greater evils than a loved one's death. While it is true that there are greater evils the conclusion that grief is too strong depends additionally on the claim that an affect's strength should be solely a function of the importance of the evaluated thing; that is, that the strength of the affect should be in proportion to the extent of the evil (or good, as the case might be), and that this should be the only factor. This additional claim is discussed in Chapters Thirteen and Fifteen.

In different ways, comforters using these consolations fail to understand the beliefs of the griever and the sorts of objects to which the grief is a response. Grievers are frequently responding to a believed deprivation suffered by their loved ones. Some of these consolations ignore the alleged deprivation ("arbitrary"), and some posit other evils for the loved one ("dreary"), such as greater suffering before death. In addition, aspiring comforters who remark that death prevented a more terrible sequel do not understand that grievers are "wishing revisionists."

Study Questions

(1) What should would-be consolers know about grief?

(2) What makes a consolation a good one?
- How do we know whether a consolation is a good one?

Three

"SHE HAD A GOOD LIFE"

The Hard Rock Cafe is a popular international chain of restaurants catering to "baby boomers" and their children. The decor is rock and roll memorabilia. The bar, at which Jeff and Connie stood, was guitar shaped. On the walls around the bar hung gold and platinum records and posters of many recording artists, including the Beatles, Buddy Holly and the Crickets, Elvis Presley, the Rolling Stones, the Doors, Jimi Hendrix, Janis Joplin, and Otis Redding. Also displayed were framed "WAR IS OVER (If you want it)!" handbills, which John Lennon and Yoko Ono distributed during 1969.

Billy Joel's "James" played in the background.

"Since you're not receptive to consolations, maybe I should just listen," Connie offered.

"If you want to help me, listening is important. But you are listening. But I also want your *honest* reactions—what you really think. If it were possible, I would love to be consoled. Sometimes the grief is so great . . . so inescapable! Everything about it! Not only knowing I'll never see her again, or that she'll never see anything again. The dying itself . . . the final thirty-three hours. It's so horrible seeing someone die whom you love! Seeing her die, feeling her die, at the very end her temperature went way up; hearing her die, her breathing was forced; even . . ." Jeff could hardly say it, but it came out in a whisper, "smelling her die."

Jeff averted his eyes and Connie fidgeted.

Jeff continued, "And the interminable, lonely trip from the Bronx to New Jersey after finding out she was dying. You know how anti-superstitious I am. Well, nonetheless, on that trip I repeated, uninterruptedly, like a mantra or a magic spell, 'Get well, get well, get well . . .' as though it could save her. . . . I need consolation!"

Jeff sighed and turned toward Connie. "When you heard of your dad's death you had to travel, all alone, halfway around the world. That must have been agony."

"It was miserable," Connie confirmed.

"More than anything, I need to be consoled!" Jeff exclaimed, but then continued with a restrained, however somber, tone. "One of the many things upon which I have focused my grief is an afghan she hadn't finished. She knitted beautiful afghans you know. That particular unfinished project haunts me. Actually, another person finished the afghan, in a cursory manner. Mom had made so many afghans that another wasn't needed. She was making it as 'therapy,' so to speak. So I think she enjoyed making it."

Connie noted, "Then her labor wasn't wasted. It's true that she didn't have the satisfaction of finishing it. Do you infer from this that it would have been better had she never begun the afghan?"

Jeff answered, "No, I suppose it is good that she began it. She enjoyed making it, and, since I have it, I could enjoy it, but for the sadness it gives me because she didn't finish it."

"Aren't *you* being 'arbitrary'? Your emotional response seems to be based solely on the sad fact that she was deprived of the satisfaction of finishing it. You acknowledge but don't emotionally respond to the good things about the afghan, even though these outweigh the bad," Connie said, gently scolding Jeff.

"What you say makes sense. Now that I think about it, I suspect that my attitude toward the afghan has more to do with a symbolic function that it has. It reminds me, as do other things, but this especially, that her life is over, and that her life ended 'unfinished' and with more living to do," Jeff said.

"Think of the Good Things"

Connie continued, "Perhaps some consolers would have you not focus on anything bad at all. But you focus too much, and one-sidedly, or 'arbitrarily,' on what is bad. Just before we arrived here at the restaurant, you indicated that 'Think of the good things,' while perhaps a good distraction, is a bad consolation because the more good things there were in her life and between the two of you, the more has been lost. Well, it does follow that the more has been *lost*. But is that any reason to grieve more than if less had been lost because her life hadn't been so good to her or you? Your mom had a good life, but you no longer respond to that. Or rather, you respond to the loss of those goods but not to the fact that she had them.

"If we define 'grief' as a response to *lost* goods, the end of a very good life *might* be an occasion for greater 'grief' than the end of an only so-so life which had fewer goods to lose. But it is worse to never have goods than to have them and lose them. By definition of 'grief' perhaps one cannot grieve over goods never had, and therefore never lost, but a person might still feel sorrow and distress about never having enjoyed them. And the definition of 'grief' is not important. What's important is the distress—that's what a consoler is trying to alleviate. So, my point is that there is less *reason* to feel distress about goods lost than goods never enjoyed since it is better to have goods and lose them than to never have them."

Jeff said, "You've made a good point, but I'm not sure how to react to it. I have two thoughts. First, although my mom's life wasn't as rewarding as some, she was able to enjoy it. She enjoys *nothing* now. So, I had no reason to be distressed that her life wasn't as satisfying as some since her life was still worthwhile, but I have reason to be distressed now.

"Second, many things deprive people of goods, either of a kind which they once enjoyed or of a kind which they never enjoyed either because of lack of ability, missed opportunity, and so on. And then there are goods lost by death. Any of these deprivations might cause distress."

Jeff continued, "Let me explain why I'm more disturbed by the loss of goods by her death than about the fact that there were goods she did not have in life. There are many good things which my mom was either incapable of experiencing or enjoying, if she did experience them. For example, she had an irrational fear of the water which prevented her from enjoying either boating or swimming. She also had a fear of cats and dogs. I guess she could have overcome these fears, although I suspect that they were somehow linked to central features of her personality. On the other hand, I don't think she could have ever experienced the thrill of some really 'daredevil' activity like skydiving! She would have had to have been a *very* different person to do and enjoy such things!"

Connie said, "Yes, one's personality can limit one's capacity for good experiences. And other personal characteristics, besides personality, can limit one's capacity for good experiences. For example, some experiences depend upon one's gender. I hope that someday I'll know what it's like to breastfeed."

Jeff said, "Yes, there are many sorts of characteristics which a person has which determine the kinds of goods they can and cannot enjoy. Some of these characteristics could change while one remained 'the same person,' but other changes would make one a 'different person.' While Michael Jordan's life is probably better than mine it would not make any sense to wish that I were him. I don't simply mean that the wish is fruitless, I mean that the wish is meaningless. If I were Michael Jordan, there wouldn't be any me."

Connie said, "Though these points need further elaboration, I agree with them. Some changes which a person would have to undergo for it to be conceivable that that person enjoy some good experience are so radical that we might as well speak of a different person. But how would this explain why you are more distressed by the goods your mom lost by death than the fact that she missed out on things while alive?"

Jeff explained, "Death deprives a person of goods which they conceivably might have enjoyed while remaining 'the same person.' I do not grieve because death entails or means that my mom will never go boating again, or skydive, or view the earth while standing upon the surface of the moon. I grieve, in part, because her death entails that she will never again enjoy a joke, a soap opera, or the company of her family and friends. I grieve because she'll never again make an afghan.

"On the other hand, many deprivations in life are of goods which the person could not have enjoyed while remaining the same person. And I'll admit that it doesn't make sense to be distressed about something if there is no conceivable alternative. For example, it would not be rational for me to be distressed that my mom was not Neil Armstrong because that's inconceivable.

"But it is conceivable that my mom didn't die. As I've claimed, the better for my mom was her life, the worse for my mom was her death. As you've said, it also follows from the fact that her life had many goods that she had fewer deprivations within life. Now, any statement, which implies that her death is even worse, 'adds fuel' to my distress. Unfortunately, the only way to avoid this implication is by saying that her life wasn't so good, which is also distressing. But the loss of goods by death is the more distressing of the two because these lost goods were all possible for the person who died.

Connie said, "This can't be right! According to you, the better the person's life, the more good things which existed, the greater the reason for distress. How can that be? That sounds like you would advise a person to have a miserable life in order to make death acceptable!"

Jeff replied, "I agree that a person should have many goods rather than few. But the loss of many goods is more distressful than the loss of few."

Connie said, "How can it make sense to be greater distressed by the better of two possibilities?"

Jeff attempted an explanation, "Another reason that I'm more disturbed by my mom's losses entailed by death than any losses she suffered in life is that my mom's losses in life happened a while ago, whereas the losses entailed by her death are fresh and even ongoing. If she were alive *now,* she could enjoy what this moment has to offer. If she were alive tomorrow, she would have been able to enjoy what tomorrow has to offer, and so on. Death has brought her infinite losses."

Connie objected, "I doubt that you are really grieving over an infinite loss. Certain expressions to the contrary, as when grievers lament 'We shall *never* see each other again,' grievers are really only responding to the loss of that person for the next several years, not for all future time.

"But besides objecting that you're not really grieving over an infinite loss, I also want to object that the fact that your mom's death is fresh is not a good reason for being more greatly disturbed by this than by any ills that she suffered in life, necessarily more remote."

Jeff responded, "It's true that a remote evil is not any less evil than a recent one, but sometimes one should respond more strongly to one evil rather than another even if they are equally bad. And I think that temporal proximity might be a reason for responding more strongly. Not only should one respond more strongly to a present or recent evil than a remote one, one should also respond more strongly to a present or recent evil than to a remote *good*. That my mom's life was good implies that she had some goods which are now past, mostly long past; but it also implies that she has an ever ongoing loss. Therefore, if emotional responses are justified by temporal proximity, then the goods she enjoyed in life give me more reason to be distressed than to be cheered."

"As you say, I do believe that grief, even if it is the most intense and prolonged sorrow in a person's life, does not presuppose that the loss is the worst thing that has happened. But even if I thought that sorrow should always be proportionate to the evil suffered, so that we should respond equally to equal evils, it would not follow that I should be grieving less than I am. If there are evils greater than death, or the death of a loved one, then perhaps we should feel *more* sorrow over these evils, whatever they are. If there are such evils, then perhaps, preserving proportion in our affects, we should feel less sorrow over death than we do. Or perhaps we should feel as much sorrow over death as we do, and more sorrow over these other evils."

"Yes, I forgot," Connie said, "You made that point earlier. I certainly hope that either there aren't any evils worse than death, or that, if there are, we should not feel greater sorrow over these. I wouldn't want our discussion of consolation to lead to further anguish!"

"I don't either. But I don't see the way out. What I do see is that we must explore the subject of consolation more deeply and more systematically than we have thus far. We need to have a better understanding of evaluations, emotions or affects and the relation between emotions and evaluations, in general, and a better understanding of grief and death, in particular."

"It's funny where the simple remark 'She's not suffering' has led us," Connie observed.

"That's right," teased Jeff, "Are you sorry you offered it?"

Instead of answering, Connie offered, "Jeff, you really are inconsistently defending 'negative' emotions, such as grief and guilt. In defending grief you've said that you should not be cheered by temporally remote goods enjoyed by your mom. But earlier, when expressing guilt that you haven't accomplished more and didn't give your mom the pleasure of seeing you successful in your career, or having additional grandchildren, you were responding negatively to temporally remote deprivations. It seems that you respond to temporally remote evils but not temporally remote goods. Now, I don't know whether temporal remoteness is a justified factor in limiting emotional response, but I do know that you should be consistent!"

Enter Phil

As Jeff hesitated in making a response, Phil arrived and was greeted warmly. "The way you drive I would have thought that you'd either have gotten here before us or never have gotten here at all," Connie joked.

"I thought I'd let you guys wait for the table and then show up just in time!" Phil joked back. "How are you Jeff?" Phil said, adopting a serious tone.

As though on cue, the three were called to their table.

Summary of the Conversation

The remark "She had a good/full life" is discussed as an argument against grief responses, especially inhibition, instead of as an argument against any evaluation made by the griever. The characters argue whether we should enjoy recalling the good things in our loved one's life.

The remark "She had a good/full life" is also discussed as a possible grievance, a reason for greater grief. The better the life, the more good is lost in death. This might not be a reason for greater grief, or greater sorrow. For the lack of goods in life might be a proper object of sorrow. On the other hand, as long as a life had enough goods to make it worthwhile, distress over death appears to be more reasonable than distress over a limited, though valuable, life.

Issues are raised instead of resolved in this chapter. The only resolution is that a systematic treatment of evaluations, affects, death, and grief is necessary. The characters have only begun to articulate the factors which influence grief.

Using terminology introduced and developed later in this work, "She had a good life" is a counterproductive "evaluation consolation" because it implies that death is bad. But it is a somewhat promising "response consolation" as it provides one basis for criticizing the grief responses of sorrow and inhibition. Partly for not having made this distinction, Jeff and Connie were unable to reach a consensus about this consolation.

Two important ideas that recur throughout the dialogue are introduced in this chapter. First, for a state of affairs to be evil for a person, it must be conceivable that a better state of affairs exist for that person. Second, some characteristics of a person are "central" to him or her, such that if they were changed, the individual would no longer be the "same" person (in some sense).

Study Questions

(1) Why does Jeff resist consolation?

(2) What is a "full life"?

(3) What is a "fulfilled life"?

Four

TYPES OF GRIEF AND COMFORT STRATEGIES

As Fleetwood Mac's "I'm So Afraid" played, the trio ascended the stairs to the restaurant's mezzanine level. They walked past four TWA flight bags used by the Beatles during their 1965 United States visit. Only Paul McCartney and Ringo Starr's bags faced forward. Jeff, Connie, and Phil sat at their table. Upon the wall hung the white Vox "teardrop" guitar played by the Rolling Stones' Brian Jones, with clearly visible pick-marks on the body. Next to it hung a photograph of Jones, standing in front of a studio console, holding this guitar.

The waitress introduced herself. "Hi, I'm Barbara. I'll be back in a minute to take your order."

Connie turned to Phil and said, "Maybe you can help me. I need your philosophical expertise."

Phil replied, "I'm out of philosophy. Now if there any 707s you want me to direct as they approach for landing, I'm your guy. Why don't you borrow some of Jeff's expertise?"

"That's just it: it's Jeff's philosophical training that I need to oppose!" Connie protested.

"What do you want me to help you to do?" Phil asked.

"Console Jeff," Connie said.

Jeff looked at Connie for her approval and asked, "Should I fill him in?"

"Go ahead."

"Connie has been offering me some consolations, but I find them to be, upon the whole, unhelpful and irrational. Nonetheless, I desperately *need* to be consoled. I want to go on with my life and be happy and feel like a good person, but I'm so upset, so distraught. I can't forget the past, I don't even want to forget it, but I feel that no matter what I do, I'll never be happy, that it's too late for that, that the past will always 'cast a pall over my future,' that what I've lost and know another to have lost will always trouble me. I'm not even sure that I wish to recover.

"The way I've been feeling reminds me of some things I've read about John Lennon. It's funny. You both know how sentimental I am. Before mom's death I used to feel some sorrow at Lennon's death because I've enjoyed his music, admired his public positions, and he was a source of many pleasant childhood memories. But now that mom's dead I have 'no room left in my heart' to feel sorrow about his death. In fact, in light of my mom's death, I keep thinking that it was absurd that I grieved for a stranger, even slightly. Anyway, as I was saying, I'm reminded of some things I've read about Lennon. In a poem composed for a friend, Stu Sutcliffe, he wrote:

> I can't remember anything without a sadness
> So deep that it hardly becomes known to me.

"A year later, three days after Sutcliffe's sudden death, John said to Sutcliffe's fiancée, 'You can't behave as a widow. Make up your mind, you either live or you die. You can't be in the middle.' And then, the last words reportedly spoken to John, by the police officer in the back of the patrol car rushing him to the hospital after the shooting: do you know who you are?[1] Just as John seemed undecided about his attitude toward grief by recommending stalwartness to Stu's widow but earlier confessing to great sadness, I don't know who *I* am, or rather, I don't know *what* to do. I hate my grief, but it seems inescapable. I don't even want to escape it if the only way is by lying to myself. I want to do the right thing, if it's not too late."

Some Basics: Consolation and Other Comfort Strategies: Some Grief Responses and Objects of Grief

Phil rolled up his sleeves, which provoked a laugh from Jeff and then Connie, and Phil began, "First," Phil requested, "What do you mean by 'consolation'?"

"I use it more specifically than the way people generally use the word. According to the way the word's usually used, a consolation is a person or thing that alleviates misery or distress of mind. However, as I say, I'm using the word more specifically."

"Okay. How do you use it?"

"By 'consolation' I mean an *argument* that grief is wrong or mistaken. This differs from the way that the word is usually used because *my* definition specifies *how* a consoler tries to alleviate distress. *One* way in which a person might try to alleviate distress is through reasoning, or an argument, that the distress is wrong or mistaken. It is this way which I call 'consolation.'"

Phil said, "Before I would even consider offering you any consolations, Jeff, I'd like to get even clearer about this definition. Let's start with what you mean by 'grief' so that we understand what it is that a consolation is supposed to be alleviating."

Connie protested, "Come now, Phil! Although you're fortunate enough to have both your parents and all other loved ones alive, you understand what grief is. It's a feeling, a terrible feeling. Jeff won't be helped by defining the word."

Phil replied, "I'm not being obtuse. We can't begin to evaluate arguments against something we haven't analyzed, even a little. Perhaps the thing a consolation is trying to alleviate is really desirable. I'm not being naive, either. I realize that, however we define 'grief,' it's something which hurts real bad. But just how bad it is, and whether there's any thing desirable about it remains to be seen, and initial definitions can't hurt."

Then Jeff settled it, "Thanks for your concern, Connie, but Phil's right. 'Grief' stands for different things. Before we can evaluate even one of them we've got to make some distinctions. It's true, all the things called 'grief' hurt very bad in some way or another. But perhaps that common factor isn't the only important thing about these different things called 'grief.' Anyway, as Phil knows, I enjoy being analytical."

Phil added, "A minute ago, when Jeff told us about his concerns for his future, he offered several different thoughts, anyone of which could be part of grief. Some of these are: sorrow when he thinks of the past, fear that he'll never be happy or that he's not or won't be a good person. So, let's be careful."[2]

Connie agreed, "Okay. When Jeff and I were discussing this earlier, a distinction arose between the feeling of sorrow, on the one hand, and inhibition, that is, a lack of feeling or apathy toward having good experiences, on the other."

"Yes," Phil said, "inhibition is a 'numbness' or incapacity to enjoy oneself. And of course this is different from the *feeling* of sorrow, though they often go together. Jeff, which responses are you experiencing?"

"Both. I'd like to be rid of both attacks of sorrow and inhibition. The attacks of sorrow are so overwhelming, and seem relieved only by fits of crying and yelling. Inhibition comes in different degrees, and I suppose, different grievers are inhibited about different things. I'm inhibited with respect to several things, but my inhibitions are fewer than they were a couple weeks ago. Obviously, I wouldn't be out with my friends in a pop culture restaurant were I still totally inhibited. And during no crisis in my life have I ever been prevented from enjoying food. However, there are certain meals which I used to enjoy, which I'll *never* have again, since they're associated with mom. My mom used to enjoy the way I savored a beer and cheesecake. I'll never have them again. My sense of humor is returning. My libido is still strong—I suppose because I'm grieving over my mom, not over a lover. I still enjoy music, although some of it too has acquired unpleasant associations, and this worries me because the more I've liked something the more unpleasant associations it now has. You see, I tried singing to my mom as she was dying. I've become uninterested in sports, or more accurately, I now wish the Yanks would lose, since I hate to think of mom missing out on their success. I'm less interested in politics . . . well, that's perhaps a benefit, since it's more often a source of aggravation.

"An illustration of my being partially inhibited is the following: before my mom died I purchased tickets for a Paul McCartney concert which was three weeks ago. I went, but derived much more bitterness than pleasure from the show, although the set and performance were excellent. While my feet tapped to nearly every song, I couldn't get my mind 'into' any of the songs, apart from the melancholic 'Yesterday.' I was still reeling in anguish and wasn't able to feel the vivacity or abandoned joy in the music.

"In sum, others suffer from inhibition more than I do, and I suffer slightly less than I did a month ago. But I still have the apprehension that my enjoyments, while not totally inhibited, or prevented, will always be accompanied by an ill feeling—that I won't have the satisfaction of reflecting positively on my enjoyments. One wants to not only have good experiences, one wants to be able to enjoy reflecting on them, reflecting on one's life. I'm terrified that I've lost that for good, and I'm unwilling to lie to regain it."

"Is there anything else about your grief which you'd like to tell us?" Phil asked.

"I'd just like to re-emphasize that when I'm reminded that she's dead the distress can be overwhelming," Jeff added.

"Perhaps you can receive some comfort from the recognition that you're not totally inhibited," Connie said.

Phil said, "So, the misery a consoler is trying to alleviate is at least twofold: first, the pangs of grief, second, the inhibition of enjoyments. In your case, that inhibition is partial, and mostly specific to enjoyments associated with your mom. You're also very much inhibited from enjoying reflection on your life and enjoyments, and sad reflection might even be one cause of these pangs of grief."

"Yes."

Smokey Robinson and the Miracles's "I Second That Emotion" ended, and Phil said, "In order that I know what to think about consolation, would you contrast consoling with other kinds of efforts to reduce or eliminate grief?"

Connie interjected an initial answer, "There's sympathy which is sharing the sorrow or the inhibition. Also, there are distractions of different kinds. First, there's the distraction by activity, in which the griever is kept busy . . . ."

"I've found that returning to my work schedule has been both a distraction and a reminder. A reminder because prior routine supplies many opportunities to realize afresh that things will never be the same. No more phone calls to home before leaving work to get any last minute requests for grocery items," Jeff commented.

"Yes. I guess the activity shouldn't be too closely associated with the lost loved one," Connie continued.

"But there are no alternatives. One either returns to his prior routine . . ." Jeff said.

"There are other distractions, such as enjoyment" Connie said.

"Vacations are of no use," Jeff complained.

"Of course, were any griever totally inhibited, this method for alleviating grief would be unavailable." Connie conceded.

"Distraction by enjoyable activities provides a little relief from the horrific attacks of sorrow," Jeff admitted.

"And worthwhile for its own sake," Connie said, although unnoticed.

"But I don't see how it could help a griever to overcome the inability to reflect positively on enjoyments," Jeff continued. "If one has a negative attitude toward one's life, toward the shape or direction of one's life, how would more enjoyments help?"

"Perhaps the idea is to distract you from reflection. Even if distraction by enjoyments doesn't enable you to reflect happily on your life, it provides a good substitute! But one should go further: surely, the more one enjoys, the happier should be one's reflection on one's life. Even if one can't eliminate the feeling of loss, reflection on a life with many and varied enjoyments should be better than a reflection on a life lacking these, everything else being equal. That is, enjoyment is not only distraction from morbid or sorrowful thoughts; it is what constitutes a good life, so review of one's life should reflect that."

"Okay," Jeff replied to Connie, "we're returning to an earlier point in our discussion: that one should be cheered by good things, yet the loss of these is reason for remorse. And I need to eliminate the feeling of loss. I need to be consoled. Yes, there are other methods to try to comfort. There's sympathy and various distractions, as you've mentioned. And there's listening, which we talked about earlier. And in some cases, a griever uses psychotherapy. But these are halfway measures. I need to be consoled. And yet I prefer these other methods to irrational consolations."

Connie said, "There's another, as yet unmentioned kind of distraction: self-medication. . . ."

The waitress returned and asked for their orders. They apologized for not being ready to order their entrees, as none had even glanced at the menu, though all agreed on the appetizer: Buffalo chicken wings with blue cheese and celery. After the three ordered soft drinks, rather than hard liquor, the waitress left their table expecting a small tip.

As the Rolling Stones' "Mixed Emotions" ended and Paul McCartney and Wings's "Daytime Nighttime Suffering" began playing, Phil continued to organize the discussion. "I want to know a little more about grief before we begin assessing consolations. We've distinguished two grief responses, inhibition and sorrow. This distinction deals with the types of reaction a person might have to the death of a loved one. Of course, there are probably more responses than just these two; we can discuss other grief responses as they come up in our conversation. But now I want to be clearer about the *object* of grief. *To what* are the sorrow and inhibition responses? As we're using 'grief,' it is a set of unpleasant or distressful responses to the death of a loved one."

The others nodded.

"Death causes a number of unpleasant or distressful responses. These seem to be based on *evaluations* made by the grieving person. While all these evaluations are made by the griever *because* of death, only some of these evaluations are directly *about* death."

Jeff developed, "Yes, I see what you mean. The death of a loved one can trigger unpleasant responses to several things. Fortunately or not, death is a common occasion for a loving one to evaluate the life of the dead loved one, since that life is finished. It is also a common occasion for the loving ones to evaluate their own past, since their future will be quite different from their past. One might feel pangs of sadness or be inhibited from enjoyments depending upon the evaluations one makes of either of these.

"Death also commonly makes the loving ones evaluate their relationship with the dead loved one. This often leads to pangs of sadness and inhibitions, that is, guilt, as in my case.

"The process of dying, even considered apart from its consequences, if witnessed, or even imagined, by the loving one, is often an object of evaluation which leads to sadness and inhibition. The same can be said about the aftermath of dying: the appearance of the corpse, the behavior of the mourners . . ."

"As for instance, whether they offer irrational consolations?" Connie asked.

Evaluation Consolations and Response Consolations

"Right, Connie. Lastly, and this is what I most urgently wish to discuss, is grief's relation to beliefs about a loved one's death itself. Not that life, per se, or their relationship, or the cause of death, or circumstances of the wake or funeral, but what death 'means' to the dead person and the lasting effects it has on the loving ones. As a grieving person, I am convinced that the death of my loved one is a terrible thing, both for my loved one and for me—not to mention that it is also terrible for those of her survivors whom I also love, my sisters and my nephew. These convictions cause me frequent and intense pangs of sadness, and, in ways already detailed, some inhibition.

"The claim that death is a great evil for the dead loved one we'll call the 'sympathy evaluation' because, after the fact, it is, by necessity, an evaluation made by one person about another person's well-being. The claim that a loved one's death is a great evil for those that loved him or her, we'll call the 'ego evaluation.' We'll call it the ego evaluation since this is the bereaved persons' evaluation of the effect of their loved one's death on themselves."

Phil suggested, "Let's start piecing together what we've got thus far and we'll know where to go from there." Phil was about to pick up on his own suggestion when the waitress returned and the three finally ordered their entrees.

"Though I hesitate to introduce a further complication at this time," Connie said, "we must realize that while perhaps some consolers think that *all* grief is wrong or mistaken, I think that many more consolers think only that someone stricken with grief should feel *less* grief, not that the bereaved should feel none at all."

Jeff partly concurred, "Some consolations, especially by philosophers and other writers, are meant to be 'total' consolations, I believe. That is, some consolations are intended to *eliminate* grief. The views of a conventional consoler, a 'man or woman on the street' are more difficult to specify, because they're undeveloped, in part because they're oral. . . ."

"Then you'd better write down everything I say!" Connie advised.

Phil continued with Jeff's point, "Conventional consolers, as you've called them, haven't thought through what they think regarding the extent or degree or type of grief which should be felt. For that matter, neither have philosophers. Anyway, I believe that conventional consolers have very unclear ideas on this subject. They definitely believe that a loving one should feel some grief, for we often hear people criticized for being too carefree when a loved one has just died; yet, get a conventional consoler in a room with someone grieving, however little, and the consoler wants to cheer the bereaved up."

"Perhaps we require loving ones of the dead to be inhibited, but not sorrowful?" Connie said.

"Or perhaps we want them to be sorrowful, but not around us," Phil said.

"Or maybe we want them to be sorrowful but for our heroic efforts," Jeff said sarcastically.

"Let's face it," Phil concluded, "we have unclear ideas on this subject. Nevertheless, your distinction, between 'total' consolers who oppose all grief and 'partial' consolers, is important, Connie. As we review consolations it might be helpful to keep in mind, not only whether a consolation is directed against both types of grief responses, or one only, but also whether it should eliminate or just limit grief."

"Yes," said Connie, "but I believe in resorting to distinctions only as they come up."

"I like to have an overview before setting out. It prevents mistakes later, even if it sometimes involves unnecessary precautions. It reduces the risk of unintentional omissions and the risk of confusing separate issues, but I'm sure that some distinctions will come to us only as we survey consolations," Phil added.

As Phil continued, the Beatles advised "Let It Be." "Just as there are different types of grief responses, and these we should perhaps either limit or eliminate, we've seen that these grief responses have different objects. Jeff wants us to discuss the evaluations about the death of a loved one that make him grieve. They are the sympathy evaluation, that death is a great evil for the dead loved one, and the ego evaluation, that death is a great evil for the dead person's loving ones, that is, the survivors. So, a consolation might be an argument to show that either or both these evaluations are wrong."

Jeff said, "Let's call these 'evaluation consolations.' An evaluation consolation is an argument that an evaluation, upon which grief is supposedly based, is false."

"One thing I'm not yet clear about," said Phil, "are there any strategies for consolation besides evaluation consolations? That is, is there any other way to argue that grief is wrong or mistaken besides arguing that the evaluations made by the griever are false?"

Jeff said, "I think a survey of consolation will reveal that not all arguments against grief are directed against the evaluations. In addition to a survey, the issue itself seems to require the possibility of another approach. Connie suggested that perhaps people approve of inhibition immediately following a loved one's death, but disapprove of sorrow. Grief is, in part, a *response* to these evaluations. This not only raises the question of the truth of these evaluations but also whether the response is appropriate or correct, or wrong."

Phil said, "Inhibition and sorrow are two different responses to the loss of a loved one. Either these are based on two different sets of evaluations, which I doubt, or else the same set of evaluations yields different responses. This *suggests*, but it does not prove, that either one or both of these responses is not justified by the evaluations. This raises the question of the proper relation between evaluations about the loss of a loved one on the one hand, and sorrow and inhibition on the other. Arguments which criticize the grief responses themselves, rather than the griever's evaluations, we'll call 'response consolations.' This unspecific and negative definition will do for now, but we'll sharpen it when we turn our attention toward response consolations."

More Basics: Intrinsic, Consequential and Organic Value

Phil continued, "Okay. Now, in considering whether the sympathy or ego evaluations are true or false, we must consider at least two types of evaluations."

"Please explain," Connie requested.

"Sure, but it's a lengthy explanation. According to a classification often used by philosophers, something is good or bad, either intrinsically or consequentially. The intrinsic value of a thing is its value considered independently of everything else, the value of the thing itself, the value that it has in itself. Please, somebody nod!" which Jeff and Connie dutifully did.

Phil resumed, "For example, the taste of barbecue sauce is intrinsically good, and so is the taste of chocolate cake. . . ."

"Please, I'm hungry! No more food examples! Where are those chicken wings?" Connie exclaimed.

"An example popular with undergraduates and myself is that an orgasm is intrinsically good, worth having for its own sake, desirable in itself. Likewise, the feelings of joy or contentment," Jeff said.

"I think I'm getting what you mean by 'intrinsically good,' but to be sure, may I have some contrasts?" Connie said.

Phil offered, "Examples of things widely regarded as intrinsically bad or evil are toothaches, itches, thirst, the feeling of frustration. These are things worth avoiding because they are in themselves bad."

"Consequential value is the value of a thing insofar as it causes, or is either necessary or sufficient for, something with intrinsic value. Something is consequentially good which causes, or is either contingently necessary or sufficient for, something intrinsically good. Something is consequentially bad which causes, or is either contingently necessary or sufficient for something intrinsically bad. So, our money is consequentially good for us in that it will enable us to eat our food, which will be intrinsically good, I hope. The taste of my soda, which is intrinsically good for me, is, I hope, consequentially good for my companions, if it makes me more exuberant."

"But is consequentially bad for you insofar as it contributes to tooth decay," Connie added.

"Is that payback for my mentioning food again?" Phil joked.

Connie stated, "All right, I understand intrinsic good and bad, at least as far as your examples go, and I understand consequential good and bad. I also understand that something intrinsically good could be consequentially bad, and that something intrinsically bad could be consequentially good, for example, when toothache alerts a person to tooth decay and so better dental care is practiced."

"Furthermore," Phil continued, "among those things with intrinsic value, some have organic value."

"What is organic value?" Connie asked.

Phil answered, "This is an especially controversial category, even in an area of philosophy replete with controversy. The organic value of a thing is not its consequential value, it is an intrinsic value; organic value is the value of a whole insofar as this value differs from the sum, or aggregate, of the intrinsic value of its parts. Colors, for example, have an intrinsic value, let's say that red is more pleasant than beige, but the value of a painting is not simply the aggregate of the value of the colors from which it is composed. If not, then a canvas covered in red would have greater value than a Rembrandt.

"Here's another example contrasting organic value and the sum of the intrinsic value of the parts of a whole: a single note of music, say from a pluck of a string, has a certain value unto itself, an intrinsic value, which is probably slight. A musical composition consists of notes, each with its particular sound, and pauses organized in certain ways. The value of the piece consists more in the way these are organized, the rhythm, the melody, and arrangement than it consists in the sum of the intrinsic value of the notes in the piece."

"Otherwise my piano playing would be as good as Connie's!" Jeff said.

Phil added, "An interesting consequence of organic value is that a whole can have greater value because it has some parts of little, or even negative, intrinsic value. We already saw an example of this in contrasting a somber Rembrandt painting with a canvas awash with red. Red is intrinsically more pleasing than the somber tones in a Rembrandt painting, but a completely red canvas would have less aesthetic value than a Rembrandt. Music also provides examples. Supposing that some notes or chords are 'sweeter' than others, a composition might nevertheless be better for including some less sweet, or even 'sour' notes or chords. An inharmonious chord can make a composition more interesting."

"The dissonance at the end of the Beatles' 'Mother Nature's Son' is a good example," offered Connie.

"Actually, I believe that that's discord, not dissonance, at the end of 'Mother Nature's Son' since it is not resolved," said Jeff.

"An example of organic value applicable to this evening is given by the philosopher, Clarence Irving Lewis, when he says:

> The pleasure of good company and the concert is not the pleasure of the company plus the pleasure of the music, but is the pleasure found in the total state of affairs including these constituents.[3]

Adapting this quote, we might say that the value of the experience of the two together differs from the value of both considered separately."

"I thought we might go the entire evening without a philosopher being quoted, but some erudition won't hurt!" Connie joked. "But, Phil, you said that the category of organic value is especially controversial. But, as you've explained it, that there is organic value seems as obvious as that there are intrinsic and consequential values."

Phil explained, "One thing is clear. From these and other examples, we know that the value of a whole is sometimes different from the value of the sum of its parts. What is not clear is how to understand this. How is it that the value of a whole can or does differ from the sum of the value of its parts? Different explanations have been offered. But determining the precise nature of organic value is a difficulty worth avoiding."

Connie reassured, "Your examples, if nothing else, make me think that I know how to use 'organic value.' Now, if you've finished explaining intrinsic, consequential and organic value, how is this going to help us comfort Jeff?"

The Billy J. Kramer and the Dakotas's version of John Lennon and Paul McCartney's "I Call Your Name" took over after the Jive Five's "My True Story," as Phil explained.

"If death is a great evil, either for the dead person, or the loving ones of the deceased, and if our classification of values is comprehensive, then either death is intrinsically evil for the dead person or the survivors, or, it is consequentially evil for the dead person or the survivors; and if it is intrinsically evil, it might be organically evil for the dead person or the survivors. Evaluation consolations challenge some or all these evaluations as made by the griever. We might help Jeff, if we look at the grievers' evaluations in turn, and perhaps offer evaluation consolations."

Jeff said, "I'm not optimistic, but I certainly think we should try. If nothing else, it might do some good to articulate the evil which has befallen my mom and me. Now that we have an overview, I'd like us to begin by looking at evaluation consolations, and afterwards we should examine response consolations."

Connie and Phil agreed and at that moment their appetizer arrived.

Study Questions

(1) Can you think of any objects of grief not mentioned in this chapter?
- Can you think of any grief responses besides sorrow, inhibition, and the phases of grief (denial, anger, bargaining, depression and acceptance or resignation) mentioned in this volume?

(2) Does Jeff's grief appear normal to you?

(3) We see a wide range of emotional response to "bad news":
- What is the difference between genuine grief and the mere somber acknowledgement of a misfortune?
- How do we make somber acknowledgement of a misfortune?
- Are these acknowledgements like "small-scale" grief responses?

(4) This chapter introduced an area of philosophy sometimes termed the theory of value.
- *Do* intrinsic and organic values exist?
- Do all intrinsic goods have anything in common with each other?
- Do all intrinsic evils have anything in common with each other?

Five

THE ANNIHILATION CONSOLATION

The three dug in. Jeff listened as the Beatles' "Julia," penned by John Lennon for his dead mother, began:

> Half of what I say is meaningless,
> But I say it just to reach you, Julia.

"My mom died on the same date as Julia, the fifteenth of July," Jeff said, as though speaking to himself. He then apologized for the remark.

"That's okay," Connie stressed, "Obsession is part of grief. That's one reason why it's such a drag and can't last. Don't apologize for whatever is on your mind."

"Okay, as long as you're just as frank," Jeff replied and they agreed.

Phil began, "Let's examine each possible evaluation in turn. We have the sympathy evaluation, that the loved one's death is a great evil for the loved one, and we have the ego evaluation, that the loved one's death is a great evil for the ones who loved the dead; and both of these alleged evils might be understood as either intrinsically, or consequentially evil. Now, I can't understand what could be meant by 'Loved ones' deaths are intrinsically evil for their loving ones.' It might *lead* to things intrinsically evil for their loving ones, but that would mean that death is consequentially evil for the loving ones; it would not mean that death is intrinsically evil for them. For something to be intrinsically good or evil for someone, it has to be a state or condition of that person. I don't think this is profound; I'm just trying to understand 'intrinsically good or evil for someone.'"

Jeff said, "I think you are right, but I am not sure. At this point, I know no meaning to 'My mother's death is intrinsically evil for me.' But as far as I can see, my grief isn't based on a belief that her death is intrinsically evil for me."

"All right, I just don't want to leave any loose ends. . . . There is a more ambitious evaluation consolation which concludes that the death is not intrinsically evil for the dead person," said Phil.

"Why isn't death intrinsically evil for the dead person?" asked Connie.

The Annihilation Consolation

"I believe we three agree that a dead person no longer has consciousness. A dead person doesn't sense, feel or think. And that's not because of the absence of external stimuli, that's because the person no longer exists," Phil answered.

"I see," said Connie, "the examples you've given of 'intrinsic value' are all examples of a person's state of consciousness: sensations or emotions. Since a dead person neither senses nor feels, nor even thinks, nothing can be intrinsically evil for the dead."

Phil continued, "Yes, Connie. We try to imagine death. Of course, one can imagine corpses, various funerary practices, such as burials, and so on. Further, one can imagine one's own body being a corpse, being placed in a casket, buried and such events. But the corpse doesn't experience these things. When we imagine the corpse, if we imagine these events as experienced by the corpse, then we imagine something which doesn't happen. The person who died doesn't experience these or any things. Therefore, common pictures of death are misleading because they make it seem as though death is intrinsically evil for the dead person. Death, considered as the cessation of consciousness, cannot be pictured.

"The dead person, that is, the person who no longer exists, does not experience darkness, for example. The dead don't feel cold, or their flesh being consumed, or smell it rotting away. A dead person isn't afraid, frustrated, lonely or bored. They don't feel like they are plummeting into an abyss. Many of these pictures seem to come from imagining what the experience of a corpse would be like. But, as we agree, corpses don't have experiences. We picture darkness because a dead person can't see. We picture cold because the ground is cold. We picture fear or boredom since a living person with such limited stimuli would feel these emotions. The fourth picture, of plummeting into an abyss, is more difficult to explain. Perhaps it's an imagined consequence of, or risk incurred by, a body walking around in total darkness. Perhaps this picture is connected with burial."

"I wonder whether societies which customarily cremate their dead have the same pictures of being dead," Connie conjectured. "With the corpse quickly reduced to ashes maybe they refrain from imagining death as though it were experienced by the corpse. If they do picture it, perhaps they picture heat or pain or choking. Perhaps they think the dead soar rather than plummet."

Oddly, this pop restaurant played Fleetwood Mac's almost "medievally" morbid "Dust," and as the three friends continued to enjoy their appetizer, Jeff commented on Connie's speculation. "That's interesting. But darkness, with its psychological effects, still seems to be the closest picture to the cessation of consciousness; not that they are anything alike. It's just that, when we try to imagine being dead, if we proceed by eliminating stimulus after stimulus, since we are visually oriented, we end up with darkness and its psychological effects. Therefore, I would suspect that, regardless of the funerary practices of one's society, many of these pictures would still be common."

Jeff continued, "Everyone, including myself, lapses into the mistake of trying to picture the cessation of consciousness. But I'm aware that this is a mistake; it's a mistake to suppose that an annihilated person experiences anything. Yet I still can't help but think that death is intrinsically evil for the dead person even though he or she'll never be conscious again. Let me put it this way: as paradigmatic of 'intrinsic value' as your few examples seem to be, even to me, I suspect that there is another sense of 'intrinsically evil' which does not refer to disagreeable states of consciousness, such as pain or fear, and that death is intrinsically evil in that other sense."

"What other sorts of intrinsic evils might there be?" asked Connie.

Jeff hesitated and then spoke. "I am reluctant to contest Phil's claim that all intrinsic evils are states of consciousness since that would require us to discuss thorny issues in metaphysics and value theory."

"Go ahead," urged Connie.

Phil concurred, "We'll do what is necessary to try to console you," and he added, "Maybe we need to discuss these 'thorny issues' less than you fear."

Thus encouraged, Jeff began, "Some things which are not states of awareness might possess an intrinsic value. For example, one *might* claim that the physical universe as a whole is beautiful. It is vast and contains great variety, order, and so on. This beauty, when perceived, causes pleasure or intrinsically valuable states of consciousness. Perhaps the *contemplation* of the universe has an intrinsic value, or perhaps intrinsic value belongs to the feeling of grandeur which results from its contemplation; but besides these intrinsically valuable states of awareness, the universe itself *might* possess an intrinsic value which *makes* its contemplation worthwhile and its admiration justified.

"One might claim that the universe is intrinsically valuable, and, through the intrinsic value which it possesses, causes states of consciousness which have intrinsic value. In other words, the universe has consequential value through its intrinsic value. While the universe causes appreciation, saying that it is valuable is not just an elliptical way of saying that it causes appreciation.

"Besides the grand example of the beauty of the universe as a whole, there are other things which are not states of awareness which might be thought to possess an intrinsic value. For examples, radiant sunsets and floral fragrances might themselves be intrinsically good, and not just the awareness of these. Noxious odors and bitter tastes might be intrinsically bad, not just the awareness of these."

Phil commented, "As you warned us, these examples raise controversial issues which are almost as old as metaphysics and value theory. 'What exists other than states of awareness?' and 'Does it possess intrinsic value?' I certainly hope that consolation will not require solution of these perennial problems."

Connie said, "We do not need to settle any disputes about what exists besides states of awareness. Because what does any of this have to do with whether death is intrinsically evil *for* the dead person? Okay, I realize that we began with an argument that death cannot be intrinsically evil because intrinsic evils are all states of consciousness and that death, rather than being an intrinsically evil state of consciousness, is the cessation of consciousness. It makes sense that you two have been discussing whether it is true that all intrinsic evils are states of consciousness; however, by this point it should be clear that the counter-examples proposed by Jeff in no way support his claim that death is intrinsically evil for the dead person, or *for* anyone. Because an intrinsic evil which is not a state of consciousness, even were it possible that there are such, would not be an intrinsic evil for anyone. Even if the physical universe has intrinsic value it doesn't become valuable *for* anyone until one experiences it. Even, for example, were there something intrinsically evil about the state of a corpse, it would not be an evil for anyone, least of all for the dead person."

Phil concurred, "Yes, Connie. To affirm that there are any intrinsic evils for the dead person assumes that the dead person is conscious."

Jeff said, "I agree with Connie that my counter-examples, whether successful or not, were irrelevant to your consolation because they could not show that death is intrinsically evil for anyone. I took a wrong direction. But I was led to it because I can't but feel that the consolation based on annihilation aimed at the griever's intrinsic sympathy evaluation is facile. I can't help but think that it avoids a profound but obvious truth."

"We'll give you every opportunity to express the truth which you suspect is being overlooked."

Jeff added, "Besides pleasant experiences being regarded as intrinsically valuable for a person there are other things regarded as intrinsically valuable for a person: 'possessing a good will,' 'achieving or pursuing human excellence.' These theories about the intrinsically valuable emphasize a person's *activity* rather than simply an enjoyable state of awareness or consciousness."

Phil replied, "I shall forego the question as to whether these theories as to the intrinsically valuable are really alternatives to the view that all intrinsic values are states of consciousness. Certainly at least, these theories require *some* reference to states of consciousness, even if, according to them, intrinsic value does not consist entirely in states of consciousness. Instead, I'll make the following comments: first, on the theory which identifies the good will as that which is worthwhile having for its own sake, what is intrinsically evil? The evil will? Being vicious or selfish? But the dead are not inflicted with an evil will. They aren't wicked. So, the supposed intrinsic evil of death for the dead cannot be explained in this way. Second, though, of course, it's true that an annihilated person does not achieve or pursue human excellence, this doesn't mean that the dead languish in mediocrity or plunge into a state diametrically opposite that of excellence. The dead person does not exist in an extreme state of inactivity; the dead no longer exists."

Imagining the Dead as Conscious

Jeff said, "Although I am still not convinced that death is not intrinsically evil for the dead person, I do agree that I have not yet found a way to explicate this. In particular, I am convinced that the dead suffer no intrinsically evil states of consciousness. Though I'm convinced of this, I am still haunted by images of the dead being aware of their plight. Still, my grief is not based on this absurd idea. In fact, I believe that *consolers* as well as grievers surreptitiously suppose that the dead person retains consciousness.

"First, it is not unusual for comforters, philosophers, and 'average Joes' alike to refer to the dead or annihilated, those whose loss of consciousness is permanent, as being 'at rest' or 'at peace.' Nevertheless, the cessation of consciousness is altogether different from the feeling of tranquility or untroubled existence. Yet, as 'rest' and 'peace' often refer to either untroubled existence or the feeling of tranquility, these *words* have a power to comfort which has nothing to do with what might truly be said of dead persons. The words are comforting rather than the truth."

Connie and Phil nodded in agreement. Connie added, "The famous line from Tacitus, 'They made a wasteland and they called it 'peace,'' refers to a very similar equivocation on 'peace.'"[1]

"Yes," said Jeff. "Second, I believe that consolers offer comfort by imagining the annihilated person as having a continued existence as a disembodied observer, observing events of both personal and historic significance."

Asked to explain, Jeff continued. "We agree that we cannot imagine, that is, form images of, being dead, the permanent cessation of consciousness. But we can imagine what the world is, or would be like after a person's death. We might imagine that person's corpse, the burial, *et cetera*. We might also imagine the subsequent lives of loved ones. We might further imagine strangers to that person carrying out their routines, or suffering their own losses, or we might imagine turning points in history, turning points which come after their deaths. One might imagine any of these things even if one imagines that it is one's own death which precedes these imagined events.

"Of course, in that case, one must not imagine oneself in these events other than as a corpse. However, while one cannot include oneself within the imagined events as a conscious being, one is imagining these events oneself. Probably one is narrating. At the very least, one is the editor of these events. No, indeed, one is the animator, the creator of these imaginary events. Therefore, when one imagines the continued existence of the world, loved ones, strangers, or human history after one's own death, despite the stricture that one is not to be included, one does include oneself, at least as observer, but in fact, in several roles.

"I am not saying that 'The world continues to exist after my death' entails that 'I exist after my death.' I am saying that, when one attempts to imagine the world continuing to exist after one's own death, since one imagines it oneself, one has an emotional response to the imagined events as though one were able to witness them. While 'I will not exist' does not entail 'The world will not exist' we cheat an understanding of 'I will not exist' when we imagine the continued existence of the world.

"By analogy, and partly because it can be less difficult to identify with loved ones than with others, when we imagine the world minus a loved one, we imagine the dead person's continued existence, if only as an observer. That is, when one imagines the world after one's own death one receives comfort from one's status as observer, despite the fact that one's continued existence contradicts what we seek to imagine, namely, the world after one's annihilation. Then, granting the modest assumption that one is not an exception in these matters, we surreptitiously imagine others, especially loved ones, continuing as observers, even though it is oneself who imagines the posthumous events.

"In sum, certain words, images and conceptual activities have an affective power beyond, and perhaps even contrary to, the propositional content of what we conceive or imagine. This power is abused by grievers and consolers alike."

Connie suggested, "Perhaps continued existence as a disembodied observer would be particularly satisfying to academics."

Phil said, "It's possible that both consolers and grievers draw comfort and grief respectively from the absurd continued existence of the annihilated. Be that as it may, annihilation is neither intrinsically good nor evil for the dead person."

Summary of the Conversation

No sense is yet given to the intrinsic ego evaluation, that death is intrinsically evil for the loving ones of the dead.

With respect to the intrinsic sympathy evaluation: if intrinsic evils for a person must be, or require, states of that person's awareness, then death is not intrinsically evil for the dead. Even if there are intrinsic values which are not states of awareness, these cannot be intrinsically valuable for anyone, unless concerning states of that person's awareness.

Grievers and consolers alike surreptitiously introduce the continued existence of the annihilated. Grievers sometimes think of the dead as experiencing entombment, and so on. Comforters sometimes think of the dead as disembodied observers. Even if comforters acknowledge that the dead do not survive as spectators, the mere act of imagining events after one's death (or a loved one's death) might have the same comforting effect as though one believed in continued existence as a spectator. This might explain some of the comfort one might receive from imagining the continued existence of the world after one's death.

Assuming that it is worse to be afraid, lonely, and in the dark than it is to be annihilated, the grievers' surreptitious supposition makes death appear worse than it is. On the other hand, assuming that it is better to be a disembodied observer than it is to be annihilated, the consolers' surreptitious supposition makes death appear better than it is.

Some consolers also use "peace" and "rest" equivocally to mean nonexistence on the one hand and tranquility or untroubled existence on the other.

Study Questions

(1) Is the sympathy evaluation largely based on absurdly imagining that the annihilated are still aware?

(2) At one end of our ideas about death we have ideas of the afterlife; at the other end is the idea of annihilation.
Do people sometimes derive comfort from an unarticulated in-between image or concept?

Six

DEATH AS DEPRIVATION

The Guess Who's alternately breezy and desperate "Undun" played as the conversation resumed.

Diametric and Deprivation Evils

"Okay, we've just gone through the annihilation argument against the intrinsic sympathy evaluation, that death is intrinsically evil for the dead person" Phil began.

"Though I'm not convinced by the argument," said Jeff.

"*What* evil is entailed by being dead, or annihilated?" Phil asked.

Jeff answered, "The paradigms of 'intrinsic evil' which we've been using do not reveal the evil intrinsic to being dead. The evil entailed by being dead is not like the intrinsic evils of pain, feelings of boredom, confusion or frustration; it's unlike any of the examples we've used. Rather, death is evil as a *deprivation* of things which are intrinsically good. Death is a 'deprivation evil.' I would insist that we accept, as an axiom, that if something is intrinsically good, that is, worth having for its own sake, without consideration of anything else, then the deprivation of that thing is worth avoiding, without consideration of anything else, in other words, intrinsically evil. Nothing can be worthwhile in itself the non-existence of which is indifferent."

"That sounds like it must be right, though I'm not convinced," Phil said.

Connie said, "Jeff, *earlier* we were discussing the lost goods or deprivations entailed by death. This seems to be a crucial point."

Jeff said, "Let's get a little clearer about deprivations and intrinsic evils generally. Let's suppose that we can precisely compare, or weigh, goods and evils to each other. Let's say some good—for example, the experience of eating some tasty food—is 'equal' to some evil—for example, a mild stomachache—in the sense that they 'cancel each other out.' Now a stomachache isn't a deprivation evil; a deprivation evil would be not having the tasty food. In other words, the non-deprivation evil—a mild stomachache—is as bad as the good—eating the food—is good. Because of this relation of 'canceling out,' which non-deprivation evils, our heretofore paradigmatic intrinsic evils, have to these goods, we might call these goods '*diametric* goods' and non-deprivation evils '*diametric* evils.' They are diametric opposites, you might say."

"I think I understand. A diametric good is like having a credit for a dollar. A diametric evil is like being a dollar in debt. They cancel each other out. If you were fifty cents in debt the evil would only partially cancel out the good. Whereas a deprivation evil is like being penniless," Connie said.

Phil exclaimed, "The difference between diametric and deprivation evils is important! Jeff, you claim that death is a deprivation evil. I have some questions about that. But before I get to those, let me say that even if death is a deprivation evil, it would be worse if it were a diametric evil. Everything else being equal, it is worse having a diametric evil than merely being deprived of some good."

Connie continued with her analogue, "It's worse being a dollar in debt than penniless."

Jeff remarked, "Slow down. Yes, it's worse being a dollar in debt than penniless. But that's because being a dollar in debt is *two* evils: the deprivation of not having any money—being penniless—and indebtedness. Likewise, it's worse having a diametric evil and being deprived of the good which would cancel it out than merely being deprived of that good. Everything else being equal, two evils are worse than one. This obvious point does not show that, everything else being equal, diametric evils are worse than deprivation evils.

"Having a good and an evil which cancel each other out is neither better nor worse, intrinsically, than having neither, that is, having the deprivation evil only. Having both credits and debits for a dollar is neither better nor worse than being penniless. In other words, when the diametric evil is not combined with the deprivation it is not worse to have the diametric evil than it is to have the deprivation. More precisely, with respect to the same diametric good, its deprivation and its diametric evil are equally worth avoiding, apart from consideration of anything else. Having 'nothing but troubles' is worse than having neither pleasures nor troubles, but losing a good can be just as bad as having some trouble. So, there's no consolation to be found against death's being evil as a deprivation by claiming that deprivation evils are not as bad as diametric evils. Of course, death might have been worse than it is: deprivation evils *and* diametric evils."

"So," Connie summed, "the claim that death is intrinsically evil for the dead means that death inflicts *either* deprivation or diametric evils on the dead. I take it that we agree with the annihilation consolation that there are no diametric evils for the dead, following their death. So, your claim is that death inflicts deprivation evils on the dead."

"As Though" the Dead Never Existed

"Yes," Jeff said, "as there are no diametric goods for the dead person, death is a deprivation evil for the dead person. Death deprives a person of all possible goods. Look, you both have creative and expansive attitudes toward your own lives, so I know that I do not need to *itemize* the goods a dead person might have continued to enjoy had life continued. The dead have been deprived of beauty, pleasure, love, joy, the excitement of discovery. . . ."

Then Jeff interrupted himself. "Here's something about a dead person's loss which is worth emphasizing because it's easy to overlook: the dead are not only deprived of their future, they are also, in a sense, deprived of their past. For example, when listening enjoyably to a familiar song, the complex good of that experience is a combination of the present hearing of that song and the present recollection of other occasions when one heard the song. In other words, persons' futures contain two temporally different objects for them to enjoy. In the future one can enjoy future events or objects—then present— and one can enjoy past events or objects by recalling them. By depriving the dead of their future they're deprived further enjoyment of their past."

"Hold on," Phil requested. "Let's be careful to avoid confusion. Let's not make death appear to be any worse than it might be. The dead are deprived of all future goods. That means that they cannot, after their death, enjoy recalling things which occurred before their death. But of course, dead or not, people cannot literally *relive* their earlier enjoyments. There are many pleasures which I wish I could relive, but I can't—and death has nothing to do with that. So, death has not deprived the dead of reliving their former pleasures. Furthermore, death doesn't change the past. That the person has died does not mean that he or she hadn't enjoyed what he or she had earlier enjoyed. Whether one lives or dies, the past can be neither relived nor undone. I agree that the dead are denied any recollection of their previous experiences. I just don't want us to get carried away by confusions and magnify the evil of death."

"I completely agree," said Jeff. "My mom's dead, but it's still true, the truth is unaltered, that she enjoyed raising a family, watching soaps, having a husband and friends and so on. Were this not true, death could not have deprived her of them. Her death does not mean that she never existed, or never enjoyed, but part of the terrible evil of death is captured in the phrase 'It's *as though* she never existed.' Among other things, this phrase captures the fact that persons 'accumulate' their past in their memories, in their skills, and in their personality, and that they lose this entire 'accumulation.' This could also be part of the meaning behind the statement that 'We go out as we came in.'

Jeff continued, "It's important to emphasize the loss of the accumulation of the past if for no other reason than that a prospective consoler might overlook this loss because it is a future good dealing with the past. That is, it might be easy to overlook the goods of recollection even when admitting that the dead are deprived of all possible goods following their deaths.

"And the deprivation by death is quantitatively great. For, while we reject the solipsistic idea that when a self dies the entire world ceases to exist, it is true to say that *an* entire world so to speak, a world of future experiences, has been lost by the dead. Because of death we are deprived of our 'inner world,' the story we tell and retell to ourselves about ourselves. That internal monologue which ties together the parts of one's life and integrates the past and present is silenced."

Connie warned, "Okay, but the phrase 'it's as though the dead never existed' is a phrase with a *heart rending* sound and unless one is careful the phrase can make death seem even worse than as you've explained it."

"Yes, thank you," Jeff said. "My mom did exist and her death does not change that. I need to keep reassuring myself of this."

As Roy Orbison's "It's Over" began, and the three friends awaited their entrees, Phil commented, "I have several questions about the claim that death is a deprivation evil for the dead person. At the outset, however, let it be clear that I agree that a dead person no longer experiences any good things. My concerns about the claim that death is a deprivation evil for the dead person do not come from a belief in the afterlife. Rather, my concerns are that grievers confusedly characterize the annihilation of their loved ones by saying that death is a deprivation evil for the dead and thus assimilate death to diametric evils, and so grieve unnecessarily. Your characterization of the fact that a dead person is annihilated, namely, that death is a deprivation evil for the dead person, might be a false or meaningless and misleading characterization. And this characterization might be stimulating your grief," warned Phil.

"Okay, Phil," asked Connie, "what are your reservations?"

Conditional Value

Phil began, "First, death does not deprive the dead person of any goods, if all the goods of life are conditional upon the person's being alive."

"That sounds peculiar," Jeff interrupted, "Of course, the *attainment* or enjoyment of any goods in life is conditional upon the person's being alive. You can't enjoy something unless you're alive. But I don't see where this could lead to a consolation."

Phil continued, "Thanks for pointing that out. However, what I meant was that if all the goods of life are *good* only on condition that one is alive, then death is not a deprivation of goods. I did not mean that if all the goods of life are *attainable* only on condition that one is alive, then death is not a deprivation of goods. I meant that the things lost were good only on condition that one were alive."

"We must be careful not to confuse these," Jeff cautioned.

"I'm not clear about the distinction," Connie remarked.

Phil responded to Connie's request for clarification. "At least some good things are only conditionally good. By calling something 'conditionally good' I mean that it is only good on condition that something else exists."

Connie said, "You mean like money? Money has little or no value except for the fact that people will give you things for it. So, money's *good* only on *condition* that people give you something for it. Money's a conditional good."

Phil continued, "Right. Now let's suppose that a person were plunked down into a society where money had no worth and yet people still obtained what they wanted. Well, under those circumstances the person should not regret losing money."

Connie added with a smile, "Or a woman gets stranded alone on a deserted island without her birth control pills."

Phil and Jeff just looked at each other.

"It wouldn't make sense for her to be upset over the loss of her birth control pills," Connie concluded. "But what does this have to do with consolation over death? Guys? Guys?"

Phil smiled. "Well, just suppose that *all* of life's goods are conditional, that is, worthwhile only on condition that something else exists. And let's more specifically suppose that all life's goods are worthwhile only on the condition that one is alive. Therefore, just as it wouldn't make sense for our stranded island girl to regard the loss of her pills as harm, the loss of life's goods due to death would not be harm because they're worthwhile only on the condition that one exists. The things lost through death wouldn't be goods anymore anyhow."

"Explain to me why, if the value of all life's goods is conditional upon being alive, that death would not be a deprivation of goods," Jeff requested.

Phil explained, "Let me more formally express my reservation about 'death deprives the dead of goods.' 'Y is a conditional good, and conditional upon X' means that if X, then Y is good, but not otherwise. Now suppose that Y's *existence* also depends upon X. If X does not exist, then neither does Y. But then, if X does not exist, Y would not be good anyhow. So, the loss of X would not involve the loss of something which is good, but would instead involve the loss of something which *would* have been good. So, the loss of X would not have deprived one of a good."

"I'm still not sure that that isn't a loss. But please continue," Jeff requested.

Phil obliged. "Jeff, the loss of a conditional good, *along with* the loss of that upon which it is conditionally good, is not regrettable. Let me be clearer than I had been: the loss of a conditional good is not the loss of something which would have been good had only it existed, it is the loss of something which would have been good had only something *else* existed. Using the money example, loss of money is the loss of a good, which is regrettable only in a society which assigns money exchange value. It's not that money would have been good if only it existed, it would have been good only if something else, its exchange value, had existed.

"Here's an analogy: let's say you've enrolled in a course. Well, of course getting an A is better than getting an F. But if you don't enroll at all, you're not missing something because you don't have an A. The person who doesn't enroll is not worse off than someone who does enroll and gets an A. Of course, the person who gets an A is better off than the person who gets an F. So, the consolation that I'm offering states that while a life with many goods is better than a life with few goods someone who's dead isn't worse off than someone alive with many goods."

Connie said, "The consolation sounded better when I couldn't follow it!"

Jeff smiled and said, "All right. So, there are two questions. First, whether the value of *all* goods is conditional. Second, whether being alive is one of those conditions," Jeff summarized.

"As to the first question, I believe that only consequential goods, things good only for what they produce or ones that lead to some end, such as money or medicine, can be conditional. I believe that some goods in life are desirable or worthy of being attained, *apart from consideration of anything else*. In other words, intrinsic goods cannot be conditional. Otherwise they would not be good apart from consideration of anything else. And I believe that I observe that there are intrinsic goods. The feelings of excitement, joy, tranquility, sensual pleasures and much more are good not just for their consequences, but intrinsically, in themselves. I do not pretend that this is an argument. It is a report of my experience.

"As for the second question, I think that there is a very strong *ad hominem* argument for the conclusion that it cannot be the case that all life's goods are conditional upon being alive. A person who chooses to continue living in the hope that he or she will continue experiencing goods does so because these goods would be good, that is, would be worthy of being attained, regardless whether one chose to live. That is, these things make living good, rather than that life makes them good. Life makes them possible, but it does not make them good. We live so that we can enjoy the good things in life; it's not that these things are good because one happens to be alive anyway. Using Phil's analogy, the possibility of getting an *A* does not give anyone a reason to enroll. Likewise, according to this consolation, life's goods are not a reason to continue living.

"In other words, were all life's goods good only on condition that one were alive, there would be no reason of this kind to refrain from suicide. I believe that this is a strong *ad hominem* since few consolers would wish grievers to draw the conclusion that there are fewer reasons to refrain from suicide."

"On the contrary, few consolers, at least in literature, have expressed a clear commitment to the idea that we should choose to live because life has unconditional goods," Phil suggested firmly. "Many philosophers have written that we should choose to live because it is our *duty* rather than because of the idea that life has unconditional goods which we should pursue."

Jeff replied, "Still, I think that few consolers, especially these days, would wish their consolations to limit the number of reasons for a griever to not commit suicide. But the consolation that all life's goods are good only on condition that one is alive has the effect of severely limiting the number of reasons for a griever, or anyone else for that matter, not to commit suicide. For if all life's goods were good only on condition that one were alive, then if one were dead, such as by suicide, these things would not be worthy of attainment. And if they were unworthy of attainment, there would be no reason for one to live so that they could be attained. Therefore, if all life's goods were good only on condition that one were alive, there would be no reason for one to live so that they could be attained. Living would be the reason they were good, rather than these being reasons that living is good.

"The problem with this and other consolations is that the facts which justify the choice to continue living are the same facts which make death a great evil!" Jeff concluded excitedly.

Death as a Deprivation

"Phil, what *other* reservations do you have about the claim that death is a deprivation evil for the dead person?" Connie asked.

"Earlier, Jeff argued that deprivations are intrinsically evil, that is, worth avoiding, apart from consideration of anything else, since there are intrinsic goods, states which are worth being, apart from consideration of anything else. This is a forceful argument. I nevertheless have some concerns about understanding death as a deprivation evil. If these reservations can help Jeff in his grief, then I would be happy to share them.

"First, death is not a typical deprivation. It is *total*. This means, among other things, that the people thus deprived are unaware, after the fact, of their deprivation."

"But Phil," said Jeff, "though perhaps diametric evils for a person are impossible without some awareness of them by that person, awareness is not necessary for deprivation evils. We can imagine people who lose their sight and their memory of what it is like to see. Nevertheless, their blindness is a great loss for them. In fact, memory loss itself involves some unawareness of what has been lost. To be exact, people who lose a memory might be aware of having lost it, but are unaware of the particulars of that loss. These are evils though persons are unaware of them.

"In addition to these plausible counter-examples to the claim that deprivation without awareness by the deprived person is not an evil for the deprived person, there is the following argument: you seem to implicitly grant in your doubt about the evil of *total* deprivation that the *awareness* of a deprivation is an evil. Do you grant this?"

"Yes, I do," answered Phil, "the awareness of a deprivation often causes various forms of anxiety."

"Do you think persons aware of their deprivation are justified in feeling anxiety?" Jeff asked.

"I'm still not certain. Isn't that part of what we're trying to find out in our conversation tonight, whether the awareness of a loss justifies anxiety?" Phil dodged.

Jeff said, "Fine, you're right. We're not yet in a position to settle whether the awareness of a deprivation justifies anxiety, but let's make this implication clear: if anxiety due to the awareness of a deprivation is justified, then deprivation must be an evil. And if deprivation is an evil, then total deprivation is an even greater evil."

Phil replied, "All right. But keep in mind that many consolers would deny the antecedent of your first conditional. They would deny that awareness of a deprivation justifies anxiety."

"Granted, but as I've already argued, if anything is worthwhile, its absence is worth avoiding," Jeff reminded.

"True. And although I agree that life is abundant with good things, we mustn't overlook the fact that some consolers would deny this," Phil indicated.

"Then they're not welcome to join us!" Connie exclaimed.

"And I wonder how consoling they would be! For instance, they would deprive us of some reasons for not committing suicide," Jeff added.

"Hmm. The denials that life has any goods and that life has any goods unconditional on one's being alive have the same implication," Connie observed.

"Yes. Both denials limit the kind of reasons to choose to live," Jeff said.

Death and Prenatal Non-Existence Compared

Phil began. "I have a *second* reason for doubts about the claim that annihilation, or total deprivation, is an evil. And that is that annihilation is the same as prenatal non-existence. That is, before one was born one didn't exist. Yet people's attitude toward prenatal non-existence is very different from their attitude toward death. People are not in the least distressed by their prenatal non-existence. This suggests that prenatal non-existence is not an evil. And if it isn't, then neither is annihilation," Phil argued.

Jeff began, "You seem to think that indifference toward prenatal non-existence is justified while concern over death is not. I think that different attitudes toward prenatal and postmortem non-existence are justified, at least to some extent. But before I reconcile comparative indifference toward prenatal non-existence with the belief that death is a great evil, let me note something about the two reasons you've thus far offered for doubting that annihilation is evil for the dead person.

"Your first reason was that awareness after the fact of death or *postmortem* non-existence by the annihilated is impossible and therefore death cannot be evil. Your second reason includes pointing out that people typically show comparative indifference toward their prenatal non-existence. These reasons are ironically conjoined, to say the least. For people do have awareness, after the fact, of their prenatal non-existence. This makes me suspect, though it does not prove, that *either* the evil of deprivation does not consist in the awareness, after the fact, of the deprivation or that there is a justified difference in one's attitudes toward prenatal and postmortem non-existence. The first alternative contradicts your first reason, and the second alternative contradicts your second reason for doubting that total deprivation is an evil for the dead person.

"Before discussing differences between prenatal and postmortem non-existence which justify, to some extent, differences in attitudes toward these, I must first say that I think that a *complete* difference in attitudes toward these is unjustified, and *I* do not in fact have completely different attitudes toward these. I do regard my prenatal non-existence as, in some ways, evil for me. . . ."

"I'm not surprised!" Connie exclaimed.

"Really! There are so many things I've missed! Civilizations and natural phenomena! I wish I had witnessed so many events, or at least had the kind of reliable information you can only get by witnessing them yourself. Who wouldn't want to witness many historical events? That's one reason that we make movies about them. If life contains goods, as we agree, then *any* limit on these is evil. . . ."

"But not necessarily evil *for you*," Phil slipped in.

Jeff continued without responding. "As I've been promising, now I'll turn to those differences which might justify partially different attitudes toward death and prenatal non-existence. First, there is nothing which we can do to prevent our prenatal non-existence; we can't even arrange it that we were born earlier. Now, while death is inevitable, it can be postponed. Thus, there is an instrumental or consequential value in more concern over death than prenatal non-existence."

Phil replied, "Your explanation was that the difference was due to the consequential value of concern over one's death because it can postpone one's death. But how does this make sense of grief? More specifically, *reactive* grief, that is, grief *after* the death of a loved one, cannot postpone that death. The problem is that, given your explanation, people should expect that their attitude toward the death of loved ones, after their death, would be like their attitude toward their own prenatal non-existence, yet grievers do not take that attitude. If only they did!

"Let me state my objection to your explanation again. Supposing that death is an evil, or, at least, that life contains goods, there would be a consequential value to concern over death which would not belong to concern over prenatal non-existence. I concede that this is generally true. But there is no such consequential value to concern, after the fact, of the death of a loved one. If this difference in attitudes toward prenatal non-existence and death is justified, which you think it is, it cannot be justified by such a consequential value."

Jeff replied, "We're getting ahead of ourselves. Issues are now being raised which would be more efficiently discussed when we turn to response consolations. However, there are a couple things I'd like to point out right now. First, it's possible that concern over one's own death is in some sense inseparable from grief over the death of a loved one. If this were true, then grief would be necessary for the consequential value in postponing death. That is, concern for future death might be psychologically inseparable from concern over past death.

"Second, the task your argument gave me, Phil, was not to reconcile belief in death as evil with different attitudes toward one's own prenatal non-existence and a loved one's death. My task was to reconcile belief in death as evil with different attitudes toward one's own prenatal and postmortem non-existence."

"But you accomplished your task only in such a way as to burden yourself with the further task of explaining the difference in attitudes toward a loved one's death, after the fact, and one's own prenatal non-existence," Connie said.

"Not to mention the difference in attitudes toward a loved one's death, after the fact, and the loved one's prenatal non-existence," Phil added.

Jeff replied, "I'll try to explain. Greater concern for the death of a loved one, after the fact, than for one's own prenatal non-existence is entailed by the more general observation, which I believe to be often true, that one is less troubled by one's own sufferings or evils *once they're past* than one is concerned with the past suffering of a loved one. The important exception to this is when one's past suffering is still vivid. But of course, there is nothing vivid about non-existence. Thus, this exception is nothing to the present case. If it is largely true that we are more concerned about a loved one's past suffering, as I suspect, it might be due, in part, to moral beliefs that great concern with one's own past suffering is cowardly or indulgent self-pity, whereas concerns about a loved one's past suffering is charity or magnanimity.

"In fact, people are so concerned to avoid the appearance of self-pity that when they recount their own long past sufferings, unless trying to be dramatic, they either *boast* of their sufferings or they affect an attitude of humor, attitudes they seldom take toward *future* suffering. This suggests an even deeper, and an inevitable basis for greater concern over past sufferings not one's own, and that this explanation is confirmed by the exception where one's recollection of one's own past evils is vivid; and that basis is, that we do not experience the evils which befall another. Since we experience the evils which befall ourselves, apart from non-existence, it makes a very great difference whether they are past, present or future. But since another's evils are not experienced by us the difference between past, present and future is less important, except insofar as one identifies with that person's point of view. The feelings of anxiety or relief which we feel toward our own suffering, future and past, respectively, normally exceed any such feelings for the suffering of others. This difference itself might only be justified by its consequential value, but that doesn't alter the fact that there is such a difference and it explains different attitudes toward a loved one's death and one's own prenatal non-existence consistent with the claim that total deprivation is an evil.

"Assuming that people have a greater concern for the present or recent past, whether this greater concern is rational or otherwise, we can easily explain greater concern for a past death than for anyone's prenatal non-existence, because the goods which a loved one loses through death are, or would have been, present or more recent than any goods lost through prenatal non-existence."

"Hold on," said Phil, "The goods lost by the loved one through death are more recent only in comparison to a person who was born before the loved one's death. In other words, the deprivation to someone through prenatal non-existence is more recent if that person was born since the other person died."

"No," replied Jeff, "in the case of a person whose deprivation through prenatal non-existence is recent because that person was recently born, at least that person has present goods, unlike a dead person.

"Now, getting back to my explanation of less concern over one's own prenatal non-existence than over one's own death, which I attempted before the digression contrasting prenatal non-existence and the death of one who has already died: while we cannot arrange to be born earlier, as I said, we can, to some extent, *remedy* our prenatal non-existence, though we cannot, to nearly the same extent, remedy our postmortem non-existence. That is, we can *learn* about that which occurred before our existence. I already mentioned the appeal of historical movies. Of course, this is no substitute for earlier existence, but it does lessen the resultant deprivation. In this respect, we are lucky to live in an age in which the discipline of history has advanced as much as it has. More than any earlier generation we can thus remedy our prenatal non-existence. In fact, I envy those who will live after us because they will surpass our *understanding* of history and thus be better able than ourselves to remedy the deprivation due to their own prenatal non-existence."

Connie observed, "Earlier you spoke of death as depriving us, not only of our futures, but in some sense of our pasts. Here you observe that, in some sense, prenatal non-existence need not deprive us of the past."

"Yes, Connie," Jeff said, "and, in the sense in which we can remedy this deprivation the passage of time actually helps us to remedy it because we develop a greater understanding of the past."

"The passage of time helps and hurts," Connie objected. "It's true that historiography has become more sophisticated, and the natural sciences generally, and this helps us to learn about the past. But the everyday experiences of people of our generation are less like the everyday experiences of its predecessors than any preceding generation. Thus, while our understanding of history is greater, we are less *acquainted* with the way life was before we were born than any other preceding generation."

Jeff said, "You're right about that, although this does not affect my main point. We can remedy the deprivation due to prenatal non-existence, whereas there is nothing comparable when it comes to remedying the deprivation, through death, of future goods. Of course, we can *speculate* about posthumous historical and natural events, but I think that speculation stimulates more than satisfies our desire to know the future."

Phil said, "I agree that there is a difference between remedying prenatal and postmortem deprivation, and I concede the principal point that it could explain, in part, our different attitudes toward these. I just want to make sure that we express ourselves carefully so as to not get carried away by this contrast of prenatal and postmortem non-existence. Learning about the past does not 'bring us there'; what it does is lessen the detrimental effects of not having 'been there.' As you said, learning about the past is not a substitute. Nevertheless, I agree that there is nothing closely parallel to this when it comes to death. Earlier I cautioned you not to overstate the deprivation due to death by making it seem that death makes it false that we ever existed. Likewise, do not exaggerate death's difference from prenatal non-existence by making it seem that learning about the past which preceded our births makes it true that we did exist then.

"However, I will say that this explanation of our different attitudes toward these two periods of our non-existence does seem rather esoteric. Remedying our ignorance of the past is not the sort of concern which would make a difference to people's attitudes toward prenatal non-existence and death. As Connie teased earlier when discussing the comforts which result from considering oneself as a disembodied observer after death, remedying our ignorance of the past is a consideration mostly appealing to academics!"

Jeff said, "There's a lot to your objection, Phil. But you know, when you first expressed doubt about the evil of death on the ground that people don't have a great concern over their own prenatal non-existence, I suppressed the objection that lack of concern by people over their own prenatal non-existence was irrelevant in determining the evil of total deprivation because concern with prenatal non-existence was too esoteric for people to even think about. I might say that people, rather than having an attitude of comparative indifference to their own prenatal non-existence, have *no* attitude toward it. We don't even have a name for prenatal non-existence! I'm sick of having to use that cumbersome phrase every time! Some of my explanations *are* esoteric, but I suspect that it's an esoteric problem."

"Maybe we should call prenatal non-existence 'd-e-a-r-t-h' or 'd-i-r-t-h'" Connie facetiously suggested, "a cross between 'death' and 'birth!'"

Jeff continued, "In sum, your argument against the claim that death is intrinsically evil goes like this: in itself, prenatal non-existence is no different from death. However, people are little troubled by their prenatal non-existence. This indicates that non-existence is not intrinsically evil, nor perhaps evil in any way. Thus, death is not evil for the dead person. Isn't this the argument?"

"Yes," answered Phil.

"In a systematic manner, these are my replies: first, prenatal non-existence does somewhat trouble me, and would trouble many people if they had the occasion to think about it. Second, there is a difference in the sequence between prenatal and postmortem non-existence, one preceding, the other following life."

"But this difference in sequence cannot make a difference to the non-organic intrinsic evaluation of non-existence," Connie objected.

Jeff replied, "True, but it could explain the difference in attitudes. The difference in the sequence could explain the comparative indifference toward prenatal non-existence without concluding that it is not intrinsically evil. I agree that the two 'periods' of non-existence are intrinsically the same, so I need some other difference to explain the different attitudes. Now, since sequence makes no difference to non-organic intrinsic value, the difference must lie in either a difference in the organic value of prenatal non-existence and death, or in a difference in the consequential value of one's attitudes toward prenatal non-existence and death. And we agree that differences in sequence *can* make a difference to organic and consequential value.

"We haven't yet systematically looked at the specific issue of the organic value of death, so let's leave a comparison of the organic value of prenatal non-existence to death to that time. But I want to say now that if death is a greater organic evil than prenatal non-existence, then that could, in part, explain the difference in these attitudes.

"Furthermore, besides possible differences in organic value between prenatal non-existence and death, the difference in the sequence gives a value to concern over death, because it prolongs life, which it does not give to concern over prenatal non-existence.

"Third, not only are these two periods of non-existence differently related to one's life as a whole, one coming before, the other after, prenatal and postmortem non-existence are also differently related to the present. Already existing persons past prenatal non-existence does not entail that they do not exist *now*; persons past death does entail that they do not exist now. Thus, past death disturbs us more than past prenatal non-existence. For people have a 'bias' to the present, that is, people respond emotionally as though the present were most important. As a result, anything which entails *present* non-existence will be regarded as more important than anything which does not entail present non-existence, if non-existence is an evil, as I maintain."

"Yes, but why should it matter emotionally that these two periods of non-existence are differently related to the present?" asked Phil.

"That's an intriguing question. Fortunately, we do not need to answer it. Rational or not, and whether rational only in its consequential value or rational in some other way, our concerns are, in fact, shaped by whether they concern the past, present or future. In general, my strategy in proposing alternative explanations for our different attitudes toward prenatal non-existence and death, alternative to the conclusion that non-existence is not intrinsically evil for that person, has been that this difference in attitudes can be accounted for by other differences in attitudes which we *in fact* have. I suppose that it would strengthen my defense were these general differences in attitudes rational, and were they rational in more than consequential value alone, but that is not necessary to my defense."

At that point, the waitress brought their entrees. "If only they had arrived sooner!" said Connie to her companions.

Posthumous Predicates

As the three dressed, seasoned and sliced their entrees, Phil said, "I have one final reservation about the claim that total deprivation is an evil for the person deprived, that is, an annihilated person. My reservation is that this claim seems to require one to attribute a predicate or property to something or someone at a time when it does not exist. In other words, 'X is deprived of all goods' is an attribute which, if it could exist, could only exist when the subject does not. But that is nonsense. The dead do not exist. Therefore, they can't be subjects of evils, deprivations or otherwise. 'X is deprived of all goods' is what we might call a 'posthumous predicate' or 'posthumous property' when X is a dead person.

Phil continued, "The total deprivation of which you complain and which we are trying to understand must be a posthumous predicate, that is, belong to a subject only after that subject no longer exists. But since an attribute cannot belong to a subject after it exists, posthumous predicates make no sense. So, 'X is deprived of all goods' does not make sense."

"This consolation seems totally *depraved*!" remarked Connie. "If 'X is deprived of all goods' is meaningless, doesn't that mean that everyone will always continue to enjoy some goods? But that's a denial of annihilation."

"I haven't explained my thoughts clearly," Phil responded. "'X is annihilated' isn't a predicate at all. It is a denial of an existential claim, which, when used after the fact, has a posthumous reference. 'X is annihilated, that is, X does not exist from such a time on' is not ascribing a property to X after that time. X cannot have any properties after that time. Rather, 'X is annihilated' merely denies the existence of X from a certain time. So, Connie, it does not follow that we will continue to enjoy some goods forever. That would be ascribing a property to something nonexistent. For the same reason we cannot say that, after that time, X is deprived of goods or X has a deprivation evil."

"Why not? What's the difference between 'It is not the case that X enjoys any more goods' and 'X is deprived of all goods?'" Connie asked.

Phil continued, "Look at the progression of our discussion of the intrinsic sympathy evaluation. We began with what we *now* call 'diametric values.' At the time we thought that the only intrinsic values were diametric. Jeff then extended the concept of 'intrinsic values' to include deprivation evils. One implication of this extension was that intrinsic evils need not be a state of awareness of the person affected by them. But annihilation is *not* just a *mass* of deprivations. It is the non-existence of the subject. Now, less extreme deprivations, such as blindness or the loss of a few memories, while *not* being *states of awareness* of the person afflicted with them, are *states* of the person so afflicted. Therefore, when you claim that death is a deprivation evil for the dead person you entail that death is a state, or characteristic, of that person. But that would be a posthumous predicate. You've almost convinced me that something can have an intrinsic value for someone though it is not a state of that person's awareness. However, something can have an intrinsic value for someone only if it is a state of that person, whether or not it is a state of awareness. So you see, life can contain goods without death being a deprivation evil for the dead person, for the latter is meaningless. So, one needn't offer pessimistic consolations. Life is *good* for the living person, but death is *nothing* for the dead person."

Connie objected, "Can't we even say that life is better than death? Can we make sense of the decision to stay alive without entailing that life is better than death? It is not sufficient to justify the decision to continue to live that life contains some goods. For the decision confronting people contemplating suicide must be based on a *comparison* of their alternatives. We saw that both the denial that life has goods and the denial that life has goods unconditional upon being alive severely limited the reasons for continuing to live. Doesn't the denial of death's being an evil entail the same limitations?

"On the other hand, if we can say that life is better than death, doesn't this imply that death has a value? Then where has this consolation gotten us? Further, if death is worse, mightn't this be enough to justify grief? That is, if death compares unfavorably to life, apart from whether or not this is expressed by 'X has a deprivation evil,' mightn't this be a reason to feel bad for a dead loved one?"

In the background Blue Oyster Cult's "(Don't Fear) The Reaper" lured its listeners to self destruction. And all the while that Phil and Connie spoke Jeff completely ignored his plate. Jeff took a deep breath and began. "We're getting to the nub of it, aren't we?" He looked from Phil to Connie. "*Slowly*, we're getting to the nub of it. My grief is based on the facts entailed by 'My mom is annihilated,' not a confused description of it. My grief is not based on a linguistic illusion that my loved one exists in a state of torment, tormented by deprivation evils. Nor do I believe that my mom exists or 'subsists' in a shadowy refuge of confused ideas."

Connie and Phil listened intently as Jeff continued. "Phil gave a fair, but brief, analysis of 'X is annihilated.' I'll add a little to it, but with no alteration in principle. Remember, in the relevant case, X is a person. A person existed from one time to another. In that time she enjoyed many things. From the latter time that person does not exist.

"These are the facts toward which my grief is directed, insofar as it is sympathetic toward her. I believe these facts justify my sympathy evaluation. In particular, these facts justify the intrinsic sympathy evaluation.

"Of course, Phil is well aware of these facts; he's well aware that my mom no longer exists. But, he says, this cannot be an evil for her because in order for something to be an evil for someone it must be a state of that person, and non-existence is not a state of that which does not exist.

"I agree that my mom no longer has any states. However, not only are some deprivation evils not states of awareness for the person who has these evils, but at least one deprivation evil, death, is not a state at all of the person who has this evil. This sounds very odd, I admit. However, it is not unique. I'll explain.

"Certain facts can be bad for persons without being a state of those persons. After death there have been and will be goods which they would have enjoyed, such as a warm spring day. Further, had they continued to live they would have enjoyed other good experiences such as Thanksgiving dinners they prepared or Christmas mornings with presents opened that they purchased. Since they no longer exist they won't enjoy these goods. So, there are goods the *existence* of which is independent of our existence, and there are goods the existence of which does depend on our existence, but in either case, our *enjoyment* of these goods requires our existence. These enjoyments will not exist. This is the basis of my intrinsic sympathy evaluation. These statements follow from the facts of our existence and non-existence.

"Your difficulty in understanding the intrinsic sympathy evaluation stems from the fact that the evil entailed by these statements is not a state of the person who has this evil. But these facts, which entail this evil, do *concern* us. If a person were alive, there would be goods which the person would experience. It is our earlier existence which we've described. It is the dead's current existence which is denied. It is the dead person who is the subject of these counterfactuals, for example, 'If Mom were alive, she'd have enjoyed this.' In fact, their death concerns that which *would have been states* of their awareness. It is in this sense that the deprivation is an evil for the dead.

"Is a consolation to be found in the fact that the intrinsic sympathy evaluation requires the loved one to be the subject of counterfactuals? How? The counterfactuals are true, aren't they? If she were alive, she would have enjoyed these goods. If she were alive, she would have produced yet other goods which she also would have enjoyed.

"This type of deprivation evil, which *concerns* a person's state but is not a person's state, is not unique to the case of death. Not all deprivation evils are like blindness or the loss of a few memories which are states of the person who suffers the deprivation. There are other deprivation evils which are not states of the person deprived. For example, a person can be deprived of opportunities without even knowing it. In fact, not knowing of one's opportunities is a common cause of being deprived of them! This deprivation is not only *not* a state of the person's awareness, but also, I don't think that it is a state of the person at all, though the lost opportunities deprive the person of particular states of awareness. That a person loses opportunities does support counterfactuals in which that person is a subject, such as 'If she had been in the right place at the right time, she would have enjoyed various goods.' Likewise, while death is not a state of a person it does entail that the person does not have states.

"Death differs from these deprivation evils only in two ways. First, by being more extreme, that is, a total deprivation of all goods. Second, because the deprivation is the result of non-existence."

Jeff concluded, "We've been analyzing '*X* has a deprivation evil,' and in particular, when it is due to annihilation, or total or absolute deprivation. I am unmoved by any suggestion that '*X* has a deprivation evil' even when total is senseless. However, I appreciate the caution that a griever must not misunderstand the intrinsic sympathy evaluation; specifically, that I must not imagine diametric evils for the dead."

Connie agreed. "I still wish to console Jeff. But I'm concerned by the consolation that a total deprivation is not an evil for the deprived person, after conceding that a partial deprivation is an evil for the deprived person. It seems as though it is claimed that it does more harm to a person to injure than kill that person. Such a consolation gives a strange, altruistic twist to the *awful* old insurance and tort cynical advice that, because payments to a severely injured child are usually higher than payments to the parents of a dead child, if you run over a child you should back up over the child to make sure it's dead!"

Summary of the Conversation

Even if the dead are annihilated, death is intrinsically evil for the dead if death is construed as a deprivation. This deprivation is of goods to which we refer in the counterfactual: if the person were alive, then that person would have enjoyed certain goods. After the person's death, this counterfactual has a posthumous reference, but it is not a posthumous predicate. The deprivation concerns the posthumously referenced person in that it concerns the absence of states of awareness of that person. (I shall further scrutinize this concept in Chapter Ten).

A deprivation is intrinsically evil in the sense that it is worth avoiding for its own sake, apart from consideration of anything else. If something is intrinsically good, worth having for its own sake apart from consideration of anything else, then its absence is worth avoiding for its own sake.

Death is not a diametric evil for the dead, but we can find only so much consolation in that since death is a deprivation and we cannot state that, as a rule, diametric evils are worse than deprivations. But a combination of diametric and deprivation evils is worse than either alone.

Life contains unconditional goods, things the goodness of which do not depend upon any other thing. If all life's goods were conditional, and further, conditional upon being alive, then death would not be the loss of something which was good regardless whether we lived to enjoy it. The dead are unaware, after the fact, of this deprivation. However, one can be inflicted with a deprivation evil without being aware of it.

Death is not a state of a person or a state of that person's awareness. However, a deprivation evil need not be a state of a person or a state of awareness of that person. Nevertheless, a deprivation evil for a person does *concern* states of awareness of that person; it concerns states of awareness which *would* have existed.

People have different attitudes toward prenatal non-existence and death. This difference can be explained without resorting to the conclusion that death is not intrinsically evil for the dead person. We should consider the consequential value of concern over our own death, whereas we have no such concern over our own prenatal non-existence. Also, the harmful effects of prenatal non-existence are more easily remedied than the evils entailed by death. Our greater concern for the future over the past can explain our greater concern for our own death more than any concern over our own prenatal non-existence.

Finally, our greater concern for the present over the past can explain a greater concern over a loved one's death as compared with the loved one's prenatal non-existence. While a person's prenatal non-existence might be a necessary precondition for that person to exist, our own death might not be necessary for our own existence. Some difference in organic value may exist between prenatal non-existence and death. I only hint at these last two points in Chapter Six, which are discussed more fully in Chapter Eight. Still, I hold that prenatal non-existence is an intrinsic evil, regardless whether people care about it. I will discuss a further difference between prenatal and postmortem non-existence in the next chapter.

Study Questions

(1) What do you think about Jeff's axiom that if something is worth having for its own sake, then the deprivation of that thing is worth avoiding, without consideration of anything else, in other words, intrinsically evil?

(2) What do you think about Jeff's argument that diametric evils, simply by being diametric, are not worse than deprivations?

(3) Give other examples of conditional value, things which have value only because of something else, such as money which has value only because it can be exchanged for other things.

Seven

WOULD IMMORTALITY BE GOOD?

Consolation over Premature Death

"Now that I have a better understanding of the nature of the evaluations we should make about death, that it is a deprivation evil, we should consider the *extent* of the deprivation entailed by death," Jeff suggested. He continued, "I'm claiming that death is a great deprivation evil because it involves the loss of so many goods by the dead person. And just as one mustn't argue that the annihilated are not losers because their losses must be posthumous, one must not argue that, because the dead have no experience of time that the goods lost over a hundred years are to the dead as the goods lost over a moment.

"In fact, I think that the loss entailed by death is *infinite*.

"My mom did not have a long life for one in her demographic group. Thus, I've not been subjected to 'She had a long life' consolations."

"As though an even longer life would not have been better," said Phil, perhaps slipping from his role as consoler.

"But it is better to live long, so a 'She had a long life' consolation does somewhat *mitigate* the evil of death, when it is applicable," interjected Connie.

Phil continued, "There are consolations specifically directed toward grief over premature deaths. One goes like this: there is no difference between a long and a short life, that is, a premature death is not worse than death after a long life, since all deaths are of equal duration."

"What does 'all deaths are of equal duration' mean?" asked Connie.

Billy Joel's "Only the Good Die Young" faded and another song by the Guess Who, "No Time," played and Jeff suggested an answer to Connie's question. "It could mean something to which I referred a moment ago, that the dead have no experience of time. In this sense, with respect to their own experience, all dead are dead for an equal time because they are dead for no time. That is, the experience of being dead, because there is no such thing, might be awkwardly expressed as of zero duration. But, this does not mean that their losses are equal. Their losses are not zero, even though their continued experience of time is zero."

"It could also mean that all dead are dead for an equally *long* time, that is, for *all* time," suggested Phil.

Jeff commented, "But that is a fallacy. The length of time following the death of an old person is infinite, assuming, as this consolation does, that future time is infinite. And the length of time following the death of a young person would also be infinite. But one infinite series can be smaller than another, in the sense of being a proper subset of the other."

Phil replied, "So, there is a sense in which the infinite times following the deaths of the young and old are unequal, but there is still a sense in which they are equal. That is, there is a one-to-one correspondence between the years following the death of the young person and the years following the death of the old person. Therefore, the question remains, should a comparative evaluation of the deaths of a young person and an old person be based on the sense in which the times after their deaths are equal or in the sense in which they are unequal? If the former, then the deprivation evil due to a premature death is no greater than the deprivation evil due to a death in old age."

"You're both wrong!" exclaimed Connie. "The amount of time following a person's death is a function of *when* the person died, it is not a function of how long that life was. The time after Methuselah's delayed demise is greater than the time after Mozart's early death. Only for people born at the same time is the amount of deprivation due to death a function of how long or short were their lives."

"You're right," remarked Jeff. "The controversy has been placed on the wrong footing, if one makes it seem that the longer the time after one's death, the greater is the deprivation. But I should remind you that I think that prenatal non-existence is also a deprivation evil. So, an elderly person who dies earlier than the death of a young person has not suffered a greater deprivation than the young person who died, despite a 'longer' time following the death of the elderly person.

"So, on neither interpretation of 'All deaths are of equal duration' has a good reason been given for regarding the deprivation as equal—at least, for every sense of 'equal'—for short-lived and long-lived persons," concluded Jeff. "The first interpretation falsely assumed that the deprivation could be measured according to the duration of the dead person's continued experience of time. The second interpretation, besides the difficulty of the sense in which one infinite series can be greater than another, ignored the fact that the extent of a person's loss is partly a function of prenatal non-existence."

"But when one considers the extent of the deprivation by including prenatal non-existence, it is not only death which is the proper object of the complaint," noted Connie.

"Again you're right!" said Jeff. "But switching the object of complaint from death to the combination of death and prenatal non-existence, like all consolations which attempt to alter the object of complaint, is of limited value."

"However," Connie replied, "unlike consolations which attempt to shift the object of complaint from death to, say, a terminal illness, a consolation which shifts attention away from death to prenatal non-existence, shifts attention to a temporally distant object, and is therefore likely to have greater psychological effectiveness."

"You have a point. But this whole discussion strengthens my earlier remark that prenatal non-existence, though not as evil as death, is still an evil. After all, the length of a life is a function of death and prenatal non-existence.

So, when people complain of the shortness of life, prenatal non-existence is implicitly an object of their complaint, despite their apparent indifference toward prenatal nonexistence. Perhaps we should characterize people's usual attitude toward prenatal non-existence in this way: first, any complaint they make of it is implicit. Second, most people would never complain of it, implicitly or otherwise, except for the fact that there is death. That is, the deprivation entailed by prenatal non-existence is usually, for some reason we haven't yet explained, regarded as acceptable except for its combination with the deprivation entailed by death.

"And this interpretation of people's attitudes toward prenatal non-existence strengthens my other point. If people find prenatal non-existence acceptable by itself, and only objectionable in conjunction with death, then any attempt to shift the object of complaint from death to prenatal nonexistence emphasizes the wrong member of the pair."

"I haven't yet given up on the second interpretation of the consolation 'All deaths are of equal duration,' namely, that an infinite time follows all deaths," Phil argued. "The infinite time following all deaths, while not proving that all deprivations due to death are equal, in more than the 'one-to-one correspondence' sense of 'equal,' might nevertheless provide a consolation for premature death. The point of the argument might be that, considering that all deaths are followed by an infinite deprivation, the finite difference between the deprivation of short-lived and long-lived persons is comparatively insignificant.

"And so therefore, a grief which emphasizes the unusual brevity of a loved one's life is 'blowing' the added deprivation 'out of proportion'?" Connie asked.

"This is another dreary consolation!" Jeff insisted. And then he said sarcastically, "Cheer up! What's a finite loss compared to the infinite one we all suffer? Attention to the infinity of the loss is a better reason for rejecting the 'She had a long life' consolation than it is for being consoled about the unusual brevity of a loved one's life."

"Again, I think you're both off!" emphasized Connie. "As I was saying to Jeff earlier . . ."

"Gee, I missed a lot!" exclaimed Phil with sarcastic alarm.

"Oh, sure," continued Connie, "we had this all figured out before you showed up! As I was saying to Jeff earlier, despite some expressions such as, 'She'll *never* see anything again,' which are seemingly to the contrary, grievers don't really concern themselves with an infinite loss, with an eternity following death. Phil, you pointed out that the finite difference between a short and a long life is comparatively insignificant. That is, in comparison to the infinite deprivation we all suffer. Jeff correctly replied that that's not a rational consolation.

"But grievers never compare the loss to an infinite one. They compare losses to other losses with which they are familiar, or that they can imagine.

Perhaps the limit on the imagination in this case has something to do with the familiar extent of the good that was lost or the good that has come to an end."

"Huh?"

"I'll explain. When a person dies at a young or middle age we sometimes estimate the loss by comparing it to the death of an elderly person. We imagine that the young person was deprived of forty to sixty years. When an elderly person dies we sometimes estimate the loss by comparing that person's death to that of a person with the greatest realistic longevity. So, we imagine that the deprivation was ten or twenty years or so. But we also sometimes estimate the loss by imagining the person, no matter how elderly, as having another lifetime. I don't mean that we imagine them starting all over again, being reborn. I mean we imagine a future, which includes them, lasting as long as a familiar lifetime."

"I think that this *might* be a fairly accurate description of what we think in such situations, but is it rational?" Phil asked. "Why estimate the loss in this way? I realize that it's easy to compare things with the familiar. I'm not sure what the psychology would be behind wishing the person had an additional lifetime, estimating the loss as equal to a lifetime. Is it akin to 'second chance' wishing? In other words, in wishing for a second chance for someone else we imagine the loss as equal to a second lifetime? Is it some sort of bargaining? 'Let's not wish for too much—a doubling of life's time wouldn't be too pushy, would it?' Is that the underlying thinking? But that's not rational. One can't estimate the extent of a deprivation evil by pretending to bargain for a reprieve.... Can I have a fry?"

"Don't bite the hand that feeds you!" warned Connie. "I'm suggesting that even grievers don't really regard the deprivation as infinite. Jeff contends that the loss is infinite."

Jeff stated, "The loss needn't be infinite for my grief to be justified. And frankly, I'm not sure what meaning one could, or should, give to 'infinite deprivation'; however, I do think the loss exceeds any particular limit. That is, after no finite length of time is life necessarily not worth living. It follows that, whenever life ends, one's loss is greater than any particular finite amount. In that sense, then, the deprivation is infinite.

"I agree that death is not a diametric evil. But I believe that it is an infinite deprivation evil. Earlier I argued that everything else being equal, a deprivation evil is as bad as a diametric evil. In other words, with respect to some diametric good, its deprivation is as bad as its diametric evil. Therefore, an infinite deprivation evil is infinitely worse than any finite amount of diametric evils."

"A Long Day; A Short Life"

"At the risk of offering you a dreary consolation," Connie said hesitantly, "It's always struck me as odd when people complain both that life is short and that each individual day is too long."

"Like the joke beginning *Annie Hall*: complaining that one's food served at a restaurant isn't very good *and* that there isn't much of it!" Phil added, "You've used the term 'dreary' before, but what exactly do you mean by a 'dreary' consolation?"

"That's something else you missed. A grieving person is upset over an apparent evil befallen a loved one. A dreary consolation tries to limit the response to that apparent evil by referring to another evil," said Connie.

"I see. If apparent evils are upsetting someone, it doesn't help to mention other apparent evils. And in this case, it is dreary to point out that people's days often seem too long!" Phil confirmed.

"Yes," continued Connie, "but isn't it irrational to complain both of the shortness of life and the tedium, or even pain, of one's days?"

"Do you want me to respond to the 'She's not suffering anymore' consolation all over again?" Jeff threatened, teasingly. "These arguments have a lot in common!"

"No, not that!" Connie begged.

"Something else I missed" muttered Phil.

"But really," Jeff insisted, "coupling the complaints about life's brevity and one's sometimes impatience for the day to end is ironic, but it's not necessarily irrational, even if we imagined an insufferable complainer who never enjoyed anything, or never enjoyed anything but the prospects of a future which isn't enjoyed when it arrives.

"First, some of the oddness of 'life is short, days long' might come from peculiarities in the subjective awareness of the passage of time. A single day can feel 'like forever' and yet a week can seem to fly by, even a week which contained the 'endless' day! But the contradiction which you allege between 'life is short, days are long' has, rather, to do with the evaluations intended by these complaints."

"Yes."

"Second, the evaluations involved in these complaints need not be contradictory. The evaluation in 'one's days are too long' is that there isn't enough good in one's days. The evaluation in 'life is too short' is that a finite, or a normal-length, life is not long enough to encompass all *possible* goods. These evaluations are not contradictory. In fact, the first evaluation offers some support for the latter. Were one's days more delightful, life would come closer to encompassing all possible goods; though it would still fall far short, of course.

"'Life is too short' can mean *either* that life is too short though not worth living; *or*, that life, as good as we could conceive it to be, is too short, when it is only as long as it usually is. Now, it's true that it doesn't make sense to say that a life not worth living should be longer without being better. But you *can* complain that life should be both better and longer.

And then Jeff continued. "People can be impatient for their day to end, or even for weeks or months to pass, for several reasons. One reason is that one is looking forward to something. Now whatever might be said against such an attitude as either unjustified or counterproductive, clearly such a person thinks that life contains some goods and therefore might rightly complain of life's shortness.

"Others might complain of the lengthiness of their day because it was a bad day. But again, while a life filled with such days might never be short enough, we can conceive of a life which would be worth living, however long.

"Finally, people often complain that their day was too long either from tedium or physical exhaustion. But sleep restores our strength and even our fascination with life. By the way, contrary to some consolers who trivialize death as sleep, this is an important difference between sleep and death. Of course, there are other remedies for tedium.

"In sum, it *would* be inconsistent to complain *both* that life, as it is, is not worth living *and* that such a life should be longer. But it is *not* inconsistent to complain that a *better* life should be longer."

Would Immortality Be Good?

"Okay, Jeff," said Phil, "now you'll have a chance to have a bite, while my dinner gets cold. I doubt that the deprivation suffered by the dead is infinite. Or, to be more precise: I do not think that, were it not for death, that a person's goods could proceed without end. Contrary to what you have said, I suspect that after some finite length of time a person's life necessarily becomes not worth living. I don't know what finite length that is, and I'm sure that it would vary from individual to individual. But I suspect that an individual's life would necessarily lose its value."

"Are you referring to the infirmities of old age?" asked Connie.

"No, I'm referring to something even more inescapable, because, knowing Jeff, he'd object that we could *conceive* an old age, even a very ripe one, an unlimited age, without physical and mental infirmities, such as loss of memory and other cognitive skills, and that whatever causes these infirmities, whether death or degeneration, is a terrible evil. Then he would say that this is a dreary consolation for it presents us with another evil for the loved one, namely, degeneration."

As Phil said this, Jeff drank deeply from his soda glass and pointed, with a barbecued chicken leg, to Phil, in order to make known his agreement.

Phil continued, "So instead of talking about elderly infirmity or dementia, I want to argue that, for an immortal person, life would lose its value, and even become a burden because after a finite length of time life would become a meaningless repetition. There would be a kind of tedium, but I'm not talking about the *feelings* of boredom or restlessness which everyone has every now and then, because Jeff will ask us to conceive of a life minus these feelings. No, I'm referring to a point which an immortal would eventually reach in which no experience would offer anything new, or from which that immortal would learn nothing new.

"In complaining of death, evaluating it as evil, Jeff is asking us to conceive of beings like ourselves, except that they are deathless. For several reasons, I think that this is either inconceivable, or if it is conceivable that there be immortal human beings, then I believe that at some point their lives would cease to be worth living. Consequently, I do not think that death entails an infinite deprivation since human lives cannot conceivably have more than finite development.

"There are processes essential to human beings which, even in the course of finite, normal lives, diminish the goods which life has to offer. It is inevitable, therefore, that an immortal human being would find life progressively less worthwhile...."

"I don't want to interrupt, I can see that you have a lot of explaining to do, but I must object at the outset that even a life of progressively diminishing goods could still be worth living. But please go on," Jeff said.

"Again, I'm not referring to infirmities. It's true, the laws of nature make these inevitable. But we can conceive of human beings who do not degenerate in these ways, people who do not lose their sense of hearing, who do not lose their sense of taste, etc. There is nothing in the concept of the *progress* of a human life which entails these infirmities. But diminished goods are entailed by the very human processes which make life worth living.

"This unhappy result of immortality is complex. And it is caused by processes which occur in normal, mortal lives. Because of genetic predispositions and our experiences we develop particular personalities. In some respects, it seems, such as quickness of temper, we might say that a person has the same personality 'from cradle to grave.' In many other respects, a person has the same personality from adolescence, and especially, from young adulthood, until that person's death. 'You can't teach an old dog new tricks' does not refer, as it sounds it might, to learning disabilities through central nervous system degeneration; rather, it refers to the fact that once certain habits are formed it is extremely difficult for incompatible actions to be learned. I shall call this result a 'fixed or stagnant character' and the phenomenon 'character fixity or stagnation.' Stagnation has several dimensions. For one, there is a fixed *moral character*. Many of us, and all of us to some degree, even long before the end of our brief lives, cease to modify our conduct according to what further reflection and additional experience of distinctions and similarities would recommend. It's true, people cease to develop their moral character at an unnecessarily early age, partly because of the need to make moral decisions before we've morally matured, partly because of the 'politicalization' of moral views which petrifies them, and for other reasons, but isn't it *inconceivable* that a person 'freed' from death, and even freed from infirmities, would not eventually reach the final stage of a fixed moral character?

"There is also fixed *intellectual character*. This is the condition of no longer learning new *kinds* of things. Intellectual stagnation has many causes, but I shall ignore most causes since Jeff would ask us to conceive them away. The one cause of intellectual stagnation upon which I will insist is the paucity of kinds of things to be learned."

"What?! We have an infinite number of things to learn!" objected Connie.

"Yes, let's assume that's right. And we may also say that there are an infinite number of good things, given an infinite time. But there aren't an infinite number of *kinds* of good things, and there aren't an infinite number of kinds of things to *learn*. We have to be careful, I don't want to overstate my case...."

"Too late!" Jeff sniped, as Fleetwood Mac played "Woman of a Thousand Years."

Phil continued, "Even for an immortal, there will always be new things to learn. I grant this. It's reasonable to suppose that there are an infinite number of things or objects. Certainly there are an infinite number of events, given the supposition of immortality. And depending upon what is meant by a 'kind of thing,' it might follow that there are an infinite number of kinds of things. There is a use of 'kind of thing' according to which two things are of different kinds however slight the difference. But this use is pedantic rather than interesting. Anyway, according to this use, if there are an infinite number of things, it is possible, though still not certain, that there are an infinite number of kinds of things.

"However, if the difference between two things is slight enough, it cannot teach a human being a new kind of thing. That is, the pedantic use of 'kind of thing' is something below the threshold of our ability to learn kinds of things. For example, let's suppose that there are an infinite number of shades of blue. It follows, I believe, that there are shades which even immortals have not seen. Suppose a five thousand year old woman sees a shade of blue which she's never seen before. By the pedantic use of 'kind of thing,' she's seen a new kind of thing. Of course, she wouldn't realize that she has seen a shade of blue she'd never seen before. Has it given her knowledge of a new kind of thing? Well, she now has *acquaintance* with a 'new kind of thing.' But this acquaintance will not enable her to better differentiate or assimilate shades of blue or colors in general. Not only does she not have knowledge by *description* of any new kind of thing, but her unarticulated *skills* are not enhanced by this experience. We couldn't even speak of her *remembering this* shade as opposed to remembering any other similar shades. This 'kind' is below the threshold of human intellectual capacity or discernability; it's 'indiscernible.'"

Connie said, "All right, let's use this example. Our five thousand year old woman sees this new shade of blue. I agree if she's human, she couldn't learn anything about kinds of blue or kinds of colors from this acquaintance, because of the 'discernability' threshold. But let's more fully describe the situation. She saw a blue *what*? Let's say it's a flower . . . of a species that she already knows. But maybe it's a variety she never knew before. She didn't know there were blue thingamabobs," Connie stated.

Phil said, "Okay, so she did learn a new kind. But after another five thousand years, during which she has learned everything about this genus of plants, not by examining each individual, of course, but by learning all the basic, underlying characteristics of all the species of this genus, she would *not* be in a position to learn any new kind of thing from this plant."

"But species and even genera aren't fixed; they evolve," Connie said. "So, an immortal's knowledge of kinds would always develop."

"So, in another ten thousand years, our woman botanist has become expert in chemistry and physics, far beyond our knowledge of these subjects. If she's careful, there would be no *unanticipated* kinds of things which would be discernable. Therefore, no new species could surprise her," said Phil.

"But I don't think that the human discernability threshold is fixed. That is, the more we learn, the more discriminating we become, the more we can discern. Maybe no new species will be able to surprise her, but she'll be able to be interested in things which would have earlier escaped her notice," Connie responded.

"I think this is true. However, there must be a limit to our ability to lower this threshold. I suspect that any being with a finite mind, even an immortal with an infinite future, requires *some* threshold. Further, even if we could conceive of a being with finite intellectual capacities that did not have such a threshold, it would not be human. In fact, it's difficult to conceive how different from us it would be. And remember, we're discussing whether there are any conceivably better alternatives to death for human beings. Perhaps immortal humans would develop into such beings, but they would not be like us anymore."

Phil went on and said, "I'm suggesting that once the preliminary work of getting the right methods and paradigms is complete, and it can be complete, these methods will accelerate intellectual progress to the point that even a finite mind, if it's been 'around' long enough, could only learn particulars. This is my 'Malthusian' conclusion: *knowledge* of discernable kinds—that is, kinds which are above the discernability threshold—would increase 'geometrically,' so to speak, while the *number* of kinds above an even lowered discernability threshold could only increase 'arithmetically.' Assuming only that the latter hasn't an infinite head start, the former must eventually catch up! In fact, it would push ahead, by anticipating new kinds, until it exhausted the possibilities."

"You assume that there are only a finite number of discernable kinds. If this is not true, then it would still be possible for an immortal human to learn new kinds," Jeff said. "Earlier, Connie suggested that an immortal could lower the discernability threshold through knowledge. Even if, as you replied, there must be a limit to this, there is another way that an immortal could discover new kinds through her increase in knowledge. If she exhausted her environment, she could find another, thanks to her increased knowledge and unlimited time."

"You've only partly grasped my argument," Phil said. "At a certain stage of knowledge, there could not be any unanticipated kinds. I assume only that an immortal can grasp enough basic physics far advanced of our own that there could be no kinds which she could not anticipate. That is, so long as the most basic kinds are finite, even an infinite number of less basic kinds could be anticipated."

"You're committing a fallacy of composition," Jeff said. "Assuming that an immortal human would necessarily grasp the most basic kinds, it follows perhaps that she could anticipate *each* of an infinite number of less basic kinds. However, being finite, she could not anticipate *all* the less basic kinds. Therefore, there would always be room for learning new kinds."

"Ah, but is there? Yes, immortals would always have ignorance, but would there always be 'room' for improvement, that is, limiting their ignorance?" Phil said. "I've been arguing that an immortal would reach intellectual fixity even though my argument took a fairly favorable view of human abilities. However, despite optimistic assumptions about our ability to learn, I argued that, because of an exhaustible supply of basic kinds to be learnt that the eventual result would be a halt to the learning of new kinds of things. If one chooses to take a more pessimistic view of human abilities, as you have in your present objection, then the more certainly and quickly would human immortals reach the end of their intellectual progress. Therefore, I do not think that you do your view a favor by mentioning inherent limitations in our abilities.

"I caution to add that, however optimistic I suppose our abilities to be, I am not supposing that a human immortal would become omniscient. There are things that will never be known. But this ignorance is an obstacle to continual intellectual progress.

"I've been arguing that immortality would present us with diminishing returns. Perhaps I have overstated my case by claiming that an immortal would eventually reach the point of learning no new kind of thing, either through complete success or incorrigible limitations; but I'm confident that there would be diminishing goods returning from further discoveries. For example, to make any discovery in biological taxonomy anywhere near as interesting as the ones we've already made we'd have to find multicellular organisms which were neither plant nor animal. Are such discoveries likely?

"There will always be new equations. But will they require solutions which are different in kind from the old equations?"

Connie reacted, "If we took the progressive road to intellectual fixity, it would be quite a ride, and one I'd *love* to take! I'd much rather take this ride and spend the rest of eternity intellectually fixed than die before I could take this ride!"

Connie added, "I must say, however, I don't like the sound of it: morally and intellectually 'fixed.' Sounds like something we do to a dog!"

"Connie is right," Jeff said. "Even if immortality has its flaws, in pointing them out, you've made me despise an early death even *more* than I had! More carefully, I should say that, even if you've shown that even an immortal's goods are finite—which you haven't—and therefore that death is not an infinite deprivation evil, these finite goods are so precious that I feel 'death's sting' all the more.

"Besides, despite your wish to make it appear otherwise, an immortal's character stagnation, if reached after much progress, does not seem bleak. It would be good to live with this knowledge, even stagnant. Our fixed character immortals needn't be 'couch potatoes!'"

Phil said, "Let me take another tack. I've been arguing that fixity must be reached by an immortal. It must result from either unabashed success or from failure when a person stops learning well before having reached the limits imposed by the environment. If immortals were like most humans, fixity would probably be the result of failure. But conceiving the best possible human immortals, I argued that fixity would result from success.

"However, I agree that fixity is not inevitable. But the only alternative is not satisfying. Strictly speaking, what is inevitable is that *either* a human immortal would reach a limit of development, that is, fixity, or else would continue to change to the point of ceasing to be the same person. Earlier, I spoke of a person acquiring habits, which together with genetic predispositions, gives one a character. And, as I said, these are difficult to change. But what if they could be changed? And in the course of an immortal's life, most of them would be changed. In fact, unlimited intellectual progress, if there were such, would change much of our character. In a very important respect, the original person would no longer exist.

"I repeat: either people continue to develop, or they do not. A person who continued to develop would eventually cease to be the person he or she was originally, which would be, almost quite literally, dying a slow death. Or, the immortal would at some point face eternity after already having become a finished product, so to speak. In either case, the person you love would have necessarily ceased to develop, even though she was to live forever. Because, in the first case, she would cease to be the person you love, and in the second case, she would cease to develop."[1]

Just then the Casinos's "Then You Can Tell Me Goodbye" began.

Phil continued, "Thus much as regards the sympathy evaluation. For a moment let me bring the conversation back to the ego evaluation. Suppose that both you and your loved one were immortals. Either you'd both continue to change, and if you grew apart, you would lose the loved one despite her— and your—immortality; or, only one of you continues to change, in which case you would certainly lose your loved one. Or finally, you might both remain the same. You would still have the loved one but I suspect that much of the value of the relationship would necessarily be lost were neither of you modifying yourselves.[2] That is, not only would you and your loved one find life in general less interesting, your relationship would be less rewarding. Even though freed from death, on each alternative, you would still lose the relationship as precious to you as it is now."

Connie responded, "Regarding the second alternative, in which only one person changed: the parent-child relationship is unlike any other, and as long as the memories remained, the relationship need not lose its value. Remember, even in our finite lives the child changes much. This doesn't appreciably alter the value of the relationship."

Phil replied, "Not for the parent, at least. But the value for the child often decreases."

Connie replied, "Unless the relationship becomes really sour, the unique basis of this relationship preserves some value."

Jeff responded, "As to the first alternative, that we both continue to change, what if we didn't grow apart? What if we changed together, in 'complementary' ways?"

Phil answered, "If you didn't grow apart from each other, you'd 'grow apart' from your present selves. The person you would have become is quite different from the person you are. The person your mom would be is quite different from the way your mom was. These two people—the immortal Jeff and his immortal mom—would continue to enjoy each other's company, but what concern of that is yours, that is, what concern is that of the person you are now?"

Phil summarized, "People think how nice it would be to exist forever and how wonderful it would be for their loved ones to exist forever. But as with some other philosophical errors, the illusion of an ideal, blissful and still personal immortality is preserved because the imagined situation is underdescribed. That is, people do not go very far in describing what it would be like to be immortal."

Connie interjected, "That's an example of the point I've been making. People talk about 'forever' but never mean more than a 'long time.' Now, character fixity need not occur for a 'long time,' but it might be necessary eventually. Unless, that is, one developed until one was a different person altogether."

Jeff rubbed his face with his left, sauce-free, hand, and began a reply to Phil's consolation as Elvis sang "I Forgot to Remember to Forget." "First, your point about facile conclusions based on under-described or under-imagined situations is very well taken. However, even your argument is based on insufficiently analyzed concepts. Not only have people under-described what it would be like to lead an unending life story, we do not yet understand, except by acquaintance, what it is like to lead a terminal life-story. Despite your efforts, in your initial developments of the concepts of 'character fixity' and 'discernability threshold,' we have yet to adequately articulate what it is like experiencing a life of normal length! Not having adequately articulated this, it's easy to say that were we immortal we must either cease changing or become an altogether different person. But even in a normal lifespan it is necessary that we cease developing with regard to some things, begin development with regard to others, forget what we learned, relearn it, forget it again, etc. That is, our changes do not all go 'linearly' in one direction. It's possible that we go on learning and backsliding forever. . . ."

"Like a character on a sitcom that, each week, learns the same lesson, over and over," Connie remarked.

"To an outsider this might appear either comical or boring. And presumably we would ourselves become aware of this situation; and perhaps we would then have a laugh at ourselves, or a sneer, maybe. But that wouldn't change us! Even that view of ourselves from which we appear comical or incorrigible would be forgotten, relearned, and forgotten again, and so on. And this 'resilience' might be something else for us to chuckle or sneer at," Jeff continued.[3] "Nevertheless, you *might* be right when you claim that an immortal must either get bogged down or become a very different person. There are several unclear concepts here, such as 'character development' and 'leading a life.' The point of my first objection to your consolation is that this crucial claim of yours is unproven. We're not yet in a position to determine either the soundness of your argument or my objection.

"Second, surely you don't wish to offer a theory of value according to which character development is either the only valuable thing in life or an essential ingredient to anything being valuable. Granting that one who has learned all *kinds* of things would receive less value from her billionth ripe strawberry, unless the immortal's fixity *necessarily* and altogether altered taste sensations, he or she would receive some intrinsic value from the strawberry. And I deny that fixity would necessarily altogether alter taste sensations.

"Furthermore, you made much of your claim that an immortal would eventually run out of kinds of things to learn, admitting that she or he could always learn more particulars. But knowledge of particulars is still valuable.

"The point of my second objection is that, even conceding that, after a certain length, life would necessarily offer 'diminishing returns,' we could still conceive it to be valuable.

"Third, this consolation too is dreary. You argue against my evaluations about death because you insist that the reasons for which I complain about death, the loss of goods by my loved one and the loss of the goods offered me by my loved one, would likewise apply to the alternative—immortality. But again, that there is no better alternative to death, were it true, would not make death less bad. At best the consoler has substituted a logically more complex object for my sympathy and ego evaluations, not death alone, but death *or* character fixity *or* inevitable growing apart from loved ones *or* 'death' by metamorphosis."

"But Jeff," Phil urged, "there's a difference between this consolation and others, such as the consolation that an immortal would grow progressively infirm, or that the dead would have continued suffering had they lived. With these other consolations you're being asked to consider a contrary to fact alternative which is also bad. You object to them by saying that there are other conceivable contrary to fact alternatives which would be better than death or any of these other bleak alternatives. But my argument has been that there are no conceivable alternatives which would be better than death. And certainly there is none which is *infinitely* better than death."

Jeff replied, "*One* way that I realize that something is bad is by conceiving of something that is better. But I can realize that something is bad even if nothing better is conceivable."

Phil, in turn, replied, "Remember our earlier discussion. Deprivation evils are deprivations of some good, that is, a conceivable good. And in this case, what is the conceivable thing which is worth having which death prevents? Immortal life, wherein we retain our personalities and yet continue to grow? If I'm right, this is inconceivable; and we fail to realize it because we under-describe what it would be like to be an immortal."

Jeff said, "Okay, you've convinced me of this much: a deprivation evil must be the loss of a conceivable good. But according to my previous objections: first, I'm uncertain that the good we're considering, continual character development with a recognizable personality retained, is inconceivable for immortals. Second, character development's not the only conceivable good from which death deprives us, anyway. It deprives us very simply of pleasant experiences," Jeff said. "Besides these objections there are others. Even if there were no conceivable alternative to eventual deprivation, it is conceivable that it happen much later. And so, death is a much worse way to suffer this deprivation."

"I grant it. But the difference between losing these goods through death and eternal life would not be infinite. So, I've been arguing against your claim that the deprivation evil is infinite. In other words, I've been arguing that, even if an infinite time follows the death of a particular person, it is inconceivable that that person could have enjoyed an infinite number of goods had they continued to live. In general, one cannot infer from the fact that an infinite amount of time has been lost that a conceivably infinite good has been lost. Nevertheless, I must accept your criticism that life would still possess some value, even were one already quite familiar with every kind of good," Phil said.

"This is just a thought. I very strongly agree with Jeff that we haven't yet explained the concept of 'forming a character,'" Connie said. "Phil, you make it seem that character fixity is an attainable state toward which we make eventual 'progress,' however slowly. Jeff makes it seem rather more like Sisyphus rolling a rock up a hill only for it to roll back down. But maybe it's neither. Maybe character fixity is an unattainable limit which we approach, but never reach. In trying to determine whether character fixity is inevitable we must be careful how we describe an immortal's life. Of course, by definition, that life will be infinitely long. But at no time in that life will an *already* infinite time have been lived. We suppose the immortal to be deathless, not 'birthless.' Therefore, at no time in his or her life will a fixed character be attained, if it is an unattainable, though approachable, limit. This is just an idea. I have no grounds for thinking that this is a superior model for understanding 'character development.'"

Phil said, "If your model is correct, an immortal's life would still offer only diminishing goods, as I've been arguing."

Jeff seized on Connie's idea. "Your model of 'character development' gives us an additional reason for regarding death as worse than prenatal nonexistence. On Connie's model, had we always lived, we would already have fixed characters, and that would be bad—if even conceivable. But, still following Connie's model, a future infinite life would never bring us to the point of fixity,' or 'tedium,' as Phil has called it."

Consequences of the Prospect of Death

Phil said, "Let me take a new approach. Thus far we've been arguing about whether death is an intrinsic evil for the dead person, and how extensive a deprivation this is. But, in order to form an adequate evaluation of death for the person who is dead, we must not only consider death itself, we must also consider the consequences for that person of the *prospect* of dying or death. That is, we must consider the consolation that the prospect of death, or rather, the certainty of eventual death, was consequentially good for the person who is dead while alive. Of course, one cannot have the prospect, or especially the certitude, of death unless one eventually dies. So, one's own eventual death is necessary for any consequential value which the prospect of one's own death had for the person who is dead."

"Be careful," warned Connie, "that you don't aggravate the evil of death, rather than mitigate it!"

Phil continued, "Most recently, I offered the argument that immortality would become, in a sense, tedious. Now, part of what I'm suggesting is that, without the prospect of death, even a fairly short life would be tedious, although in a slightly different sense of 'tedium.' Life without a foreseen, eventual death would be like 'a game without stakes.'"

Jeff jumped in before Phil could continue. "To begin, there's surely something wrong with the idea that the prospect of death gives life its value. Young children, unaware of mortality, enjoy life. Although we are discussing my grief while enjoying dinner, the morbid content of our discussion does not add to the sweetness of the barbecue sauce. Generally, people try to exclude morbidity from their enjoyments.

"'The prospect of death gives life its value' must be clarified. Is it being claimed that *all* life's value is the result of the prospect of death? Surely this is false. Were one to insist that death's eventuality is necessary for all life's value one would have to ignore intrinsic value, as with the recent consolation that an immortal's life would not be worth living. If such a consoler did not simply overlook intrinsic value, he would have to offer an implausible theory as to the causes of our awareness of good things. Certainly, our meals are good, not because we realize we must die, but because they *are* good! Furthermore . . ."

"I agree that the prospect of death is not necessary for all life's value. . . ." Phil said, getting a word in edgewise.

"Then death can still be a great evil," Jeff replied.

Phil continued, "The prospect of death is necessary for the attitude of urgency which we have in life. And this attitude feels intrinsically good and it is consequentially good, too. Urgency is consequentially good because it strengthens our desires for good things; it makes us more efficient in achieving good things, and forces us to establish priorities amongst the objects of our desires so that we waste less time on trifles."

"Oh boy! Have I got a lot to say!" exclaimed Jeff. "You've already agreed that some of life's value is independent of the prospect of death. And well you should, since your argument that the prospect of death introduces some value into life by creating urgency in large part presupposes that life already has value conceptually independent of the prospect of death. For your claim that urgency is consequentially good presupposes that some things, which are produced by urgency, are already good. Furthermore, rational urgency presupposes that something is good. In other words, 'Person A feels it is urgent that event e occur' entails that 'Person A thinks that e would be good.' And if life possesses goods *conceptually* independent of the prospect of death, then surely some of these goods *exist* independently of the prospect of death."

"I agree," Phil said, "and that means that I must concede that death deprives us of goods. . . ."

"Even further," Jeff interrupted, "even if all life's goods did come from the prospect of death, death would *still* deprive us of life's goods. That is, death would deprive us of the goods provided us by its prospect!"

Connie added, "That *would* mean that death was necessary for a finite amount of goods, that is, all the goods we have before death. But it also entails their cessation. Is that enough to console?"

"Yes, it *would* be enough to console," Phil answered. "Death entails that one's goods are finite. However, without death there would be no goods, if it were true that the prospect of death is necessary to all life's goods. In other words, death would mean a net gain. However, as I admit, there are goods independent of the prospect of death.

Phil continued, "My consolation that the prospect of death adds value to life is meant only to *mitigate* the evil of death."

Jeff said, "I agree that the feeling of urgency can be intrinsically good. Sometimes it includes the feeling of excitement, which is intrinsically good. However, the feeling of urgency can also be intrinsically bad. It often takes the form of anxiety. Is this a net gain? Are the effects of the prospect of death really benign?

Jeff continued, "I also agree that the knowledge of our eventual deaths sometimes makes us feel urgent about obtaining goods. However, I think that it is seldom that the prospect of death is *necessary* to make us adopt an urgent attitude. That the prospect of death sometimes causes this attitude does not show that it was necessary in order for us to have this attitude. And if this attitude is usually produced or producible in other ways, then one cannot significantly mitigate the sympathy evaluation with the claim that the prospect of death sometimes causes the attitude of urgency. In fact, the prospect of aging, another evil, part diametric, part deprivation, gives us urgency. It has more of an influence than death's prospect, perhaps because death is, we hope, more remote.

"Even for an immortal, some goods would be irreplaceable. The prospect of a person's annihilation is not necessary to regard things as irreplaceable. No moment ever comes again. And an immortal who enjoyed two-thirds of his or her days would be far happier than one who enjoyed one half of his or her days.

"Without getting into infinite proper subsets all over again, while both of these immortals would have an infinite number of enjoyments, one would have more enjoyments than the other," Jeff concluded.

"Yes," Connie added, "and as, at any moment in their lives, they both would have had up until then only a finite number of enjoyments, there would never be a retrospective one-to-one correspondence between their enjoyments."

Jeff said, "Even though an infinite future would provide unlimited opportunities to try *some* kinds of things again, as long as the past cannot be undone, life would offer irreplaceable opportunities for some good or bad."

Connie asked, "Why do you say that an infinite future would provide unlimited opportunities only to try 'some kinds' of things again? Wouldn't one have the opportunity to try every kind of thing again?"

Phil said, "Good question. Apart from that pedantic use of 'kind of thing' in which every particular is a unique kind of thing, wouldn't an infinite future provide *inexhaustible* opportunities for every kind of thing?"

Jeff answered, "No. First, assuming that one reaches a point where one's character develops little, as Phil has urged, one might be no longer able to avail oneself of future opportunities. Certain things are closed to fixed persons. Second, an infinite time need not repeat every opportunity. This is especially true because of human 'historicity.' In a roundabout way, I'll explain what I mean by this term...."

Jeff was interrupted when the waitress came over. "How are you guys doing? It seems like you're having an intense conversation," she said. The three muttered and nodded in response that their meals are fine.

Harry Chapin's "Old College Avenue" concluded and the Grass Roots sang "I'd Wait a Million Years."

Jeff resumed, "As Connie reminds us, an immortal, having been born, has only lived a finite time. Let's suppose that in that finite time an immortal fell in love with another immortal. Suppose also that this opportunity for happiness is lost. Is it necessary that another opportunity for this happiness eventually present itself?"

"Both being immortal, there are unlimited opportunities for them to meet again," Connie said.

"That depends. Other intentions, desires and obligations of theirs might forever be obstacles to such an opportunity," Jeff replied, "We're not dealing with the collision of randomly moving particles, but with the reunion of rational organisms. As such, our immortals would still have physical constraints and even conflicting intentions."

Phil said, "You asked whether there would be an opportunity for '*this* happiness' again, without explaining what you meant. Did you mean 'happiness with this same individual' as Connie took it, or did you mean 'happiness with a similar individual' or 'similar happiness with another individual?' If you meant happiness with a similar individual, then any obstacles to such an opportunity would be very unrealistic."

Jeff said, "Now, what do *you* mean by a 'similar individual?' Similar appearance? Similar personality? Similar preferences? Even similar experiences? I agree that, given an infinite time, only very unrealistic circumstances would prevent a meeting with a person similar to your original lover in all these respects. In fact, I'll even drop my objection to Connie, and admit that one would eventually meet again with one's original lover. Furthermore, the reunion might be a very happy one. However, this would not be the same as had they stayed together when they first met. Their reunion might be better or it might be worse than had they never parted, but it would be very different. It would not be the same as had they stayed together when they originally met. People have *histories*. And since their pasts are finite, even immortals, their histories would always be more or less unique, and furthermore, include unique experiences. Our lovers' histories would have been quite different had they always been together. And if one had found another who was similar only, but not identical to one's original lover, even when it came to her experiences, she would still have a different history from one's original lover. So you see, the original opportunity never again presented itself.

"What's more, you can see *Casablanca* for the first time only once. This unique experience is possible because even immortals have only finite pasts. Everything they've done, they once did for the first time, and only once did they do it for the first time!

Billy Joel's "Get It Right the First Time" played as Phil said, "This supports my earlier point that an immortal's life would eventually receive dwindling returns. This is because there are only so many kinds of things to do for the first time."

"And I agree, only I think that you tried to make too much of the point. Life would still have value for an immortal. I admit, also, that an immortal would *always* have further opportunities for *many* kinds of things. However, they would not have the further opportunity for all kinds of things," Jeff said, "Or, perhaps I should say that the opportunity for all kinds of things is not the only kind of opportunity which contributes to the value of a human life. Some of the things we value are *unique* because they and we have histories.

"Returning to your sports or gambling metaphor, that life without death would be like a game without stakes, let me state emphatically that there are stakes *within* life and which we would still have even if we were immortal."

Phil said, "Jeff, you argue that death is not necessary for us to feel urgent about life's goods. And you offered a plausible, although hopelessly romantic, example of this. But death is necessary for us to feel urgency about *some* of life's goods. Let's use sports examples. You have certain favorite teams. Although your grief makes you indifferent, you usually root for these teams to win their respective championships. . . ."

"Like the Bills, Mets or Yanks, Knicks and Islanders," Connie listed.

"Yes," said Jeff warily.

"Now, assuming that these teams and their leagues and their championships will exist forever, it follows that the fortunes of each team against their opponents within each their own league would eventually more or less even out. Assuming further that you were immortal, the fortunes of these teams would even out in the course of your lifetime. So, your desire could not be that your teams fare better than their respective opponents during your lifetime," noted Phil.

"The most mind-boggling implication of infinity is that eventually, the fortunes of the Knicks will equal that of the Celtics, that the Yanks will pan out equally to the Cubs or Bosox, or that the Bills or Vikings would *ever* win the Super Bowl!" Jeff joked.

"Given that their fortunes versus the fortunes of their opponents will approach equality in your own, if immortal, lifetime, what difference would it make to you that one team wins now and the other later?" Phil asked.

"Assuming also that he continued to be a fan of the same teams throughout his immortal life," Connie noted.

Jeff replied, "As I said before: each moment, or in this case, each season is irreplaceable. Although twenty-five teams in the same league will all average over an infinite time one championship every twenty-five years, only one team can win the championship in any particular year. Were we immortals, life would be different, and though we can only begin to imagine the many ways that it would be different, were we otherwise the same as we now are, we would still lead our lives one moment, one day, one season, one year at a time."

Phil replied, "But earlier, you claimed that, comparing two immortals, one who enjoyed two-thirds of his or her days and another who enjoyed only one half, the former would be far happier, despite the fact that both would have infinite enjoyments. Now, I've been arguing, using as an example the long—haul success of sports teams, that over the long run the fortunes would be equal, and not just in the sense of a one-to-one correspondence, for any two immortals. And I ask, what could justify urgency when one's fortunes are inevitable?"

Jeff answered, "Not all life's goods are like the enjoyment which comes from one's team winning the championship. Goods which are beyond one's control and sufficiently random would be equally distributed between the lives of different immortals. An example of this is the success of one's favorite teams. However, goods within one's control or not random need not be equally distributed between the lives of different immortals.

"Furthermore, insofar as the prospect of death makes us urgently avail ourselves of the opportunity to achieve goods, this morbid prospect does so because death is a great evil, that is, because death deprives us of life's goods. I find it, therefore, a strange consolation! In sum, death deprives us of goods. Consequently, it heightens our desire to achieve goods. This benefit of death's prospect therefore proceeds from death's being evil.

"In addition, you claim that the prospect of death maximizes goods by motivating us. Even if this were so and death's prospect caused us to 'pack in' more goods into sixty years or so than an immortal would in any sixty or so years in his or her life; since death is a deprivation, and not necessary to all life's goods, it follows that death limits the goods that each of us will receive, no matter how efficient its prospect motivates us to be. Therefore, death would still be a loss, even if it made us more efficient.

"Specifically, you said that the prospect of death motivates us to waste less time on trifles. My argument is that even were there no death life would offer us reasons to prefer significant goods to trifling ones. But now I wish to add that, although even an immortal would be well advised to ignore trifles, for an immortal 'wasting time' would be impossible, anyway. Though I've argued that, even for an immortal, certain precious opportunities could be wasted, because they would be unique, despite an infinite future, time itself could not be wasted, for *that* an immortal has in unlimited quantity. The point of this observation is that, while death's prospect might discourage the wasting of time, it is only because of death that time *can* be wasted. I'm not contradicting my position that, whether we die or not, each moment is irreplaceable. My point is that so long as an immortal is not missing a unique opportunity for a significant improvement in its life, or the lives of others, there would be nothing seriously wrong with trifling. An immortal could afford to trifle more than a mortal.

"So, to some extent death creates the *value* of urgency. One cannot then turn around and appreciate death for causing us to feel urgency. Our knowledge of eventual death, or prospect of death, merely mitigates some of the evils entailed by death. This prospect would *not* be *missed*, if there were no death to foresee. Contrast this point about death with the point we've made about life. There are goods in life which are worthwhile antecedent to living, that is, their value is not conditional on being alive. However, part of the value of urgency is conditional upon eventual death. In other words, if there were no death, urgency would be less important. We cannot therefore use the value of a heightened sense of urgency to mitigate our evaluation of death.

"It's the same fallacy which I believe is committed by smokers. They say that they smoke because it relaxes them, but it probably relaxes them only because they're addicted to it. Are they more relaxed than non-smokers? The addiction creates the value of the nicotine. You can't credit cigarette smoking for creating that value. Likewise, you can't credit death for creating urgency since the urgency it creates would have no value were it not death. The non-smoker isn't missing something; the smoker is only mitigating the stress due to the addiction. Likewise, an immortal would not be missing out on some good by lacking the urgency specifically caused by death."

"The consolation Phil's been offering has been put by some as follows: death teaches us the preciousness of life," Connie said, "That's another way to express this urgency to make one's life good."

"Baloney!" Jeff said impatiently, "*Life* teaches us that life is precious. Death teaches us that life is *fragile*. It's a truth about human psychology that one effect of the awareness of life's fragility is a heightened desire for life's goods. On the other hand, another effect, of course, is depression. The fact that people are sometimes moved by a close shave with death or by another's death to heighten their appreciation of life only shows that immortals, were they in other respects just like humans, would lead their lives one day, or one year at a time. For, although we mortals all know very well that we are mortal, we seldom take that into consideration, unless death comes uncomfortably close. And just as we mortals don't constantly consider our mortality, contrary to the exaggerated claims made by your consolation, were we immortal, I don't think that we would often consider our immortality.

"Unfortunately, I know too well how easy it is to not even consider our mortality. As obsessed as I am with her death after the fact, though I knew she had an incurable cancer, I hardly gave a thought to her mortality before her death.

"People say death teaches us the preciousness of life, but consolers, arms full of dreary consolations, would teach us otherwise!" Jeff said indignantly.

"Some consolation it is that death teaches us life's preciousness for it entails that death is bad, as it deprives us of something precious!"

In contrast with Jeff's anger, Climax sang its melodically sweet, "Precious and Few."

Connie took a deep breath and summarized, "There are many unresolved points regarding Phil's consolations based on comparing immortal lives to ourselves. This is due largely to the sketchiness of our picture of what it would be like to be an immortal human, which in turn is due, at least in part, to an incomplete understanding of what it is like to be us, mortal humans! The uncertainty chiefly concerns the concepts 'character,' 'character formation,' 'the value of character formation,' and 'the prospect of immortal life.' Nevertheless, I would conclude that an immortal life could be worth living. First, it is not necessary that immortality would deprive one of all intrinsic values. Pizza might be good even for the billionth time. Second, though immortals have an infinite future, people like us, even if immortal, must live one moment after the next, and would never have an infinite past. The preference which we all have for the present, near future, and recent past does not come from death's inevitability."

"Immortals put their pants on one leg at a time, eh?" Phil joked.

"Yes, that's right, you pest," Connie continued. "Finally, I want to say that there is something peculiar about comparing the fortune of conceivable immortals to ourselves. I know that Phil got into it, at least initially, because of Jeff's claim that death is an infinite deprivation. But death could be terrible even if it is a finite evil, and so, the comparative plight of immortals, even if unfavorable in the comparison, could never prove that death was not a great evil, unless the supposed evils besetting immortals would necessarily accrue when an immortal reached an age comparable to a normal human life span. And unless one argues, drearily, that old age is not worth living, one could not argue that immortals' lives become not worth living at about the age an average human dies."

Phil cautioned, "That's dreary as long as the evils necessarily plaguing an immortal were the result of processes present in old mortals. Admittedly, such is the case regarding my consolation that an immortal's character would become permanently stagnated, for stagnation is the result of a process regrettably begun early in life."

Jeff said, "In sum, the eventuality of death doesn't make non-valuable things valuable, it makes them urgent or momentous. Death does this by making our opportunities fewer, sometimes even making them 'once in a lifetime.' This consequence of death is bad as well as good. It aggravates the suffering inflicted upon those who loved the dead, especially when the dead person is a parent, because our significant relationships with others, especially parents, are each unique or nearly so. This is because people have histories. Certainly one of the most important things in our histories is our relationship with our parents.

"It's been argued that immortality would be tedious. Well, if life had nothing of intrinsic value, it would be tedious whether it was short or long, mortal or immortal. On the other hand, if life has intrinsic value, immortality couldn't be altogether tedious.

"As a result of our conversation thus far," Jeff concluded, "I have articulated my sympathy evaluation as follows: death is intrinsically evil for the dead person as a deprivation evil, which I believe to be of infinite extent. I want to thank you both for helping me to articulate my anguish, but I'm not consoled."

Summary of the Conversation

The principal topics of this chapter are the extent of the deprivation entailed by death and the consequences of the prospect of death.

The topic of the extent of the deprivation includes the issue of whether the deprivation is greater for a person who died at an early age than it is for a person who had lived to a later age. While to be dead *longer* is not a greater diametric evil, a death occurring earlier in life causes a greater deprivation than a death occurring later in life. The consolation that the difference in the lengths between any finite lives is insignificant compared to the universal infinite deprivation is a dreary one for introducing the loss as an infinite one. Discussion of this consolation led to consideration of whether the deprivation entailed by death for the dead person is infinite.

The characters examined the consolation that every person must either change "beyond recognition" in the course of an immortal life, or become fixed to such an extent that life would cease to be worth living. This consolation relies upon the principle that in order for eventual death to be an evil for a person there must be a conceivable and better alternative for that person than eventual death.

Several concepts, such as "character development" and "character fixity," crucial to this consolation require further analysis. However, I conclude that a person need not change as drastically as to become "a different person" to prevent life from ceasing to be worthwhile. Even an immortal life would remain worthwhile because not all enjoyments depend on character development, and immortals, like mortals, would still have desires pressing for satisfaction. Presumably, immortals would share our preference for recently past and near future events rather than those which are more remote, though they could afford to take a "longer view' as they would be less susceptible to dangers.

However, we still have room to doubt that death is an infinite deprivation for the dead person because of the above mentioned need for further analysis of certain crucial concepts, such as "character development." It might also be the case that an immortal's life, though never necessarily worthless, might necessarily become less worthwhile.

The prospect of death causes a sense of urgency, which can be intrinsically and consequentially good. As a consolation, this is insufficient for several reasons. First, this sense of urgency can also be intrinsically and consequentially bad; second, the prospect of death is not necessary to feel urgency; third, urgency is not necessary for every good in life to be good; fourth, death deprives us of all life's goods, including any supplied by its prospect. Finally, much of urgency's consequential goodness is conditional upon the certainty of eventual death. Therefore, this goodness is not "to the credit" of eventual death. The prospect of eventual death merely provides a partial remedy for the evils which death entails. This consolation commits the smokers fallacy.

I examined the complaint "Life is too short, but days are too long" and found it to be objectionable only on one possible interpretation, that a life full of unhappy days should be longer without being happier.

Study Questions

(1) Would immortality be bad?

(2) For a healthy individual at what point would life cease to be worth living?

(3) Is immortality conceivable?

(4) Much of American popular culture endorses faith. So, it was refreshing and daring that an episode of the television program *Murphy Brown* showed characters with nothing but either doubt or puerile belief in the afterlife. One character however, Eldin the housepainter, opined that he did not want to be immortal because otherwise he'd require an infinite number of pairs of pants. Comment.

Eight

LIFE AS A WORK OF ART

Several waiters and waitresses converged on a family seated two tables away from Jeff, Phil and Connie. The staff sang and clapped as they brought a cake to a girl who was celebrating a birthday with her parents and siblings. All the nearby patrons clapped, too; except for a handful which included Jeff.

Because of their intense conversation, Jeff, Phil and Connie were still eating their entrees.

Jeff reflected, "I want to remind you that I really wish to be consoled. I wish for it more than anything—except, that is, that there were no need for me to be consoled, I mean—that my mom were still alive."

Organic Value and Death

Phil said, "I think that we can find a consolation in your admission that an immortal's life might have fewer and fewer goods as character became more and more stagnant. My new version of this consolation uses 'organic value.' Organic value, you'll remember, was a specific type of intrinsic value. Organic value is the value of a whole and it is not simply a function of the summing of the value of its parts. Organic value depends upon the relations of the parts of the whole. Remember, from our earlier discussion, the value of a piece of music, or a painting, is more a function of the relation of the parts to the whole than a sum of the value of all the parts considered separately. Prettier or livelier colors don't necessarily make a better painting. One song can have more pleasant sounds than another but also have a forgettable melody, sloppy rhythm and a poor arrangement. These are faults in the relations between the parts. And just as there are many types of relations, there are many types of organic value.

"Now, some consolations might be based on the claim that the value of death is organic, considering the dead person's life as a whole. That is, some consolations might claim that death entails a good for a person's life considered as a whole. A person's life can be seen as a whole and the stages within life as its parts. Also, a person's entire life can be seen as a part of a larger whole, such as the human race. Now, it might be the case that either of these wholes, the person's entire life or the human race, is organically better through death."

"You lost me!" Connie said.

"I'll give you examples of such consolations to make these points clearer," Phil promised.

"The argument, which I earlier offered, that eventually an immortal would experience fewer and fewer goods could be taken in two ways. Simply, it might mean that, at a certain point, an immortal's life would have so few goods as to be no longer worth living. That is, apart from consideration of the earlier and better part of an immortal's life, one would evaluate that life after some time as being no longer good. . . ."

Connie said, "Yes, we've already examined that idea."

Phil continued, "Right, but the consolation could be taken in a direction which we have not yet examined, which concerns the organic value of the relations of the parts of an immortal's life as compared to the organic value of the relations of the parts of a mortal's life. There are two ways to evaluate a stage or period of a person's life. One way, not essentially organic, is by considering that stage in isolation from the other stages of a person's life. Another way, which is essentially organic, is to consider that stage with respect to certain relations which it has to other stages. Now, as I've said, there are many organic values. Let's begin by looking at one which we might call 'value direction.' There are various possible value directions: one where the person's life improves, that is, where the value within later stages is always or on average better than the value within earlier stages. A second value direction is 'declining' in which a person's life worsens. A third would be 'oscillating' in which the value fluctuates, et cetera."

Connie said, "Ok, I think I understand 'value direction.' A person's life gets better or worse or goes back and forth. And I understand what you mean by calling it an organic value of the person's life. It depends upon a relation or comparison of the value of the parts of that life."

Jeff said, "All right, what's the consolation which you wish to offer me based upon the concept of value direction?"

Phil said, "An immortal whose life has fewer and fewer goods has a life which is in decline. And a life of declining value is organically worse than a non-declining life. Therefore, because of the latter part of an immortal's life, an immortal has a life of less organic value than a mortal who died without a decline. Thus, even if immortal lives continued to have some goods, as you argued against my earlier version of this anti-immortality consolation, if the goods became fewer and fewer, as you all but conceded, then their lives would be organically evil, or at least would have a bad value direction."

Simon and Garfunkel's "Leaves that are Green" played as Phil continued.

"Let's face it: a declining life is organically worse than one that is not declining. We regard as significant the difference between a story with a happy beginning and a sad ending and one with a sad beginning and a happy ending. We prefer the latter. That is, we do recognize value direction as an important value. So, if death prevents a decline in life's value, then that must be regarded as significant. Now, the preference for happy ending stories, or an inclination for 'improving' stories rather than declining ones is not a prejudice. Yes, people do place more importance on proximate or recent events than a more distant time. But the preference for happy ending stories, or improving stories, is not due to this emphasis on more proximate times, for we prefer improving stories to declining ones even in stories about the future. In stories about the future the ending is further from us than the beginning, but we still prefer a happy ending after a sad beginning than a sad ending after a happy beginning."

"Yes, but we're *told* the ending last," Connie objected. "That's why we think a series of events with a happy ending to be better than a declining series with a happy beginning. The final and most recent impression received by the audience is the one which lasts; it's the impression which they have once the entire series is in front of them. So naturally people prefer an inclining story to a declining one. But I don't see that this preference is rational."

"I agree," said Jeff, "I would add that in an engaging narrative the audience adopts the point of view of its participants, and from that point of view, the ending is the most recent event, no matter when the narrated events take place."

Phil asked, "So, you both think that an evaluation with respect to the direction of fortunes is irrational, and therefore, it is no consolation that death prevents a decline which an immortal would suffer?"

Jeff answered, "I'm not sure that the direction of one's happiness should not be a consideration in evaluating a person's life, however, I am inclined to believe that as long as an immortal's life still contained goods it would not matter at all that there were more goods earlier in life, except insofar as the awareness of this decline might depress the immortal."

Phil looked puzzled. "But isn't it you who grieves because of a decline in life's value? The greater the loss, the worse your grief?"

Jeff explained, "Declining value justifies grief because it shows one the goods which could have conceivably continued. It's not the sequence itself which justifies grief. An inclining sequence also shows one the goods which might have been. This might also justify sorrow, except that people respond less to former evils than present ones."

Jeff continued, "I suspect that value direction is unimportant in itself. People prefer improved to declined value direction because the former seems to be predictive of further diametric goods, while the latter seems predictive of further diametric evils. Happy ending stories proverbially tack on 'And they lived happily ever after.' But, of course, that does not apply to a dead person. The dead have neither diametric goods nor evils. Therefore, our preference for inclined value direction cannot be used to evaluate death."

Phil looked at Connie. "Have you abandoned trying to console Jeff? You've opposed my consolation based on value direction, and several of my recent consolations."

"No, but after Jeff defended the view that death is a deprivation evil for the loved one, I'm becoming more diffident of evaluation consolations," Connie answered. "And I'm suspicious of evaluating death in terms of the organic value of the whole of a person's life. From the examples you first gave me of organic value, I can see that it is crucial in evaluating works of art, but I think it is quite a bit . . . I don't know . . . erudite . . . 'academically clever' to evaluate life and death in this way."

Jeff said, "Phil, you're playing with dynamite when you seek to console me by arguing that an immortal's life, because declining, would be organically worse than a mortal's. For, first, as Connie cautioned you earlier, you must be careful, when comparing immortality unfavorably to mortality, not to entail that an early death is better than death at a ripe old age. Now, your consolation with respect to life's value direction fails to heed this caution, as aging is a decline in many respects. Second, in my mom's case, not only did she decline as a result of the usual aging processes . . . in fact, not so much because of these, since she was vigorous and only seventy when the cancer struck, rather, her life declined principally because of the damned cancer. So, I am not comforted by insistence on value direction as a distinct criterion for evaluating a life.

"Third, even were an immortal's life declining and therefore, in that one respect, organically worse than a life which does not decline, I believe that death with respect to value direction is organically worse than immortality, even as bleak as you've imagined immortality.

"An immortal's life is in decline because goods diminish. But a dead person loses far more than an immortal! You might reply that an immortal would be aware of the loss whereas the dead are not. But I remind you that the awareness of a deprivation evil is not necessary for its existence. So, the organic evil of decline does not require awareness of the evil, although awareness of it might compound the evil. Nor can I see that it matters whether the decline would be gradual, as with immortals, or sudden, as when it comes through death. Perhaps I should say that a sudden decline is a greater organic evil than a gradual one; and that would not assist your consolation!"

Phil reacted, "Agreed; I would not argue that a sudden decline was organically better than a gradual one. However, I would reply that you have misunderstood the use of 'value direction.' The whole, of which this is an organic value, is the person's life from start to finish. This whole does *not* include comparison with what comes either before or after a person's life. In this sense, death is not a decline at all."

Jeff objected, "You can use the term 'value direction' in this way, if you like. According to your use, the only comparisons to be made are not only *of* stages of a person's life, but also only *between* stages of a person's life. But there is another relation, between one's life and each of its stages on the one hand, and all time, including that which precedes and follows life, on the other. Call this relation, because more encompassing, '*greater value direction*,' if you like. Death entails a decline in greater value direction.

"Further, I don't see that value direction is a more important relation than greater value direction. The only argument which I can think of that value direction is a more important relation than greater value direction would rely on the rejected claim that the value depends upon the person's awareness of that value. It's true that, whereas a person later in life can compare the quality of life at different stages, the dead do not sit around comparing life with death, but the organic relation does not depend on the dead drawing comparisons. A person can be aware of the value direction of one's life and either gladdened or saddened by it. If saddened, this sadness is an additional evil, but it is a consequence of the awareness of the organic value, not a part of it. Likewise, awareness of greater value direction is not a part of it; the organic value exists independently of any awareness of it."

Comparison between Death and Prenatal Non-Existence Reprised

Jeff said, "Your attempted consolation supplies another explanation of why people regard death as worse than prenatal non-existence...."

Connie said, "I remember that earlier you said that one possible explanation for the difference in people's attitudes toward prenatal non-existence and death has to do with differences in their organic value."

Jeff continued, "Prenatal non-existence, unlike death, does not entail that one's greater value direction is declining. In fact, I think that prenatal non-existence might be organically good in some respects. Besides an improving greater value direction to which prenatal non-existence contributes, another organic value is *individuality*, or *uniqueness* or *originality*. Individuality is an organic value. People are called 'unique' because they contribute variety to a larger whole, such as the human race.

"A unique individual entails the organic value of variety for the whole of which it is a member, and a finite past is necessary that people are unique. One way that people are unique is by being born at different times, thus growing up under different influences and entailing that not everyone will be the same age with the same amount of experience and the same types of experiences. In other words, prenatal nonexistence is necessary for the organic values of uniqueness and, in turn, variety."

"Ah! But then death would be organically good as well. For immortals would either cease developing or they would eventually become more and more alike. The more their experience, the less unique would the experience of each become. Immortals would lose their individuality or uniqueness," Phil claimed.

Jeff remarked, "It is plausible that with respect to some things immortals would become more alike. Their preferences, knowledge and principles might converge. But it is conceivable that they retain their individual memories and consequently, a special intimacy for only a few other immortals. No matter how homogeneous their experiences became people would still remember only a few persons as having been intimate with them *throughout* their lives, mostly parents and older siblings.

"Admittedly, much uniqueness would be lost. Yet, however organically evil this might be, I do not think that this would be an overall bad thing. The search for wisdom is, in some respects, a shedding of individuality. At this table we're trying to reach a consensus, that is, remove individual differences.

"You raise a good point, Phil, but a finite past is, I think, more important for uniqueness than a finite future; and I'll add that an infinite future contributes more to uniqueness than no future at all! Remember, some consolers argue that death is good because it treats all alike! Drearily, it impoverishes us all. Again, whatever organic evil immortality might hold, I believe that death holds it in spades!"

Connie mused parenthetically, "Anyone who thinks that death is egalitarian never studied an actuarial table, never compared private with public health care, and never compared the homicide rates of different neighborhoods!"

Phil added, "Or they regard as insignificant the difference between long and short lives, especially when that difference is contrasted to the difference between finitude and infinity."

Jeff continued, "Having a finite past was crucial to my mom's having been the person she was, a finite past is crucial to my being the person I am, and a finite past for us both was crucial to our relationship having been what it was. An infinite future might change all these drastically, although you have not convinced me that this is necessary, but an infinite future cannot change what we have been nor what we were to each other. That is, a finite future is not necessary to that which has been, whereas a finite past was."

Others' Deaths Makes Our Lives Possible

Phil responded, "Not only was a finite past necessary in order for you to be the person you are and your mom to have been the person she was and your relationship to have been what it was, it was also necessary for all these that, until some recent time, *other* people died. That is, although your own and your mom's futures need not have been finite for you to be the people you were, it was necessary that virtually everyone else's futures were finite.

"Succinctly, human mortality is a condition of your identity, your mom and your relationship, just as was prenatal non-existence."

Joe South sang his popular song "Rose Garden."

As Jeff reflected Connie said, "This sounds like you're imagining a 'Dialogue with Death.' Death says, 'I am a condition of your existence. You would be nothing without me! I am you! How dare you complain of my prospect! How could you curse me when I claim a loved one!' Then the griever would say, 'I complain that you have come too soon,' to which Death replies, 'I must come sometime, and whenever I would come you would make the same complaint! Besides, I am not the only condition of your existence. This *other* condition has many names: Fortune, Fate, and Chance. I am indifferent to the time of death, I can wait longer than you can imagine, but she, Fate, has no patience. But without her also you are nothing!' Death gallantly would defend her. . . . Very theatrical, huh?" Connie asked teasingly.

"Very good performance!" Phil said sarcastically.

"Is there a point to your little play?" Jeff said.

"Of course there is! I'm not here for comic relief! I'm here to straighten you two out!" Connie said. "By the way, what do you think the point of the play was?"

Jeff answered, "Phil seems to personify death when he says that it is a condition of myself and my loved ones, even those I've lost, and concludes that I should not grieve, or complain that death is evil. But death and I have made no contract, no bargain, and no agreement. On the contrary, I'll take what I can from life and still complain when I can't get anymore! Phil's right that human mortality has made me possible, but I'll still complain that it means the deaths of my loved ones."

"No, you miss my point," Phil replied. "Of course, there is no bargain between you and death. The point is that human mortality is necessary for your existence and for all the dear and valuable things you've lost. Death is necessary for *all* life's goods."

Jeff noted, "We're moving beyond the consolation that death is necessary for uniqueness. Now you're claiming that death is necessary for all goods that I or my mom enjoyed."

Phil concurred.

Jeff said, "Strictly speaking, it is not either my death or my mom's death which is necessary for my mom's or my own existence. The necessary condition for these is the mortality of others. I agree that were all humans immortal there would never have been persons such as my mom or myself. Were all other persons immortal, history and society would be so vastly different that there would be no sense in identifying my mom or myself with any individuals in that possible world. A large part of what identifies us is our histories. And no persons with my own or my mom's histories could exist in this world of immortals.

"Although it is not conceivable that she and I exist in a world in which everyone who ever lived never died, it is conceivable that she and I and others of our contemporaries are immortal. When it comes to this, the parallel between death and prenatal nonexistence breaks down. My own prenatal nonexistence, and hers, is necessary in the strongest sense for my existence and hers. And I grant that the deaths of billions of others were necessary for our existence. But not my own death—not my mom's."

"What about your dad's death? It was a long time ago. You were barely an adolescent. You hadn't yet discovered philosophy. You had never been in love. So, you've changed a lot since he died. Isn't it plausible that the way you've changed, the person you've become, would have been quite different had your dad not died? His death must have altered, in some way, your relationship with your mom. You never had a loved one die before your dad's death, for that matter. The death of your dad itself must have changed you, and in ways that you would not have otherwise changed," Phil said.

"That's a very intriguing and perhaps disturbing point. But I'll pass on your claim that my dad's death is necessary for the existence of the person you see before you, as it would require analysis of the concept of a person's continued existence which is an analysis better delayed," Jeff said.

"Ok, but it's an issue you'll have to address," Phil insisted.

Jeff halfheartedly offered, "There are some things about me which would be different were my father still alive, but other things would not have changed. In a sense, therefore, his death was necessary to my existence. However, the person I am as a result is probably less good than the person I would have become, so I take no comfort in his death's being necessary for the me you see before you. But again, the point you make raises issues which we're not yet prepared to tackle.

"I'd rather make the point that, even if my own and my parents' deaths are necessary for any of the goods we experienced, this does not change the fact that my mom, having died, has lost any possible future goods and that I have lost any possible future goods stemming from her. And this fact is sufficient for my grief. Let's be clear on all this: death, as annihilation, entails deprivation evils. Your consolation that death is also necessary for the goods which have been lost does not change that. I concede that, were it not for the deaths of many others, the goods which I cherish would have been inconceivable. However, I maintain that it is conceivable that at least something very much like me and my loved ones would exist, although immortal.

"But of course, the laws of nature make it impossible that my loved ones and I exist and turn out immortal. So, while the laws of nature make all my cherished goods possible, they also doom every one of them. Should this change my evaluation of her death? Her death is part of an *incredible, marvelous, fantastic* system without which she would not have existed. Nonetheless, her non-existence is still an evil for her. I evaluate the laws of nature as good insofar as they are bountiful, and I evaluate them as evil insofar as they are not."

Death Is Part of Nature

Connie said, "You *acknowledge* that death is a part of a system which is necessary for all goods, but it doesn't *show* in your affects that you acknowledge the goodness of this system."

Jeff replied, "My sympathy and ego evaluations are that my mom's death is a terrible evil for her and me, respectively. My evaluations are not that the entire system of nature is, upon the whole, evil for my mom or me. Now, do you think that every *affect* should be a response to the entire system of nature? I doubt that even a *single* affect should be a response to the entire system of nature. What would such an affect be?"

"A general feeling of approval, of being pleased . . ." Phil began.

"We're getting ahead of ourselves," Jeff said, interrupting an answer to his question. "We're supposed to be examining evaluation consolations now; after we've finished discussing the sympathy and ego evaluations I want us to examine response consolations. Our discussion is getting us into that prematurely. Without being drawn into response consolations, let me restate my view. I still believe the sympathy and ego evaluations despite the facts that the mortality of others is necessary to my most cherished goods and that my own and my loved one's mortality is part of a system which is necessary for these goods. My loved ones' deaths, or more precisely, the events of their deaths, is not itself productive of these goods. On the contrary, it eliminates them."

Phil said, "All right, I haven't shown that the griever's evaluations are false. However, perhaps we're a step *closer* to showing that something is wrong with grief. But we can wait to consider that."

Connie noted, "Jeff, a minute ago you conceded something you did not need to concede. You said that others' mortality is necessary for the existence of you and your mom. This is true in one sense of 'mortality,' but false in another. Others' *deaths* are necessary for the existence of you and your mom. But others' *annihilations* are not necessary for your existence or hers. Because world history could conceivably be the same as it has been, including the lives of Jeff and his mom, even if people survived death, that is, were not annihilated, continuing to exist in an afterlife but without affecting human history. This is an important point since your primary complaint is against annihilation, not against survivable death."

Jeff said, "You're right. The things I have cherished do not require anyone's *annihilation*."

Phil cautioned, "*Assuming* that it even makes sense to say that a person can survive death."

Jeff said, "I think that survival of death is conceivable though almost incredible, but rather than argue for the conceivability of the afterlife let's get back to the topic of the organic value of death. In discussing that subject we were led away from it. Let's return to considerations of organic value."

Connie dissented. "There might be organic values *within* lives, such as value direction. But an entire life as a whole does not have organic value, such as uniqueness."

Phil said, "No, I think that there is such a value to our lives. Jeff and I agree that life must be finite for it to possess the organic value of uniqueness. Jeff and I disagree in that he believes that, for uniqueness, life need be finite only at one end—it must have a beginning."

Connie maintained, "Once again, I think that you are both going overboard in considering the organic value *of* a person's life as a whole and whether death improves or worsens that value. Even if a person's uniqueness entails a good of the whole such as variety, this does not mean that one's uniqueness is a good of the part, that is, a good *for him or her*. Just because someone had a unique life and contributed to the species' variety doesn't entail that this person had a happier life. In fact, often the experience and skills which make a person unique make life challenging and uncomfortable. And so, if either prenatal non-existence or death contribute to uniqueness or prevent uniformity, and this increases a good of the whole, even then these things are not necessarily a good of the part, considered separately. Remember, the deficiency of a part can contribute to the organic good of the whole, as exemplified by musical discord. And if an evil or flaw of a part can enrich the organic value of a whole, then a person's uniqueness is not necessarily good for that person."

Jeff said, "You are right on this point. It does not matter to the sympathy evaluation whether death alters in any way the organic value of the human race, or nature, or whatever. It doesn't benefit the person that one's uniqueness added to the variety within the species."

Life as a Work of Art

Phil agreed and added, "But I do think that other organic values of a person's life as a whole do merit consideration. So far, we've considered two organic values which a life as a whole might possess: value direction and uniqueness. But furthermore, as an entire life resembles a *narrative* more closely than it resembles any other art form such as music or painting, in trying to determine the organic value of a whole life it would be most helpful to consider the organic value found in narratives."

As the Browns' "Three Bells" played, Jeff said, "Despite Connie's protests, I do think that the comparison of life as a whole with narrative might be relevant to evaluating death. But we must remember that it is only a small part of the evaluation. I think it is relevant to compare life to a narrative because people do think of their lives as a story. People are constantly, though for the most part secretly, relating and revising bits of their own biography. People go over their pasts and their plans again and again. They think 'This was a turning point,' 'This was a high point,' 'This led to that,' almost as though they were editing a film."

"Also, any good story needs an *ending*," Phil said. "So, if a life as a whole is a good story, not just something that contains good stories, life must have an end. The organic value which requires an ending we might call '*narrative structure*.' Death is necessary that life possess a good narrative structure."

Connie replied to Phil, "We cannot learn anything about the value of death by employing criteria appropriate to works of art. Another example of the absurdity of applying criteria of narrative structure to life as a whole is that life, contrary to the rules of drama, is highly episodic, no matter how rich with recurring themes. Life would have to be either very short or very narrow for its events to have the causal connectedness required by drama or comedy.

In life events do not have the close interrelatedness that they have in a narrative work of art."

Phil replied to Connie, "I would like to use the criterion of interconnectedness which you've mentioned. The events of an immortal's life would gradually become less and less tightly connected. One might say that immortal life would 'unravel.' In the course of their lives their relationships with persons, places and things would change drastically, however gradually the change might occur. To some extent, as long as a story possesses a high degree of interrelatedness, its telling can be lengthy. However, it must come to an end sometime otherwise it will unravel for sure."

Passing over the specifics of Phil's last point, Jeff said, "I'm coming to agree with Connie that we cannot evaluate life by the criteria for narrative structure. For example, one reason for storytelling is to teach. Therefore, a story's length should be partly determined by however long it takes to teach whatever it is the storyteller wishes. But a lesson which requires an infinite story before it can be learned would never be learned. A story without an end would be, in this respect, like a proof of a theorem of infinite length. Even an immortal would not learn from it. But how could this reason, that a story's length must be long enough to teach something, be used to justify death?"

Phil said, "As I argued before, life is sufficiently long once one has learned all that one can; life's length is adequate according to how long it takes to learn. This is a variation of my consolation that an immortal would reach intellectual fixity and that an intellectually fixed life would not be worthwhile."

"If life's length is justified by one's capacity to continue learning then I'm glad I'm a slow and voracious reader!" Connie joked.

"And I'm glad I'm a philosopher, since it takes us forever!" Jeff added.

"Sorry, but your deaths will just have to be unjustified!" Phil said.

Jeff said, "Well, I've already argued that there would always be something to learn. I won't get into that again. Instead of that, let me give one reason why the criteria for a good narrative, such as that it have an end, are not applicable to a life as a whole: the end of a story is very different from the end of a person's life. An ended story is incorporated into the ongoing life of the person to whom the story is related. In view of this incorporation, storytelling has rules. But the end of a person's life is not incorporated into that person's life.

"Furthermore, an immortal's life might have finalities *within* it. Within an immortal's life there would be an unending series of events, many of which would have a narrative structure. Immortals would not lack this organic value within their lives.

Value *of* a Life Contrasted with Value *for* a Life

"Finally, picking up on a point that Connie made, even if it were proven that death increases the organic value of a person's life as a whole, it would not follow that death increases the value of that person's life *for* that person. It is one thing to show that a person's death increases the organic value of that life as a whole, but it is another thing to show that a person's death increases for that person the value of life. The latter is necessary for one to mitigate the sympathy evaluation. It is of no interest to me that death increases the organic values of my mom's life unless it made her happier, that is, made her life better *for* her, benefited her. The supposed increased value of the person's life as a whole does not entail that the person is benefited, everything else being equal. The increased organic value *of* a person's life might make a spectator happier, yet not increase the happiness of the person who has this valuable thing. A beautiful but blind person has an organic value which can make others happier, but it does not necessarily benefit that person. Awareness of one's beauty is not necessary to possessing it, but awareness of one's beauty is one way to be benefited by it."

Phil said, "I still don't fully understand. Although your example seems like a good one, I still wonder whether it is *possible* to increase the value of a person's life without increasing the value *for* that person."

Jeff said, "In order to explain let's begin with a different case. The *consequential* value of a person's life might be increased without an increase in the value of that person's life for that person. We can imagine a person's death having considerable consequential value; for instance, a democrat who dies while sabotaging some war effort of a fascist regime. That person's life, and even death, might have considerable consequential value. But this value would not be for the dead democratic heroine. The value would be for her fellow democrats. It would be they who would receive the benefit. Now, perhaps the consequential value of her death should comfort her loving ones, but it would not mitigate the sympathy evaluation."

Phil said, "According to our classification of consolations, it would be a response consolation to argue that the griever should respond to more than just the sympathy and ego evaluations, that other evaluations take precedence over the griever's evaluations."

Jeff said, "But some consolers would not appreciate this clarification. They wish the griever to *confuse* the consequential value which some deaths have with a value *for* the dead person."

Phil objected, "Under some circumstances of death, usually martial, consolers have offered as comfort the good consequences of the death. And this consolation *might* be a result of treating consequential value like intrinsic value, thereby mistakenly mitigating the sympathy evaluation. However, a second strategy would be to leave unaltered the sympathy evaluation and argue that one's affects should not be determined solely, or even predominantly, by the griever's evaluations. That strategy will have to wait until we get to response consolations. But a third strategy would be to argue that a heroic death, for example, has consequential value through the dead person's *virtue* and that there is no greater good for a person than to be virtuous. In other words, virtue not only has consequential value for others but also the greatest intrinsic value for the virtuous person. I admit that I do not subscribe to the theory that possessing virtue necessarily benefits its possessor. My point is that consolers need not be simply confused who oppose your sympathy evaluation on the ground that there was something virtuous about a person's death."

Jeff replied, "I suspect that someone who maintains that virtue is the greatest intrinsic good for the person who is virtuous confuses consequential and intrinsic value *somewhere* along the line. But be that as it may, even assuming that one's own virtue were the greatest good for oneself, death would still be a deprivation evil. For it would deprive a virtuous person of the continued exercise of virtue."

Phil responded, "A consoler who maintained that virtue was the greatest, or even only, intrinsic good would have to admit that an annihilated virtuous person was deprived of future virtuous acts. However, they might still argue that the value of a person's life for that person is not only a function of the *number* of virtuous acts performed by that person, but also that the value of a person's life for that person is a function of the 'magnitude' of the virtue of his or her actions. So, while a heroic death deprives one of future acts of virtue, since such a death would be an act of *exceeding* virtue it is an overall increase in the value of a person's life for that person."

"Fine," Jeff said confidently. "First, a dead heroine would still have been better off had she made the ultimate virtuous act after having lived a very long life filled with virtue. In other words, as long as the *number* of virtuous acts *partially* determines the value of a person's life for that person, there would be something evil about death coming when it does.

"Second, if a consoler is going to avoid confusing consequential value for others with intrinsic value for oneself, and they are going to make the magnitude of one's virtue a partial determinant of the value for that person, there must be some basis for determining the magnitude of one's virtue which would be independent of its consequential value for others. We can't say that the heroic death is greatly virtuous because it was of great benefit to others because that's its consequential value."

"That need not be a problem," Phil said. "The magnitude of the virtue of one's acts need not be a function of the consequential value of the acts. A heroic death saving thousands need not be more virtuous than a heroic death saving one. In fact, one might argue that the latter is more virtuous since it requires even more self-denial. It would be easier to count oneself as less than thousands than to count oneself as less than a single other person."

Connie added, "The 'magnitude' of the virtue entailed by a heroic death might be increased by the brevity of the hero's life because it requires greater self-denial."

"Then is the magnitude to be determined by self-denial or self-sacrifice?" Jeff asked. "But our imaginary consoler tells us that a virtuous death is a great good for the dead. Where then is the self-sacrifice?"

"Maybe the magnitude shouldn't be measured by self-sacrifice. Perhaps the magnitude of the virtue of one's acts is determined by the extent to which they triumph over one's inclinations," Phil suggested. "Even if a heroic death greatly benefited the hero, the willingness to die does show opposition to a very natural inclination."

Jeff objected, "If virtue's magnitude were simply a function of the strength of the inclinations which one's determination needs to overcome, then a suicide which benefited no one would be exceedingly virtuous."

"Another consolation that limits the kinds of reasons for refraining from suicide?" Connie asked.

"Then perhaps the magnitude of virtue is a function of one's commitment to *duty* over one's inclinations, such as self-sacrifice which benefited others. And as pointless suicide is not a duty, pointless suicide would not be exceedingly virtuous," Phil responded.

Connie added, "The magnitude might be increased by the heroic person's youth, as it implies a triumph over one's inclinations at an age in which one is usually less 'mature.'"

Jeff concluded, "All right, I have not proven that the concept of virtue's magnitude is either senseless or dependent upon the consequential value of one's virtues. Therefore, I have not disproved the consolation which seeks to mitigate the evil of death for the dead in cases in which the death displays virtue. On the other hand, you have not proven it. In any case, such a consolation would have limited application and none at all to my mom's case, since her death involved no commitment to duty on her part. It was not heroic."

Phil observed, "We've been digressing again, although importantly. For whatever we think of the consolation criticizing the sympathy evaluation on the ground that the death involved some virtue, we can all agree to the point which led to this digression, namely that the consequential value of a person's life need not be a value for that person. Jeff's suggested example of this, that of a heroic death, led us into this digression about virtue's value for its possessor, but I think other examples could be found which would avoid such a digression. For instance, if a person *accidentally* benefits others at a cost to oneself, no question of virtue, and consequently, the value of virtue to its possessor, can enter in. Such a consequential value need not be a value for that person. But I still do not see how an increase in the *organic* value of a person's life might not be an increase in the value of that life for that person."

"I'll continue with my explanation," Jeff said. "For starters let's take some intrinsic values, ones which do not have a person's whole life as their subject. Of these, some are diametric. We've agreed that a diametric value for a person is a state of that person's awareness. But not so for deprivation evils. Deprivations are evils for a person without necessarily being states of that person, let alone states of awareness of that person. However, I do *not* think that an increase in the organic value of a person's life as a whole entails a value for that person unless that person *is* aware of this organic value of his or her life as a whole. That is, the only thing the person could get out of the organic value of life as a whole would be the enjoyment derived from awareness of it. In sum, whereas a deprivation evil is evil for the deprived person whether or not that person is aware of it and whether or not that person reacts badly to the awareness of the deprivation, the organic value of a person's life as a whole is not a value for that person except insofar as that person is aware of it and insofar as that person reacts to it with either enjoyment or distress."

Phil said, "I object. Aren't you being inconsistent? And aren't your inconsistencies designed to perpetuate your grief? You make awareness necessary when it suits your grief, and you make it unnecessary when that suits your grief. For a deprivation to be evil for a person, you deny that awareness is necessary. But for an organic good of the person's life as a whole to be good for that person you insist upon awareness and appreciation."

Jeff remarked, "No, I'm not contradicting myself, let alone contradicting myself for the purpose of prolonging my grief. But I am getting clearer about my grief.

"A deprivation for a person need not be a state of awareness of that person. It needn't even be a state of that person at all. However, it must, like any other value for a person, at least *refer* to a state of that person's awareness. It must *concern* that person's awareness. Death and some other deprivations concern a person's awareness. That is, they are deprivations of that person's awareness.

"A person can be benefited by one's consequential value for others by being aware of it, if it pleases one.

"And an increase or decrease in the value of a person's life as a whole is not good for that person unless that person is aware of it. For the *only* way that the organic value of a person's life can *concern* that person's awareness is by that person's awareness of it. Thus, the increase or decrease in the organic value of a person's life by death has no implication for the sympathy evaluation except insofar as the person was aware of this increase or decrease in organic value."

Connie said, "Let's continue to work with your example of physical beauty. It seems clearly false to say that the only benefit a person could receive from her own beauty would be her own awareness and appreciation of it. A person's beauty can benefit that person if it causes others to treat that person better."

Jeff said, "You're right. But that sort of counterexample is inapplicable to the present issue. Because we are mortal do we treat each other better than were we immortal?"

Connie said, "You're just opening up again our discussion of the value of the prospect of death. Is death necessary for us to treat each other well? Would we necessarily treat each other less well were we immortal?"

"I don't think so," answered Jeff.

"The immortal gods treated each other miserably!" Phil quipped.

"But they treated us mortals even worse!" Jeff sparred.

Jeff blushed, "I'm sorry. I've misstated my view. Of course, a person might be benefited in a variety of ways as a result of possessing some organic value, such as beauty. Awareness and appreciation of it is only one way. The point I need to make was the point I started out with, but strayed from, namely, that the possession of a value such as an increase of the organic value of one's life as a whole does not *entail* that one is benefited by it."

Jeff continued, "Now, I stated that a person views and reviews one's own life as though telling and being told a story. But I do not think that for this reflection it is necessary that we have the prospect of the story's coming to an end. If we were immortal, we would still tell ourselves our life-stories, but without a thought to their end.

"However, as we are mortal, we do think, occasionally, of the end of our lives. But I don't see that this awareness of our mortality is an awareness of a value which our lives supposedly possess thereby, even supposing that our lives do have added organic value because of death. In other words, I am arguing that, even if death enhances the organic value of a person's life, that this is irrelevant to the sympathy evaluation, unless the dead person, when alive, was aware of this enhancement of the organic value of her life.

"Now, I have two reasons for doubting that a person would be aware of, or appreciate, the supposed increase in the organic value of life. First, aesthetic appreciation normally requires a degree of disinterestedness which would be lacking to a person contemplating the organic value of one's own death. Whatever organic value which death supposedly contributes, it deprives us of many goods and so we are not disinterested. Second, while I agree that people 'stand back' and look at their life-story, this is not the only perspective which they adopt toward their lives. True, people are spectators of their own lives; but they are also creators. They are artists as well as critics. And death ties the hand of the artist creating that life. It's true that works of art are finite: canvases have an edge, movies a running time, and scores have a conclusion. But do not compare death to the edges of a canvas, for a painter chooses the canvas. Furthermore, death, unlike the edges of a canvas, is not a condition of the work, though perhaps prenatal non-existence is a condition of that work which is our lives. But even this concedes too much, for one can conceive of a painting which has no spatial limit, but which grows and grows. So, a limit is not a condition of creativity. Or would you argue that death makes life better in the way that the difficulty of working with the material makes porcelain objects more prized? Is this to be our consolation?

"Death wrests from one the control of one's life-story. Upon one's death little remains of one's life-story since no one else can recall it as you, and that little is handed over to others. Our round characters become flat; our complexity becomes inconsistency; and our unspoken dreams have no part at all in our legacy.

"Death always interrupts the person creating a future, revising one's biography. Or only the dreariest lives end without an interruption of plans."

Phil said, "I see what you're doing. You're trying to turn my consolations based upon considerations of the value of a life as a whole into grievances. From the point of view of an artist, death is an obstacle to further creation. All right, suppose that death decreases the value of a life in this way. As you've argued, unless a person were aware of this decrease it might not have harmed that person. And fortunately, again as you've pointed out, people usually ignore the fact that death will come and interrupt that which they are creating."

Jeff said, "Yes, but you must admit that people are sometimes aware that death will wrest from them their projects and the control of their life-story."

Phil agreed.

Jeff added in a low voice, "Sadder even than coming across photos of my mom are finding photos of people and places which meant something to her but which mean nothing to me. These were a part of the life-story she had been making. Now they're clutter."

Phil said, "Since the loss of meaning of these photos seems also to be a loss for you, as well as your mom's, the next thing we should discuss is the ego evaluation, which until now we haven't discussed much."

Summary of the Conversation

In this chapter, I consider arguments that death improves or detracts from the organic value of a person's life considered as a whole. I have also argued that an alteration in the organic value *of* a person's life, either as a whole, or within that life, does not entail a value *for* that person. One manner in which the organic value of a person can be a value for that person is through that person's awareness of, and response toward, that value of one's life. I argued that insofar as a person was aware of the organic value of one's life as a whole, death is more baneful than beneficial, for persons are aware that death will interfere with the projects they have proposed for their life as a whole. Even if death supplied organic value to a person's life as a whole, and that person was aware of this value, that the person would have acquired much aesthetic satisfaction from the awareness is unlikely since disinterestedness appears to be a general psychological requirement for aesthetic satisfaction. A person's death harms the person's interests.

Consolations I examined are:

(1) Death is necessary to prevent a decline in value direction;
(2) Death is necessary for life as a whole to have a narrative structure;
(3) Death is necessary to prevent a person's life from losing its uniqueness.

To the first consolation I object that death is not sufficient to prevent this decline, which occurs as part of aging, unless one dies young, and thus, this consolation is dreary. Death is a greater decline than any entailed by immortality. Death is a decline of a person's greater value direction, as opposed to prenatal non-existence, which makes possible an incline or improvement in one's greater value direction.

To the second consolation I object that the reasons for which narrative structure is valuable to a story have little or no application to a person's life as a whole.

To the third consolation I object that, while prenatal non-existence is perhaps necessary to a person's being a unique individual, the person's death is not necessary to prevent an unacceptable degree of uniformity.

Consideration of the third consolation led to consideration of further consolations that death is necessary for a person's existence and also that a person's death is a part of a system that is good upon the whole. To the first point I object that a person's death is still evil for that person, and to both consolations I object that emotions are properly a response to particular events, not to the system of nature as whole. I will more fully discuss this point in Chapter Thirteen.

Study Questions

(1) Why do we enjoy theatrical tragedy or depictions of tragedy in art?

(2) Why do we enjoy some *real* tragedies?
- Is "enjoy" the wrong way to put this question?
- Why do we enjoy some real tragedies but grieve over others?

(3) In what senses might a life be more or less unified like a work of art?
- Should life have such unity?

Nine

DEATH'S IMPACT ON SURVIVORS

Paul McCartney and Wings' "Band on the Run" began:

> Never seeing no one
> Nice again like you, momma,
> You, momma, you . . . .

"A topic which has been waiting in the wings is the ego evaluation that death is a great evil for those who loved the person who is now dead," Jeff said.

"We've digressed to that issue a couple times, but we haven't carefully examined it," Connie observed.

"I'm not yet agreed to the sympathy evaluation," Phil reminded.

The Ego Evaluation

Connie said, "There's no question that, as a result of your mom's death, you are suffering a lot. That's why we're having this morbid discussion on such a beautiful summer evening."

Phil cautioned, "Yes, Jeff is suffering, but one must not use the grief itself to conclude that death is a consequential evil for the loving ones, except to the extent that grief is inevitable, because Jeff is trying to justify his grief on the basis of the sympathy and ego evaluations. So, neither of these evaluations can in turn be justified because he feels grief.

"To put it another way, apart from inevitable grief, grief is not the result of the event; rather, it is the result of the griever's beliefs about the event. If grief is the result of the beliefs, then grief should not be used to justify those beliefs.

"Now, to some extent, grief is probably inevitable. However, our whole effort this evening is based on the assumption that grief is not inevitable beyond some point, a point which Jeff has or might pass. Therefore, continuing with this assumption, the grief itself, or at least that which is not inevitable, cannot be used to justify the claim that death is consequentially evil for the loving ones of the dead.

"And if a person tried to justify *further* grief solely on the basis that the loved one's death caused some *inevitable* grief and that the grief was itself evil, so that they were grieving over the grief, then I would say that if the only evil were the grief, then stop grieving!"

Connie said, "All right; nevertheless, there is no denying that the loving ones lose many precious goods because of the death of a loved one. . . ."

"I agree," Phil said, shaking his head as if to say it was understood.

"First and foremost, the company of that person is lost. It is a dreary consolation that no one's company is always enjoyable...."

"Perhaps the nearest exceptions are very young children," said Jeff.

"Who are raised by another!" joked Phil, the father.

"and romantic partners about whom one is so much 'head over heels' that you would rather argue with that person than make love to another."

"In other words, when it comes to the loss of a person's company, there are losses worse than that of a grown child's loss of a parent," Connie said.

"Being a comptroller, you know about company losses!" Phil snapped, defensively wearing a pained expression.

Connie continued, "The loss of a beloved spouse or a child is usually worse than that."

"There are many evils greater than that over which I grieve," conceded Jeff. "I agree that on average the loss for the loving ones of a child or a spouse is much worse than the loss of one's parents. Normally, children or a spouse are more a part of one's daily routine and enjoyments. Obviously, the loss of one's spouse is usually the loss of one's sexual partner. And insofar as the bereaved is inhibited the loss of a spouse would probably involve either the loss of sexual desire or the will to satisfy it, as was earlier pointed out. However, in *some* respects, the loss of one's parents is worse than these other losses. I lost their experience. I lost their love, and in some ways, a parent's love can be more resilient than any other which we receive during life."

Jeff continued, "A parent's death, along with the others we've mentioned, but especially so, lessens the organic value of the loving one's life as a whole. Apart from older siblings and a few extended family members, the only close relationships which one has from birth are with one's parents. My mom was a resource to a part of my life which I cannot recall. Many times already, since her death, I have had questions, now unanswerable, about my own past."[1]

Connie said, "It's too bad that we wait until that resource is gone before we think to use it."

Jeff nodded and continued, "Earlier, the organic value of 'interrelatedness' came up. If both parents die before one is married, has a family, a career, *et cetera*, then the interrelatedness of the stages of one's life is greatly diminished. In particular, part of the structure of a life-story is that there are 'milestones.' Interrelatedness requires that those persons with whom one has shared one's earliest milestones be a part of, or share in, subsequent milestones."

Phil said, "I don't disagree that there is such a value; in fact, I insisted upon it when I tried an earlier consolation, and I agree that one loses this good because of a parent's death. However, there are other organic values, such as 'variety' or 'diversity' which could increase as the result of the death of one's parents. The loss of the emotionally most prominent people of the first half of one's life certainly can increase the variety of one's experiences.

One does what one can to fill the vacuum, and so one develops more relationships and of different sorts."

Jeff replied, "Since the values of interrelatedness and variety conflict when they go beyond a certain point, perhaps we should regard either, not as good in its own right, but only as aspects of some optimal 'balance' of interrelatedness and variety. And were we immortals the conflict between these two aspects would be very much lessened, or in other words, the balance more easily achieved. For our loved ones would still live, and if still loved, might share in our milestones, while at the same time we would have the opportunity to explore new relationships.

"Therefore, I conclude that the death of a loved one is organically evil for the loving ones, that is, decreases the value of the loving one's life as a whole—and all the more so when the death occurs at certain times in the survivor's life."

In the background, Paul Simon's joyful "Mother and Child Reunion" began to play.

Connie said, "This is a very dangerous conclusion for a griever to reach. Since I cannot dissuade you from it, I shall at least try to avoid a discouraging view which one might falsely claim to follow from the organic ego evaluation, that death is organically evil for the loving ones. In particular, interrelatedness is most important between milestones. And given the early emotional importance of parents a continued association with parents is an important part of interrelatedness. It follows that the death of parents is an organic evil, at least with respect to the value of interrelatedness. I shall not dispute this argument, for each of its claims are plausible, although I am somewhat puzzled about the *nature* of several of the claims. Several are contingent on human psychology. Certainly, people desire their lives to have interrelatedness, especially for milestones, and they want this to include those persons for whom they have the strongest and best feelings. How far this desire is *justified*, I cannot say.

"In any case, I'll grant that interrelatedness with the specifics you've added is a good thing which is decreased by a loved one's death. But we must be careful to avoid a misconceived and unhappy inference. An erroneous inference from this organic ego evaluation might be thought to justify inhibition."

"I'm intrigued," encouraged Jeff.

"Be careful, don't supply him with grievances you can't refute," cautioned Phil.

Connie resumed, "You point out that insofar as future milestones in your life will not include your parents the organic value of your life will be less. But you must not conclude from this that your life will be better without these milestones. For example, if you marry, have kids, get your degree, and publish, all these milestones will lack the integration you desire. But you are not better off without these milestones.

"We realize that it usually enhances an important milestone to share it with loved ones. And it is possible that the value of a milestone shared with a loved one is more than the sum of the value of the milestone itself and the value of the company of the loved one. This might be expressed as an organic value, but however such values should be analyzed, it is an experience of considerable value. A loved one's death deprives one of this good. However, even without this good the milestone itself retains value. Jeff, do you agree?"

"Yes, I do," Jeff said.

"So, you should not be discouraged from future achievements or milestones because of the prospect of weakened integration or interrelatedness. Your achievement will have less good than it would have had were your parents still alive, but it is still worthwhile," Connie concluded.

Phil said, "Jeff, I'm glad you agreed that the achievement remained worthwhile even though it can't be shared with your parents. I held my breath when Connie asked you. She was relying upon your good sense, and I thought that was a risky business!

"Fortunately, I had an argument up my sleeve, just in case!" Phil added.

"Well, I never know when my good sense will fail me, so you'd better present your argument," Jeff said.

Phil said, "You grieve, in part, because of the sympathy evaluation. You think that your mom's life was worthwhile, right?"

"Yes," said Jeff.

"Did she have milestones in her life after *her* parents died?" Phil asked.

Jeff answered, "Yes, I guess. *I* was born after her parents had died."

"That's a worthwhile milestone, I'd say!" Connie offered.

Jeff said, "I get the idea. The milestones my parents had after the deaths of their parents made their lives more worthwhile. Therefore, my reasons for grieving commit me to the view that achievements in my future will have some good, although less good than they otherwise would have been."

"Good job!" Connie said to Phil.

Can a Survivor Alter the Extent of Deprivation for the Dead?

Phil resumed, "I had a concern similar to that which Connie raised. Connie was worried that a griever would conclude from the organic ego evaluation that it would be better to avoid future achievements. It worries me that a griever might come to the same terrible conclusion from the sympathy evaluation.

"When orphans achieve milestones they are often saddened by the reflection that this experience would have been enhanced for them by the presence of their parents. But they are also saddened by the reflection that their parents missed this joyful occasion. That is, using our terms, the parent's non-existence on such happy occasions is another deprivation evil for the dead. And from your remarks, I can tell that some such thoughts are troubling you, Jeff."

Jeff nodded.

Phil continued, "I'm concerned that a loving one would be inhibited from pursuing milestones, or even less important goods, by the mistaken idea that, by achieving these goods one would be *adding* to the deprivation evils of the dead loved ones. But one cannot add to the deprivation evils of the dead by producing good things which the dead would have enjoyed had the dead person continued to live. I can prove this: Jeff analyzed the deprivation evils for the dead into either of two counterfactuals. These were 'if the dead person were alive, that person would have enjoyed X' and 'if the dead person were alive, good X would have existed and that person would have enjoyed X.'

"The intended difference between these counterfactuals is this: in the first counterfactual, the good thing exists whether or not that person continued to live. The only thing dependent upon his or her existence is enjoyment of this good thing. In the second counterfactual, the very existence of the good thing depends upon his or her existence. But if either counterfactual is true, the person has a deprivation evil. This means, because of the second counterfactual, that a person can be deprived of a good which will never exist. Therefore, if the bereaved, as a result of inhibition, for example, fails to produce some good, for themselves or others, they have not thereby limited the dead person's deprivations. To put it another way, if the loving one does produce this good, for himself or others, one has not added to the dead person's deprivation evils.

Phil concluded, "You cannot harm the dead. They cannot have diametric evils, *and* we cannot increase their deprivation. In particular, you cannot harm the dead by enjoying yourself or helping others enjoy themselves.

"There's much more to be said, when we get to response consolations, comparing inhibition and sorrow. But we can conclude this much: inhibition does not minimize the evil of death for the dead. Despite the decreased interrelatedness of the life of a person who has lost his or her parents, the survivors are better off pursuing major goods."

"Very good!" Connie said, smiling.

"As has been said, there are poor reasons for grieving just as there are poor reasons for being comforted. And I must admit that I have been troubled by such thoughts. I have had thoughts that it might be better, either for my mom or me, that my life has no further milestones. You're right; *thanks*. But I still think my grief is justified," Jeff said.

Then all three smiled, but Jeff smiled with some restraint.

Possible Benefits to the Survivor and Irreplaceable Goods

Phil began, "I agree that, in many respects, the death of a loved one is an evil for the loving ones. However, I am not convinced that it is *necessarily* a loss, *upon the whole*, for the loving ones. Let me explain: since we are primarily considering the death of persons who were loved it follows that their survivors are harmed by their deaths. As you say, the person's company will be lost; also lost will be the advantages of the other's experience; and the loving one's life as a whole will be more fragmented. But it is conceivable that, despite these evils, the lives of loving ones are *improved* as a result of the loved one's death. One set of facts which would result in an improved life for the loving ones is dreary. And since you think that dreary consolations are not rational I will make only quick mention of this dreary set of facts. If there is something limiting about a relationship, even one based on love, then a loving one's life can be improved by the death of the loved one. For instance, if the loving one were 'over dependent' on the person who has died, perhaps the death has presented an opportunity to lead a more satisfying life."

"This imagined case is ironic as well dreary," Connie indicated. "For over-dependence often prolongs grief.[2] We must be careful. For, while it is conceivable that an over dependent survivor will 'blossom,' it could go the other way. Over-dependence can multiply rather than mitigate the evils for a loving one."

"This is true," Phil said. "I'm claiming only that the effect of a loved one's death on the loving one *can* be good upon the whole. But so far I have argued for this only by using a dreary supposition, namely that the relationship included over dependence. However, I think that I can show that it is conceivable for one to benefit upon the whole from the death of a loved one, without using particularly dreary suppositions."

Connie said, "Phil, you're either a very brave consoler or a limitlessly inquisitive philosopher. Grievers deeply resent the suggestion that it is possible to benefit upon the whole from a loved one's death."[3]

Phil responded, "I don't know which I am. But I know Jeff well enough to know that he wants to get to the bottom of his grief and not allow any pretense to stand in the way."

Jeff said, "In this instance, I think you're more the 'inquisitive philosopher.' Regardless whether it is conceivable that a loved one's death upon the whole benefits the survivors, it is not so in my case. Nevertheless, I wish to pursue Phil's topic because I think it might help us to understand grief. I am, in fact, both an inquisitive philosopher and very much in search of a 'brave consoler,' so I need philosophy for my comfort."

Dr. Hook's comical "The Millionaire" played as Phil proceeded, "Supposing that the relationship with a dead loved one was good upon the whole, it is nevertheless conceivable that the death was good upon the whole for the loving ones."

"How is this possible? What benefit upon the whole could one receive when the lost relationship was good upon the whole?" Jeff asked.

Phil said, "Earlier, I kidded you that you were a hopeless romantic; permit me now to be hopelessly *crass*...."

Connie exclaimed, "Oh no, I know what's coming: inheritance!"

Phil continued, "You got it. Suppose a loving one inherits a million dollars. It frees him from financial worries, permits him to quit his job with the pushy boss, allows him to travel, enables him to buy an apartment with a spectacular view of the skyline, makes him more popular with members of the opposite sex, makes available to him and remaining loved ones the finest health care, and he can order out Chinese food from Beijing. Does this sound good?" Phil asked rhetorically.

Connie replied, "Better make that *twenty* million!"

Phil added, "Of course, none of this alters the sympathy evaluation. But it should drastically effect the ego evaluation."

"Would I be able to resurrect my parents?" Jeff asked.

"There would be serious losses," Phil reassured. "There would be no more 'Sunday dinner with the folks,' they'd be missed at family gatherings, and they'd be missed a *hundred* other times each year. But still, hasn't our imaginary heir benefited upon the whole? Unless he inflicts himself with grief, wouldn't he be better off?"

Connie winced and shook her head.

Jeff turned to Connie and said, "Really, I'm not shocked. Phil's trying to be clear. Fine. I think that a loving one, in such a situation, would be justified in grieving even between the occasions you've conceded for grieving, such as family gatherings, not only in anticipation of such occasions, but also on the basis of the sympathy evaluation. However, I agree that we can imagine 'compensations' for the loss of a loved one, some of which you've mentioned. But whatever compensations we imagine that the *loving* one has, these cannot outweigh the *loved* one's loss, unless we suppose dreary reasons. That is, the loss to the dead exceeds any imagined gain to the survivor. Therefore, upon a whole which considers *both* the loved and loving ones, the death would still be an evil."

Phil said, "I'm not sure that's necessary, but I won't press any objection."

"And here's an objection which *I* won't press, although I'll mention it," Jeff said. "I think it is dreary that the person's life lacked these good things before the inheritance. It's dreary that he had a pushy boss, little success with the opposite sex, and a poor view before his ill-found prosperity. Therefore, I don't think you've supplied a non-dreary consolation."

But Jeff shrugged as though discounting his own objection and continued, "While there are conceivable *compensations* for these great losses, such losses are nevertheless 'irreplaceable.' This is an important distinction. Because of the fact that individuals have histories and our histories are important to us, parents, who have unique roles in our histories, are irreplaceable. You've supposed in your consolation, and I've allowed it, that we can compare with each other goods of different kinds. You compared spectacular views, tasty foods, sexual relations, and so on, with family relations. You say that some amount of the former can outweigh some amount of the latter. If different kinds of goods are 'commensurable' or comparable, then perhaps we could say, as you have, that a loss of a good of one kind could be outweighed by a gain in goods of some other kinds. That is, if commensurability is possible, then compensation is possible.

"Now, I don't understand how commensurability is possible, but I won't object to your consolation on those grounds. For I think that the commensurability of values or the ability to weigh values of different kinds is a presupposition which we must make, if there is a shred of rationality in our daily decisions. When making decisions we often 'weigh' values of different kinds. In any case, I concede the principle that different kinds of our goods are comparable.

Connie interjected, "Like choosing between prospective lovers: one's cute, the other's smart. Can you compare these in order to make a rational choice?"

Phil said, "And which would *you* choose?"

But Jeff spoiled Phil's fun by continuing. "Though I allow that such a comparison is possible, so that one good can outweigh another, or one good can compensate for another's loss, it is also important to insist on the fact that these goods are of very different kinds. So, while gains of one kind can *compensate* for losses of another kind, they cannot *replace* them. And the crucial part of my objection is that it is important, in deciding whether an affect is justified, to consider not only whether there were uncompensated losses, but also whether there were irreplaceable losses."

Connie interrupted, "Let me get clear on the terminology: a 'compensated' loss is a loss which is outweighed by other things which are good. A 'replaced' loss is a loss which is outweighed by goods of the same kind."

Jeff said, "Yes. I would agree that a person should not be distressed over a replaced loss. For example, I would regard it as ridiculous for one to be upset about the loss of a dollar after the search for that dollar led one to find a ten dollar bill.

"However, it can make sense to be distressed over a compensated but irreplaceable loss. Once again, we're encroaching into the area of response consolation. Upon reflection, my view is that a loving heir should be pleased with his spectacular view, prospect of longer health, sexual success, and so on. But he should also feel grief for himself over the loss of the company of his parents and whatever other irreplaceable goods which were lost as a consequence, as well as grieving over the sympathy evaluation.[4]

"When we earlier broached the area of response consolations I said that we should not require that affects be directed toward the entire system of nature, but only events, objects and aspects within it. Similarly, I do not believe that the survivor of a loved one is required to adjust his affect in such a way that he responds only to the value upon the whole of the effect upon himself of the death of a loved one. Besides the value upon the whole, there are the values, some good, some evil, from which the sum is composed. I do not see that it is wrong to respond to each of these distinctly, supposing that they are of sufficiently different kinds.

"I believe there is some *physiological* basis for my idea that one should be distressed by irreplaceable losses, whether or not compensated. For example, plenty of water should not dispel concerns about loss of food, and plenty of food should not dispel concerns about loss of water, and so on. However, I am unsure as to whether this could lead to a justification of my view that our imaginary heir should still grieve."

Phil said, "Okay, I don't want to rush us into response consolations, especially as I'm not finished with evaluation consolations. But we've accomplished something with respect to restricting the ego evaluation. It is *conceivable* that, upon the whole, the ego evaluation is false. However, apart from dreary consolations, and upon the supposition which we've made all along, that the dead were loved, to some extent the ego evaluation is true. In some respects, the loved one's death will be terrible for the loving ones, but it is conceivable that the loving one will receive more goods than those lost. Nevertheless, you object, it might not follow that the person should stop grieving altogether. But you do concede that our imagined heir has reasons to feel joy as well as grieve."

Jeff nodded his agreement.

A Loved One's Death and a Survivor's Virtue

Phil continued, "Let me go from being crass to being some sort of so-called idealist. My crass consolation has at least two difficulties—apart from being crass. First, very importantly, it does not apply to you. Second, these crass benefits cannot replace the lost goods. Whether this second difficulty really amounts to anything, that is, whether it would justify the grief of a survivor remains to be seen. But the first difficulty is very important. With my crass consolation the most I've shown is that it is conceivable that the ego evaluation is false. But by selecting a different, non-economic possible benefit of a loved one's death I might be able to show that it is *likely*, though still not certain, that the ego evaluation is false and with a fair chance of applicability to yourself.

"Here's the so-called idealistic benefit which a survivor might receive from the death of a loved one: the loved one's death might make the survivor 'stronger' or provide an opportunity to show his or her strength. . . ."

Connie added, "As Friedrich Nietzsche said, 'That which does not kill us makes us stronger.'"[5]

Phil added, "Certain events, such as a loved one's death, might instill a virtue in the survivor or provide opportunity for that virtue to be exercised."

Jeff cautioned, "Before you go any further, you should know that I think that most, if not all, virtues have only consequential value. Courage, for example, is good to have for what it accomplishes. Further, I believe that the consequential value of many character traits is conditional upon the existence of evils. In other words, if a person was not afflicted with, or susceptible to, evils, there would be nothing good about many of these traits. If there were no dangers, courage would have no consequential value. If this is so, a person afflicted with these evils, but possessing the traits which are good conditionally upon these evils is not, upon the whole, better off than a person with neither the evils nor the appropriate traits. The bad things create the value of virtue. So, you can't turn around and say that it's good we have bad things, because otherwise we wouldn't have virtue. That's another example of the smokers fallacy."

Connie said, "Let's get specific. Which benefits to a person's character come from the death of a loved one?"

Jeff said, "In the case of a loved one's death we're not talking about heroism. In the case with which we're concerned, the loved one is already dead. In other words, the death of a loved one, after the fact, is not an opportunity for bravery."

Connie objected, "Not so fast. Yes, it's too late to save the loved one. But perhaps this experience would make it more likely that you would later save another person. It might not be something as dramatic as rescuing a drowning person. Perhaps it would be a blood donation."

Jeff remarked, "Putting aside the question of whether the donor benefits from donating, I want to point out that this effect of a loved one's death on a person's character presupposes the sympathy evaluation, that death is evil for the dead. You're saying that a loved one's death might make a person try to prevent the death of another person. But why would it, unless death is an evil?"

"I suppose the survivor would at least have to believe that death is evil for the dead," Connie conceded.

Phil objected, "That doesn't follow. Even people who believe in a blissful afterlife try to preserve life. At least they give indications that they believe in a blissful afterlife."

Jeff conceded, "All right, I have not proved my point."

Phil said, "Here's another trait which might be either improved or displayed as a result of a loved one's death: *perseverance*. Quite apart from how a loved one's death might dispose a person with respect to the possible death of a third person, there are aspects of the bereaved person's character dealing directly with the loved one's death, that is, in how they handle it. Not only might the death of a loved one *make* a person more persevering of other evils, perseverance is a trait which *conceptually* requires events such as a loved one's death."

Jeff objected, "I have two problems with your conceptual observation, if it is meant to change my mind about the ego evaluation. First, death, and more specifically, a loved one's death, is not required for perseverance. *Other* evils will do."

Phil replied, "But other things do not always 'call upon' the same *degree* of perseverance."

Jeff went on, "Second, similar to my objection to Connie's example of a possible increase in one's concern for others, I would like to point out that perseverance requires events which are *bad*. Presumably, in the case of a person persevering after a loved one's death, the evil which required that perseverance is either the loved one's death itself or its harm to the survivors. In other words, perseverance through the death of a loved one entails either the sympathy or ego evaluations."

Phil objected, "Not necessarily: persevering through some event x need not entail that x is evil. It might entail only that x is apparently evil, or *thought* to be evil. That is, there are two different understandings of 'perseverance.' According to one, perseverance is 'holding together' despite an evil. According to another notion, perseverance consists in 'holding together' despite an *apparent* evil, that is, something which might be regarded as an evil, although it is not. My point is similar to one I offered when we were discussing virtue, that the magnitude of virtue might be a function of one's ability to disregard false views of that which is bad. According to the second notion of 'perseverance,' perhaps the way in which a person perseveres is by recognizing that the event only appears to be bad.

"Therefore, in saying that a loved one's death is necessary for the loving one to have a particular degree of perseverance, one is not implying that the death is evil.

"Now, unlike the earlier inheritance example which requires rare circumstances; and unlike the heroism example, which while more common than a sizable inheritance, is still not a universal benefit of the death of a loved one; nearly everyone perseveres through a loved one's death. Thus, this benefit is a likely one and not merely conceivable."

Jeff responded, "Perseverance, or in particular perseverance despite a loved one's death, is highly overrated. Yes, it is a good thing that a survivor perseveres. But is such perseverance really an admirable character trait? Is it a virtue? It is common, as you point out. But I don't denigrate perseverance because it is common; I'm no snob. But I denigrate it for the *reason* that it is so common: namely, that it is so easy, or even effortless. It's easy persevering through the death of a loved one, not in the sense that it is painless, for it can be quite *excruciating*, but because perseverance isn't the result of effort; rather one perseveres because a loved one's death seldom drastically alters the survivor's biological functions.

"I continue to function either without choice or because there is no better choice. I continue to breathe because that's what a healthy organism does. I continue to eat because a healthy organism gets hungry and because I still enjoy some, although fewer, foods. I sleep, though with disturbing dreams, because I become exhausted or bored. You said perseverance was 'holding together.' Well, I hold together because, with no assistance from me, time passes, and so far, I continue my biological functions. Furthermore, I hold together, not because of religious faith, or anything of the kind, but because I am an organism without a better choice. I suspect that people often falsely attribute their perseverance to their faith or their virtue.[6]

"It's true, I go to work, I don't jump out windows, and I look both ways when I cross the street. And these are voluntary. But is there a better choice? What great virtue is it that I go on living, or that I don't become a raving lunatic?"

Jeff lowered his voice as he realized that the couple at a nearby table was looking at him. Spanky and Our Gang lamented, "Sunday Will Never Be the Same."

He continued, "Am I to regard myself as blessed by my mom's death because it reveals to me that I have little aptitude for self-destruction? Realize this: her death was not necessary for me to have the desire to live. In fact, her death has the contrary tendency.

"As I said, this sort of perseverance is overrated as a virtue. I speculate that this overestimation comes from a desire to make the mundane seem noble. I've noticed in recent years that the media labels persons 'heroes' simply because they survived some terrible event. A person who survives having fallen down a well is proclaimed a hero. A person who survives captivity is a 'hero.' Yeah, these things must have been *ordeals*, but what would they have done if they weren't heroes? Hold their breath until they explode?"

Connie objected, "There's more to 'holding together' than 'getting through.' There's more to it than the uninterrupted operation of biological functions. There's more to it than the passage of time. There's more to it than not killing oneself. There's even more to it than returning to one's daily routines. It includes retaining some joy, a sense of humor for example."

Jeff replied, "Do you mean 'not grieving?' Well, maybe the cessation of grief is a part of perseverance, but we have not shown that a person should not grieve. That's what you're trying to show. So, we cannot use the cessation of grief as an example of a good character trait which is made possible, or revealed, by a loved one's death."

Connie said, "Phil, you began our discussion of perseverance through a loved one's death by distinguishing the claims that this loss is conceptually necessary for a certain degree of perseverance and that this loss increases a person's perseverance. We have not discussed this latter claim. I take it that you meant that it enables one to better persevere in the face of other losses, whether subsequent or even precedent."

"Yes, that's what I meant," Phil confirmed.

Jeff said, "But *why* does the loss of a loved one make one better able to persevere through other losses? When we understand this we will see that the evil of a loved one's death to the survivor cannot be appreciably mitigated by this supposed increase in perseverance.

"As I've said before, there are evils greater than a loved one's death. An earthquake in a populated area of China is a far greater evil. However, human nature being what it is, I do not need 'perseverance' through such a disaster. Unless, that is, perseverance would include simply ignoring an evil or apparent evil. . . ."

Phil said, "No, I agree. Whatever the full analysis of perseverance is, this would not be a case of perseverance."

Jeff continued, "Not only would such a disaster not affect my interests, so far as I know, it doesn't affect anyone I know personally. So perseverance isn't even an issue, so to speak, unless I am harmed (or apparently harmed), or someone I really care about is harmed or apparently harmed. Now, the death of a loved one is very nearly the greatest realistic evil that will befall me or someone I really care about. It follows that the death of a loved one cannot help us persevere through realistic evils which are very much greater than a loved one's death.

"I doubt that losses minor in comparison with a loved one's death can do very much to prepare one for that terrible loss, so that one could not receive any such benefit from small losses. But if it *were* possible to receive such a benefit from small losses, then at least it could be said of these losses that the benefit we received exceeded the loss entailed by them. But when a great evil, such as a loved one's death, is the means by which we learn to better persevere through lesser evils the lesson has been learned at too high a price. The price is so high for the comparatively slight benefit that it's a lesson I'd gladly forego.

"Besides, it's dreary to console someone by saying 'It's good for you that your loved one died since there'll be more evils in store for you, or because there already have been great evils for you, which you can handle better, because they are minor compared to a loved one's death.'"

Jeff concluded, "Furthermore, perseverance is one of those character traits, of which I spoke earlier, which is valuable only on condition that there are evils, or, as Phil might say, apparent evils. In other words, using our example, if there were no death, perseverance of death would not be valuable. Not only is perseverance conceptually dependent on evils, as Phil first pointed out, but its *value* is also dependent upon them. Perseverance is valuable only insofar as it is a limitation of the evils consequent to the awareness of an evil. Therefore, were there no such evils, or apparent ones, then perseverance would have no value. The conclusion is that were one to suffer no evils, not even apparent ones, which require perseverance, then one would not be missing a good."

Phil reminded Jeff, "Many philosophers would disagree. They think that the *goodness,* though not the existence, of perseverance is independent of the apparent evils persevered. Therefore, without these apparent evils a person would lack something valuable, namely, perseverance."

"I realize that some say this, but they are wrong!" Jeff said. "The death of a loved one, for several reasons, causes harm to those who loved the person who died. That the loving one perseveres means that this harm is less than we could conceive it to be; they don't kill themselves; they don't go raving mad. Perseverance is not a diametric good. It is a good only in the sense that it is a limit to the diametric and deprivation evils suffered by the loving ones.

"So this is my conclusion. A loving one who perseveres suffers fewer evils, but they still suffer terrible evils. Perseverance, not being a good, other than in the sense that it is a limit on evils, cannot even begin to compensate for—let alone replace—the evils suffered. This is another instance of the smokers fallacy."

"The ego evaluation is that death is a terrible evil for the loving ones. This does not mean, of course, that all loving ones suffer to the same extent. Those who better persevere suffer less, everything else being equal."

Phil restated, "Many philosophers think that perseverance is valuable as more than a limit to evils. Some think that it is consequentially good as a way of earning rewards which are dished out according to some cosmic or transcendent principle. Still others think it is a diametric intrinsic good."

"Okay, go into the kitchen, and stick your face in the deep-fryer for a minute. If you think perseverance is a diametric, intrinsic good, then that's enough. If you think it's good as a way of earning rewards, then come back and have dessert," Jeff replied facetiously.

"Fortunately, I'm not one of those philosophers!" Phil said, laughing, pretending that he narrowly avoided the plight proposed by Jeff. "But seriously, that's not much of a response!"

Jeff said, "I'm not sure that it isn't. But if you want another response, I'll give you one. If my earlier comments were correct, that perseverance requires little effort, then there isn't much merit to perseverance. Therefore, I don't see how perseverance can be consequentially good as a way of earning cosmic rewards.

"As far as perseverance being a diametric intrinsic good, I have no proof it isn't. Of course, cheerfulness is a diametric intrinsic good. It *feels good* to be cheerful. And cheerfulness is a diametric intrinsic good under either adverse or favorable circumstances. And cheerfulness under adverse circumstances is one of several related ideas which might be called 'perseverance.' But it is not perseverance itself which is the diametric good, it is cheerfulness. That is, cheerfulness is not intrinsically better under adverse circumstances than under favorable ones.

"Furthermore, every moment is, at least theoretically, an opportunity for cheerfulness. It is only perseverance which requires evils. Therefore, one cannot mitigate an evil by claiming that it is an opportunity for cheerfulness.

"Of course, as with most claims about what is or is not intrinsically good, I have no argument for my claim that cheerfulness under adverse circumstances is not intrinsically better than under favorable ones. All I can do is to criticize poor arguments to the contrary."

"Such as?" Connie asked.

Jeff said, "During misfortune, cheerfulness is rarer. Likewise, during misfortune we think that we must encourage cheerfulness. One might mistakenly think that that which is rare, or that which we must encourage, is intrinsically better than that which is common or which needs no encouragement, and consequently, is not encouraged. On the basis of this mistake one might infer that perseverance is intrinsically better than a pleasant disposition under good circumstances.

"Remember, I do not denigrate perseverance as a virtue because it is common, but for the reason that it is common, that it does not require great effort," Jeff said.

Summary of the Discussion of the Ego Evaluation

Daryl Hall wailed "She's Gone" as the three paused to consider the direction of their conversation.

Phil suggested, "Perhaps we can use our distinctions of evaluations into intrinsic and consequential to summarize our views on the ego evaluation."

Connie said, "I think we agree that there is no sense in saying that the death of a loved one is intrinsically evil for the survivors."

Jeff said, "At the outset of our systematic discussion I had agreed that the intrinsic ego evaluation had no sense, but I no longer agree. Since the time that I agreed we've become clearer on the concept of 'intrinsic value.'"

Phil said, "Reviewing this interim clarification: diametric evils are states of awareness, and some deprivation evils are states of those who are deprived. But death, or total deprivation, is not a state or property of those who suffer this deprivation."

Jeff added, "Now, if total deprivation is worth avoiding for its own sake, then it meets our definition of an intrinsic evil, even though it is not a state of its 'victim.' If we can accept this clarification of 'intrinsic value,' then I don't see why we couldn't say that death is intrinsically evil for the survivors. That death is not a state of the survivors can no longer deter us from this conclusion, as it had, since we now recognize death as intrinsically evil for the dead even though it is not a state of theirs either. A person's death is evil for that person, apart from consideration of anything else. Thus, it meets our definition of an intrinsic evil. Now, the loved one's permanent absence is entailed by death. So, as the loved one's permanent absence from the loving one is worth avoiding for its own sake, death is intrinsically evil for the living, loving ones.

"Further, for the survivors the intrinsic evil of a loved one's death would also be a deprivation, the loved one's absence. Now, consequential evils for the survivors might include loss of financial security, the loss of the parent's experience, the loss of other relationships which one had through the dead loved one, such as the loved one's friends and immediate family. By the way, these consequential evils of the loved one's death are also deprivations."

"Great!" said Connie sarcastically. "Jeff had agreed that the intrinsic ego evaluation was meaningless, but now defends it. Our efforts at evaluation consolations have been a huge success!"

Phil reassured Connie, "Jeff is very well aware of how much he misses his mom. That is, he is aware that her permanent absence is an evil for him.

By giving this use to 'intrinsic evil for the survivors' he has not been made aware of any previously unknown reason for grief. Instead, I half hope that by extending 'intrinsic value' in this way, separating it so far from the original assumptions bound up with what we now call 'diametric evil,' that Jeff will reconsider separating 'intrinsic evil' from 'diametric evil' in the case of the sympathy evaluation.

"Originally, when we considered 'death is evil for the dead' we implicitly restricted its meaning to 'death is a diametric evil for the dead' which required not only that death be a state of the dead, but also a state of awareness of the dead. We then extended 'death is intrinsically evil for the dead' to include 'death is a deprivation evil for the dead,' which not only need not be a state of awareness of the dead, it need not be a state of the dead at all. So, the dead can have intrinsic evils which are not their states. Formally, X's death is intrinsically evil for X, though it is not a state of X. Now, we conclude that X's death is intrinsically evil for Y, for though X's death is obviously not Y's state, X's death entails deprivations for Y. Clearly, the concept of 'death being intrinsically evil for some person' has undergone quite a transformation. We went from it not being intrinsically evil for anyone, not even the dead, to its being intrinsically evil for others! Since the analysis which led us to the first revision or clarification leads to the second, Jeff might be wise to reconsider the analysis which led to the first, that death is intrinsically evil for the dead."

"The analysis seems correct, however unfamiliar sounding are its conclusions," Jeff said adamantly.

Phil promised, "I haven't given up on evaluation consolations. I'm still not sure about either the sympathy or ego evaluations."

Summary of the Conversation

Examples were supplied to illustrate and support the ego evaluation in its three forms: intrinsic, and more specifically, organic, and consequential. Through the clarification of the concept of "X is intrinsically evil/good for person P" sense can be given to the intrinsic ego evaluation because X need not be a state of P.

Among the examples for the ego evaluation, prominent was the evil for a survivor of the absence of the loved ones during further milestones in the survivor's life. However, it is not the case that the survivor would be better off without further milestones. The argument for this was that the grievers' parents' lives were benefited by further milestones after the death of *their* parents. This removes a possible reason for thinking that inhibition is justified.

Also, a loving one does not increase the dead person's deprivation by enjoying life. This also removes a possible reason for thinking that inhibition is justified.

Despite the many ways in which death is an evil for the survivor or loving ones, it is conceivable that a loved one's death is *good* overall for the loving ones, assuming that it is possible to make comparisons between goods of very different kinds. Nevertheless, it is likely that, apart from dreary estimates, the net benefit to the loving one cannot exceed the net loss to the loved one. Therefore, it is likely that the overall value of a person's death for the subjects of the griever's evaluations is an evil, unless drearily, the lives of either the dead person, or the loving ones before the death, were very bad. However, even if the loved one's death is good overall for the survivor, emotions need not be a response to the overall value of some state of affairs. Thus, grief *might* be justified even though the bereaved reaped benefit from the loved one's death. I address this point further in Chapter Thirteen.

It is unlikely that the loved one's death will increase the well-being of the bereaved, sufficiently to compensate for the evils entailed and produced by death, by promoting or occasioning the survivor's exercise of virtue. For, even assuming that the exercise or development of virtue is intrinsically good for the virtuous person, the most likely virtue exercised or developed by the loving one is perseverance. And, ranking virtues by the *effort* required to exercise or develop them, perseverance is a minor virtue. Therefore, if there is a supposed correlation between the effort required for a virtue and its intrinsic value for the one possessing that virtue, then perseverance, the most likely virtue exercised or developed by a loved one's death, has comparatively little intrinsic value for the loving one.

In addition, even though it is useful to develop perseverance, since adversity is not unusual, a loved one's death is usually so much more evil than any distress which could be produced by any other misfortunes, that any advantage derived from an increase in perseverance from a loved one's death is easily overshadowed by the usual evils of a loved one's death. Of course, some philosophers—stoics—would maintain that distress, such as grief, is the *only* evil, so any apparent evil is worth it, if it develops "perseverance," in the sense of a disposition to not be distressed.

While it is good to persevere of course, perseverance is primarily just a limit upon one's suffering. Therefore, the claim that an evil is an occasion for perseverance primarily means that an evil is an occasion for limited suffering. But it does not mean that it is primarily an occasion for a diametric good.

Cheerfulness, or the exercise of this disposition, is an intrinsic, diametric good. However, anytime is an opportunity for cheerfulness; only perseverance (one sense of which is "cheerfulness despite apparent evils") requires adversity. Therefore, evils cannot be mitigated on the ground that they supply occasions for cheerfulness.

Study Questions

(1) Is it good that there are (apparent) evils to test one's virtue or to provide opportunity for the exercise of virtue?

(2) Are goods or evils of different kinds comparable?
- If not, then is *rational* decision making possible when choosing among alternatives that offer incomparable goods or evils?

Ten

IS CONSTANT CHANGE CONSOLING?

> I've never been to heaven,
> But I've been to Oklahoma.
> For they tell me I was born there,
> But I really don't remember.
> In Oklahoma, not Arizona.
> What does it matter?
> What does it matter?

"Never Been to Spain," by Three Dog Night, playfully warmed the patrons as Phil and Connie continued to try to console Jeff. The three dallied over their entrees.

Personal Identity

Phil began, "Obviously the death of Jeff's mom is an upheaval. But I wonder whether we can console Jeff through the fact of constant change. More specifically, I believe that consolations against both the sympathy and ego evaluations can be found in the proper understanding of the concept of a 'person.' I believe that the concept of personal identity provides serious difficulties for the sympathy evaluation and greatly limits the evils claimed in the ego evaluation."

"It's been apparent for some time that we'll have to grapple with the concept of personal identity, but I do not think that we will find any consolations there," Jeff predicted.

"Would you please explain this concept before using it in any consolations," Connie requested.

Phil began, "Personal identity deals with *individuating* and *identifying* persons. By saying that people are 'individuated' all I mean is that each person can be distinguished, or differentiated, from all other persons. For example, we know that you are not me . . ."

"Otherwise, I would already know what 'personal identity' means!"

"Right. Besides individuating persons, it is possible to identify—or perhaps better to say, *re*identify—these individuals over the course of time, even over many years. For example, you were born in December 1973. Where?"

"Westchester Square Hospital."

Phil continued, "You, the person I see eating a ranch bean, attended Cardinal Spellman High School during the late eighties . . ."

"You've memorized my life!"

"You don't even know about the private detectives!" Phil kidded.

Connie said, "Okay, I understand. People are 'identifiable' or 'reidentifiable.' I am the same person who did x, was at place p, had y happen to at time t. I understand the terminology," Connie said.

"Do you notice how impatient Connie is *for* clarifications yet how impatient she is *with* them?" Phil teased, addressing Jeff. Jeff smiled.

"It's because your clarifications are so clear," Connie countered with a contrived sarcastic tone.

Phil continued, "The person who was born in that hospital, on that day, continues to exist. And what we mean by 'person continues to exist' is that there is still someone 'identifiable' as that person. To introduce some ugly, but helpful, terminology: the person I see before me, the baby born in the hospital, and the high school student are '*relata*' or related things, which are identified or reidentified. When reidentifying a person the *relata* or terms are that person at different times.

"While we can speak of a person being reidentifiable whenever that person is referred to by different descriptions, such as 'the person I now see eating a ranch bean' can be reidentified as 'the person who is now trying to grasp my terminology,' *our* discussion will emphasize reidentifying a person when the different descriptions refer to different times."

"Okay, whatever. I understand your slightly cumbersome terminology. People are being reidentified whenever referred to by different descriptions, and a person can be reidentified over time," Connie said.

"Using one of your examples, in 'I am the same person as she who was born in Westchester Square Hospital on a particular date' the *relata* are me and that baby, and what is said about she and I is that we are the same person, in other words, we have the same personal identity. I am being reidentified."

Phil said, "Okay. I have some observations about personal identity which we can use to console Jeff. I'll *try* to restrict myself to only those observations which will be necessary for the ensuing consolations," Phil said.

"Good."

"But the necessary observations will be several and somewhat lengthy."

"The important thing is that we do this right, even if we err on the side of thoroughness," Jeff reminded.

Phil said, "For years Jeff and I have been discussing the concept of personal identity. And he and I have come to agree on the following observations. Jeff, if I overlook something important, please remind me."

"Certainly," Jeff promised. "But I am unaware of any comfort to be derived from the proper analysis of personal identity."

"We'll see."

Phil began, "*First*, the criteria for personal identity must be guided by what it is to be a person. A person has both physical and mental characteristics and abilities. Most aspects of the family of concepts 'person,' or more cautiously, 'human person,' need little elaboration. The criteria for being a person, though they are not all either necessary or sufficient, include: physical characteristics, such as a face, torso and limbs; abilities such as walking erect, grasping, and omnivorous ingestion; other abilities such as consciousness, recollection, anticipation, language use and deliberation; and as we've said, people have histories. Therefore, the relations, which normally hold between the same person at different times, are both physical and mental.

"I'll use another example from your life, Connie. The statement 'You are the same person who broke her arm when slipping on some stairs as a girl' has two *relata*, the person who is sitting in front of me, wincing at my example, and the person who, at an earlier time, suffered this unfortunate accident. These *relata* are, as we say, 'the same person.' Now, as the *relata* are both a person, and persons normally have both physical and mental characteristics and abilities, the relations, on the basis of which these are the same person, must, in *normal* cases, be both physical and mental. Normally, both physical and mental relations will hold between the *relata*."

Jeff offered examples of several such relations. "You bear an outward physical resemblance to that girl who broke her arm; specifically, in facial features, complexion and hair texture. Also, any scars which that girl had resemble some scars which you have. You have resembling fingerprints, and you have the same genetic code, unless you've been exposed to heavy doses of radiation."

"I dislike being an example!" Connie jokingly snapped.

Phil smiled and continued with more relations. "In addition, you remember that girl's fall, and the subsequent hospital visit. Perhaps you even remember the pain, fears and thoughts which that girl had. Perhaps you can readily visualize the incident *from* the girl's point of view. That is, perhaps you can picture the stairs and ceiling swirling as the girl tumbled, and the momentary silence in the stairwell as she trembled after the fall before letting out a scream. The view of her brother rushing in from the next room . . ."

"Gee, maybe *you* are that girl!" Connie exclaimed.

"I'm just *guessing* at the experience. I'm only imagining; you *remember*," Phil replied.

Connie said, "Actually, I don't remember the fall itself. I do remember going to the hospital."

Jeff continued, "Okay, the relations which hold between the same person at different times could be even more complex than already sketched. You do not remember the fall, but you do remember going to the hospital. This introduces a *third* term in the relation 'same person,' the girl going to the hospital, in addition to the first two—you now and the girl who had the tumble. Supposing further that the girl going to the hospital remembered the fall, though you do not, the situation would be that you remember some of the experiences of the hospital-girl who, in turn, remembered the experiences of the tumbling-girl. Memory 'directly' relates you with that girl on her way to the hospital because you recall that event. Since you don't recall the fall you're not directly related by memory to that, but we can say that memory 'indirectly' relates you to the girl who fell because there is an intermediary, the hospital-girl, whom you directly remember and who directly remembered falling.

"A somewhat different indirect relation involved in personal identity is illustrated by altering the example thusly: you still do not remember the fall, but suppose that the girl who fell did so because she was excited by that winter's first snowfall because it made her remember the fun she had the previous winter. And suppose that you even now remember the fun that that girl had that winter before the accident. Here again, memory holds between you and the girl experiencing the accident, but only indirectly. And in this altered case, the intermediary, that is the girl having winter fun, comes before the injured girl, being identified. That is, the intermediary does not have to be chronologically in-between.

"In sum, memory normally holds between the same person at different times. It can be direct; or indirect, that is, involving an intermediary related to the extreme terms by direct memory, and in different ways: the intermediary might or might not be chronologically between the indirectly related terms."

Phil said, "Thus far, all our examples have concerned reidentifying present with past *relata*. Let's also use an example reidentifying present with future *relata*. 'You're the person who will act as a comptroller at a particular place when Monday rolls around.'"

"A less unpleasant example," Connie sighed.

"Well," Jeff said, "besides all the close physical resemblances between you tonight and you on Monday morning, you now and the Monday-morning comptroller both remember the girl going to the hospital after she broke her arm."

"Not *her* again!" Connie objected.

"And you can anticipate, better than any other person, taking the train in on Monday, going up to the comptroller's office, knowing what to do, and having no one call the police to remove a delusional trespasser!" Phil added.

"Also, suppose you spend part of the weekend deliberating about some financial report which you will work on next week," Jeff said. "That would be another way that you are related to that person."

"That connects the weekday comptroller with a person over the weekend. What connects her with me now?" Connie said.

"For one thing, the deliberating person over the weekend looks like you," Jeff said.

Phil added, "And there will be a spatio-temporal 'path' continuous from you, the person who just asked this question, and the person who we suppose spends part of the weekend deliberating over a financial report."

Connie asked, "By 'continuous spatio-temporal path' do you mean that if one were to trace my movements, perhaps with one of Phil's private detectives, they would 'lead to' a person, looking just like me, who deliberates about a financial report, *et cetera*?"

"Right. And besides a spatio-temporal 'path,' there will be a series of 'overlapping' short term memories, which, with few interruptions such as due to sleep, will 'connect' you and our diligent executive. While awake a person's experiences are 'connected' by overlapping short term memories. Each second you remember the previous second."

Connie said, "I've got the main idea. These are the sorts of relations which normally hold between the *relata* and upon the basis of which people are reidentified. I think I understand all this," Connie ventured. "In sum, some relations that hold for normal uses of 'same person' are: physical resemblance; spatio-temporal continuity; memory, direct or indirect, and especially memories of a uniquely privileged kind, that is, remembering something from a unique point of view-even several people at the same event will have different memories of it; there's also a connecting series of overlapping short term memories, with interruptions for sleep; and anticipation and deliberation.

"Resemblance, anticipation and deliberation, like memory, can be either direct or indirect. I might not very closely resemble that baby born in Westchester Square Hospital, but I do closely resemble a young girl who closely resembles that baby. I might not be deliberating about next year, but I might deliberate about next month, and next month, deliberate about next year."

"Good, you got it! It is also important to note that these relations, and especially deliberation, involve causal relations. For, using deliberation as an example, any serious deliberation assumes a belief on the part of the one deliberating that there is some causal influence over future *relata*. For example, when you plan a vacation it's because you assume that your plans will have an influence over your later self," Jeff said.

"Besides the relations already mentioned, we could add similarity of character, beliefs and skills. While some beliefs, traits and skills vary considerably over a single person's lifetime, and even over a brief period, others are stable. Therefore, similarity of character normally holds between most *relata* which are reidentifiable. All these relations, which normally hold between the same person at different times, we'll call 'reidentifiability relations,'" Jeff added.

Connie summarized again, "The same person at different times usually has these relations between him or herself at these different times, either directly or indirectly: resemblance, long term and short term memory, anticipation and deliberation, spatio-temporal continuity, character similarity and causality.

Connie said, "Even before this analysis I knew how to reidentify people. So far we've taken something we do simply and automatically, and articulated it but made it seem harder. Is that wise?"

Phil promised, "There will be a payoff, I assure you. The analysis will lead to consolations."

Johnny Rivers' "Secret Agent Man" played in the background.

Phil continued, "The *second* observation which it is important to make is that the reidentification of a person can have several purposes. For examples: there are legal purposes for reidentifying persons, such as for enforcing contracts, paying taxes, the use of the rights of citizenship, and criminal prosecution, to name a few; there are communal or social purposes for reidentifying persons, such as for class reunions, veteran reunions, romantic reunions, and again, many more.

"The *third* observation actually deals with the first two. As we've said, in normal cases, a wide variety of relations hold between 'the same person at different times.' And reidentification has several purposes. Consequently, depending upon the purpose involved, the different relations, which normally hold between the same person at different times, that is, the criteria for reidentifying persons, take on varying comparative importance. Here's an example of memory being given no importance in determining personal identity: you're an American citizen by birth. You're the same as that girl born in December 1973 at Westchester Square Hospital. Because of this reidentification, a particular person will be permitted to vote. But this reidentification has nothing to do with the later *relata*, the voter, recalling that birth. Further, this particular reidentification between the newborn and the voter has little, although something, to do with physical resemblance, and a whole lot to do with spatio-temporal continuity. What entitles you to vote is your continuity with that baby, even if the board of elections does not actually 'trace' the spatio-temporal path. They don't trace the path, but they *assume* it."

"Sounds plausible. The grownup me is allowed to vote in this country because it's believed that my spatio-temporal path goes back to a baby born in this country. The path isn't traced; they use my possession of a birth certificate as evidence of this path. But of course no one ever spells it out like that."

Jeff added, "For social purposes memory becomes very important. The board of electors doesn't care what the voter remembers, but friends, lovers and family do."

Phil resumed, "My *fourth* observation is partly an addendum to the third. I observed that the comparative importance of relations involved in reidentifiability varied with the purposes of the reidentification. Further, to some extent, the purposes vary according to *whom* is making the reidentification. Specifically, reidentification of a person is sometimes done by that person, and sometimes it is done by another person. It is likely that the comparative importance of these relations depends, in part, on who is reidentifying whom, specifically, whether one is reidentifying oneself or another. For example, it is possible that memory is more important when reidentifying oneself; that is, the claim 'I am the same person who did x' is more likely to be based upon a direct memory of the event, recalled in a uniquely privileged way. For example, you know that it was you who was rushed to the hospital not because you remember that that person resembles you, but because you remember the event only as that person would."

"That seems oversimplified, but there probably are connections between the different purposes of reidentification and the need to reidentify either another or oneself," Connie said.

Phil said, "Another difference between reidentifying oneself and reidentifying another is that whereas we need to reidentify others only more or less periodically, we always need to be able to identify ourselves. People who could not always instantaneously identify themselves would be largely dysfunctional."

Jeff concurred, "Yes, reidentifying oneself is indispensable for deliberation and deliberation is one way that people function. A functioning person has to be able to ask 'What should *I* do later?' One must have some idea *whose* future one is planning. Pointing this out sounds odd, but only because we take it for granted.

"Let me add that when one is close to others one has to be able to reidentify them with great frequency, though still not as much as one must be able to reidentify oneself. Near one extreme, the state needs to be able to reidentify me only a few dozen times in my entire life, unless I become incarcerated or become a public employee, and at the other extreme, I have to be constantly able to reidentify myself. In between, but closer to the latter, is the need for loved ones, associates and other intimates to be able to identify each other."

Phil stated, "I'm finally in a position to make a set of observations on these relations that will bring us directly to the sympathy and ego evaluations."

"Good," Connie said.

Annihilation Consolation Reprised

Phil continued, "In various ways, the *relata*, the same person at different times, are different from each other. Simply, the same person at different times is different. For example, while your appearance today is similar to your appearance of two years ago, the resemblance is far from exact."

"Don't mention it! We're here trying to comfort Jeff, not depress me!" exclaimed Connie.

"Of course, there's even less resemblance to you as a young child," Phil continued.

"Furthermore, while some memories which you have today are the 'same' as memories you had five years ago, many are different. Not only have you added memories, you've lost some. In fact, just as a person's 'sameness' is consistent with many changes, so is the 'sameness' of memories consistent with many changes. Not only does a person's *set* of memories change, but *individual* memories change as well. For example, memories lose vividness and poignancy . . ."

"Or gain poignancy," Jeff added.

"Details are lost, others are substituted, and perspectives alter. So, while some of your current memories are the same as those you had five years ago, this is consistent with the fact that these memories are not alike in all details or aspects.

"Also, many projects which you had five years ago, and concerning which you anticipated and deliberated, you no longer have. You no longer have them either because you completed them, gave up on them, or decided against them. Also, your roles have changed greatly during your life. Twelve years ago you were a high school student and a pianist; seven years ago you were an accounting student going into grad school; now, you're a comptroller."

Jeff added, "Continuing with Connie as an example: her tastes have changed. In high school you balked at the artificiality of Hollywood musicals, now you can't get enough of them.

"Twenty years ago we were very religious. But adolescence and scandals changed our ideals and our confidences."

Phil concluded, "The point is that we must not be misled by statements of the form 'x and y are the same person at different times.' It only means that there are various relations between x and y, but these *relata* are different from each other, sometimes greatly. In fact, in some cases, some of these relations which normally hold between these *relata* do not hold at all. Memory cannot connect anyone with his or her own birth, directly or indirectly."

Connie challenged, "I agree that in some respects a particular person changes quite a bit, and that in nearly all respects a person changes somewhat. But there are still other respects in which a person does not usually change at all. For example, a person's DNA. Although it can be altered, as Jeff said, it needn't. Another example is fingerprints."

Phil said, "A person's fingerprints do vary. For example, they expand as your fingers grow. However, for the purposes of reidentification, such variation does not matter. But anyway, DNA does not individuate, as in the case of identical twins. But yes, people have the same DNA and the same fingerprint pattern throughout their lives. But these are not the things which we care about regarding a person. Jeff's grief has nothing to do with fingerprints. We care about a person's appearance, memories, plans, fantasies and beliefs—Jeff mourns the loss of these in his mom's death. Though DNA contributes to these things, the person is these things not the DNA. A person's DNA, in part, causes people to be what they are, but it is not them. They are changing things.

"In conclusion, a person in the course of his or her entire life, or even a part, is a series of *relata*, which differ from each other in many ways. There is no changeless thing 'inside' us which underlies all these changes. There is no single, changeless 'core' to which all these changes occur. Yes, you have the same DNA, but that's not *you*. You are a series of *relata*, different from each other, between which various relations normally hold."

Jeff agreed; Connie hesitated, but did not object.

Phil said, "I believe that this forms the basis of at least three evaluation consolations. The first two will be directed against the sympathy evaluation and the last will be directed against the ego evaluation."

"Preliminaries over?" Connie asked.

"Preliminaries over," Phil answered as Paul McCartney sang "Too Many People."

Phil began, "Previously, I argued that all evils are predicates—or properties, or states—and that death is not a predicate of any subject, but that 'X is dead' is a denial of X's existence. Or, if death is a predicate, the subject is the corpse, not the person, and that all evils for a person must be a predicate of that person. Jeff objected that these arguments are not sound when directed against some deprivation evils.

"Now I shall take a slightly different approach. I shall argue that death does not have the dead, beloved person as its subject because a person is not a single subject but a *series* of subjects. In effect, I shall argue that death has too many subjects! This will be the first consolation drawn from our lengthy analysis of personal identity."

Phil asked, "What is the subject of the sympathy evaluation, that death is a terrible evil for the dead person?"

"The dead person, of course," Connie answered suspiciously. "This is just one subject. Why do you say that there are too many subjects?" Connie asked incredulously.

"There are too many subjects, in the sympathy evaluation, to which we can attribute the evil of death, since the dead person was a series of subjects, that is, a series of greatly varying *relata*," Phil said.

Phil explained, "Jeff, of course we agree that your mom was reidentifiable throughout her life. That is, even as a baby she was the 'same person' as an adult. But we've concluded that the *relata* which constitute this reidentifiable person vary greatly throughout her life. Your mom, though one reidentifiable person, was very different at different phases of her life."

"Yes, she was an infant, a toddler, a girl, an adolescent, a student, a worker, a single woman, a wife, a young mother, a middle-aged wife and mother, a grandmother, a widow, a retiree and a semi-invalid. Of course, some of these phases overlapped somewhat," Jeff surveyed.

Phil resumed, "Her appearance, thoughts and abilities were quite different during these different phases, I assume. Since these *relata* differ, despite the undeniable resemblances, continuity and causal connections between them, I ask you, '*Who* is the subject of the sympathy evaluation?' That is, for whom does her death entail deprivations? We agree that your mom was not a single, unchanging thing. So again, who is the subject of the sympathy evaluation? Certainly not the infant. And yet since this infant is reidentifiable as your mom, why couldn't we say that the subject is the infant? But that would seem clearly wrong. You see the difficulty one gets into when trying to determine the subject, and thus make sense of, the sympathy evaluation. So, are *any* of these selves, or *relata*, the subject of the sympathy evaluation?"

"Perhaps the subject of the sympathy evaluation is the last phase of a person's life," Connie said.

Jeff commented, "I don't think I can give that answer, Connie. My mom wasn't well in the last phase of her life. And although I believe, as I told you, that she is worse dead than as unwell as she was, when I think of the person for whom I feel sorry, that is, the subject of the sympathy evaluation, I do not restrict myself to the last phase of her life. In fact, I'm haunted by something my Uncle Jim said at the wake. My mom was the youngest and Uncle Jim the oldest in their large family. Uncle Jim told us that when my mom was two he would toss her into the air, and when he caught her she would say, 'Do it again, Jamie.'" Jeff stifled a sob.

Phil and Connie looked at each other with concern.

Connie spoke. "I can understand why this story saddens you. But the sadness need not come from a belief that that little girl is dead, or that that little girl is the subject of the sympathy evaluation. Just because your mom's death makes you think of other parts of her life, and these thoughts sadden you, does not mean that these parts of her life are the subject of the sympathy evaluation. Remember, grief has several objects. In an effort to begin to understand your grief we've focused on the griever's evaluations.

"Any number of things could explain why your uncle's story saddens you. It vividly contrasts the difference between having one's life ahead of one and having one's life behind one."

"*Whose* life ahead or behind?" Phil asked.

Jeff responded to Connie. "Perhaps some of the sadness comes from this contrast. Some of it also might come from the story's implication that my mother died comparatively young as she was survived by a much older brother. Some of it also comes from sympathy for my uncle, who, though grieving not nearly as much as I, felt sadness when he told the story."

Phil asked, "Sadness for *whom*?"

Jeff continued, "Perhaps the story saddens me because I heard it, charming as the story was or might have been, only after my mom's death. I wish that I could have shared the potential pleasure of this anecdote with her. I don't know whether she recalled the 'rides' her big brother gave her. I wish I knew whether she did. And if she did, this is one more pleasant recollection which death deprives her."

Connie reminded, "That little girl ceased to exist long before your mom died, though either is reidentifiable as the other. Death did not make that girl cease to exist."

Jeff said, "Still, I do not think that the last phase of my mom's life is the only or primary subject of the sympathy evaluation. There was so much more to my mom before she became a semi-invalid. It is inadequate to regard only the last part of her life as the subject of the sympathy evaluation. I grieve more because my healthy mom is dead than that my ailing mom is dead."

Connie said, "That doesn't sound right."

Phil said to Connie, "I agree that the infant cannot be the subject of the sympathy evaluation. You propose that the subject is Jeff's mom in the final phase of her life. Jeff is reluctant to agree. Please explain why you propose the final phase as the subject."

Connie complied, "This phase was the one which was ended by her death. During this phase, which lasted four years, she was most like the person who died."

Phil objected, "But then why not take the principle even further? If you did, the subject would be Jeff's mom in her final hours, rather than in her final years. Also, if her death had come as soon as a month after the onset of her illness, wouldn't it be correct, on your reasoning, to conclude that the subject of the sympathy evaluation had a duration of only one month? It seems strange that the subject could vary in this way."

Jeff objected, "The subject is certainly not the person she was in her final hours. If it were, I would be grieving over a person who was unconscious and barely functional biologically. But I do not grieve over the non-existence of this."

"You're making my point," Phil said. "Since the *relata* which constitute a person are different in many ways any attempt to identify the subject of the sympathy evaluation must fail. The sympathy evaluation lacks a subject for having too many candidates.

"The attempt to find a subject must fail because: the person during phases remote from death cannot be the subject because that phase ceased to exist for reasons having nothing to do with death. But the criterion of proximity, when pushed to the extreme, does not leave a suitable object of grief. But it seems arbitrary to not employ this criterion to the extreme, if it can be employed at all. Anyway, even before this criterion is pushed as far as it can go, it has already gone too far to suit Jeff's sympathy evaluation. For it has already eliminated as the subject that phase of the person for whom Jeff feels most sympathy, namely, his mom when she was healthy."

Jeff said, "I have a few objections to your consolation. First, you said that persons during phases not proximate to death cannot be the subject of the sympathy evaluation. But in cases like my mom's, in which the healthy and happier phase was ended by the same thing which caused her death, it is not comforting. For you've just shifted from one evil, her death, to another, her cancer."

Connie added, "In another case, where a person dies suddenly and in the 'prime of life' Phil's consolation would fail. The final phase of such a person's life would be very valuable and it's loss regrettable."

Phil replied, "I'm not concerned that my consolation would fail in such a case, as long as I can find a consolation which fits Jeff's circumstances.

"By the way, Connie, are you sure that you haven't gone over to the other side?!"

Connie answered, "No, I still wish to console Jeff. But after having found some of these evaluation consolations promising, only to be disappointed, I'm getting suspicious."

Jeff said, "I have a second objection to your consolation. If it is an error to attribute the deprivation of death to the infancy of a person who died in later life, this might be because the subject of the deprivation is not any particular phase of that person's life. Instead, the subject might be the person's entire history rather than some subset of *relata* within that history. After all, it is possible for an entire life to be a subject. For example, 'Her life was seventy-four years.' This is a statement about the entire series. So why couldn't the subject of the sympathy evaluation be the entire life? Why couldn't the entire series of these *relata* be the subject? Why must it be a single phase, or even worse, a single momentary *relata*?"

Connie observed, "Jeff, your two objections were on behalf of two different subjects of the sympathy evaluation. First, you defended the idea that the subject was your mom during that phase of her life which immediately preceded her illness. Second, you suggested a yet unconsidered possibility, that the subject was her entire life. Now I'm beginning to wonder if Phil wasn't right all along, that there are too many possible subjects. All in all, we've had three serious suggestions. In addition to the two just mentioned, it's been suggested that the subject is the final phase of a person's life. Maybe there *is* something incoherent about the sympathy evaluation."

Phil said, "Let's look at your suggestion that a possible subject of the sympathy evaluation is the person's entire life, that is, the entire series 'tied together' by relations of resemblance and memory and so on, but differing over time in many ways. This series is not an appropriate subject of the sympathy evaluation. In fact, none of the proposed subjects will do. One criterion which we used to try to determine the subject was proximity to death. This was because death is the cessation of only the final phase. But even though death marks the end of the final phase of a person's life, strictly speaking, since death is not a state of the living, there is no moment in a person's life in which one is harmed by death—except possibly by its prospect.

"An infant is not harmed by eventual death in later life. A thirty year old is not harmed by eventual death at eighty. Even in one's final phase of life, one is not harmed by subsequent death. Therefore, I cannot see how the subject of the deprivation entailed by death could be the person's life as a whole, or any part of that life. Neither the series, nor any of the *relata* which comprise it, were deprived of anything by subsequent death. You say that death is a deprivation evil. But for whom? Someone who has been deprived. But subsequent death does not deprive any *relata* within this series, nor the series itself considered as a whole."

Jeff commented, "I agree that, except by its prospect, death does not deprive any of the *relata* within the series. For example, her eventual death did not deprive my mom of anything in her fiftieth nor in her seventieth year. But it did deprive her of the rest of her seventy-fourth year, and her entire seventy-fifth year, and so on."

Phil asked, "Who was deprived of these? Not your mom as a seventy-three year old."

Jeff said, "I've already agreed that the subject of the deprivation is not any of the *relata* within the series. It is the entire series which has been deprived."

Phil countered, "It's true that death is a *limit* to the series. But that just means that instead of the existence of a series of one length, there is a series of another length. That is, death is not a deprivation for the actual series; it is only that death entails that the actual series is of some finite length, and death at a particular time entails that the actual series is one particular length rather than another. Again, death limits the series, making it as long as it is, but it does not deprive the actual series of anything.

"Furthermore, I do not see how it would be possible to deprive a *series* of anything without depriving any of its *relata*. And we agree that none of the *relata* within the series are deprived by eventual death. Therefore, the entire series cannot be the subject either.

"Jeff, you've said that a deprivation evil for a person need not be a state of that person. You gave as an example a person missing opportunities. Now, I concede that a missed opportunity is a deprivation evil for a person though it is not a state of that person. But later, even you said that the evil must concern a state of the person for which it is an evil. In all cases of deprivations, besides death, the evil is *concurrent* with that person. I'll explain my meaning with examples: if a person misses an opportunity to make love on a particular day, the person deprived of this is that person on that particular day. If a person misses a once-in-a-lifetime career opportunity, the deprived person is him or her from that time onwards, perhaps until death. In neither case is the subject of the deprivation that person at other times in life. In sum, for concurrent deprivations, unlike death which is an alleged deprivation *subsequent* to life, there is less difficulty in determining the subject of the deprivation.

"Here's a sad but paradigmatic case which shows that the subject of the sympathy evaluation is neither the entire series nor any *relata* within the series, because death is subsequent to all the *relata* and the series as a whole. Consider the death of a very young child. This person has not been deprived of infancy . . ."

Jeff said, "This person's been deprived of the rest of its life."

Connie nodded.

Phil continued, "But who has been deprived of the rest of his or her life? Not the infant. Not any *relata* within this actual, brief series, nor the actual series itself. The person who has been deprived is an imaginary person who, it is supposed, would have been reidentifiable with this infant. In other words, the subject of the sympathy evaluation is not the series which did exist, nor any *relata* of this series. It is an *imaginary* thing which never existed, despite imagined reidentifiability relations to that which did exist. We imagine an older person which looks like this child or had this child's memories.

"Now, my point about the child is true even for a person who dies in old age. The deprived person is an imaginary extension of the actual person. However, I began with the example of a very young child because it makes my point more conspicuous. When imagining a very young child's deprivation, if we imagine the deprivation to be extensive, we must imagine the continued existence of the series involving *relata* not closely resembling the child. That is, we must imagine the deprived person as growing up and changing in many ways. Whereas, when imagining the continued existence of a dead adult, or one whose *relata* show less variation than a child, it is easy to confuse the deprived person or 'correct' subject of the sympathy evaluation, which is merely an imaginary thing, with the 'incorrect' because not deprived subject of the sympathy evaluation, which was a real thing.

"Now, if the 'correct' subject of the sympathy evaluation, the deprived person, is not the actual series, nor any real *relata*, but only an imaginary extension of this series, then the sympathy evaluation is about merely fictitious, imaginary evils. For real evils, whether diametric or deprivation, must have real subjects.

"In sum, unlike your example of the deprivation evils of missed opportunities, death is not merely not a state of its 'victim,' it concerns only an imaginary victim. It is not merely the case that some of the goods lost to a dead person, such as Thanksgiving dinners she would have prepared, are merely conceived and not real, because these goods never came into being as a result of that person's death, but the person who is the subject of these lost goods is likewise merely conceived and not real.

"Since the imagined extension of a person's life is not that person, but only an imaginary thing, and since this imagined extension is the 'correct' subject of the sympathy evaluation, the actual person, whom you loved, is not the 'correct' subject of the evaluation."

Phil concluded, "One thing which I've learned from our conversation is how many variations there are on the annihilation consolation. This last version makes use of the fact that the actual *relata* must be distinguished from imaginary *relata*."

Jeff paused then spoke. "We keep coming up to this point again and again. How we can understand the sympathy evaluation. Before your most recent consolation I thought I had understood it fully. Let's see whether we can settle it now. To meet your most recent criticism of the sympathy evaluation, I now understand it for the first time. I still say that death is an extreme deprivation evil for the dead person, whether that deprivation is finite or infinite. But I now have an understanding of the subject of this deprivation evil. It is not an imaginary being. It is the fact that she is dead. In other words, it is the state of affairs which are the truth conditions of the statement 'She is dead, she no longer exists.' This state of affairs contains an intrinsic evil which is 'captured' by the intrinsic sympathy evaluation."

Phil said, "I'm confused. The subject is this state of affairs subsequent to her life *and* the subject is the person who is dead? This seems contradictory."

Jeff proceeded, "I'll have to be careful in my explanation. According to our analysis, what does it mean that some person continues to exist?"

Connie answered, "It means that the world continues to contain *relata* which are reidentifiable as that person. These are 'connected' by some of the reidentifiability relations."

Jeff asked, "So what does it mean that some person is dead?"

Connie answered again, "It means that the world no longer contains *relata* which are thus related to that person."

Phil asked, "Yes, but how could this be an evil for that person, the actual *relata*, other than perhaps as a prospect?"

Jeff answered, "It doesn't harm the *relata* which did exist. I agree with that. But the world, the entire state of affairs, is intrinsically impoverished, everything else being equal, because it does not contain *relata* connected to that person."

Connie looked puzzled and said, "You grieve for the *world*'s loss? I thought you were grieving for your mom's loss. The world has many such losses, why grieve over this one? I thought you were grieving because someone you love has had a terrible loss. But if the sufferer is the world, then the personal connection is lost."

Phil added, "And the world isn't a person at all."

Jeff cautioned, "It seems I'm explaining this paradoxically. But it's not paradoxical. Let me continue. What does it mean that some person will suffer some diametric evil, such as a toothache?"

Connie answered, "According to our analysis, it means that there will be *relata* reidentifiable as this person that includes a toothache."

"And what does it mean that some person will suffer some deprivation evil, such as blindness?" Jeff asked.

Connie, the teacher's pet, answered again, "It means that there will be *relata* reidentifiable as this person but that awareness of colors, or sensitivity to light, will not be among such *relata*."

"The world will contain this person, but sightless, without visual sensations," Jeff added.

"Where is this leading?" Connie asked.

Jeff answered, "To an understanding of 'Person P has good/evil X,' or 'X is good/evil for Person P.' Statements of this form are about goods or evils related to P and about whether they exist or not.

"So, 'Death is a terrible evil for the dead person' means that there will not be any *relata* reidentifiable as the person who died, and this *relata* would have been very good and extensive. Thus, the intrinsic sympathy evaluation has a real subject, the world minus the loved one, that is, the state of affairs which are the truth condition for 'That person is dead;' but it is still personal to the loving ones. For this evaluation is only about the world *insofar* as it lacks *relata* reidentifiable as the loved one."

"This is a bit clearer, but not entirely. The world's no longer containing your mom involves evils, but are they evils *for her*? It's evil for her loving ones, but how is her absence bad for her?" Connie asked.

Jeff began his answer asking, "How would her continued existence be good for her? The world would contain *relata* which are intrinsically good and reidentifiable as her. Her death means the non-existence of these intrinsic goods, that is, her death is a deprivation evil for her."

Jeff suggested, "Let's have a brief review of the griever's evaluations. Afterwards, I hope the meaning of the intrinsic sympathy evaluation will be clear. There are several evils involved in a person's permanent absence from the world. There are even some goods—I know, you're surprised to hear me say that without it being dragged out of me. Of these evils and goods, some are 'for her.' Her absence can be intrinsically or organically bad for herself, and intrinsically, consequentially, and organically bad for others. Let's review each of these, in reverse order from our earlier lengthy discussions of them.

"A loved one's absence, that is, the non-existence of *relata* reidentifiable as that person, is intrinsically evil for the loving ones. It can also be consequentially evil for them. But let's face it: not everyone who is affected by the death is harmed by it. Bluntly, some people benefit from it. The point needn't be subtle. Some people profit from another's death. Some kid's tuition, or braces, or blue jeans are being paid for in part because my mom died.

"Continuing, the death of a loved one can 'misshape' a survivor's life. It deprives it of interrelatedness. It can produce a decline. In short, it can be an organic evil for those who loved the dead.

"Returning to the sympathy evaluation, a person's death could be organically good or evil in two ways. We could compare the entire life to other's lives, asking, for example, 'Was it unique?' Or, we could compare the parts of that entire life to each other, asking, 'Was it declining?' Either of these evaluations concerns the whole series of reidentifiable *relata* which is that person's life. *Here* the subject might be the entire series of a person's life. The subject is not any state of affairs subsequent to that person's death. And the subject of these evaluations is not an imaginary extension of the series. In the case of these organic evaluations, the subject might be just the whole, actual series. The life was unique, declined and so on. I argued, against Phil, that the series had less organic value because limited by death. In any case, we agreed that any such organic value, good or bad, was irrelevant to the sympathy evaluation, unless the dead person, while alive, was aware of this value. That is, unless people are aware of their uniqueness or the value direction of their lives, these would not have affected their happiness. I then argued that, insofar as people are aware of the entailments of eventual death for the organic value of life, this awareness was probably baneful."

"Fair summary," Phil said, and Connie nodded.

"Now we come back to the intrinsic sympathy evaluation," Jeff directed. "In my brief review I referred to various ways that the world is better or worse because of this death. But the review has left something out. It leaves out the goods which would have existed, that is, the good experiences which the dead person would have had. And this is, considered by itself, a terrible loss, because these are of great value and would have been extensive, perhaps infinite. These facts alone are terrible, whether or not their evil is outweighed by entailing or causing goods which exceed it. If it were the case that intrinsic evils for the dead person were outweighed by goods it entailed or caused, this would not change the fact that the non-existence of these goods is a terrible evil. If one argued that the death was good because of its benefit to others, *et cetera*, this would be a response consolation not an evaluation consolation. Death's benefit to strangers does not concern the griever's evaluations.

"I grieve because of evil suffered by those for whom I have the most concern. The sympathy and ego evaluations claim that the death of a loved one is evil for those for whom I have the most concern. An argument that death benefits others for whom the griever has less concern cannot be a successful evaluation consolation, because, as we're using the term, an evaluation consolation is an argument directed against either the sympathy or ego evaluations. Therefore, consideration of a death's effects on others for whom one has less concern must be an argument against the griever's concerns, that is, a response consolation.

"The reason I now draw attention to the distinction between evaluation and response consolations is that I am trying to isolate the facts which are relevant to the sympathy evaluation from everything else. The relevant facts to the intrinsic sympathy evaluation are the world's lack of goods reidentifiable with the loved one.

"Again, if we ask why a griever cares so much, or reacts so strongly to these goods and their loss of them, then we are getting into response consolation 'territory.'"

Jeff concluded, "In sum, that some person has some deprivation evil means that there does not exist some good reidentifiability related to that person. This can be true whether or not that person still exists. The subject of the deprivation evil is that person, construed either as the entire series of its life, or some actual *relata* therein, in the sense that the deprivation concerns states which would have been reidentifiable with that person. But the subject, in another sense, is the state of affairs which is the truth condition of 'The person is dead;' even though this state of affairs does not include, nor is included within, the actual series or *relata* of that person's life. My mom's continued existence would have included great and extensive goods."

Jeff deeply inhaled and exhaled.

Connie scratched the back of her neck and Phil rubbed his eyes, both frustrated in their hopes to console Jeff.

Continued Existence Is Not So Different from Death

As Buddy Holly's "Not Fade Away" rocked the restaurant, Phil tried again. "All right. We now have a better understanding of what it means for a person to continue to exist, and thereby, what death is. But from a proper understanding of these, consolations can be found. In fact, we can see that continued existence and death are not so very different, and can be made even less so."

"I'm listening," Jeff said, suspiciously.

"The continued existence of a person means that there continue to be things related to this person, such as resembling this person, having the same memories, and these have spatio-temporal continuity. But we also said that throughout life the *relata* differ in many ways. The death of a person means the absence of such *relata*. But, to be more precise than we have been thus far in our understanding of death, there are always *relata* which bear some reidentifiability relations to the dead person. For instance, after a person's death, there will still be people who outwardly resemble that person. Also after one's death, there will be people who have had experiences similar to the dead person, and thereby, similar memories. Further, after a person's death, there will be people similar in character, skills and beliefs.

"Admittedly, some reidentifiable relations will be discontinued upon a person's death. That is, in some respects there will be no further *relata*. For example, after a person's death there will be no person spatio-temporally continuous with that person. Of course, *something* will be spatio-temporally continuous, namely, the corpse or ashes. And of course, if a person donates organs, then there will be a person at least partly spatio-temporally continuous with part of oneself. And I suppose that children are in a sense spatio-temporally continuous with their parents, or their mothers, up until conception or birth. Of course, the parents' 'path' after conception or birth is not continued through that child's life. Thus, there will be some *relata* partly continuous with oneself, some of which will be part of another person's life.

"After one's death there will not be any *relata* related to one by overlapping short term memories. But this happens every time we go to sleep. So death cannot be claimed to be so different from continued existence just because it concludes an overlapping series of short term memories.

"In short, since there is considerable variation between these *relata* over the course of a life, and since some reidentifiability relations continue to hold even after death, death is not altogether unlike continued existence. That is, the world will not completely lack things bearing reidentifiability relations to the dead person. Therefore, death is not such a terrible evil for the dead person; the world will not so much be intrinsically impoverished through this death. Since a person, throughout life, is not a single, changeless thing, death is not an abrupt change from the existence of this changeless thing to its non-existence."

Jeff protested, "You *greatly* exaggerate the similarities between continued existence and death, between a world in which the person continues to exist and one in which that person does not. But before I object, I'd like to hear more of what you have to say."

Connie said to Phil, "We despise death as the *opposite* of life. But in effect, you are saying that 'opposite' has different meanings, and that in the sense in which life and death are truly opposites, the contrast is not so great. If life and death were opposites like good and evil, true and false, existence and non-existence, the contrast would be sharp. Instead, the opposition is rather like north and south. Something like that."

"The world goes on, but in a different 'direction'," Phil mused.

Phil continued, "Not only are there many differences between the *relata* which constitute a life, but also, many of these changes are desired and desirable. For instances, increase in knowledge, growth, sexual maturity, parenthood, additional and varied experience all entail or produce changes and weaken the reidentifiability relations which 'hold together' a life and contribute to personal identity. And if a person is unhealthy, unattractive or impoverished, further changes would be welcomed. Therefore, either there are major differences between such changes which weaken personal identity and the weakening of these relations entailed by death, or death is not a terrible evil for the dead."

"You know which disjunct I'd take." Jeff said.

"No, wait," Connie said. "Yes, we desire many changes in the course of a lifetime, but many changes are unwelcome. For instances, aging, forgetting, and I can't remember the third . . ."

"Ugh! That's an old one!" Phil groaned.

"Disillusionment is a third example," Connie added. "Therefore, to the extent that weakening of personal identity is bad, I find it a dreary consolation that death is like continued existence because even continued existence is replete with change.

"I would go even further because it strikes me as dreary that all we are is an ever changing series of reidentifiable *relata*, without a changeless core," Connie concluded.

Phil said, "Jeff and I agree that the concept of a person can be 'reduced' or analyzed in terms of relations of reidentifiability. We are 'reductionists.' Therefore, this has been the assumption of my consolations based on the concept of a person. But I do not agree that it is *dreary* that, *in general*, we change, even though some *particular* changes might be bad. Remember, we agreed that something was evil only if a better could be conceived. Now, I don't know anything better than a series of *relata*, related in such ways that change can be conceived. Yes, there are conceivably better types of changes which could happen, but the general facts of change itself, contrary to Plato . . ."

"Who?"

Phil continued, "do not seem to me to be worse than some conceivable good. Even if something better, something changeless, were conceivable, it would still not be conceivable that *people* be this better kind of thing. Applying this remark to the present case, it is not an evil for Jeff's mom that she was a series of reidentifiable *relata*, which relations weakened, because it is not conceivable that there be anything better than this for her, this condition being so general and basic to 'person.' Therefore, I disagree with your further point that a consolation relying upon the general facts of change is dreary."

Jeff pronounced, "Phil is right about this, but Connie was right in her first point, namely that insofar as *some* changes in life are undesirable, a comparison between death and life can be dreary unless the changes in death are somehow generally better than those in life. But if death is like life's flaws, then death is not made any less terrible."

Phil reminded, "Not all changes in life or weakening in relations involved in personal identity are bad."

Phil continued as Peter, Paul, and Mary's "Puff the Magic Dragon" concluded and the McCoy's "Hang on Sloopy," penned by Bert Berns using the pseudonym Bert Russell, played.

"Not only are death and continued existence not altogether different, one can *further* minimize the difference between the two. One can minimize the difference between the world succeeding one's death and the world with one's continued existence, if during life one expands one's interests, thoughts and projects beyond oneself. In part, what constitutes a particular person is what that person is aware of, what that person thinks about, *et cetera*. For example, Jeff and I have been thinking about philosophy for years; you've been concentrating on your career. In a very real way, these projects become part of a person's identity. These are things which link stages of a person together over years. Therefore, to the extent that one thinks about things which one's survivors will think about, to that extent one still exists, or one's death is not different from one's continued existence.

"People's plans and thoughts can be about themselves, for example, what they'll do or what they'll wear; the object of plans and thoughts I'll call 'personal.' Alternatively, one's plans and thoughts could be about others, such as what one's children will become, object of which I'll call 'impersonal.' Finally, they could be about things other than persons, for example, curiosity about nature, which I'll call 'nonpersonal.' Now, the less involved in personal projects, and the more involved in impersonal or nonpersonal projects, the less is the difference between one's continued existence and one's death. After one's death, it cannot be expected that others will make one the object of their thoughts, unless perhaps one was a celebrity. But if one concerns oneself with nonpersonal objects, such as astronomy or mathematics, or impersonal objects, such as politics or one's descendents, one can expect that others will continue to make these objects their concerns.

"In sum, if my reidentifiability as someone in the future is based, even in small part, on the similarity of the projects and thoughts which we share, then I am reidentifiable, to some at least small degree, with anyone who shares these projects and thoughts. Remember, anticipation and deliberation are two reidentifiability relations. Part of what makes two *relata* part of my life is that they are 'linked' by anticipation and deliberation. But it is possible for this 'link' to survive one, if one anticipates and deliberates concerning future nonpersonal and impersonal things."

Jeff objected, "But the relations which I have to some person reidentifiable with myself is not just that the object of our thoughts are similar; the relations include my ability to influence the future, to shape the *relata* which is reidentifiable with me. Causality, remember, is an important reidentifiability relation. And I am no more able to influence either the mathematical or political theory of people who live after me by thinking about these than had I never thought about these topics."

"Unless you publish," Phil rejoined.

"Publish or perish?" Jeff sarcastically interjected.

Jeff added, "An ironic implication of your consolation has become apparent during our discussion. If one could minimize the evil of one's eventual death by developing impersonal and nonpersonal interests, because they could be more easily shared by others following one's death, then one would be better advised to cultivate an interest in soaps than in mathematics or politics, which were your examples. For you're better guaranteed of a large number of people 'carrying on' your interest in soap opera characters than carrying on your interest in imaginary numbers or unemployment figures."

"Another imaginary number!" Connie interjected.

Jeff continued, "Philosophers who offer such a consolation probably do so in the hopes of interesting us in 'grand' things. So, if your argument instead tended to encourage gossip concerning fictitious, implausible and stereotypical characters, I think philosophers would wish to withdraw it!"

"I think you should concern yourself with rice! That's what most people think most about!" Connie teased.

Phil said, "But it is still desirable that people make their interests more impersonal and nonpersonal."

Jeff added, "By the way, there is an important difference between the advice to *substitute* impersonal and nonpersonal concerns for personal ones and the advice to *add* impersonal and nonpersonal concerns without dropping personal concern. The latter advice can be better followed. You see, even impersonal and nonpersonal concerns are one's concerns. And one's concerns usually make one desire continued existence, even if these concerns are not personal. For examples, if a person is concerned about a child, and one's death might harm the child, one has a reason to desire continued existence. If a person wants to understand astrophysics, then one has a reason to desire continued existence. But a desire for one's own continued existence is a personal concern. Therefore, an increase in impersonal and nonpersonal concerns, everything else being equal, entails also an increase in personal concern. That is, there is a strict limit to the abandonment of personal concerns, apart from the unusual cases in which a person's impersonal and nonpersonal concerns are better served by death. Therefore, even when people expand their interests to impersonal and nonpersonal objects, since they have thereby also increased personal concern, they have not significantly lessened the difference between death and continued existence."

Phil reconsidered, "Perhaps it is a mistake to think that one can lessen the evil of death by expanding one's concerns. We must not confuse this evaluation consolation with the good, though simple, advice that the more expansive one's concerns the less *worried* one will likely be about one's death.[1] But that a person with impersonal and nonpersonal concerns is less likely to worry about death because there is so much more to think about does not mean that death would be less evil. I admit that. One thing which repeatedly surfaces in our discussion is the importance of distinguishing that which justifies an evaluation from that which justifies an affect or feeling. Greater impersonal and nonpersonal concerns might not justify the claim that one's death has been made less evil for one, although it might justify the claim that one should be less concerned with one's death."

"Maybe" Connie said.

Jeff began, "Actually, I find our discussion about minimizing the evil of death by changing one's concerns a bit fantastic. The advice, some of the objections to it, and the replies on behalf of it all give much too much credit to the idea that death is like continued existence."

"Frankly, I wanted to say that too. But I thought I'd let you guys do your philosophical thing, and I even joined in," Connie said.

"Well now my 'philosophical thing' is to criticize the philosophical idea we've been indulging until now," Jeff said.

Phil said, "I know you've been holding back objections. Please don't hold them back any longer."

Jeff said, "Your consolation is that an improved understanding of 'continued existence' and its opposite, 'death,' reveal that the difference between these is not as great as often supposed. Therefore, you conclude that death is not a terrible evil. Connie was concerned that if the difference between death and continued existence is not great, then maybe continued existence is not as good as we previously believed. You replied that the general fact that we change has no conceivable better, and therefore is not evil; allowing that *particular* changes might conceivably not occur, and so might be evils.

"I shall try to establish two points: first, that normal continued existence is *very* different from death; and second, that, in general, the few similarities between death and continued existence are emotionally less important than the differences.

"Before offering my objections, I'll recap some of the specifics of Phil's consolations. Phil compared 'death' and 'continued existence' by looking at several reidentifiability relations, one by one. And he asked whether these relations altogether ceased to hold when a person died. He noted that death does not entail that there will be no one who looks like the dead person. And others will have very similar personalities, skills and beliefs. Again, others will have similar experiences and thus similar memories . . ."

Phil interrupted, "I would like to add that the significance of many of our memories, perhaps especially childhood ones, is not primarily in the details of the events; as mentioned before, the details of memories alter and fade. The importance is rather how the events made us feel.[2] Whether or not every child broke a bone falling down stairs, everyone was terrified by something when a child. In fact, most people's earliest memory is of something unpleasant. My point is that, to some extent, the importance of memories is something about memories which is universal rather than unique. The importance of an event is largely how it made you feel, and everyone has much the same feelings, whatever the differences in the events which produced them. So, whether I live to remember my happy childhood or not, others will live who remember their own happy childhoods. The world without me will not be so different from the world with me. While my memories involve images of different faces and different rooms, and different aromas in the kitchen, there is common content to the memories of everyone with a fond childhood."

Jeff nodded and resumed his survey, "Death ends a series of overlapping short term memories, but a countless number of such series is concluded by sleep during continued existence.

"The point is, as far as this survey goes, there are no relations of reidentifiability which hold throughout a life which do not also hold in *some* way after death."

"Yes," Phil said.

Jeff, having concluded his survey, began his objections. "There will be people who resemble the dead person. However, none will be qualitatively identical. Nevertheless, there will even be a few people who resemble the dead person at the 'prime' of life more than the dead person in old age. But death entails that, everything else being equal, there will be one less person who looks like you. But that's exactly what we thought death was all along: the dead person no longer exists. It matters naught for the dead that others similar to them continue to exist. That is, the world is as intrinsically impoverished by the loss of this person as we thought all along. Properly understood, it is this loss which is the object of the sympathy evaluation. Your analysis has not reduced this loss one jot. If instead your consolation is that this loss should not be the focus of such concern because there are others who are qualitatively similar, then that is a response consolation. We'll get around to that. But for now, my objection is that this loss is the same as it was prior to your analysis. Regardless of some qualitative similarity to others, the loss is quantitatively the same as the griever thought at the outset.

"As with physical appearance, the same can be said for memories. Others will have similar, but different, memories. But even though others will have similar memories, death entails that, everything else being equal, there will be one less person with such memories. And this is intrinsically important.

But in addition to this point which I also made concerning physical appearance, a person's memories are irreplaceable by similar memories in a special way. Memories have objects; memories are *about* individual events, places and persons. Another's memories, although similar, will have different, although similar, objects. So, in three ways memories by others are different from one's own. They are not entirely alike; they are numerically distinct; and they have different objects.

"A crucial relation that normally holds between the same person at different times is causality. While a dead person might have some influence over the lives of successors, normally, this posthumous influence is very slight compared with the amount of control which one has over one's continued existence. In fact, even a married person has more control over his or her continued existence than over his or her successors!"

"Don't be so sure!" cautioned the married Phil.

"Even a prisoner has more control over his future than a person has over survivors. Besides this control, a prisoner can anticipate events in his life. In fact, given the routine of prison life, I imagine that a prisoner can anticipate his future better than a free person. In contrast, I think there is little that a person could realistically anticipate concerning survivors."

"I don't know, Jules Verne didn't do so badly!" Connie sniped.

"Finally," Jeff said, ignoring the counterexample, "in addition to the already mentioned differences, there is another big difference between 'death' and 'continued existence.' There are various relations which normally hold between the same person at different times. Usually, *several* relations connect the same *relata*. For instance, I am the same person who, as a one and a half year old, was taken by the police to a doctor during a blizzard after having cut open his forehead. Between these *relata*, myself now and that baby then, there exist several relations: spatio-temporal continuity, direct memory, resemblance, and causality." So saying Jeff brushed his bangs off his forehead, revealing a scar.

Jeff continued, "As we've said, direct memory does not connect all the *relata* of a person's life with each other. Nevertheless, in all normal cases of personal identity several relations hold; minimally, spatio-temporal continuity, resemblance and causality. In short, in continued existence, there is a strong tendency for several relations to hold between the same *relata*.

"But death is quite different. Yes, some people will look like the dead person, some will act like the dead person, some will have similar memories, and some *thing* will be spatio-temporally continuous. But these relations 'follow' separate 'strands.' The relations are 'diffuse.' That is, to the extent they hold at all, the relations hold between *relata* which are individuated from each other. In life, a person is individuated as well as reidentifiable. But the reidentifiable, individuated person *altogether* ceases to exist with death."

Phil said, "All right, I agree with your first point, that death is very different from continued existence. Please go on to your second point that the differences are more important than the similarities."

Jeff began, "This second point is relevant to our emotional responses. But first let me point out that the causal relation which one has to oneself at different times is of tremendous consequential value. I can, to some extent, determine my own happiness and others' through my future actions. I can influence my own future actions much more than I can influence another's. Furthermore, one often knows that oneself at a future time will recall one's present thoughts, and that oneself at a future time will have similar thoughts. We know that, when others misconstrue our words or actions, or perhaps construe them correctly but unfavorably, that there will be someone who understands, someone who gives one the benefit of the doubt, namely, one's future self. Control and anticipation justify one's concern for this *relata*, as well as facilitating mutual sympathy between them.[3]

"Such control, anticipation and mutual sympathy are possible, or possible only to such a degree, only insofar as one continues to exist. The diffuse continuation of reidentifiability relations after death does not justify them as important. They are important when conjoined, as in continued existence, making influence and intimacy possible."

Phil nodded.

Jeff appended, "However, I will agree that if it could be proven that immortals would necessarily change so much that they became not reidentifiable with their original selves, then immortality would at some point become like death. That is, since a person's continued existence is a matter of reidentifiable *relata* which differ over time, it is possible that immortality, while not a biological death, would be a reidentifiability 'death.' Normal continued existence is not like death except for people with severe dementia, although immortal continued existence might conceivably become like death. Therefore, our analysis of 'same person' might add some support to Phil's earlier claim that immortality is not a conceivable alternative to death.

"However, it would still have to be shown that it would be necessary that immortals would change so much from the people they were originally. And there might be considerable difficulty in showing this. For, even supposing that an immortal's appearance, memories, beliefs and character had to change radically, there will still be spatio-temporal continuity. And even more importantly, as long as these radical changes were gradual, they would allow for deliberation and anticipation through every phase of the change, making influence and intimacy possible the whole while. So, although *relata* on either end of this wide gulf might be unable to influence, understand or appreciate the other, they would be connected by a series of *relata*, each of which had these relations with others. And the abruptness of the change entailed by death would importantly distinguish death from an immortal's gradual transformation."

Phil said, "I can see how it would not comfort a person with respect to the prospect of death that following death there will be scattered *relata* bearing some reidentifiability relations. One's special concerns are not for these *relata*. But our issue is whether the survivor should be comforted by the posthumous existence of things which bear some reidentifiability relations with the dead. I agree that I exaggerated the similarity of death and continued existence, and in ways which concern the emotions of a person toward the prospect of death. But why are the differences so important to the loving one, unless the loving one is just sympathizing with the point of view which the loved one had to death before it came? And, I add, this is unusual sympathy: with a person who does not know of, or receive the sympathy, and after the time when that person felt distress. We usually sympathize with people *while* they are feeling distress."

Jeff answered, "I think that my grief is *partly* sympathy with the formerly living person, which perhaps contributes to the error we have already discussed of imagining dead people as currently aware of their own deprivations . . ."

"Or that error causes the sympathy," Phil interjected.

Jeff continued, "But the reason which a person has to feel bad about prospective death *is* the same, only greater in degree, as the reason that a loving one has to feel bad about the loved one's death, after the fact. For a loving one had some mutual understanding and some mutual influence with the person who has died. Granted, the loving one has considerably less mutual understanding and influence with a loved one than people have with themselves at different times. Nevertheless, generally one has greater mutual understanding and influence with respect to loved ones than with respect to anyone else, other than oneself.

"In sum, I grieve in part in sympathy with the affects which my loved one had toward her prospective death, and I grieve in part because I have lost a person with whom there was mutual sympathy."

"Time Heals"

"All right, I see your point. Well, at least I can mitigate the *ego* evaluation based upon our understanding of 'same person,'" Phil said.

"Really? Clearly, there is a subject of the ego evaluation. Therefore, the consolations based upon the supposed difficulty of identifying the correct subject of the sympathy evaluation do not apply to the ego evaluation," said the subject.

"Yes, but your precise nature is not as clear as the fact that you exist. And your precise nature, upon examination, supplies a mitigating consolation," Phil said.

"How so?"

"The loving survivor is an ever changing thing, too. Your personal identity does not consist in some unchanging core," Phil explained, "Right now and in the near future the permanent absence of your mom is a great evil for you. This is because you are, and have always been, her son. I do not refer to your biological relationship. I refer to your *role* as her son. Actually, this is several resembling and overlapping roles: her infant son, her toddler son, her pre-school son, her grammar school son, her adolescent, rebellious son, her young adult son . . ."

"A role which I never assumed comfortably," Jeff interjected.

Phil continued without pause, "her caring son. Much, though certainly not all, that you have been, and yet are, is contained in these roles. The different roles involved different skills, responsibilities, habits, memories and projects, for example.

"But eventually, just as each of these roles more or less succeeded the other, you will, more or less, cease having any of these roles. You will change with the consequence that the intrinsic evil to you of her permanent absence will diminish. Her death is intrinsically evil only for certain persons, and for you, but not for your entire future."

"Though the evil will never entirely go away," Connie added.

Phil said, "In a manner of speaking, this evil will be less for the person you will be than it is for the person you are now."

Phil continued, "Why is a person's continued existence so especially important to close family and friends, aside from the consequential value of that person for them? That is, what is it about that person's existence itself, or that person's company, which is especially important to a few?"

Jeff answered, "A fair answer to your question would be very lengthy. Nevertheless, I'll give you a short answer. There is a mutual adjustment of routines and enjoyments. When a person is a part of your life, the habits which you develop for enjoying life often involve the participation of that person. When that person is absent, not only might you have difficulty finding another to cooperate, but another will not 'play the part in the same way,' and thus, those habits you developed will not bring enjoyment."

Phil reflected, "Yes, when I was dating, I remember that if I didn't make an effort to change some habits which I developed with a previous girlfriend, then the next girlfriend would not enjoy my company, nor I hers...."

"Good, dating tips!" Connie joked.

"For instance, some women liked it when I 'brought out the little boy in me,' while . . ."

"No, please. Spare us!" said a now red-faced Connie.

"Great, we can discuss morbidity, but not this!" Phil said pretending to be disappointed.

Phil cleared his throat, and assuming a more serious tone said, "All right, the special intrinsic value of a person's company depends upon habits. But your habits will, and have already begun to change. This is a safe prediction. Since your mom is dead, your habits involving her, the ones which made her company of special value to yourself, will have to change.

Jeff said, "On the other hand, there is one change in me which makes an earlier loss worse. That is, as I am getting older I resemble my father more closely. This reminds me of the loss of my dad."

Phil objected, "I understand that, as you get older, you look more like your father, and that this reminds you of that loss of many years ago. However, while this makes you *feel* that loss once more, it is not actually increasing that loss for you. Does the fact of your greater resemblance to him make you such that his company would now be more valuable to you?"

"No, I suppose not," Jeff answered.

"Again, we must distinguish between whether or not something changes the evaluation which one should make of a thing and whether or not something makes us feel different about it. This is a lesson which we are each teaching the others," Phil said.

"Yes," Jeff said, "But be careful you do not make the same mistake. I agree that, as survivors change, they drop habits which centered on the dead person. Similarly, memories fade and anticipation no longer includes the dead person. However, although the survivors no longer feel the loss so mightily, it does not follow that the loss for the survivor has become any less. If one drops old habits centered on the absent person and those habits used to bring enjoyment, and does not substitute other productive habits, the loss will still be as great, though felt less."

Connie said, "Unfortunately, this is true. However, you seem to concede that if the person *does* develop other productive habits, then the loss of the loved one will become less for the survivor."

Connie added, "You must admit that it's been awhile since you have *felt* the evil for you of your dad's death."

"Yes, although now I feel it again. Partly because my mom's death, although coming many years later, has compounded the evil for me of my dad's death," Jeff said.

Connie continued, "But not only has it been awhile since you had felt that evil, it has been a long time since his absence has been a great evil for you."

Jeff said, "Be careful, one does not follow from the other. But I admit that it follows from our analysis of 'same person' that his death was less evil for me in my twenties than it was soon after he died. As Phil observed earlier in our discussion, I changed a lot after my dad's death. However, I do not think that the same can be predicted for me now. It will be tougher to adjust to mom's death. When my dad died I was just an immature teenager: my character had not yet 'fully' formed. But the kind of person I now am will be pretty much like the person I will be when I die. It was easier for me then to develop habits which did not depend upon my dad. But my character is now more or less 'fixed.' I have no choice but to drop my old habits centered around my mom; but it will be harder for them to be replaced by other productive ones."

Connie urged, "Well, you'll have to take some of your greater maturity and 'unfix' that character a little! I understand the problem you are outlining, but you also have greater resources today. The prognosis need not compare unfavorably to one that might have been made when your dad died."

Jeff said, "But part of the problem is that I do not *want* to develop other habits. I do not want to become a person for whom my mom is comparatively obsolete.[4] This is connected with the fact that I am not comforted by Phil's consolation that this evil for me will be lessened as I will become a different person, so to speak. This is a dreary consolation. I want to continue to be a son! I know that I will make some adjustments, but I don't wish it! It's not that I do not wish to adjust under *these* circumstances, I know that my future will be happier if I do adjust, but I am saddened that I must adjust. I *dread* the day when this loss will seem like 'it happened to someone else!' Connie was right that some changes within personal identity are evil. I don't like being 'disconnected' from my childhood, and this loss will increase that 'disconnection.' Also, this loss has assured that I will eventually be more 'disconnected' from my young adulthood."

Connie spoke calmly, "I know that people feel this way. I feel this way, too. But is it justified to not want to become a person for whom the dead are less significant?"

Jeff said, "Earlier, we said that one value a life can have is interrelatedness. And I said that a parent's death limits life's interrelatedness. For example, one will not be able to share the milestones of one's later life with one's parents, with whom one shared most of one's early milestones. But now, as a result of our analysis of 'same person' I realize that a loved one's death entails a limitation on interrelatedness which I had not articulated. The loving one changes."

Connie objected, "But is that really evil for the loving one? I know it makes a person feel bad, but that does not automatically make it evil?"

Jeff replied, "Perhaps you are right. Perhaps these changes in a person are not evil for that person. However, the prospect of such change is not comforting. As I said, one's special concern for a particular person is based upon one's ability to influence that person and one's intimacy with that person. But the person I was before my mom died neither deliberated about nor anticipated this person I am becoming. I will become a person who remembers vaguely and with less poignancy those things which I now remember well and deeply. In short, there has been less influence and there will be less intimacy or sympathy or understanding between these *relata*. I do not want to lose influence with my future self, or lose intimacy with either my future or former selves."

"But is one justified in not wanting to lose this control? Is there any evil in it?" Phil asked.

"The loss of sympathy and mutual understanding harms me now and later because these things are good," Jeff said.

There was a pause after which Connie said, "Have we been discussing the famous 'Time heals all wounds' consolation? Who said that, anyway?"

"Terence in *The Self-Tormentor*,"[5] answered Jeff, "I think that 'Time heals all wounds' usually means that, over time, the pangs of grief, obsession of grief, and numbness or inhibition of grief become less frequent, intense or extreme. And this happens, in part, because the survivor drops the old habits."

Phil added, "But the consolation which I offered is that the loss itself, the evil itself, will lessen over time. The survivor will develop into a person for whom the dead loved one is less precious. And this too happens, in part, because the survivor drops the old habits."

Phil concluded, "Of course, the lessening of the evil might *explain* why pangs and other grief reactions become less frequent and intense. So, my consolation was that the *evil* of this loss will decrease, whereas 'Time heals all wounds' usually just means that one's grief responses will decrease."

Connie said, "You know, Jeff, you are concerned that you will change in ways you don't like. But perhaps death accelerates change in the survivors not only because former roles must be abandoned, but also because grievers lose a bit of themselves in a useless attempt at retaining the dead person by mimicking the dead. I do not refer simply to mimicking some mannerisms, phrases or pronunciation of the dead person. These things are harmless in themselves, if not taken to 'Norman Bates' extremes, and do not represent a serious loss of one's own personality. In fact, if some trivial mimicking eases the transition between one's former life with the person who died and one's future life without that person, then it would be worthwhile. The dangerous mimicking to which I refer is when a person adopts as his own another's principles or wishes for no other reason than that they belonged to the dead loved one."

"She Wouldn't Want You to Grieve"

Jeff said, "One conventional consolation which bugs me terribly is 'She wouldn't want you to grieve.' For one thing, I doubt that it is entirely true! Don't we really want people to miss us terribly when we die? Not to the point of destruction, but we still want them to be a mess! Don't we want people to sympathize with us for the deprivation death entails for us? And another objection which I have to the consolation is that it is irrelevant. Though I suspect that we all desire others to grieve over our deaths, I am not grieving *because* I want to fulfill my mom's wishes."

Phil said, "Don't be so sure. Grief is a complex phenomenon and we don't know all its causes. But I'm no psychologist so I'll just pursue consolation strategies."

Connie said, "A better consolation than 'She wouldn't want you to grieve' might be that one should not adopt goals simply for the reason that a dead loved one wished for these."

The Foundations shook the restaurant with their song "Baby, Now That I Found You."

Jeff said, "You know, similar to mimicking, when I enter my empty apartment in a very loud voice I say hello to my mom and even my dad."

"I guess you're pretending that they're there," suggested Connie.

"Or maybe you're trying to defy the silence," suggested Phil.

"Maybe it's to frighten ghosts," muttered Jeff.

Summary of the Conversation

A reductionist analysis of the concept of personal identity fails to provide satisfactory evaluation consolations, especially with respect to the sympathy evaluation. According to this analysis, a person, during the course of a lifetime, is a series of *relata* between which several relations normally hold. However, these *relata* differ from one another in many respects.

We examined the consolation that the sympathy evaluation was senseless because neither any of the *relata* that compose a person's life, nor the series itself, can be the subject of the deprivation supposedly entailed by death. The "correct" subject of the sympathy evaluation is an imaginary extension of the formerly living person: it is not real, according to this consolation. This consolation concludes that imaginary beings have only imaginary evils.

However, the evil of death is not imaginary. The formerly living person—I'll call P—and the conceivable extension of that person are "subjects" of the sympathy evaluation in that the deprivation entailed by death is the non-existence of goods which might have been, but are not reidentifiability related to P.

The deprivation for person P entailed by P's death is the absence of goods that would have had reidentifiability relations with P, the formerly living person. Any deprivation evil for a person consists in the non-existence of some good which would have been reidentifiability related to that person. Any deprivation is bad as the absence of something worthwhile. A person's death—not considering its other entailments or effects—is bad as the absence of goods which would have been reidentifiability related to that person. This *is* the intrinsic sympathy evaluation.

The sense of the issue, "*Who* is the subject of the sympathy evaluation?" amounts to the following:

What is the evil? The absence of goods.

Which goods? Those which might have been reidentifiability related to P. This is the intrinsic sympathy evaluation.

Further, *why* do P (in prospect) and P's loving ones care so much about this absence of these goods? These goods would have been part of a series with which P and P's loving ones would have had mutual influence, sympathy and detailed knowledge.

Beyond these questions and answers, I believe that "Who is the subject of the sympathy evaluation?" is a senseless question. Neither the sympathy evaluation nor grief depend upon an answer to a senseless question.

Whether the concern that P's loving ones have for these lost goods justifies grief responses, such as sorrow and inhibition, is a consideration relevant to the affect or responses not the evaluation. But if we believed that a further fact existed, perhaps a pale, ghostly substratum of deprivation evil, which might be needed to justify grief, we would be stuck trying to answer a senseless question.

Grievers might mistakenly imagine that death itself—not the prospect of death—harmed their loved one when still alive, or that the subject of the intrinsic sympathy evaluation is a ghostly extension of the dead person. These misleading pictures might exacerbate grief, but they might also be useful in that through them we appreciate the importance of the intrinsic sympathy evaluation.

Consider the following possible alternative lives (P series) and suppose that each life contains goods as long as the life lasts:

P_1 has a beginning but no end.
P_2 lasts one hundred years.
P_3 lasts seventy years.

Series P_2 is better than series P_3, and series P_1 is infinitely better than either.

We might ask, "Better for whom?" Better for P_2 at one year old than P_3 at one year old? No, these are equally good.

Better for P_2 at ninety-nine years than P_3 at sixty-nine years. No, they are equally good.

Better for P_2 at ninety-nine years than P_3 at seventy-one years? No, because there is no P_3 at seventy-one years.

The intrinsic sympathy evaluation does not depend upon answering the question "Better for whom?" though it is expressed as "P's death is bad for P." The reason we are tempted to ask "Better for whom?" is that we wish to explain the personal concern directed toward this loss.

That the actual series was P_3 rather than P_1 or P_2 entails that there is a better conceivable alternative than the actual one. This is the intrinsic sympathy evaluation.

It is conceivable that the P series had been P_2 rather than P_3. However, in Chapter Seven it was not definitely shown that it is conceivable that the P series had been P_1 (infinite) rather than any finite series.

Are grief responses justified because there are better conceivable series than the actual one?

Adding to the discussion of this chapter, a consoler might object that it is not an evil that an actual series is shorter than a conceivable series, for otherwise it would be an evil that an actual P series was zero, that is, that it would be an evil that some person was never born. But that's absurd. Therefore, it is not an evil that an actual series is shorter than a conceivable series.

The reply is that it is not absurd that it is an evil that some person was never born. This only *appears* absurd on the following *false* assumptions:

(1) Deprivation evils are just like diametric ones. But only diametric evils "cancel out" diametric goods (see Chapter Six). Therefore, even an infinite deprivation evil does not cancel out a finite diametric good (for example, it can be better to be born and die than never to have been born at all).

(2) Deprivation evils are indistinguishable from fictitious evils. But fictitious evils are based on false statements whereas statements of the forms "P is dead" and "P was never born" can be true.

An example of a fictitious deprivation evil would be "P is blind" said of a sighted person. An example of a fictitious diametric evil would be "My third eye is sore from reading this."

Although someone never having been born might be an evil, grief over this loss is more problematic than grief over a person's death because we cannot have detailed knowledge about a life that never began. Mutual influence or sympathy is not possible in this case.

Holding that no great difference exists between death and continued existence is a great exaggeration since, even on a reductionist analysis, many differences exist between them. The differences are crucial to the loving ones of the dead person. Most importantly, though there will be others who resemble the dead person, others with similar memories, and others with similar personalities, the survivors will not have detailed knowledge of these other persons. No mutual influence or sympathy will exist between them.

With respect to the ego evaluation, since the loving ones change, the evils entailed or produced by the loved one's death will likely decrease over time.

To learn that the evil will be decreased due to drastic changes that will occur in the griever is not comforting to the griever because this results in decreased mutual understanding between the loving one's present and future "selves," and less influence of the present self over the future self. Understanding and influence are perhaps the primary factors in determining the special concern people have for particular individuals—even the special concern we have for ourselves.

Study Questions

(1) This chapter discussed many characteristics about people which change. In addition to these changing characteristics, is there a "changeless core" within each person? Why or why not? What difference would it make were there some changeless core?

(2) Which is worse: death in which a changeless core ceased to exist, or death which ends a constantly changing person? Please explain.

(3) Which would you most miss about the deaths of loved ones? Their physical appearance? Memories? Habits? Explain.
  - If you had the choice, which would you prefer: that after your death your body were revived but with different memories, or that your memories survived in a different body. Explain your choice.

(4) Even without sudden and drastic changes such as those that occur to a survivor upon the death of a loved one, how do you change over a lifetime such that you lose influence or mutual understanding between yourself at different times?
  - How would your life have to be different to *retain* this influence and mutual understanding?
  - Is it good to lose this influence and mutual understanding? Explain.

(5) According to Buddhism, desire and impermanence are two main sources of suffering.
  - How do desire and impermanence separately *and* combined weaken influence and mutual understanding between oneself at different times?

(6) Can you minimize fear of death by having interests in things which will survive your death? Explain.

Eleven

IS PRESENT EXISTENCE BETTER THAN PAST EXISTENCE?

Dreams and Time

Jeff and Phil continued the conversation though Connie excused herself from the table.

"I don't want to miss anything important while I'm gone!" Connie chided them.

"How could you? We wouldn't consider saying anything important without you present!" Phil kidded.

"That I know! I was concerned that I would miss dessert!" Connie retorted.

"We won't order without you," reassured Phil.

Billy Joel advised "Tell Her about It" as Phil said to Jeff, "Earlier you said something about your dreams. . . ."

Jeff stated, "Yes, I have disturbing dreams."

"What are they?"

Jeff answered, "Every night, or so it seems, I dream about mom."

Phil said, "That doesn't sound surprising. I bet if Connie were here she'd tell you she had a lot of dreams about her parents after their deaths."

Jeff said, "In some ways these dreams are similar to ones I had soon after my dad died. I would dream that he had been restored to life either by some experimental medical technique or by an outright miracle. In other dreams he was alive but another loved one was dead. In my recent dreams about my mom she has either been brought back to life or else saved while on the brink of death; in some dreams she only has a reprieve of a month or two."

Phil questioned, "In these dreams, do you get to tell her you love her?"

"Yes. And hug her and cry with her and pamper her and respect her for the time which remains to her," Jeff answered.

"Sounds like wish fulfillment dreams. First, you wish she were alive, and second, you wish to express your love to her," Phil suggested.

Jeff asked, "Is it wish fulfillment also that, in some dreams, her recovery is only temporary?"

Phil scolded, "What? No! No! The reason her recovery is only temporary is because reality intrudes upon the dream. Or perhaps the dream is like the bargaining phase of preparatory grief, that is, grief before the death. Your wishes are bargaining with reality, so to speak. Really, you're being too hard on yourself!"

Jeff said, "You are right that my dreams are modified by an intrusion of reality. Perhaps this does explain why her recovery is sometimes only temporary. I'll give you an example of reality intruding into my dreams. In part I dream about her so much simply because, since her death, I think about her so much. But at some point in the dream I remember that she is dead, or had died, and so I have to 'rationalize' the dream; I have to make sense of her being in it. So some vague, *post hoc* explanation is given. Somehow she recovered. Sometimes while I do not deny remembering that she came near death, I do deny that she died. Or I accept the memory of her death, but deny the consequence that she couldn't be alive afterwards."

Phil observed, "It's interesting that there is an 'imperative' in these dreams to try to make them correspond, as much as possible, to reality. Again, that's because these dreams are your attempt to fill a very real absence. Also interesting are the strategies which you use, or the strategies which you don't use, to reconcile the dream with the intrusive reality. For instance, why not reconcile your mother's being alive in the dream with her death which intrudes by 'saying' that the events dreamed happened *before* her death? Granted, the dream is after her death, but why must the dreamed events be regarded as occurring after death? One explanation would be that the dream is meant to fulfill the wish that your mom is *still* alive. This wish eliminates any reconciliation strategy placing the dreamed events before her death."

Jeff said, "It's ironic that our conversation has taken this direction. Because I had a dream which tinkered around with time and was flagrantly fantastic. And while the inspiration for this dream was my grief over mom, the protagonist of the dream was Bertrand Russell!"

Phil laughed.

Jeff related the dream as "Twist and Shout," penned by Bert Berns and performed by the Isley Brothers, entertained the diners. "Before going to bed I indulged in some light reading- a biography of Russell. When I went to sleep I dreamt that Russell was scheduled to receive an award a few months 'down the road.' However, because of conflicting obligations, he knew ahead of time that he would be unable to attend the award ceremony. So, he used a time machine in order that he could be at the award ceremony after all. Of course he returned in the time machine to the day in which he began his time travel. Unfortunately, before the night of the award ceremony he died. However, since he had already traveled to the ceremony in the time machine, he was at the ceremony. Of course, he did not know that he had died in the meantime. I was in the audience, and so was a woman who despised Russell's views. She walked onto the stage, went right up to Russell and cruelly and triumphantly told him of his death. Distraught, I hurried to him, threw my arms around him, and crying, told him I loved him."

"Wow! That was some dream!" Phil said. "You are certainly right that your mom's death was the inspiration for this dream. Ironically, her absence from this dream confirms that your dreams in which your mom is present have a wish fulfillment function. You wish to tell your mom you love her.

Your dream about Russell retains the emotional ending of your dreams about your mom."

Theories of Time

Phil paused, his eyes rolled up in thought, and then excitedly, he spoke, "Perhaps consolations can be found in an understanding of time. When discussing consolations based on an understanding of personal identity we had the advantage that we are both reductionists. But, as neither one of us has a definite opinion on the proper analysis of 'time,' rather than offer consolations based on a single, comprehensive view, I shall offer different consolations based on a couple different analyses of 'time.'"

"Let's get started."

The Monkees warned, "Look Out (Here Comes Tomorrow)."

"The two theories of time which we find most plausible are the so-called A and B theories.[1] According to A-theory, whether an event or thing is past, present or future makes a very great difference to its 'reality'; the past and future are in some sense 'less real' than the present. Only present events exist. Not simply in the trivial sense that only present events exist in the present, but that only present events exist in a tenseless use of 'to exist.' The past is 'gone;' it's less real. Future, present and past are properties which events have, but these properties change. According to A-theory, events have the property of being in the future until they become present, and after which they have the property of being past. In other words, each event is, at different times, past, present and future; and future events become present, and afterwards past. We might say that, on A-theory, the set of past events 'grows' as the set of future events 'diminishes.' And as time passes existence is, so to speak, a property passed along from one moment to the next. As the future becomes present it acquires existence and loses it as it becomes past. Existence accompanies being present and 'moves along' with it.

Phil continued, "B-theory differs from A-theory in a couple ways. B-theory states that the only *necessary* difference between a thing or event's being past, present or future are the relations 'earlier than,' 'later than' and 'simultaneous with.' In other words, 'X is past' means only 'X is earlier than this moment—this thought, this utterance.' 'X is future' means only 'X is later than this moment—this thought, this utterance' and 'X is present' means only 'X is simultaneous with this moment—thought, utterance.' Alternatively, X is named, for example by a date—hour, minute and second. According to this theory, tenses—past, present and future—are just relations between earlier and later events. Events don't become present then pass into the past. The future is just any event later than some reference point; the past is just any event earlier than some reference point. And every moment is its own reference point. Whereas on A-theory there's only one reference point- *the* present, but the reference point is constantly moving on to the next later moment, and with it, existence.

"These relations, 'earlier than,' 'later than' and 'simultaneous with' are the 'order' of events which are intrinsically indistinguishable as regards their being past, present and future.

Phil continued, "Again, according to B-theory, calling some event either past, present or future is not stating a changing or unchanging property of the event. Similarly, with regard to space, saying that something is to the left or the right does not tell us anything intrinsic about the thing, but only a spatial relation it has to something else. In sum, on B-theory, being past is intrinsically no different from being present or being future. The past or future is not 'less real' than the present. Instead of an intrinsic difference between tenses, events are just ordered according to certain relations. All events, past, present, or future, are equally real. Existence does not belong to the present anymore than to the past or future. In fact we could say that B-theory does away with *the* present. *Each* moment has things simultaneous with each other.

"Finally, let's not omit an extreme version of A-theory, or what might be regarded as such, which infers from the claim that only present events exist, in a tenseless use of 'to exist,' that true or meaningful statements can only be about the present. Most A-theorists think that true statements can be made about past and future events; though fewer say this about the future. However, some A-theorists say that no statements about either the past or future are true because the past and future do not exist and so are 'like' fictions. This *extreme* A-theory we might call the 'M-theory' for its stress on the *moment* or present.

"I have the healthy suspicion that all these theories try to press philosophical analysis further than it can go. For one thing, it seems as though there's no empirical difference between A- and B-theories. Any fact of our experience of time can be described by using either theory," Jeff said.

Phil agreed, "It's a very problematic area. Anyway, we should see whether these theories have any implications for the griever's evaluations, or grief in general. We should look at the A-, B- and M- theories. I'd like to begin with B-theory and determine whether it provides any comfort."

"Okay, go on."

First B-theory Consolation

"According to B-theory, 'A person—I'll call *P*—is mortal' means 'All events of *P*'s life are earlier than some non-*P* events' and 'P is dead' means 'All *P* events are earlier than at least this moment and all later moments.' Or we can remove the 'this,' by replacing it with a date, and say, in this instance, all events of your mom's life, are earlier than at least 30 August 2004 and all later moments. On the other hand, we are alive. That is, we exist on 30 August 2004. Unfortunately, your mom does not. But on B-theory, the only difference between us and your mom is that we exist *later* than your mom. We exist now, but according to B-theory, the present does not exist—in a tenseless use of 'to exist'—*anymore* than the past. On B-theory 'P exists' means that P exists at some time, but not necessarily now. You and I exist now, but your mom exists in the past. We *all* exist; she earlier, we later.

"In contrast, according to A-theory, existence belongs only to the present. So, on A-theory, there is a big difference between us, on the one hand, and your mom, on the other. Indeed, short of the difference introduced by M-theory, it would seem that there is no greater difference than that between present things, which alone exist, and past and future things, which do not exist.

"Thus, A-theory comparatively maximizes the difference between 'being dead' and 'being alive,' whereas B-theory comparatively minimizes that difference. We might conclude that, on B-theory, death is a less terrible evil than on A-theory."

Jeff said, "Assuming that analysis of this kind has sense, I agree that death seems less terrible on B-theory than it does on A-theory. Your claim that the difference between 'having tenseless existence' on B-theory and 'having *had* tenseless existence' on A-theory is an extremely important difference requires scrutiny, but I'm frankly not sure what to say about it.

"Anyway, I am suspicious whether any satisfaction deriving from a B-analysis does not equivocate on tensed and tenseless senses of 'to exist.' As you say, on B-theory my mom exists, in the past. But as 'exists' is usually used in the present tense, rather than tenselessly, that is, as designating present or simultaneous events, perhaps the B-theory claim that my mom exists (tenselessly) is confused with 'My mom exists—present tense.' In other words, B-theory might *sound comforting*.

"In general, one cannot estimate the rationality of a consolation by thinking it to oneself and detecting a feeling of comfort. It is easy to alter feeling by stating the same thing in different words. For example, the words 'She is dead,' under my present circumstances, make me feel sick, whereas 'There are no relata reidentifiable as her' is so unfamiliar as to have little or no effect. Yet these mean the same thing. You see, it is easy to manipulate affect by stating the same thing in different words or different things with the same words. Therefore, we had better explore B-theory's consolation further, or else we risk a comforting equivocation with 'exists.'

"Contrary to your consolations, I have a conviction that the griever's evaluations need not be based on any conceptual confusion. Therefore, when confronted by any theories of time, the same in all their empirical entailments, as we believe the A- and B-theories to be, I suspect that the choice between them has no bearing on the rationality of my grief.[2] Therefore, if one theory seems to make death less terrible, I suspect an equivocation in the drawing of this conclusion."

Phil said, "I join you in puzzlement. We have two theories seemingly acknowledging the same empirical facts, yet seeming to lead to different evaluations. If the value of things is something we experience, that is, empirical, how can two theories empirically the same make a difference?"[3]

Phil continued, "You're unsure whether the conclusion that B-theory 'death' is less terrible than A-theory 'death' is rational or rests on an equivocation between tensed and tenseless senses of 'to exist' because you and I are unsure whether the key difference between these theories has evaluative significance. The key difference is that B-theory denies that existence is a property only of present events. To put it another way, an A-theorist denies that past or future things exist, whereas this claim lacks sense, according to a B-theorist. For an A-theorist, a thing loses existence by becoming past. This is the relevant key difference between A- and B-theories. Therefore, the question is 'Is it bad losing existence?'"

Jeff exclaimed, "It would seem that nothing could be worse! But we must examine this more carefully."

The Spiral Staircase's optimistic "More Today than Yesterday" cheerfully played as Phil and Jeff continued.

Jeff said, "A B-theorist wouldn't allow the question 'Is it bad losing existence?' since a B-theorist denies sense to 'losing existence.' An A-theorist might allow the question. I think an A-theorist would be agreeable to the claim that it is bad for a good to lose its existence. If this were an entailment of A-theory, A-theory 'death' would seem to be worse than B-theory 'death.'"

Phil said, "Frankly, I can think of no meaning for 'It is bad for a good to lose its existence' which would be *peculiar* to A-theory. What could it mean? Does it mean that it is bad that a good is temporary, that is, finite? But this can be expressed in B-theory. On either theory a life of seventy years is just that-seventy years long."

Jeff added, "Yes, a life on B-theory is not longer than a life on A-theory; the temptation to think that a B-theory life is longer comes from confusing tenseless and tensed 'existence.' It creates a misleading image of my mom existing at all times but in something like suspended animation."

"Does 'It is bad for a good to lose its existence' mean that a good thing *becomes* bad by becoming past? And what would that mean? It sounds as though it would wreak havoc with our evaluations and sensible advice. For that sounds like every temporary good automatically becomes a bad once past. Sounds like one step backward for every step forward.

"Does 'It is bad for a good to lose its existence' mean that a good becomes *less* good, or becomes neither good nor evil, when it becomes past? But what do either of these mean? A vivid thing does not become a faded thing when it becomes past, although our awareness of it does fade. A green thing doesn't become red or gray or transparent when it no longer exists. So, how is it that a thing loses its goodness, or becomes less good, when it is past? How is a thing intrinsically better present rather than past?

"If it means that no true evaluation can be made of a past thing, that the good thing is a fiction once it's past, then this brings us to M-theory."

"Can you give any meaning to 'It is bad for a good to lose its existence' which would be unique to A-theory?" Phil asked.

"I cannot," Jeff said.

Phil said, "We have not been able to articulate a difference between the value of A-theory 'death' and the value of B-theory 'death.' This result reassures me. I was concerned that the consolations which I shall give based on B-theory would not comfort you, since neither one of us is convinced that B-theory is more likely than A-theory.

"In sum, according to B-theory, death does not entail that the person hasn't any existence. And while death does entail this, according to A-theory, we've been unable to understand any additional evil supposedly entailed by this."

Jeff said, "Therefore, I need an argument that death is not a terrible evil if a dead person has B-theory existence."

Randy Newman's song, "Short People" began as Phil said, "B-theorists admit that death entails that a person's life is temporally finite. . . ."

Jeff interjected, "Therefore, death is still a terrible evil. Everything we've agreed to thus far is still true. Death is an extensive, perhaps infinite, deprivation evil. Although the dead are not deprived of B-theory existence, they are deprived of existence beyond a particular date. They are as much deprived of later goods as they are on A-theory."

Phil conceded, "I agree. But since a dead person exists tenselessly at some time, which is no less than the living, does it make sense to be *horrified* by death? Does it make sense to dread its prospect, or react to it with grief?"

Jeff observed, "This is now a response consolation. You agree that death entails extensive deprivation evil. This is sufficient for the sympathy evaluation.

"What is it about B-theory that makes you think it is irrational to respond with dread or grief to temporal finitude?"

Second B-Theory Consolation

Phil answered, "Because, on B-theory, temporal finitude is much like spatial finitude, and we would agree that it is irrational to be horrified by our spatial finitude, that we exist in only part of space."

Jeff said, "I agree that it would be irrational to be greatly upset, or usually, even mildly upset, about spatial finitude. But in what way is temporal finitude, on B-theory, like spatial finitude?"

Phil said, "B-theory 'time' is much more like space than is A-theory 'time.' Just as space is an ordering of points, time is just an ordering of moments, on B-theory. Just as there are no necessary, intrinsic differences between points, there are no necessary, intrinsic differences between moments, on B-theory. No points of space exist more than other points. Likewise, no moments exist more than any others, on B-theory. It is not necessarily better existing now, that is, 30 August 2004 than existing at the turn of the century. Just as it is not necessarily worse existing in one place rather than another, it is not necessarily worse being in the past than in the present or future, on B-theory.

"So, just as it would be irrational to be horrified by the fact that we exist only in some places, it would be irrational to be horrified by the fact that we exist only at some times."

Jeff said, "Hold it. I can think of two possible meanings of 'We exist only in some places,' and in neither sense does our attitude toward our own spatial finitude create problems for the rationality of grief. 'We are spatially finite' or 'We exist only in some places' means either that our bodies are finitely big, or that we can travel to only a finite number of places."

Jeff continued, "The fact that we are of finite size is certainly not horrible! First, the mere fact that we are finite in size does not deprive humans of anything. Of course, our *particular* size produces, and maybe even entails some deprivations, but I'll get to that in a minute. Were it conceivable that there were a being infinite in size, it would not be us! The argument that death is not dreadful because limited size is not dreadful is like your argument that death is not dreadful because prenatal non-existence is not. Both prenatal non-existence and limited size are necessary for the type of beings which we are. And even if temporal finitude at both ends were necessary for us, as you think, it is a conceivably much greater finitude. Whereas, for most usual purposes, the particular sizes which we are suit us fine. I admit, however, that a person's particular size causes or entails a finite amount of deprivation. I also admit that some person's particular size causes greater deprivation for that person than the particular size of some other persons causes them...."

"Hey! No short people remarks!" Phil objected.

Jeff smiled, then continued, "But these deprivations are finite. Second, it is only a contingent fact that most people would be better off if they were larger. If it weren't for social prejudice, and the occasional need for additional strength, virtually everyone's size would be adequate. I have no complaints about size, either on my own or my mom's behalf.... Although, come to think of it, her grandson teased her when he finally grew taller than she was. In contrast, temporal finitude entails extensive, perhaps infinite deprivations."

"Spoken like a six-footer. Have you ever been unable to see in a crowd? That's a deprivation," Phil said.

Jeff said, "But at least you still exist. You can do other worthwhile things that do not require any great stature or great size in any respect."

Phil laughed.

Jeff continued, "This is the third difference between a particular temporal finitude and a particular size. A dead person *necessarily* has *no* more goods. It is not merely that a dead person is deprived of this or that good. The dead person is deprived of all goods."

Phil conceded, "Yes, you're right. There is at least one important difference between living fifty years and being five feet tall which favors the latter."

Jeff went on to his next point. "The restrictions on our mobility do involve us in extensive deprivation. Wouldn't it be wonderful to travel throughout the universe, or even see the world? Of course, world travel is possible for some of us, like our absent friend."

Phil said, "She's not seeing much of the world right now!"

Jeff continued, "However, there are still great differences between temporal finitude and limited mobility. If we lived longer, then most of us could experience more places. In other words, we're limited in traveling not just because of gravity and because we're busy working and because we have limited budgets, but because we don't live long enough.

"And similarly to my remark concerning our limited size: a life can be worthwhile even with limited mobility. Even if stuck in Königsberg! But death entails an unalterable deprivation.

"However short you are, or however earthbound, you can still study the stars," Jeff concluded.

Phil said, "Very dramatic. Like the end of *The Incredible Shrinking Man*. Though the film-maker had a more religious meaning in mind, the tiny protagonist realizes his worth when he looks at the night sky.

"I get your point. Spatial finitude, of either sort, does not entail that a person's goods are finite. Spatial finitude might entail, or at least cause, that a person is incapable of this or that particular good. But spatial finitude does not entail, and without temporal finitude, would not cause, that life's goods are finite," Phil said.

"Exactly!" Jeff exclaimed. "In short, temporal finitude *as such* is an evil for us, while the mere fact of spatial finitude is not an evil for us at all. And further, one's particular temporal finitude is a much greater evil than one's particular spatial finitude. Therefore, I think it might be rational to have different feelings toward these. Besides, your sensitivity about your height, although partly feigned, reveals that you and others are not completely content with your particular spatial finitude either!"

Phil grinned.

Our "Bias" Toward the "Present"

Jeff resumed, "Earlier, we could not find a meaning, unique to A-theory, for 'It is bad for a good thing to lose existence,' or as we might put it, 'It is better for a good to be present than past.' However, while I cannot articulate this idea, I still have the inkling that it is correct. In fact, I think that a person's choices make more sense, if it is the case that 'It is better for a good to be present than past.' You've used B-theory to try to comfort in part by claiming that there is no intrinsic difference between a good's being present and its being past. But I wonder whether a present good on B-theory is less good than a present good on A-theory. If this were so, B-theory would console one for a good's being past only by denying the added value that A-theory might allow present goods. In that case, B-theory would entail that life is less good. And this is not comforting.

"I would argue that present goods are intrinsically better than past ones, as A-theory might allow. This claim is not the triviality that present goods are better *at present* than past goods. That is, it is trivial that only a present good can make the present good. Rather, the claim is that present goods are tenselessly better than past ones; or, everything else being equal, it is tenselessly better that a good is present than that it is past.

"My argument for this claim is simply based on an analysis of our actual preferences. Consider the following examples: you wish to play a particular song, one you've heard a hundred times before; or perhaps you want to eat a dish you've eaten a thousand times already; or perhaps you wish to make love to a long familiar partner. We might suppose that, in none of these cases it is likely that the experience will be different in kind from many previous experiences, for example, listening to this song, eating this dish, or making love with this partner. Now, let's compare possible reasons on A-theory which one might have for fulfilling these wishes with possible reasons on B-theory which one might have for fulfilling these wishes."

Phil said, "Assuming that all these experiences are good, then both A- and B-theories might regard these wishes as justified. On either theory, by having these good experiences one would increase the quantity of one's good experiences. This would be the case on either theory, whether or not these experiences were very similar to many previous experiences.

"In addition, if these experiences satisfy a desire which one has difficulty controlling, such as lust or craving, and if it would be bad to continue in a state of unsatisfied desire, then one would decrease one's bad experiences, by satisfying these desires, again on either temporal theory."

Jeff said, "True, either theory could allow either of these reasons for wanting to repeat these experiences. But A-theory provides a *further* reason which B-theory cannot. Why repeat an experience when another instance will reveal nothing new—as you asked when we discussed character fixity? A-theory can answer that all other experiences of these kinds are past. Only if one experiences it now will there be a present experience of that kind. If, as A-theory might allow, everything else being equal, present goods are better than past ones, then one has an additional reason to repeat the experience."

Phil responded, "B-theory can supply an additional reason as well. Even on B-theory, each moment is numerically distinct from every other, thus each moment is unique. Therefore, each moment offers a unique reason for repeating the experience at that moment. At 9:40 p.m. on 30 August 2004 the A-theorist says 'I want to repeat the experience now because no other instances of this kind of experience are present,' but a B-theorist can say 'I want to repeat the experience at 9:40 p.m. on 30 August 2004 because no other experiences of this kind are at 9:40 p.m. on 30 August 2004.' Any reason expressed using tense can be expressed with a date."

Jeff replied, "I agree that the uniqueness of moments can be expressed in either theory. But what kind of *reason* is 'No other experiences of this kind are at time X?' Why, on B-theory, should it matter that you have the experience at this unique time? A-theory might explain that one should repeat the experience at the present time because present goods are better than past ones because only present ones exist. On A-theory, the present is very special, and that is why it is worth repeating a good experience.

"In sum, A-theory helps to account for our choices."

Phil objected, "Maybe so. But it is help which we don't need. As we've agreed, with or without this extra justification, there are already two good reasons for wishing to repeat experiences of these kinds. Thus, our choices can be explained without resorting to this idea which we have not articulated, that a good loses goodness by being past.

"In addition to the above justifications, allowable by both theories, for repeating an experience in the present, there is the following important reason, again explicable on either theory. Despite the lack of necessary, intrinsic differences between past, present and future acknowledged by B-theorists, they could allow that past, that is, earlier, events cannot be altered. Therefore, there can be no deliberation concerning past events. Deliberation can only be about the future.

"Furthermore, deliberation is usually most effective concerning proximate future events. This is true for several reasons. First, remote events are usually more susceptible to alteration by unanticipated factors. Second, a necessary condition for effective deliberation concerning remote events is control over and effective deliberation concerning more proximate events. For it is only through proximate events that remote events can be controlled.

"Therefore, it might be efficient for nature to give us a preference for the *immediate* future, even though it often spells trouble when people sacrifice long term interests for short term benefits. A preference for the immediate future, or less precisely, the 'present,' maximizes the amount of goods which exist. I should explain that in all your examples, the person was deliberating concerning the immediate future, loosely referred to as the 'present.'

"This preference for present, or rather, immediate future goods can explain one's desire to repeat a good experience, in addition to the other explanations offered, without resorting to necessary, intrinsic differences between events differing in tense. We do have preference for present goods, or immediate future ones. But this can be explained on either theory. Therefore, your analysis of our choices does not reveal a value explicable only by A-theory. A-theory might postulate a value to the present which could provide a reason additional to all reasons available to a B-theorist, but this does not show that such a value is real. That is, every good reason a B-theorist can come up with is also available to the A-theorist. And one reason more is available to the latter. But this does not show that such a reason is true."

Jeff agreed, "It has not been shown that it is necessarily better to exist at present rather than at 9:44 p.m., 30 August 2004. On the other hand, unfortunately, B-theory has still not shown anything irrational about grief."

Interlude on M-theory and Eternity

The Shirelles' pessimistic "A Thing of the Past" concluded and the Beatles' "She Said She Said" began playing, as an undaunted, because curious, Phil suggested, "Let's look at M-theory."

"Okay . . ." conceded Jeff, "although neither of us is much attracted to the theory."

Phil continued, "According to M-theory, true statements can only be made about that which exists, and therefore, true statements can only be made about the present. For, M-theory agrees with A-theory in claiming that only the present exists.

"M-theory would seem to be a series of contradictory positions. For instance, 'There can only be true statements about now,' and a moment later, 'There can only be true statements about *now*.' And these statements refer to different moments. Of course, this would make a bad argument against M-theory because an M-theorist would deny the claim that there were or will be other 'present' moments. That is, an M-theorist would deny the existence of any other moment from which one could deny the existence of the moment which an M-theorist presently affirms."

Jeff asked, "According to M-theory, it's not true that my mom ever lived? So, I'm grieving over a fiction? Is that a consolation? But it was a good fiction, and that's why I've been grieving concerning it. Therefore, perhaps I should grieve because this good thing is only a fiction.

"I don't think even you, my ardent consoler, wish to offer this consolation."

Phil said, "No, I don't. I am not attracted by any M-theory consolation, although I have no comment on your objection to it that you would have reason to grieve if you found out your memories were false. I object to M-theory because if it were true deliberation would be impossible, since deliberation requires true statements about the future, doesn't it? So, for example, you would be unable to deliberate about whether or not you should grieve."

Jeff added, "Since grief is a process, or series of states, any theory denying duration, which M-theory seems to do, would have to deny the existence of grief. My mistake would not be grieving, but thinking that I am."

The Grass Roots' "Let's Live for Today" ended and the Byrds sang, "Turn! Turn! Turn!" as Jeff continued, "Similar problems attend the consolations that the temporal is not real—including the present—, or that the temporal does not matter, that is, that there are no true *evaluations* about the temporal. A consolation on this theory would be that there exists something 'outside of time'—something neither past, present, nor future; also, this atemporal or timeless thing is all that's real or that matters. Sometimes religious discourse sounds like this. But if the temporal does not exist, then it is not the case that I am grieving, and it could not be the case that I, a temporal being, exist with or without grief. And if the temporal exists but is neither good nor evil, then my grief is neither good nor evil. The griever's evaluations would be false, but nevertheless, it wouldn't be bad for me to grieve."

Phil said, "Well, *one* idea, which *is* extreme, is that the temporal is neither good nor evil, and that would entail that neither life nor grief are either good or evil; but *another* idea, less extreme, is that temporal things when present or future are good or evil, but *become* neither good nor evil as they become past. Some people ask, 'Why pursue life's goods, whether pleasure or achievement, because all those goods will be past someday?' This is the idea which we've discussed a couple times, that a thing loses its intrinsic value."

"About which we are dubious," Jeff reminded.

"Yes," Phil continued, "the idea that temporal things have intrinsic value but lose it as the thing becomes past does *not* have the implication which you impute to the idea that the temporal is neither good nor bad. According to the less extreme idea, that the present or future has intrinsic value, grief might be bad when it is present or future. Therefore, if a person deliberates about whether to discourage grief, his own or another's, the less extreme idea does not rule out considerations of grief's intrinsic value. According to the less extreme view, grief becomes indifferent only when past, and hence beyond the scope of deliberation."

Jeff reflected then said, "Of course the duration of a good or an evil is one factor in determining its importance, that is, the longer a good the better, but it does not follow that a good or evil must be eternal for it to have any importance, contrary to the extreme view."

Phil added, "I'm not sure whether anyone sincerely offers the extreme view that temporal things have no value. I know that people will denigrate the importance of the temporal, and sometimes in extreme terms. But I wonder whether they sincerely mean that the temporal has *no* value, or only that each temporal thing has a value infinitely less than the eternal."

Then Phil muttered, "Of course, unless you believed in the eternal, I do not see how these considerations could console. For that matter, I'm not even sure you could be consoled if you believed in the eternal."

Jeff said, "If the genuinely valuable was eternal, I would not be comforted by its value, since my mom and I are temporal.

Impure A-Theory Consolation

Phil began, "I have one more rough idea from A-theory which might be consoling. But it's a *very* rough idea."

Jeff encouraged, "That's never stopped either one of us!"

Phil said, "I have not endorsed the idea that a thing loses its value when it becomes past. For I've been concerned that you would use it to support the sympathy evaluation, on the ground that the idea that a past thing loses its value entails that death not only deprives a person of future goods, but it also deprives them of the full value once possessed by the goods enjoyed during life."

"You *should* be concerned that I might think this," Jeff warned.

Phil resumed, "But even if it were true that the goods of life became intrinsically less good as they became past, this result would not be due to death, but to time itself. Even the past goods of the *living* would lose their intrinsic value, according to this theory. Of course, the past goods of the living are more likely to be remembered, but that only increases their *consequential* value; it does not 'revitalize' their intrinsic value, supposedly lost or dwindled."

Jeff said, "It's true that, according to this theory, it is time, not death, which has this effect on intrinsic value. But this is not comforting. This theory of past value is dreary, because it adds sadness over time to my sadness over death.

"But in addition, according to such a theory of lost or dwindling past value, the difference between the living and the dead goes beyond the fact which you've noted, that, as the living can recall their own past goods, their goods retain a greater consequential value, everything else being equal. For, if it is an evil that time makes a past thing's intrinsic value lessen, then the living have the advantage that at least some goods of their life, their future goods, have not yet been deprived of their full value.

"Of course, that is just a temporary advantage since the living are mortal, too. But it is still an advantage."

Phil said, "But there is no conceivable alternative for us than this effect of time, assuming that this theory is true. Therefore, it would not be an evil for us that time deprives a thing of its value when it becomes past."

Phil said, "I still haven't gotten around to the rough consolation which I promised, based on this idea that the past has less intrinsic value simply because it is past."

"Go ahead."

"A-theories have been distinguished into 'pure' and 'impure.' Pure A-theory recognizes fewer temporal distinctions than the impure version. On the one hand, according to 'impure' A-theory, not only do future events become past, future events become *less* future and past events *more* past. Past events *recede*, while future events *approach*. In other words, at one time an event has the property of being *distantly* future, at a later time it has the property of being the *near* future, then it has the property of being present, then the property of being *recently* past and then *remotely* past. In fact, by specifying precisely how future or past the event is we get even more specific properties of events. For instance, an event when ten hours from the present has the property of ten hours futurity."

Jeff said, "Yes. On the other hand, pure A-theory 'lumps' together all future events, and 'lumps' together all past events. That is, though some future events are earlier or later than others, and some past events are earlier or later than others, according to pure A-theory, all future events are indistinguishable from each other with respect to their property of futurity and all past events are indistinguishable from each other with respect to their property of pastness."

Phil said, "Right. The contrast between the two theories is that, on the impure version, futurity and pastness are properties which admit of degrees, whereas on the pure version, futurity and pastness are properties not admitting of degrees.

"As we've observed, grief usually lessens over time. According to impure A-theory, a past thing becomes more and more past. This idea, together with the idea that things lose intrinsic value with their pastness, entails that value is gradually lost, or 'fades.' Therefore, there would be two phenomena varying proportionately: grief lessening and value fading.

"This proportionate variation suggests to me that value fading might justify grief lessening. That something might justify grief but also justify its lessening over time is an intriguing idea, since most conventional views of grief seem to approve of grief, but only as a temporary thing," Phil said.

Jeff inquired, "You're intrigued because you think you've found a correlation which might justify conventional thinking. But how could the supposed fading value of receding goods justify a supposedly proportionate decrease in grief?"

Phil answered, "If the goods which your mom enjoyed became less and less intrinsically good, then the loss of these becomes less and less evil."

Jeff exclaimed, "Even if those goods somehow became less good, as this theory states, it would not follow that the deprivation due to death is less. For death did not deprive her of these fading goods, but of the goods she would have enjoyed had she continued to live. This deprivation is ever ongoing. Were she immortal, she would enjoy present and future goods. Her death has not deprived her merely of goods which would be past and fading anyhow. And these goods, which she would have enjoyed were she immortal, are not lessened by the supposed fact that the goods, which she did enjoy during her life are all fading. The goods which she is presently missing are as valuable as the goods she enjoyed while she lived before their value began fading. Therefore, her deprivation is not decreased by any supposed fading of the goods she once enjoyed."

Phil asked, "But isn't it true that each good which she would have enjoyed had she lived is itself temporary?"

"Yes."

Phil asked, "So, each of these would pass?"

"Yes."

Phil asked, "So, according to the view we are considering, each good which she would have enjoyed would have decreased in intrinsic value anyway. Right?"

"Yes."

Phil concluded, "Therefore, the view that past values decrease entails that the dead person's deprivation becomes less and less."

Jeff objected, "This does not follow. As the deprivation entailed by death is infinite, no matter how remote her death becomes, it will always be the case that, were she alive, she would have enjoyed some good. Time might make *each* good fade, but the series itself, being endless, will always supply 'fresh,' 'unfaded' goods. As one good faded, another would have 'blossomed.' Therefore, while her deprivation of this or that particular good might be lessened as time fades its value, the total deprivation will not decrease over time."

Phil exclaimed, "I warned you that the idea was rough!"

Jeff said, "I suspect that the theory of fading value is an attempt to find a metaphysical justification for our disinterest in the past, although this disinterest is selective and variable. We know that our disinterest in the past is selective because some past things fascinate us, and therefore our disinterest weakly corresponds to any feature of time itself. It might also result from confusing the evaluation of that which has happened with rules for deliberation, because values of things past are less important to deliberation."

Phil said, "Maybe. But it is also a sincere attempt to come to grips with the importance of existence and A-theory's insistence that only the present exists."

Phil added softly, "Perhaps it is a mistake for consolers to argue that grief is based on conceptual confusion or metaphysical error, that is, error about the nature of reality."

The Rolling Stones sang goodbye to "Ruby Tuesday."

Roy Orbison plaintively asked "Dream Baby (How Long Must I Dream)."

Summary of the Conversation

It follows from the B-theory of time that being alive (at present) is not necessarily better than having been alive (in the past). However, even on B-theory, death entails that a person's goods are finite, so death is still a terrible evil for the dead.

Although on B-theory, time is more like space than on the A-theory of time, temporal finitude is necessarily a greater evil for a person than spatial finitude.

Although we have a "bias" toward the present, the dialogue offered no proof that present existence is necessarily better than past existence. Despite their attempt, the speakers found no satisfactory meaning for the statement that a thing loses its intrinsic value as it becomes past. Consequently, they found no meaning for the statements that death on A-theory is worse than death on B-theory (which would have been a grievance for an A-theorist), or that on A-theory goods would lose their intrinsic value once past even without death.

Study Questions

(1) Is to exist in the present better than having existed in the past? Explain.
   - Is a future existence better than to have had a past one? Explain.

(2) Which theory of time impresses you as most plausible? Does only the present exist (tenselessly)? Explain.

(3) Would you want to survive death as a being "outside" time? What would be good or bad about it?
   - Would it still be *you*?

Twelve

GRIEF AND DEATH'S INEVITABILITY

The title song of George Harrison's first album after the Beatles' breakup, "All Things Must Pass," played as Connie returned to the table.

"What did I miss?" Connie asked, but answered her own question. "Let me guess. Jeff remains unconsoled. In fact, you don't even have to tell me the topic of your discussion because they play the same music in the rest room as they do in the dining area!"

"There does seem to be a strange, pre-established harmony between the songs they're playing and our discussion!" Phil observed. "All along I thought we were being systematic, allowing for digressions only as they might be needed for clarification, when we've really been at the mercy of management's selection of songs!"

"If only they could play a song to convince me not to grieve!" Jeff said.

"Maybe it would be an instrumental!" Connie exclaimed.

Barbara came by the table to take dessert orders.

Connie said, "I'd like an espresso, and a brownie sundae please. We need plenty of caffeine."

Phil said, "I'd like a cup of tea, and the brownie sundae sounds good to me, too! Jeff, what will you have?"

Jeff mumbled, "Tea for me, please."

"How about beer and cheesecake?" Connie suggested.

And Phil urged, "Yes, have it!"

Sternly, Jeff said to Barbara, "No, I'll just have the tea, please."

"Come on!" Connie encouraged.

"For some reason your friends really want you to have a beer and cheesecake," Barbara observed.

Jeff smiled, "No thanks, I'll stick with my order. If I'm feeling lighthearted enough, maybe I'll go for *two* tea bags!"

Connie and Phil scowled at Jeff's attempt to make light of his inhibition.

Death's Inevitability and Universality

Jeff said, "Thanks again for discussing all this with me."

Connie said, "Really, I'm glad to do it. It does stir up some painful memories, but let's face it: I'm not completely over my grief either. But unlike you, I'm not sure that I could have handled such a frank discussion early in my grief. But then, if I had, maybe it would be completely behind me. Who knows?"

Phil said, "You know I've enjoyed our discussion. Anyway, though I'm fortunate enough to still have both my parents, I'll probably suffer these losses someday. Certainly, I'll die myself. And maybe I'll have to prepare for it, or help prepare my loved ones. Maybe it's a part of my good fortune that I've been able to discuss these morbid subjects before I've had these losses."

Phil added, "I'll almost certainly have to deal with death because it is inevitable and universal. I wonder whether any consolation can be drawn from these facts about death."

Jeff said, "When people mention death's inevitability aren't they usually addressing preparation for death? But I'm trying to deal with a death which has already occurred."

Phil said, "I think it's true that 'inevitability' usually comes up with respect to future events, but the word need not be restricted to them. 'Inevitable' could mean that a thing is entailed by the laws of nature together with a state of affairs known to exist. In this sense, we can describe past things as inevitable. In addition, there is a similar idea which, some would say, *especially* applies to past events, namely 'unalterable,' that is, that there is nothing which can be done to prevent or change something."

Jeff said, "All right. But it is not consoling that death is entailed by laws of nature together with known states of affairs. Yes, everyone's death is 'part' of nature. And nature is very good. But it does not follow that a person's death is good for that person. . . ."

"Yes, we've already agreed with that," Phil said.

Connie added, "Yes, a person's death can be consequentially good for others and might entail an organically better whole, but it does not follow that a person's death is good for that person."

Jeff continued, "Furthermore, neither death's inevitability, nor its inalterability, such as with a past death, change any of the things which I have said in explicating and defending the griever's evaluations. Death is an inevitable, extensive deprivation. A past death is an unalterable, extensive deprivation. It is still an extensive deprivation. The sympathy evaluation is unaltered. The ego evaluation is also unaltered. These things do not limit the deprivation. Are they supposed to be some compensating good? Maybe, but I do not see what is good about inevitability or inalterability themselves. Do you two?"

They shook their heads "No."

Death's Inevitability as a Significant Factor in Deliberation

The Grass Roots' song "Sooner or Later" was playing as Jeff continued, "The inevitability of death can be very important for deliberation. The fact that our lives are finite, and even more particularly, that they usually do not last beyond eighty years and never more than one hundred thirty or so, has a bearing on the evaluations one must consider in making certain decisions. However, this does not have any implication for the griever's evaluations.

"Several examples come to mind in which the fact that death is inevitable is relevant to deliberation. For example, one reason it is right that comparative age is a major factor in deciding to prefer the survival of a younger person to the survival of an older person, such as in a 'lifeboat situation,' everything else being equal, is that death is inevitable, and within a somewhat definite period of time. Since death is not only possible, but inevitable as well, it is certain that both the younger and older person will die someday.

"However, the survival of the younger person should be preferred, everything else being equal, since it is probable that the subsequent life of the younger will be longer. But if death were not inevitable, or not inevitable within a roughly definite time, the chances of one person's subsequent life being longer than the other's would have less and less to do with their present ages, and much more to do with things like the relative safety of their lifestyles. . . ."

"'The meek shall inherit,'" Connie quipped.

Jeff smiled as he continued, "However, since death is inevitable, and within a fairly definite time, it is right that comparative age be a major consideration. Of course, there are other reasons for making comparative age an important consideration. But because of death's inevitability, some deaths are preferable to others. But that does not mean that death is not evil for the dead."

Connie said, "I have another kind of case in which death's inevitability should be considered when making a decision. Because death is inevitable, it might be better, under some circumstances, to risk an early death rather than protect one's life at all costs. Imagine that by donating an organ to a needy but appreciative wealthy person your life 'turns around.' You might have risked your life, which would certainly seem foolish, if your life had been at all worthwhile and were it possible for you to live forever."

Phil said, "That example's pretty farfetched, but I get your point. Here's another kind of example in which it seems reasonable to take into consideration the inevitability of death: since death is inevitable it might be rational, under some circumstances, to prefer death to continued life, especially if it were also inevitable that one's death were imminent.

"Plausible candidates for euthanasia are the sort of cases I have in mind. Perhaps a person suffering terribly should continue to live no matter how long the suffering might continue as long as there was some hope that the person would recover and live well for a longer time than the suffering lasted. But of course, it is not always the case that there is such hope as death is inevitable and sometimes inevitably imminent."

Jeff suggested, "I've got another example. In this example, the persons benefited are different from the one who risks or ends his or her life. Because death is inevitable, under certain circumstances, it would be rational to sacrifice one's life to benefit others. If a happy person were assured of immortality, apart from one act of self-sacrifice, it would be irrational to perform this action to benefit others—or oneself, for that matter—, unless the benefit were infinite, because that would be risking an infinite loss.

On the other hand, since an individual's death is inevitable and therefore has a finite life, the sacrifice of one's life to benefit others can be rational, even if that benefit is finite."

Connie added, "I've got another kind of case in which the inevitability of death should be used in deliberation. Since one must die, it makes more sense, than it might otherwise, to plan for one's death, for example, by taking out life insurance!"

Phil joked, "Is this a sideline of yours we didn't know about?"

Connie said, "And of course, another type of preparation which a person needs for death is emotional."

Phil added, "And I have another kind of case, the flip side of Connie's last. Since death is inevitable, and an outside limit can be put on a person's longevity, one should not plan for immortality. This is whatever wisdom there might be in the admonition 'You can't take it with you.' For those of you keeping score, I think that is the *sixth* kind of case which we've mentioned in which it is reasonable to include the fact of the inevitability of death in one's deliberations."

Jeff concluded, "Yes, but again: none of this justifies the claim that death is not an evil, although they justify the claim that there can be evils or goods greater than the difference between a long and short life. That is, the inevitability of death presents the following choice to a person considering a life threatening action: that between a longer life and a shorter one. And sometimes it is reasonable to prefer the shorter. But while there are evils or goods greater than the difference between a long and short life, it does not follow that it is not better to have a long life than a short one, if one is happy.

"In fact, at least the first of these illustrations, preferring the rescue of a younger person to that of an older person, everything else being equal, assumed that death is an evil, and to be delayed as long as possible. That is, it is better to have great longevity.

"In sum, these considerations do not in the least support a consolation based upon death's inevitability."

Evaluation Consolation Based on Death's Inevitability

Connie said, "Still, it seems to me that the inevitability of death could be consoling. Imagine that death was not inevitable. Imagine that immortality, and an endlessly good immortality, were *possible*, although immortality was *uncertain*. It would be much more calamitous for a person to die in such an imagined world than to die in the actual world."

Jeff said, "If by 'consoling' you mean that inevitability lessens the evil of death, then I do not agree. Isn't the deprivation the same whether the dead person had a realistic or only a conceivable chance at an endlessly good immortality? Phil has insisted, with some plausibility, that nothing is an evil unless there is a better alternative which is conceivable.

But I am not at all inclined to the view that nothing is an evil unless there is a better alternative which is 'realistic' or available. Something is good or evil because of some characteristic or relation which it has or lacks, not whether there was a realistic alternative to its having this characteristic or relation. But of course a great deal of further analysis would be necessary to justify this."

Connie said, "Even without such analysis, I still see your point. The deprivation is just as extensive whether or not it is inevitable. However, I cannot agree with you that death's inevitability is not consoling, that is, that it does not lessen the evil of death, because of the fact that it would be more upsetting were one to die, if death were not inevitable."

Jeff offered, "Of course, the extent of one's *dismay* is partly a function of expectation. And possible immortals would have less expectation of death."

Connie responded, "That might explain why a possible immortal's death would be more disturbing. It certainly would explain part of it. But frankly, there should be more to the explanation, especially as, in some sense of 'belief,' people do *not* really or 'fully' believe that they shall die. Death seems so vaguely far off that it doesn't 'sink in.' That is, in some relevant sense, though not in all relevant senses, a particular person's death is never 'expected,' especially one's own or an intimate's. If we *can* say that death is 'expected' in *every* relevant sense after a long terminal illness, at least the terminal illness itself was not 'expected' in every relevant sense. And as we said before it's impossible to *picture* death, the end of consciousness, and so we don't believe it as readily as something we can picture."

Jeff said, "And without dissecting all relevant senses of 'to believe' or 'to expect,' I agree that death is unexpected in some relevant sense. *I* am certainly not a counterexample. As you know, despite my mom's having an incurable cancer, I was surprised by her death."

Jeff continued as Simon and Garfunkel's "Flowers Never Bend in the Rainfall" played.

"Although the possibility of immortality would not make death worse I agree that a possible immortal's death would probably be more traumatic. You conclude that death would be worse if it were not inevitable. You infer this from the claim that a person's death would be more calamitous were it the case that immortality was possible. In one sense this claim is true, but in the sense in which it is true, the conclusion does not follow. It is true in one sense that death is more calamitous for a possible immortal. That is, the *event* which causes a possible immortal's death is *consequentially* worse than the event which causes a mortal's death. For an event which kills a mortal only shortens life. But in either case, death itself entails equal evils."

Phil added, "Insofar as guilt is a part of one's response to a person's death, I can imagine how much worse that response would be were one to feel guilt about a possible immortal's death. But I agree that this does not change the evil of death for the dead person."

Response Consolations Based on
Death's Inevitability or Universality

Phil said, "I think it is a mistake to offer death's inevitability as an evaluation consolation. However, I think it forms the basis of several good response consolations. First, there is one which roughly goes like this: death is inevitable or, a past death is unalterable. Therefore, do not be concerned with it. The other premise is that one should not be concerned with the inevitable (or, the unalterable). And of course, grief is, to put it mildly, concern. Concern for the inevitable (or, unalterable) no matter how evil, has no consequential value because it can't change anything. Therefore, one should not be concerned about the inevitable or, unalterable."

Jeff objected, "But while death is inevitable, it is often the case that its particular timing is not inevitable.[1] And if you countered by saying that everything was completely determined, including the time when one dies, I would reply that concern with postponing it can be part of what determines its timing. That is, it is true of only some deaths that they will occur at a particular time, whether or not one concerns oneself with postponing inevitable death. Thus, concern with death can have the consequential value of postponing it, although it cannot postpone it forever."

Phil said, "That is a fair objection to the 'inevitability' version of this consolation, but it is not a fair objection to the 'inalterability' version of that consolation when applied to past deaths. In other words, while fear, or 'preparatory' grief, grief before death, *might* delay death, 'reactive' grief, that is, grief after death, can have no such effect. I shall restate the argument restricting it to this version: A past death is unalterable. One should not be concerned with the unalterable. Therefore, one should not be concerned with a past death."

Jeff said, "But as we speculated earlier, there might be a psychological connection between grief over a loved one's past death and concern to avoid one's own death. If this is so, then grief over a loved one's death might postpone one's own."

Phil replied, "There is a *logical* connection between the beliefs that your loved one's past death is evil for her and that your eventual death is evil for you. And I agree that the latter belief has consequential value. Therefore, the former belief can be discarded only with some difficulty and some risk. But the phenomenon of grief is more than merely the *belief* that the past death of a loved one is an evil. It includes pangs of grief which, as I can see, are agonizing, and inhibitions, which are depriving. Now, you can't tell me that the inhibition of life's goods and agonizing attacks have the consequential value of making you more careful about preserving your life. They can't make your life more endearing to you. Therefore, while certain beliefs, such as the griever's evaluations, are logically connected to attitudes with consequential value, the rest of grief, the responses, not evaluations themselves, do not have the consequential value of increasing the desire to prolong one's life."

Jeff sighed, and then said, "The consequential value of grief is a topic with many aspects. One aspect is the griever's love of his or her life. Although my mom's death has not made me suicidal, there have been times that I have been so miserable and hopeless that I felt that I would let my life slip away without protest, even with a bitter gratitude, if the situation arose—such as a sudden lethal illness, or an accident, or as a victim of violence. Of course, it's possible that such reflections are mere melodrama and that I would still 'go kicking and screaming.' Nonetheless, I do have such thoughts; thoughts which I didn't have before, even through other prolonged unhappy times. I think these thoughts especially when retiring. I don't cry myself to sleep; I sort of resign myself to the lapse of consciousness."

Connie said, "That you have such thoughts when trying to fall asleep is evidence that these thoughts are insincere. I think you feign indifference to life, in order to ease your burden and get needed rest."

Phil said, "Maybe dreary consolations are good soporifics, if nothing else!"

Jeff changed the topic. "Earlier, we discussed the consequences of the prospect of death. I argued, against you, that death's prospect was mostly consequentially evil, and that even to the extent that death's prospect might be consequentially good, death was still an evil. I remind you of this discussion because it is connected with the inevitability of death. I think that our knowledge of its inevitability does more harm than good, except insofar as it is necessary for deliberation to limit the evils of death as in the previously discussed six kinds of cases. I would like to add that the knowledge of death's inevitability sometimes makes life worse, as it can produce hopelessness."[2]

Phil said, "It can make *life* worse. But death's inevitability does not make *death* intrinsically worse. I add this because you have pointed out that death's inevitability does not make death intrinsically better."

Jeff said, "I hope neither of you will argue that death is good because it spares a person continued existence plagued by hopelessness and fear of death! Don't try to console me by claiming that the foreknowledge of death spoils life, and that, therefore, when death comes we have not lost anything good!"

Phil teased himself. "Don't worry. We're perfectly capable of thinking of poor consolations on our own!"

Connie continued the tease. "Speaking of poor consolations, we have yet to consider the consolation based upon the universality of death. That we all die is a depressing consolation. Technically, it does not fit our definition of a dreary consolation because it does not introduce alternative or additional evils for the dead person or the survivors, but it does introduce evils for every other person. Also, although grievers are most concerned about themselves and their loved ones, they should not be so narrow as to feel nothing for the deaths of others, if a loved one's death is so disturbing."

Jeff said, "Actually, it does fit our definition. For 'everyone dies' entails the deaths of the griever and remaining loved ones. But I agree with your main point. A griever should be somewhat troubled by the death of some strangers and acquaintances; or if the griever 'has no room left' to feel sorrow for them, then at least he should not be comforted by the fact that others die, too.

"Death is somewhat equitable, as it comes for all, although at different times. However, I certainly do not regard inequity as the only evil. Therefore, I am not consoled by death's rough equity."

But then Jeff revealed, "I must confess that I am jealous for my mom that she has so many surviving and robust elder brothers. I resent them their life and health. By the actuarial averages, she should have outlived them. Instead, five of six outlived her, and by many years. But they have *already* outlived their baby sister, so their eventual deaths cannot satisfy my jealousy. The 'injustice' has already been done and I do not *feel* it to grow worse the longer they survive her."

Phil was a bit surprised. Neither he nor Connie was sure what to say.

Jeff continued, "But I realize that these thoughts are irrational. My uncles' continued existence is not a further evil heaped upon my mom or her loving ones. In fact, it is good to know that others live who knew her as a child and remember her so well, despite the sadness that can also bring me. Her death, making her life shorter than theirs, entails more deprivation evil for her than for them. But I do not believe that this comparison, unfavorable to her, is an added evil for her.

"So, my grief includes envy. But this irrational envy is not the source of my grief. On the contrary, envy presupposes the belief that oneself, or a loved one, has suffered some evil. It is this belief which is the source of my grief. Therefore, though I do not defend my envy, I still defend my grief, though it causes my envy."

Phil said, "I'm not sure that envy necessarily involves a belief that an evil has been suffered. One might be envious because another has a good."

Jeff retorted, "Another's having some good might highlight a deprivation evil for oneself."

Phil concluded, "Maybe. I don't know that that is true as a general rule, although it is true in this case that your envy is based on the sympathy evaluation, rather than the other way around."

Connie confessed, "I have had similar thoughts. I have an uncle . . ."

"Poor uncles!" Phil exclaimed.

"who does not appreciate life. About him I think, 'My parents are dead and he lives!'"

Phil said, "We've agreed that, just as there are poor consolations, there are also poor reasons for accepting the griever's evaluations. Jeff has just mentioned one. The comparative longevity of others is not a sensible reason for the griever's evaluations, for others' greater longevity does not contribute to death's evil for the dead or their loving ones."

Jeff said, "However, others' greater longevity might make a loved one's death less expected, and perhaps less expectation justifies greater grief, although it is not further evidence to support the griever's evaluations. That is, grief is justified only partly in terms of the griever's evaluations. Other things need consideration. It's possible that the unexpectedness of death is one of these."

"Why Me?"

Phil continued, "Another poor reason for grieving is contained in the customary question 'Why me?' or in a case such as this, 'Why her?' The idea expressed by this question is that the person being referred to has been unfairly singled out for the evil. The universality of death consolation points out that people are not 'singled out' for death. Everyone dies."

Jeff objected, "Although everyone dies, not everyone dies at the same time or at the same age."

Connie said, "So, you think that when people say 'Why me?' or 'Why her?' they really mean 'Why me-her-now?' or 'Why me-her-so soon?' You might be right. Do very elderly people who are terminally ill ask 'Why me?' So you think that 'Why me-her?' is not the wrong question, if asked concerning a person who dies before extreme old age, or at least, younger than average? But since *many* people die before extreme old age, and even before having lived an average lifetime, then why don't people ask 'Why *any*one so young?' But instead they ask 'Why me-her?' as though early death happened only to that individual. This suggests that Phil's interpretation was correct, namely, that they falsely think that they are being singled out."

Jeff said, "Maybe 'Why me-her?' is just a substitution instance of 'Why anyone so young?' And it is this instance which interests the person asking the question."

Phil said, "I still think there is something wrong about asking 'Why me-her?' as grievers often do."

Jeff said, "I agree that grievers are tormenting themselves with the wrong question if they ask 'Why me-her?' But I am not convinced that the error consists in a false belief that others live forever, or even that no one else dies so young. Therefore, I do not think that reminders of the universality of death expose the error.

"Instead, I think the error behind 'Why me-her?' is the belief that some deaths are more inexplicable than others. Sure, some deaths are more unexpected than others. Some people 'beat the odds;' some just the opposite. For example, sometimes a heavy drinker and smoker will outlive a 'boy scout,' although the probabilities favored the latter. But this does not mean that there is no explanation for the 'clean living' person's death."

"On a hike in the clear outdoors he got hit by a meteorite!" Connie suggested completing the illustration.

Phil laughed, "An unlikely event; but it certainly would explain his death. Of course, some people would ask 'What explains his being in *that* spot at *that* time?' And they would be dissatisfied with the answer 'He paused to eat some wild, pesticide-free berries.' They would say, 'But why did he pause just then, eh?' *et cetera*."

Jeff said, "Yes, another false assumption of 'Why me-her?' is that the explanation must involve a moral justification. When a person asks 'Why me-her?' that person is not usually inquiring into the mechanical or physical explanation of the befallen evil. The person usually is seeking a moral justification as part of the cause."

Connie added, "Perhaps people also falsely assume that while evil befalling others is morally justified, it is not justified in one's own case. Therefore, the often futile search for moral justification is particularly unproductive in one's own case, leaving the person asking 'Why me-her?'"

Jeff said, "Although I agree that this *particular* expression of grief is based on false assumptions, I do not agree that grief is unjustified. That death does not usually have moral justification is not a source of comfort, even though the lack of moral justification should dispel the urge to ask 'Why me-her?' or 'Why any good person?' It might be *slightly* comforting to have an answer to the question, to learn of a moral justification, but it is not comforting to be told not to ask the question because it has no answer."

Phil said, "Of course, some people do think it has an answer—religious folk—you've heard of them!"

Connie said, "Even if it is not consoling to be told that the question has no answer, it might help one to overcome grief by discouraging dead ends. In that sense it might be comforting."

Then Connie said, "Perhaps when people say 'Why me?' what they really mean is 'How *could* it be me?' As I said, people do not really expect to die. This false security can result from surviving dangerous situations."

Jeff said, "Yes, that's a possible interpretation. And one can think oneself invulnerable as a result of thinking of oneself as a necessary condition for the continued existence of the world. After all, everything one knows about the world one knows through oneself! And it is easy to confuse imagining the continued existence of the world with imagining one's continued awareness of the continued existence of the world."

Phil said, "Yes, you made this point much earlier in the evening."

Connie said, "If the error made by those who say, 'Why me?' is that they do not believe in their own mortality, then the purpose of the remark, 'Death is universal' is to remind people of their own deaths, not the death of others."

Connie concluded, "Well, we've discussed several possible meanings of 'Why me?' And I think we agree that none of these justify the griever's evaluations. On the other hand, the griever's evaluations do not depend upon any of these ideas which might be meant by this familiar lament. Still, when grief does take the form of a frustrated search for a moral justification then grief is 'barking up the wrong tree.'"

Jeff and Phil nodded.

Connie resumed, "Not only is death universal, nearly everyone loses a loved one. The observation that others lose loved ones can reassure a grieving person that, as others have endured this loss, so will you. Take me, for example. After I lost my parents the pain was frequent and bitter. But now I enjoy life again. It's not the same and not as good. But I enjoy it. The near universality of the loss shows the griever that the loss can be endured."

Jeff said, "I believe that my intense and frequent grief will pass. But I want its passing to be justified. And I do not see that the fact that it passes for others justifies its passing."

Phil said, "I think that further, more successful *response* consolations might be found in the inevitability or inalterability and universality of death. So let's pursue this topic further."

Just then the desserts and beverages arrived.

The Cornelius Brothers & Sister Rose's "Too Late to Turn Back Now" played sweetly in the background.

Summary of the Conversation

Neither the inevitability, the inalterability, nor the universality of death provides any sound evaluation consolation. The inevitability of death is relevant to some moral deliberations, and some values exist that are greater than the difference between a long and a short life. But these positions do not entail that no difference exists between them.

Were immortality realistically possible but not assured, death would not be any worse than it is if immortality were merely conceivable, although an event that caused the death of a possible immortal would be more consequentially evil than the event that caused the death of a merely conceivable immortal.

Although eventual death is inevitable, fear of death can sometimes prolong life. However, it is unlikely that reactive grief has the consequential value of prolonging anyone's life. Although a logical connection exists between the belief that a loved one's death is evil and the belief that our death will be evil for us, grief might make us more indifferent to our death instead of making us more concerned to avoid it.

Although death is universal, the difference between the lengths of different lives provides "room" for envy. But even if grief often includes unjustified envy, grief does not depend upon it.

People know that disasters befall others, which is partly why they acquire a false security about themselves. So presumably, when asking "Why me?" their error is not ignorance of the prevalence of misfortune. More likely, they falsely assume that a moral justification exists for everything that happens and that in their own case no moral justification could exist, or perhaps they mean, "How *could* it be me?"

The universality and inevitability of death are further discussed as bases for additional response consolations later in the dialogue.

Study Questions

(1) Continue the discussion begun in this chapter: Why do people say, "Why me?"

(2) Why does "misery love company?"

Thirteen

THE CYCLE OF LIFE AND THE IMPORTANCE OF EMOTIONS

Response Consolations

Phil said, "Although disagreement remains on some important points, I accept the griever's evaluations. Death is intrinsically evil, as a deprivation, for the dead. I think the deprivation is finite but extensive. I accept the ego evaluation. Like Connie, I am prepared to abandon the strategy of evaluation consolation; although I do think that death, as terrible as it is, is sometimes made to appear worse than it is. Just as there are many poor evaluation consolations, there are poor reasons for accepting the griever's evaluations.

"I am still hopeful; not to discover that a great evil has not occurred, for I am convinced that it has. But I am still hopeful that you can be dissuaded from your grief. The strategy of response consolation, although anticipated several times, has not been fully explored."

Connie said, "Yes, I'm more optimistic about some response consolations. But before examining any of these we must explain 'response consolation' more carefully than we have until this time. So far all we have said is that a response consolation criticizes the grief responses rather than criticizing the griever's evaluations as false or unjustified."

Phil complied with Connie's request as Jeff sipped some tea.

"In order to understand more clearly 'response consolation' we should remind ourselves of our analysis of grief. Grief includes the following components: belief that the griever's evaluations are true, and various 'responses' to these evaluations, two of which we have emphasized, sorrow and inhibition. These responses include overt behavior, such as crying. Sorrow also entails unpleasant or disagreeable states of consciousness, and inhibition entails the absence of pleasant or agreeable states of consciousness.

"In passing, we've noted that often grief also includes obsessive thought and behavior. These sometimes include mimicking the dead person. This particular response has already come under sharp criticism."

Jeff reminded, "However, it was allowed that perhaps some minimal mimicking might help the griever to adjust to a world without the loved one."

Phil continued, "Also in passing we referred to the fact that grief often includes anger and guilt. However, our discussion of these might have to wait until another evening."

Connie exclaimed, "Or else we'll be thrown out of here!"

Phil laughed and Jeff nodded.

Phil concluded, "Now, since we acknowledge the truth of the griever's evaluations, either we must believe them or else we must argue that it is wrong to hold such beliefs even though they are true."

Jeff interjected, "I won't play that game. Since they're true I'm stuck with them."

Phil continued, "Okay, we might criticize the responses as unjustified by the griever's evaluations, as we have done with inhibition. For example, we argued that the survivor cannot lessen the evil of death for the dead by avoiding accomplishments."

Death as a Benefit to Others

Jeff said, "The first response consolation which I would like to examine has come up before. Although the griever's evaluations are true, there are *other* evaluations also to be made of the death of the loved one which are overlooked by the griever."

Phil said, "Fine. And it is perhaps most systematic to begin with this since it is most like the strategy of evaluation consolations.

"As you have indicated, Jeff, evaluations other than the griever's can be made about a person's death. A person's death usually effects or entails goods or evils for persons other than the person who died and any loving ones—funeral directors, for example. Now, what about these other evaluations? Should a person, even the loving ones, acknowledge and respond to these? And *if* a person's death is good upon the whole, though it is evil for the dead person and any loving ones, shouldn't one's emotion reflect this? I know it sounds 'cold,' but we should consider whether grief is 'partial.' That is, we should consider the two following issues: first, whether it is good upon the whole, everyone considered, that the person is dead. Second, whether it would be rational for the dead person's loving ones to be comforted by this."

Connie shook her head in disapproval.

Once again Jeff defended one of Phil's proposals. "No, Connie. This is exactly what I want—need. I want it all on the table. Let's not prejudge a consolation. Just as I resented consolations which *sounded* soothing I don't want to ignore consolations just because they sound rough."

Jeff said, "Just to show that I'm prepared to consider these issues without sentimental hedging, I'll start us off. You can then feel bold enough to be 'cold.' But first, let me stipulate that we are discussing the death of a basically good person. If she was a villainess, there'd be no question that her death brought much benefit. But were I grieving over the death of a loved villainess, other issues would be raised for my grief: such as whether I should have loved the person in the first place. But I am not grieving over a villainess. Nevertheless, it is worth considering whether my mom's death has done more good than harm.

"Perhaps there is some organic good produced by her death, such as we earlier discussed. If she were immortal, she might have gradually lost her individuality. And this, one might suppose, detracts from the organic value of variety. But I think that it might actually contribute to variety if *some* people were immortal, and it might as well have been her! An end shared by all, and death is such an end, as you've lately reminded me, does not obviously make for variety.

"But leaving aside such considerations of organic value for which I confess little patience, the only benefit which I can imagine that strangers would likely receive from the death of a decent person would be economic. As mentioned a while ago, my mom's death benefited the funeral director and anyone who depends upon him. As regards the gravediggers, one burial more or less will not affect their salaries. However, it gave them more work to do, and on a hot summer day."

Connie and Phil looked confused by Jeff's minute, even trivial, analysis of the effects of his mom's death on others.

Jeff continued, "Her death was financially bad for her doctors. However, it did relieve the taxpayer.

"We could extend the list of pros and cons in this way, profession by profession, but maybe it would be easier and more systematic to analyze her death's impact on those other than her loving ones by examining my mom's economic 'roles.' With her death there is one less consumer to 'spur' the economy. But being retired, not to mention semi-invalid, she no longer either produced goods or provided services. On the other hand, being unable to get around much, her excess income, as slight as it was, was put in the bank. And, as we know, America collectively needs much more savings than we have. Upon the whole, during her last years, I suppose that she took from the economy more than she gave. It is irrelevant to our first question, namely, whether her death was upon the whole beneficial, that she was 'legally entitled' to the costly services provided her during her last years. Therefore, I conclude, provisionally, that her death was, upon the whole, an *economic* benefit."

A flabbergasted Connie asked, "Are you trying to shame us into being anti-consolers?" So, temporarily, Connie and Phil reversed roles with Jeff.

Connie continued, "Her death helped some and hurt others, yes. But I don't think that her net effect on the economy, in terms of consumption, investment and productivity can shed any light on whether her death was economically good for others upon the whole. For the comparative difference to the economy of her death or continued existence is too slight to either benefit or harm anyone. It is only the accumulation of such differences throughout the economy which benefits or harms anyone. Her savings did not enable any bank to invest in anything it could not have otherwise done. Her social security and Medicare benefits did not increase any tax rates, and thereby anyone's taxes. And so on, for all these roles."

Phil made another point. "Even if there was a net economic benefit of her death and even if it followed that her death was beneficial upon the whole to persons *other* than her loving ones, it would not follow that her death was good upon the whole, *everyone* considered. For even if it were true that her death had overall economic benefit, not merely 'on paper,' but actually for people's lives, it would be so slight as to not come anywhere near outweighing the evils stated in the griever's evaluations. So, even if other evaluations should be considered by the loved one's survivors, this economic evaluation would not make grief irrational."

Connie reflected, "I think that Phil has played his anti-consoler role a little too strongly. Whether or not other person's benefits compare with the evils suffered by the dead person and her loving ones depends upon the particular circumstances. As an illustration, take the undertaker. His profit is probably several hundred, or perhaps thousands of dollars. Obviously, the loss to your mother of her entire future is vastly greater than the value of hundreds or thousands of dollars. Similarly for you: your loss is much greater than hundreds or thousands of dollars. However, to be precise, the value of that money to the person who profited from your mom's death depends upon how those hundreds or thousands are used. If they are used to sustain the *life* of the undertaker or a dependent, then the benefit of a person's death *is* comparable to the loss."

Phil said, "No, I don't think I was wrong. The loss to the dead person is very great, even if not infinite as Jeff claims. And while it is true that a person might need a few hundred or thousand dollars to survive, that money can only last a short while. In other words, death is sufficient for *all* the evils we've been discussing, but sufficient for only a *few* goods of the person whose life is sustained by that death."

Connie objected, "Yes, but it is *necessary* for all the future goods of that person."

Jeff settled the dispute. "Clearly, a person's death can be beneficial upon the whole, everyone considered. For example, when a hero dies that others might live. Nothing so dramatic was involved in my mom's death. But it is also possible that one person's death is necessary to save several lives in less dramatic ways, such as through financial sustenance. If those benefited lived long thereafter, the death would have been beneficial overall. Everything else being equal, one person's death is as evil as another's. Therefore, if one death saves two lives, it is overall beneficial.

"However, not only was my mom's death not heroic, it was not the financial difference between life and death for anyone, as far as I know."

Jeff continued, "Not only does this consolation not apply to my mom, since I presume that her death had no such benefit, but this consolation has limited applicability in another way. A person who dies while still economically productive was while alive a source of sustenance for others."

Death as Necessary for the Cycle of Life

Phil stated, "A moment ago you stated that you wish that your mom was an exception to our common fate; that it might increase the variety of the species were some people immortal. So let me ask: is it good upon the whole, everyone considered, that all people die? Even if a person were productive, it might be a better world upon the whole that this person eventually dies. Because even if productive, people must 'step aside' for life's goods to be shared with others born after them."

Jeff objected, "But productive people make it possible for there to be others with whom to share the world. If productive people lived forever, then they *would* be 'making room' for others born after them. They would not need to 'step aside.'"

Phil replied, "Productive people make further consumption possible. But the future consumers can either be themselves or others who are born afterwards. It cannot be the case that both groups consume these. For our environment and resources impose necessary limits on population size. If people are to be born and grow and enjoy life, people have to die, even productive people. Someone 'has to go.' Even productive people must die in order that others being born can have consumable goods."

Jeff said, "Okay, we're comparing death and immortality again. Earlier Phil argued that eventually an immortal life would become unrewarding and no better than death. Now we'll compare death and immortality with respect to their effects on society as a whole. Since we're trying to evaluate death we need to compare it with its opposite—immortality. Of course, since death is universal it follows that immortality is *not* a realistic alternative. But it doesn't follow that we should not evaluate death by comparing it to its opposite, no matter how farfetched the alternative."

Jeff continued, "Given the constraints on population size, there are two extreme possibilities. Either at some point—not necessarily early in mankind's history—all adults stop dying, or else forever the younger generation 'takes the place of' the older generation. On the first alternative, that at some point all those already born never die, depending upon how 'advanced' those humans are, it might be better, upon the whole, than that everyone is 'replaced' by others forever."

Phil argued, "I think that it would be better, on the whole, that generations succeed one another rather than at any time the earth remain populated with the same people. I think that a world populated with the same people would become 'stagnant.' I'm not simply referring to my earlier consolation that the life of an individual immortal would become less and less valuable because of character fixity. Rather, my present point is that the *species* would cease to improve. A *result* of all the individuals' character fixity in a world filled with immortals would be lack of improvements in our knowledge, morals and physical conditions. In fact, with mortals, one of the chief *delays* in the development of their own character fixity is social change resulting from new generations. This factor would be missing in the immortal world. Thus, character fixity and social stagnation would reinforce each other."

Jeff objected. "The 'turn over' of generations has its disadvantages as well as its advantages. And its disadvantages are less speculative than the advantage which you allege, of avoiding stagnation. An unavoidable disadvantage of generations succeeding each other, and especially at the rate at which they do succeed each other, is that generally each generation must learn only from its own mistakes, if it learns at all. This is true for several reasons. First, because lessons learned cannot always be transmitted. Second, human life being as short as it is, some lessons can never be learnt in the first place, let alone passed along."

Connie said, "And with the advent of nuclear power, mankind's tendency to only learn from its mistakes becomes a staggering problem."

Phil asked, "So, we owe it to the future that it be *ours*? Neat trick, if we could do it!"

Connie said, "Don't get me wrong. I agree with you on this, Phil. Of the two extremes, it is better that everyone dies, to be succeeded by others. For, continuing with the assumption that the world can sustain only a finite population, it would follow that, in such a world populated by immortals, no one born after a certain time could live—albeit briefly. This would not only be a great loss to those newborn who die, it would be a great loss to the immortals as well. I'm not agreeing with Phil's earlier point that it would not be worthwhile being immortal, but it would be worth much less, if an immortal could not raise children. And in the immortal world, they could not. Therefore, between the two extremes of a world, such as ours, with death for everyone and birth for others, and a world in which at some point everyone already born lives forever, the former world, ours, would be better, everyone considered upon the whole."

Phil nodded.

Jeff said, "Connie, I *might* agree that our cyclical world is better, upon the whole, than a world of immortal adults and no children. But, as we've said, these alternatives are extremes. And a griever is not committed to prefer the worse of these extremes. That is, for a loved one's death to be evil, upon the whole, everyone considered, it need not be the case that a world full of adult immortals is better than a world of mortals. Better than either of these extremes might be a world in which some are immortal—maybe even oneself and one's loved ones! So, the griever is not committed to the view that it is better or best that *everyone* is immortal; the bereaved would be much happier if just they and their loved ones were immortal.

"Now, we could imagine that a world of *some* immortals would be a disaster, for instance, if the immortals 'lorded' over the mortals, or if the mortals, in their jealousy, tortured forever the immortals. On the other hand, it is conceivable that a mixed world of mortals and immortals would have a healthy blend of maturity and innovation. In sum, we can conceive that a particular person, such as myself, never loses a loved one, and that the world might be better for it. Thus, there is something conceivably better than the state of affairs which grieves a loved one's survivors, even if everyone is considered."

Connie looked startled. "Well, anyone's entitled to a fantasy, and grievers are so unhappy with reality that they entertain various fantasies, even ones which exacerbate their grief, but this fantasy does seem objectionable. I realize that it doesn't matter that it's impossible for there to be a world of a few immortals which include you and your mom."

Phil interjected, "Care to fantasize that Connie and I are among that select group, Jeff?"

Jeff responded, "Immortality would be wasted on you, Phil."

Connie continued, "I know that we're not deliberating about whether to establish such a world, but this fantasy is so egocentric that it's shocking. It's just a step above the 'only guy on an Amazon island' fantasy!"

Phil said, "I think you're right, Connie."

Jeff smiled, "Phil, you're not going to let her getaway with belittling the Amazon island fantasy? Seriously, all I'm saying is that were my mom immortal that that would not necessarily be harmful. Of course, that's true of other good people as well. On the other hand, it might be bad were all these immortal. So, I *am* being partial when I wish that my mom was the immortal exception. But I'm not wishing for something necessarily harmful."

Phil recommended, "Before going any further, let's review our discussion of whether mortality is necessarily beneficial, everyone considered."

Jeff complied. "First, it is possible that a person's death, whether that person was productive or unproductive, does more good than harm, everyone considered. Second, as far as I know, this was not the case with my mom's death. Third, given certain limitations on population size, it is better that everyone die and be replaced than that no one die. Fourth, however, it might be better still that some were immortal. And to *add* a couple points: it is evil that people become unproductive. It is evil that people must die so that others may be born and raised. These facts are dreary. Finally, even if I conceded that it is better that everyone die, I still grieve because my mom's life was not much longer than it was, unless you'll argue that our world would be better shared were our lives shorter. Knowing that good people must die that others might live doesn't console me.

"Earlier, when we were discussing the consolation that my mom would have never existed but for the mortality of others, Connie made the point that if people died, but existed in an afterlife, they would have made room for others."

Phil replied, "To which I objected: I'm unsure that an afterlife is really conceivable."

Emotions and Impartiality

Phil asked, "Suppose your mom's death did enable others to live. *Would* you still grieve? Would your grief even be *lessened*?"

Jeff hesitated.

Phil said, "I know that it is difficult to answer these questions. But I ask them to make a point."

Jeff answered, "Yes, I would have grieved. In fact, I'm not sure that I would have grieved any less."

Phil said, "Then it seems that your emotional response is to a thing's value for yourself and loved ones much more than to its value for others, even when the value for others exceeds the value for yourself and loved ones."

Connie added, "This is also shown by your wish that your loved ones were the exception to mortality even though with our limited resources it's good that we're not all mortal."

Jeff acknowledged this. "As we've said, usually a person's death affects the well-being of that person and their loving ones much more than it affects anyone else's well-being. Therefore, everyone considered equally, usually the effects on the dead person and loving ones should be regarded as more important. However, even when it is not the case that others are less affected, and they were benefited, a loving survivor will grieve.

"Furthermore, although many other decent people die, I do *not* grieve for them. I grieve because of a relationship which I have to the dead person and because it effects me."

Phil said, "Then the next issue is whether this is wrong. Since grief is an instance of this partiality, if partiality of emotional response is wrong, then grief is wrong."

Connie said, "We need to become clearer about 'partiality' and 'impartiality' before we proceed."

Friend and Lover, and then Spanky and Our Gang implored "Reach Out of the Darkness" and "Give a Damn" respectively.

Jeff said, "Right. We need to begin with some basic concepts and observations. First of all, although we haven't fully explained this, affects are responses to evaluations. There might be an infinite number of things with value, good or bad; certainly, there are very many. Earlier in our conversation it was argued that death was part of nature. And that nature is good. And it was suggested that since death is part of this magnificent system that we should have a constant attitude of approbation in response to the overall greatness of this system, whereas grief is a response to just a part of this wonderful system. So, grief is 'partial' in the *first* sense in that it is not a response to the entire system of which it is a part. It is not an emotional response to the overall balance of good and evil in the universe. It is a response to a person's death. It is a response to other related things as well, such as that person's dying, *et cetera*. We've mentioned these, but are concentrating on the death itself. Let's call grief 'directed' for its responsiveness toward a part rather than the whole system, for it is 'directed' toward a part."

Connie said, "Yes, you mentioned this in passing earlier, that you are not responding to the entire system of nature, and you promised to come back to it."

"I'm a man of my word," Jeff kidded.

"You're a man of *many* words," Connie returned.

Phil laughed then said, "Grief is or might be 'partial' in a *second* sense in that it is or might be a response toward only some of all the evaluations which are true of that person's death. That is, grief might be 'selective,' or not responsive to all the evaluations which can be made of some state of affairs. Grief ignores the benefits.

"Grief is 'partial' in a *third* sense. To a great extent, grief is selective in a predictable manner. For example, a person tends to respond more strongly to those evaluations of some state of affairs which concern persons which have a special relation to that person. To give this third sense of grief's partiality a name, grief is 'relative.' In sum, grief is directive because not aimed at the entire system of nature but only at death, selective because not based on all the facts about death and relative because selective based on a special relationship to the dead."

Jeff said, "I intend to defend grief against any criticism that it is wrong because it is a response chiefly dependent upon special relationships. An affect is not wrong simply because it is a response chiefly toward persons with whom one has special relationships."

"Would *anyone* dispute that?" Connie asked.

Jeff pointed across the table.

"Me?" Connie asked incredulously. "*Of course* feelings are based on special relationships!"

Jeff explained, "On our way over here you made the point that grief is perhaps the most intense, prolonged affect which a person experiences. You thought this was peculiar because the death of a loved one is not the worst thing that can ever happen. You were criticizing a griever for being selective and even relative; that is, responding to some evaluations while not responding to others, and on the basis of one's relationship to the person concerned."

"So I did," Connie said, shaking her head. "Well, just because I put my foot in my mouth doesn't mean I should leave it there. I suppose that I thought I was being 'philosophical,' by taking the 'broad view,' but emotions *should* be relative, or at least, it's *understandable* that they are."

Phil said, "There's a big difference between saying that it's understandable that emotions are relative and that they should be! I'd like to investigate the consolation that grief is objectionably partial. The consolation is that, contrary to Jeff, grief is objectionable because partial, and relative, in particular."

Connie hesitated. "I'm not sure that there's such a big difference, but continue with your consolation; I might support it because I'm not sure what I think about this. Emotions should be relative but perspective is good too."

Jeff anticipated the consolation and defended the relativity of emotions. "It's good that emotions are relative. Emotions help us in our daily environment. Many of our obligations are relative, that is, depend on special relationships to particular people, and relative emotions help us fulfill our relative obligations. For example, Phil's got obligations to Pam and his kids that he has to no one else. The special emotional interest which he has in them motivates him to fulfill those obligations."

Phil conceded, "Sometimes marriage and parenthood aren't easy, and without special affection it would be more difficult to do what's right. I admit that we have obligations to family, neighbors and coworkers, people with whom we have special relationships, and because we respond emotionally to things which affect these people, it's *sometimes* easier for us to do right by them than had we not these feelings."

Jeff added, "And because emotional relativity is directed toward people we well know and often people in our daily environment emotional relativity motivates us to help those that we have most opportunity to help. I'll add that because self-interest most often conflicts with those closest to us, that special emotional concern for these is essential."

Phil objected, "True. But we also have *neutral* obligations, obligations to people with whom we do *not* have a special relationship. And because emotions are relative they often interfere with neutral obligations. Sometimes we sacrifice the more important interests of strangers or foreigners to those of dear ones or countrymen or coreligionists."

Connie stated, "How often is office mood tainted by promotion of favorites, or on the other hand, the false suspicion of favoritism by those close to rejected candidates? And mustn't we blame the relativity of emotions for the obnoxious behavior of Little League parents?"

Phil joked, "I swear that my kid was safe!"

Connie laughed and returned the jest, "I have my private investigators too!"

Phil stated, "I'll indict emotional relativity by pointing out that nations measure the cost of war almost exclusively by their own casualties, and how perilous is the world because of parochial biases sanctioned by superstition?"

"True," Jeff said. "Emotional relativity can be harmful, especially when reinforced by ignorance. Still, I think that it's indispensable, even to the fulfillment of neutral obligations. But I hesitate to make my argument because of the uncertainty of the topic."

Connie encouraged, "Just *sketch* an argument. We know the difference between a sketch and a fully developed demonstration. We won't come away from our discussion thinking we've settled more than we really have settled."

Jeff said, "I'll try. Self-esteem might be necessary for a person to consistently fulfill neutral obligations. For example, a person with self-esteem is more likely to be courteous to others, whether or not there is a special relationship between them. Also, one cause of unjustifiable, relative action, such as cruelty to a stranger, is a craven desire for special favor within one's group. But a person with self-esteem is less prone to this. And perhaps it is necessary to the development of self-esteem that a person has some reciprocal and special relationships. In other words, it might be good for the development of one's character, including fulfilling neutral obligations, that a person must participate in relationships in which the participants emotionally respond more strongly to a state of affair's value for themselves than for others."

Connie said, "That sounds paradoxical. People must be made to feel special and to feel that those people are special who make them feel special in order that they do not regard some people as special!"

Jeff said, "You know, 'If you don't love yourself, you can't love anyone else'—that kind of thing."

Phil teased, "Oh, you sound *very* expert!"

Connie added, "Jeff has to stop watching afternoon talk shows!"

Phil said, "The idea which you're defending is that a group of people mutually and emotionally respond to a state of affair's value for members of that group more than its value for those outside that group. Right?"

"Yes," Jeff said.

Phil said, "But I just described a *gang*!"

Connie added, "Even worse, a political party!"

Phil added, "More precisely, what I just described could be a gang, a political party *or* a family. And as the former two groups seldom promote neutral obligations, why are you optimistic that this idea of a group emotionally responding more strongly for each other will promote neutral obligations?"

Jeff said, "Of course these groups, families included, do more than *emotionally* respond more to a thing's value for its members than for outsiders, their decisions *promote* the interests of their members over the interests of outsiders."

Connie said, "That supports our point. That there is a correlation between stronger feelings for some persons and preference for the interests of those persons strongly suggests that this emotional relativity is an obstacle to discharging neutral obligations."

Jeff said, "But my point is that we can distinguish between emotional relativity and relative *action*.[1] I think that, to some extent, emotional relativity can be a *substitute* for relative action. To explain I'll go back to the beginning. Suppose people need to feel important to treat others as *important*, not 'special,' as *you* put it. Further suppose that in order to feel important people need *either* that their interests are chosen over others or that some people respond emotionally more strongly to a thing's value for them. By caring especially about someone we can teach them that they are important without teaching them that they're more important. And this claim is supported by the fact that families tend to substitute emotional relativity for relative action more than gangs or parties."

Connie said, "Do they really? Maybe you haven't watched *enough* afternoon talk shows!"

Phil cautioned, "Jeff's claims *might* be true. In fact, Jeff has more or less described good parenting in the playground. But none of us are experts in 'ethology,' or the development of character. We should not attempt to draw conclusions about whether emotional relativity promotes neutrality. My guess is that there is an optimal level of emotional relativity, varying from one case to another. Or that emotional relativity is necessary to a *stage* of moral development, making the person care about others besides oneself; but that it should be superseded."

Jeff said, "I have at least defended one's emotionally responding more strongly to a state of affairs' values for some persons rather than others. And grief is such a response."

Phil said, "Yes, grief is one of many relative responses. But even if it could be proven that emotional relativity *usually* promoted neutrality in actions, it would not follow that a particular instance of emotional relativity, such as grief, usually promotes neutrality. Remember in your own case, that you told us that grief has made you envious of your uncles' longevity."

Billy Joel concluded his "Allentown."

Emotions and Performance

"More needs to be said," Jeff agreed. "But if I tried justifying grief's relativity only by showing that it promoted our obligations, we would not fully understand that it is right for affects to be selective and even relative. There is a justification of affective directivity, selectivity and relativity which is peculiar to the nature of an affect. That is, in part an affect can be justified or criticized like an action or a decision, in terms of whether or not it promotes our obligations. But an affect is also like sense-perception, and is therefore useful in ways similar to sense-perceptions."

"Huh?"

Jeff said, "I cannot explain my meaning all at once. Let's take it one step at a time. It's been suggested that one should not grieve because death is part of nature and that nature is overall good, and that our emotional responses should be to this overall good. But as I asked concerning this suggestion, what would an affect be like which responded only to the net overall good of nature? Presumably, it would be some single, uniform affect. But which affect would it be?"

Phil reminded, "To which I earlier answered, 'a feeling of approbation.'"

Jeff said, "Let's call the claim that a person should have only one single, uniform affect, whatever that should be, and only one object of that response, the net overall goodness of things, the 'non-directive' view of affects. First, I shall argue for directivity, and then, from that to selectivity and relativity.

"Phil, you've said that non-directed affect should be a feeling of approbation. My first objection is that it is difficult to say what sort of feeling of approval this should be. Should it be aesthetic approval or moral approval?

Should it be joy or tranquility? I think that we have different 'positive' feelings for the same reason that we have both positive *and* negative feelings, because feelings should be directed. Some good news is calming, some pleasant, some joyful, and some makes us ecstatic. Which of these should we feel toward the overall good of nature?"

Connie said, "Would it matter? As long as one has *some* positive emotion and does not feel grief."

Jeff continued without directly responding. "Second, I think it is impossible to say whether the non-directed affect should be approving or disapproving because it is impossible to know whether the sum total value of everything is good or evil. Is there more suffering or pleasure in the universe? Is there more beauty or ugliness?"

Connie said, "I don't think that we can answer that. How would one inventory all the good and bad things in the world? But imagine the perks of the CEO who had that job!"

Phil noted, "Some philosophers have argued that we can know that the entire system of nature is good, at least on balance; without having to *inventory* goods and evils. For instance, they argue for the existence of a perfect creator, without having already decided that nature is good, and infer from the perfect creator that nature is good, at least upon the whole. Or they argue that evil is not real, but is merely a limitation or privation of good."

Jeff said, "I've never understood what they mean that 'evil was not real but only a limitation of good.' Using *our* terminology, are they denying the existence of *diametric* evils, such as pain?"

Phil said, "I think that they might admit that diametric evils are real, but that they are the result of sin; that the world *as it was created* had no diametric evils, but then through sin diametric evils flooded in."

Connie said, "But with this deluge of suffering maybe the overall balance is bad, and so the door has been opened for negative emotions."

Phil responded, "I think that the reply is that because suffering is the result of sin it is *deserved* and therefore we should feel approval of it."

Jeff said, "Then *if* we accepted that view, perhaps we should feel sad that there are sinners and that they require punishment, even though we're *also* supposed to approve of the punishment because deserved. You see, that makes my point that we have many different affects and they don't all have to be aimed at the overall value of everything."

Jeff added, "Why shouldn't we emotionally respond to the limitation or privation of good, or as we've been calling it 'deprivation,' as I am doing in grieving about my mom's death? It's like 'Don't let the Big CEO know that you're not completely satisfied, unless you want to be stuck in an office in the basement.'"

Phil smiled and said, "Okay, *none* of us three subscribe to this view."

Jeff said, "I'll move onto my third argument against the non-directive view of emotions. I want to point out the obvious: *sense-perception* is directed, that is, we sense this or that particular thing rather than the universe as a whole. And of course we are able to function only because we sense particular things. Likewise, we are able to function because our emotions are directed toward this or that particular thing."

"Hold on," Phil said. "Of course non-directed *sense-perception* would be ridiculous. Non-directed sense-perception would be sensing the sum total of everything with a single, uniform sense-perception. But such a perception would be pointless; the usefulness of sense-perception is precisely that it enables us to *distinguish* objects! But this does not show that non-directed *emotion* would be pointless or unhelpful. Therefore, the absurdity of the one does not show that the other is absurd. In addition, the non-directive view of sense-perception is ridiculous because no meaning can be given to 'a sense-perception of the sum total of everything.' Several different kinds of sensible exist. There is light and sound and texture and temperature, and so on. Therefore, a single uniform sense-perception of *all* of these could not be of *any* of these. It could not be a particular visual sensation, or a particular auditory sensation, or a particular tactile sensation, and so on."

Jeff stated, "I shall forego the reply that, just as there are several different kinds of sensible, thus making nonsense of 'a single and uniform sense-perception of the sum total of everything,' there are different kinds of *value*, thus making nonsense of 'a single and uniform affect toward the sum total value of everything.'"

Jeff continued, "To avoid your objection as much as possible, I'll restrict my point to *one* sensible and I'll make it temperature, which is a sensible that varies more simply than others. In this case, the non-directive view of sense-perception is that the only object of the sense-perception of temperature should be the average temperature of everything, and that the sense-perception of it should be single and uniform.

"Now, suppose the average temperature of everything was . . . fifteen degrees Celsius, on the non-directive view, the only temperature one should sense is fifteen degrees Celsius. One should not sense the zero degrees Celsius of this ice, the thirty degrees Celsius of that object, or the hundred degrees Celsius of that steam, but only fifteen degrees Celsius. And let's suppose that the sensation of fifteen degrees Celsius would be like sticking your hand . . ."

"Which has been at room temperature?" Connie interjected.

"in tepid water."

Connie said, "This is again ridiculous, but again, for reasons having nothing to do with emotions and whether they should be directed. First, even assuming that 'the average temperature of everything' makes sense and would be knowable . . ."

Jeff interrupted, "But I think these very problems also apply to the affect parallel! I doubt that 'the overall value of everything' makes sense, and even if it did, it would be unknowable."

Connie continued, "There's no such thing as a single and uniform sense-perception *appropriate* to the average temperature. Sense-perception depends upon the sensed object *and* its relation to a perceiver. For example, one's sense-perception of the temperature of an object varies with one's distance from it. So, one could not say that one should have the sense-perception of tepid, to use your example, even if the average temperature of everything were fifteen degrees Celsius. It depends upon how close the perceiver is. How close is one to everything? It does not make sense."

"My view of affects exactly! The 'proper' affect depends upon some *relations* between the value of the state of affairs and the person who is affected by it," Jeff said. "Therefore, affects should be directed, selective and relative."

Phil cautioned, "Let's not move too fast, or we'll be speaking nonsense.
It is a contingent, causal law that one's particular sense-perceptions depend upon the relation of perceiver and object. It is *conceivable* that one experienced the same temperature sensation from an object, regardless of distance. However, it is good that this is not the case. It is good that temperature sensations vary with distance. People whose sense-perception of temperature did not differentiate between hot and cold objects or between hot objects near and far would have this tepid sensation as the flames licked the flesh from their bones! A being with non-directed sense-perception would be unable to react, let alone act, within its environment. Thus, non-directed sense-perception would be very bad. However, this is not the case for a being which responded with a positive feeling to the supposed overall good of nature. Such a being would be able to react and act. It would know what was going on in its environment."

Jeff said, "On their necessity for action and reaction sensation and affect are more alike than you think. It's true that one who needed to act and react would be utterly helpless without sense-perception of particular things rather than the whole of nature. But one who had directed sense-perception but lacked directed affect would not be much better off. Affects, such as suspicion, fear, joy and more, can determine our actions and our attention. They often assist in approach and avoidance responses."[2]

Phil said, "But we can conceive of an agent-inquirer who performs voluntary actions without directed affect. But it is *inconceivable* that a being without directed sense-perception would be able to choose and so on. In fact, such a being would not be a person at all, but a rock. But we can imagine a person lacking directed affect. We can imagine someone who is aware of their environment, but who maintains a positive feeling, even in a hazardous situation."

Connie tried to settle the argument. "There are a vast number of cases to support both sides. Performance can be benefited or harmed by emotion. According to the cliché, relative emotions can help a petite mom lift a car off her pinned child and some anxiety can assist in a public performance. On the other hand, emotion can disturb concentration and even cause indecision. So, once again, because there are so many examples on both sides and the outcome varies according to so many factors I don't think that we can settle the question of the usefulness of emotion's partiality by undertaking an inventory."

Jeff suggested, "Then let me try to settle the dispute about the usefulness of emotions without undertaking an impossible inventory of their harms and benefits. But instead of bringing in the concept of a perfect creator I'll bring in the law of evolution. Since our emotions are in fact directed, selective and relative the partiality of emotions must be helpful on balance. Were partiality on balance harmful they would have been selected out."

"Yeah, like appendicitis," Connie replied.

Phil said, "I don't doubt that partial emotion, no matter how harmful to adults, is necessary for children. So, partiality at that stage is necessary for our survival. And partial emotion also assists in reproduction. Not only because aggression can help males mate, but also because sexual selection works by preferring particular characteristics and this preference comes out as partial emotion."

Connie joked, "Oh no, this time it's a favorite afternoon talk show topic: why women like bad boys!"

Jeff said, "I'm willing to agree that there is a difference between the necessity for sense-perception and the necessity for affect. However, I'm really unsure how far it goes. For one thing, I'm not sure that your confidence in the conceivability of an emotionally non-directed person is not merely another instance of our confidence in a thing's conceivability simply because we haven't spelled out the alleged concept.

"In sum, Phil would like to console me for *every* evil there is! And he thinks that might be done if I would accept the non-directive view of affects. But I don't know that the gross value of everything is good. And even if it was and I felt undisturbed approbation of some form, I think it would be difficult for me to make decisions, or even survive. And the decisions I would make might be less reliable than the ones I make now. I might emotionally respond to the gross amount of good while *decreasing* it!"

Phil teased, "That's a lot of 'might's. And might doesn't make right!"

Jeff replied, "All right, let me argue that it is beneficial that emotions are *selective*. Affects are selective in the sense that they are often responses to only a portion of the evaluations of a particular state of affairs rather than being a response to the overall evaluation of that state of affairs. Of course, one could have several selective affects to the same state of affairs, so that one responds to all the evaluations which might be made of that state of affairs, although each separate response is selective. For instance, some responses might be toward the good aspects of a state of affairs while others are responses to the bad aspects of a state of affairs.

"Earlier, we discussed the situation of a person who inherits a fortune from a loved one's death which in many ways 'turns that person's life around.' I argued that such a person should respond to the evils for himself as well as others even though that death might have been overall good for him.

But at the time of that discussion we had not yet introduced 'selectivity.' Now I would like to add to our previous discussion of such a case considerations drawn from an evaluation of selectivity.

"First, besides the difficulties in knowing the overall value of the whole universe, there are sometimes difficulties even in ascertaining whether some *particular* thing is overall good or overall bad! However, I will grant that, in our example of the loving heir that the overall value can be known. Second, it is often consequentially good that affects are selective. Assuming that a negative affect prompts a person to change that toward which the affect is directed, and a positive affect prompts continuation of its object, and assuming that these affects are well directed, that is, the negative toward evils, the positive toward goods, it follows that selective affect motivates progress much better than emotion responsive to the overall evaluation. For example, consider the creation of a work of art. It's crucial that the artist modifies the creation by approving this and disapproving that. Selective emotions can help us retain what's good but remove what's bad.[3]

"In sum, it is consequentially good that we sometimes respond to good things with good feelings, and sometimes respond to bad things with bad feelings even when the thing is both good and bad."

Phil said, "I agree that selectivity can have good consequences. However, as with so many issues concerning the value of the emotions there is potential consequential evil in the selectivity of affects. As you say, it is sometimes difficult to discover the overall evaluation, especially of a very complex state of affairs. But affective selectivity can make it *more* difficult to discover the overall evaluation. For an emotional response to a partial evaluation often discourages or even *prejudices* an inquiry into the overall evaluation. How often do we like something or someone and adamantly refuse to consider their faults? Or,—which might be worse—we dislike something or someone, perhaps even with good reason, but then refuse to acknowledge any good in it or virtue in them."

Connie said, "Okay, selectivity has risks as well as benefits. But *I'll* be content consoling Jeff with respect to his mom's death, as long as I don't make other evils appear greater. I won't try to console for every evil. So, go ahead and direct your affects. And even be selective. But it's a long way from directing your emotions to particular goods and evils to relativity, meaning emotionally emphasizing a state of affair's value for persons with whom one has special relationships."

Jeff asked, "Is it a long way? I defended directivity partly on the grounds that it greatly facilitated performance, at least in some situations, and maybe even survival situations. And I defended selectivity on the ground that it makes us more effective in preserving good things while removing the bad. If similar benefits were also true of affective relativity, then relativity can be supported as well. And I believe that the same or similar advantages *can* also be claimed for the relativity of affects.

"As I began to explain earlier, due to emotional relativity, we are more effective in our production of good things because we are more greatly concerned with intimates. That is, affective relativity has generally good consequences. For, everything else being equal, it is better that one deliberate concerning those persons with whom one has mutual influence and understanding rather than deliberate concerning other persons. For greater influence makes one's decisions more efficacious; greater understanding prevents blunders. One can most effectively help and please those whose interests are best known. Therefore, it is better that one be motivated to deliberate concerning the interests of persons with whom one has influence and understanding. And greater emotional concern for someone motivates greater deliberation concerning that person's welfare. Therefore, it is good that one has greater emotional concern for persons with whom one has influence and understanding than for other persons. In other words, in general, affective relativity is effective."

Connie interjected, "As with interoffice gift exchanges: you never want to pull out of the hat the name of someone you barely know!"

Jeff added, "Furthermore, not only does affective relativity motivate effective deliberation, it would be more difficult to make any decision if one was not more concerned about a state of affairs' value for certain persons rather than others."

Phil objected, "No doubt that greater concern for some can simplify a deliberation, or even cause one to dispense with deliberation, but would the resulting action be *justified*? That is, if an action affected one hundred people, only one of whom I loved, and whose interests were clear, affective relativity would bring a quicker decision. But it might be the wrong decision, if the loved one's interests conflicted with the rest of the effected persons. Concern for everyone involved would require more information for a decision to be made, but more information is necessary for a correct decision."

Jeff said, "Sometimes it is better to do something, help someone, than deliberate further."

Connie emphasized, "Sometimes!"

Jeff said, "Sometimes we really cannot know whether the consequences of our actions will benefit or harm persons distant from us."

Phil replied, "Yes, but when that is so, one has a very good *reason* to conclude one's deliberation with less emphasis on their welfare. But one does not need affective relativity or emotional bias for that."

Jeff said, "Earlier, you said that it might be psychologically necessary for deliberation that we have a preference for the present and immediate future. I think it might be psychologically necessary for deliberation that we respond emotionally more strongly for a state of affair's value for intimates than for non-intimates. Deliberation must be possible before it can be made more reliable."

Phil said, "But if our decisions were better without the emotional bias toward certain persons, then affective relativity can be justified only as a stage in moral development."

Connie said, "Jeff is right that affective relativity is good at motivating effective action. The problem is that when a deliberation is *influenced*, and not merely *motivated* by affective relativity it is sometimes a bad decision because loved one's interests sometimes conflict with others' interests."

Jeff said, "If a person appreciates the dangers of greater emotional concern for some, then that concern becomes less dangerous. For instance, one could be motivated to deliberate without necessarily making the wrong decision. Affective relativity is not good or bad by itself; whether it has good or bad consequences depends upon one's circumstances and other character traits, such as how independent one's decisions are from one's feelings. In this respect, affective relativity or emotional bias is no different from any virtue. Having one virtue without others can make someone worse instead of better. For example, a *courageous* fanatic is more dangerous than a cowardly one.

"And affective relativity is less likely to produce wrong decisions, if one realizes that the rules for feeling are not identical with the rules of right action. It is not merely understandable, but right, that a person has greater emotional concern for some rather than others. Nevertheless, I agree that people are too often partial in their actions.

"In sum, I believe that you have not proven that grief is wrong *simply because* it is partial and even relative. For affective partiality and even relativity is not all bad."

Phil objected, "You've been defending affective relativity, *in general*, by arguing that it has good consequences as well as bad. All right, I agree. But this does not mean that every instance of affective relativity has good consequences as well as bad. In particular, reactive grief's consequences are clearly bad for the grieving person, and do no good for the dead."

Jeff said, "Next, we should discuss *grief's* consequences."

Summary of the Conversation

Although everyone dying to be "replaced" by younger generations is probably better than everyone already born living forever with no newborns surviving, this position does not entail that that everyone dying to be "replaced" is better than some people achieving immortality.

As grief is relative, grief is a response to the values attached to a state of affairs for persons with whom we have special relationships, a loved one would grieve even under the circumstances in which the person's death was better than any realistic alternative, everyone considered equally. (Another aspect of grief's relativity is that we usually grieve only for persons with whom we had a special relationship).

The relativity of affects has both good and bad consequences. If this relativity is used properly, its consequential value can be increased considerably. For example, it can be used as a substitute for the violation of neutral obligations, and it can motivate inquiry and deliberation without necessarily determining the outcome of these. Therefore, it has not been proven that grief is wrong merely because it is relative.

Study Questions

(1) Should ethical considerations be applied to emotions in general (and grief in particular)?

(2) Should we grieve for persons with whom we have no relationship?

Fourteen

BENEFITS AND HARMS OF GRIEF

"I'm In You" by Peter Frampton began playing.

"Before considering grief's *consequences*, I would like to apply some of the distinctions we used to understand the evil of death to appraise the intrinsic value of grief responses," Connie said. "The grief responses upon which we have focused are intrinsic evils. Specifically, inhibitive grief is intrinsically evil as a deprivation. And sorrow pangs are diametrically evil."

Phil asked rhetorically, "Jeff, you would agree?"

Jeff answered anyway. "Definitely. Those are the two most obvious, even though not the most important, reasons that I wish to be consoled. *The most important reason for wishing to be consoled is that the griever's evaluations are terribly true.* I wanted desperately to have been persuaded that they were not. But I think that it is too late to dissuade me from believing these."

Phil inquired, "We've described inhibition as the absence of positive responses to good things or as reluctance to enjoy good things. And we've mentioned some good things concerning which grievers might be inhibited. But we haven't described these attacks of sorrow. Of course I know what sadness and anger feel like, but I'm not sure that I've ever experienced anything comparable to a sorrow *attack*. What's it like?"

Jeff said, "*In my case* often I think about some aspect of the loss or its severity, and then a powerful feeling surges through me, especially through my chest, throat and head. It almost feels like my head will explode. I get literally choked up: my throat feels tight and breathing is more difficult, and I grimace, clench or bang my fists, and often bury my face, and scream and cry."

Connie added, "Yes, it's *excruciating*; so much so that thinking about grief responses is almost as painful as thinking about the griever's evaluations."

Phil saw the look on his friends' faces. "I'm sorry. I'm sorry that I asked for details."

Again Jeff defended Phil. "No, don't apologize. We need—I need—to articulate my grief."

Jeff continued, "Certainly grief is objectionable insofar as it is intrinsically evil. But I'm still unconvinced that an overall evaluation of grief, including consequential value and other standards of appraisal, would not justify grief."

Possible Harms of Grief and Consolation

Connie said, "All right, let's discuss grief's consequences. Having grieved myself, I've read some psychological studies on the subject, and I recall that many people suffer from sleep disturbances, loss of appetite, headaches, indigestion, dizziness and nervousness.[1] I suffered from all of these to some degree. There are even some cases in which grief *seems* to have led to a heart attack. And grief has indirectly caused health problems by increasing drug use."

"My least favored form of distraction," Jeff said reassuringly.

Connie concluded, "Grief can harm one's health."

Phil said, "And grief can be bad for one's character, in addition to entailing and producing one's own unhappiness."

Jeff confessed, "Since my mom's death I have been less sensitive to others' misfortunes. Connie, the other day, when you told me over the phone of your nagging abdominal problems, I confess that I really didn't care! Before my mom's death I would have been concerned. And I've already told you about my feelings of envy towards my uncles. I do not think their deaths' would disturb me. But perhaps you should approve of these insensitivities, for at least others' evils are not making me grieve!

"I think that grief can be ethologically harmful, that is, detrimental to one's character, although these examples concern narrowed feelings rather than wrong action. But I have *done* some things of which I'm not proud. As we know, anger is *one* part of grief, and of course anger can be harmful.

"Four years ago, a few days after my mom was diagnosed as having terminal cancer I blew my top at a discourteous person and I said some very nasty things which was made worse, not better, by the fact that my angry remarks were true.

"Prior to my mom's death I had problems with roaches in my kitchen and my halfway measures were no solution at all. Then, a couple evenings after the funeral, I thoroughly emptied the many cabinets in my kitchen and went on a rampage. In droves roaches were sprayed, splayed, and altogether 'slayed.' They were shriveled and dismembered. I was repulsed and thrilled while the slaughter dragged on. I was a comical version of Achilles who in his rage over the death of his beloved Patrochlus covered the battlefield with Trojan corpses.

"At least I solved my roach problem."

Phil said, "That reminds me of a scene in *Paths of Glory*. One condemned prisoner said to another, 'You see that bug. Tomorrow it will be alive and I'll be dead. It will have more contact with my wife and children than I will.' The other prisoner responded by squashing the roach and said, '*Now you've got the edge on him.*' Perhaps you had a similar motive."

Connie said, "At least you vented in a way that didn't hurt anyone."

"But I have," Jeff confessed. "An hour after I came home from the funeral I received an obscene phone call. . . ."

"Oh, no!" Connie exclaimed. "I despise them!"

Jeff continued. "Of course I was shocked and hung up the phone. But then I recalled being told that obscene phone callers enjoy shocking people, so I thought that the only way to discourage him from making these phone calls, especially to me, was by 'turning the tables'—shock *him*, and for *me* to be in control. So I planned an unpleasant response for him. Sure enough, he called back the next day. In a calm voice I advised him to kill himself and even suggested a method. He just listened, and then I calmly hung up."

Connie reassured, "I'm *sure* he didn't kill himself."

Phil said, "He messed with the wrong person at the wrong time."

Jeff replied, "It was the 'wrong time' all right. But it's the 'wrong person' part that worries me. Though my grief was a factor in my cruel response, I can't blame it all on that. But to be precise, it was *anger* that contributed to my cruelty; it was not sorrow or inhibition. And while anger is understandable, I don't want to defend *it*."

Phil said, "But if sorrow or inhibition contributes to anger, then anger's mischief counts against them."

Jeff sighed and went on. "But in addition to grief's effect on character we must consider the effect of consolation on character. Many *consolations* have the potential to harm a person's moral development. We must consider not only whether grief entails and produces more bad than good, but also whether a survivor has a better alternative. Without going into detail all over again, some consolations are potentially harmful. Minimized evils are easier to produce or tolerate, and evaluation consolations seek to minimize or even eliminate the evil of death. Particularly troublesome in this regard are the consolations that life is mostly suffering, or absurd, or pointless, or trivial."

Phil indicated, "Usually systems of thought which are dreary nevertheless contain rules designed to prevent actions in complete disregard of human life."

Connie said, "I agree that minimizing the evil of death to the point that it was not regarded as a terrible evil could have the consequence of making it psychologically easier to kill another or oneself, or at least lead to not taking proper precautions to prevent either of these. But minimizing the evil of death to the point that it is no longer regarded as a terrible evil could also encourage a person to risk his or her life for some worthy purpose, or refrain from objectionable means of preserving life."

Jeff replied, "These benefits could come from beliefs which do not have the disadvantages which belong to dreary consolations. One need not think that life in general is cheap in order to risk one's own. One need only realize that other lives are as precious as one's own, for example.[2] I suspect that a belief that misery is universal would make it less likely that one would risk one's life since it eliminates a major reason for such a risk."

Phil said, "All right, dreary consolations might be ethologically poor. And grief might be ethologically poor. But not all consolations are dreary. For example, that life is good and should not be wasted on grief. So, there might be an alternative to grief which is ethologically acceptable. In that case, grief's possible ethological damage is a reason to discourage it."

Phil continued as the Rolling Stones' "Paint It Black" played in the background. "What makes me particularly concerned by grief's pain is that grief is self-perpetuating. Emotions generally linger after, and sometimes long after, the event which triggered them. This is called 'emotional inertia.'"[3]

Jeff interjected, "I agree that there is such a thing as emotional inertia. However, in the case of grief, one is responding to an ongoing evil. While mom's death happened at a single moment six weeks ago, the losses entailed and produced by this continue.

"Furthermore, there is a sense of 'emotional inertia' which is not applicable to my grief. According to one meaning, 'emotional inertia' is the persistence of an affect after the belief upon which it was based is no longer held by that person. For instance, a person angered at another for a perceived affront might still have ill feelings towards that person even after discovering that the supposed affront never occurred. Inertia can thus be very unfortunate. However, I persist in nearly all those beliefs upon which my grief is based. Thus, this particular sense of 'emotional inertia,' a sense in which it is often bad because it is less susceptible to rational persuasion, does not apply to my grief."

Phil added, "A phenomena connected with emotional inertia, in both senses—that emotions linger, and even linger after a belief which occasioned the emotion is disproved—is that emotions are often 'magnetizing dispositions.' A magnetizing disposition is one which creates conditions to elicit the response to which one is disposed.[4] For example, a guy with a 'chip on his shoulder' looks for things to rouse anger. That is, anger is a 'magnetizing disposition.' Anger makes a person disposed to further anger by seeking or creating occasions for it. Adapting your example, when a person learns that the supposed affront never occurred he might seek being affronted. A person in love looks for things to elicit these feelings, such as the blossoming of buds in the spring. Love is a magnetizing disposition. The lover anxiously awaits and notices things a lonely person does not. I am greatly concerned that grief, like many affects, is a magnetizing disposition."

"What a sweet, romantic example! And from a married man no less!" Connie kidded.

Phil groaned, "Evidently a sense of humor is a desperate magnetizing disposition! For us at least!"

Phil continued, "My concern is that grief seeks out or causes conditions which elicit grieving."

Jeff said, "What do you mean? A grieving person is not likely to kill, for the purpose of eliciting grieving."

Phil said, "No, but grievers will find further reasons for grieving and will remind themselves of their loss. Our conversation might be an example of this. And a griever might create further losses, over which to feel sorrow or inhibition, even if none are as great or serious as the death of a loved one."

Jeff remarked, "Unfortunately, it's all too easy to be reminded of my loss, regardless whether grief is magnetizing, because, as I just said, the loss is ongoing."

Phil said, "True, but do not misunderstand or ignore my caution. A grieving person finds reasons to feel sorrow or inhibition besides those entailed or produced by the loved one's death. And I do not simply mean that a griever is more likely to feel sorrow or be inhibited by evils which already exist and which he or she might ameliorate if motivated. I mean that a griever will create other losses over which to feel sorrow or be inhibited."

Jeff responded, "On the contrary, since my mom's death I am *less* sensitive to other evils, as I confessed a moment ago. For instance, I'm in no position to grieve over anyone else's death except another intimate. The only respect in which my mom's death has 'opened me up' to other sorrow or inhibition is by rekindling my grief for my dad. But as I've already said, my mom's death has made my dad's death even worse for me. Therefore, I don't' know whether the rekindling of this grief is due to grief's being magnetizing or simply because a new evil has been added to this old loss."

Phil countered, "All right, but grievers do subject themselves to additional losses; losses not entailed or inevitably produced by the loved one's death. A griever might miss opportunities. In fact, that's what inhibition is."

Connie agreed emphatically. "Yes, not only do grievers deny themselves enjoyment as a result of guilt, and not only because they might mistakenly believe that by enjoying themselves they are increasing the loved one's deprivation or decreasing the organic value of their lives as wholes. . . ."

"Mistakes we've already exposed," Phil reminded proudly.

"but also because grief is magnetizing. Grief will perpetuate itself since grief itself is a loss. Grief not only causes one to look for reasons to grieve, and create things over which to feel sorrow or nothing at all, but grief itself is an evil. Thus, it supplies, by itself, an object over which to feel bad. Of course, it does not make sense to inflict evils on oneself for the reason that it is bad for one to have evils, nevertheless, grief makes one prone to this."[5]

Jeff said, "I admit that, in some respects, grief is consequentially evil. However, in some respects, it is consequentially good. For example, grief causes crying which is good. Crying provides relief, if only temporary. It might even be unhealthy to suppress crying."

Phil replied, "First, I agree that one part of grief, crying, provides relief from another part of grief—such as the feeling that one's head will explode. That is, one part of grief lessens the evil of another part. But that is not a justification of grief. This only shows that a great sorrow without crying is worse than a great sorrow relieved by crying. Crying is not, upon the whole, intrinsically good. Instead, the value of crying is largely conditional upon one's already being sorrowful. Therefore, a person who hasn't great sorrow is not missing out on some good by not crying."

Jeff agreed, "Yes, crying was a bad example of grief's being consequentially good. *I* committed the smokers' fallacy this time!"

Phil continued, "Second, you said it was bad to 'suppress' crying. Well, I would never intentionally advocate suppressing grief. I have heard that suppression can be harmful. But I doubt that a loving one's only alternatives are grief and the suppression of grief. If consolation has an advantage over some alternative methods to comfort, such as distraction, it is that it seeks to limit grief without suppression. To explain further, we must use the term 'suppression' carefully. In the sense in which *I* am using the word, a person 'suppresses' an affective response when that person attempts to prevent a response which, for that person, is consequent to a set of beliefs which that person continues to hold. But a consolation, as we've defined it, attempts to alter the person's responses by altering that person's beliefs, either about the griever's evaluations or about the affect per se. The consoler's trying to limit grief by changing the survivor's attitude. The consoler's not trying to stifle grief. Therefore, a consoler is not trying to 'suppress' any grief response, crying or other. It's true; a consoler might inadvertently cause suppression by discouraging grief though failing to alter the griever's beliefs.

"Of course, my definition of 'suppress' is not completely clear since I have not explained what I mean by, 'a response which, for that person, is consequent to that person's beliefs.' But fortunately, in order to distinguish consolation from suppression this need not be made clearer. The point is that seeking to comfort someone by getting him or her to have feelings and responses 'contrary' to his or her beliefs is different from consoling. A consoler is trying to alter the person's beliefs thereby freeing that person from painful responses."

Jeff said, "All right, but the key issue is whether the alleged harmful effects of suppression belong to it only as you have defined it, or whether they belong to it in a wider sense which includes consolation."

Connie stated the alleged harmful effects of suppression. "In the books which I have read it is claimed that suppression, in some sense not carefully analyzed, can lead to ill health. For example, it might cause asthma, colitis, sinus, or arthritic problems.[6] Also, some claim that suppression merely postpones inevitable grieving.[7] Thus, it supposedly harms without providing any long term benefit. However, *perhaps* there is some benefit in the postponement of grieving.

"Unfortunately, none of the studies with which I am familiar attempt to draw a distinction between suppression, as Phil has defined it, and consolation. In other words, my readings have not made clear to me whether the supposed harmful consequences of suppression would result from persuasive consolation.

"In fact, further distinctions besides that of suppression and persuasive consolation might be necessary. For example, a person consoled by a *response* consolation might suffer the same consequences as a person who suppresses, whereas a person who is consoled by an evaluation consolation might not."

Jeff added, "Unfortunately, evaluation consolations are not very persuasive, so their effect—except in a conversation like ours where we're trying to be careful, considerate and non-manipulative—might be suppression."

Jeff and Phil nodded, and Connie returned the discussion to the potential harm of grief. "Maybe" by the Chantels ended, and "Searchin'" by the Coasters began playing. "In general, painful and inhibitive states, when chronic, impair a person's self-confidence. And impaired self-confidence can decrease happiness as well as harm a person's character. Thus, grief, being sorrowful or inhibitive, has these dangers.

"Furthermore, the more terrible one's grief the greater the risk that one will eventually no longer want to be reminded of the dead loved one. And I know that you do not wish such a result."

Grief and Adjustment

Jeff said, "You are right. But as I was saying, grief has good consequences as well; although my earlier example, crying, was not a good example. Grieving does help a person who has had a loved one die. When an intimate dies the loving ones need to develop new habits. Some old habits involve responses to the dead person and thus become useless. But the development of new habits requires time. Grief assists in this adjustment."

Connie said, "Although I'm unclear how grief aids in the transition, I'm glad to hear you offer a defense of this kind. For this defense of grief makes it valuable only as a phase; grief is not justified as a permanent aspect of the survivor's life."

Phil said, "I agree with Connie that this account of grief justifies it only as a phase. But I wish to focus on the other point which she raised. *How* does grief aid one in acquiring new habits?"

Jeff said, "I'll tell you why I think grief responses can help one adjust to a loved one's loss. For example, one of my old habits was to phone my mom before leaving work. Now I still 'get the urge' to phone her, but it causes me intense sorrow. So, such old habits are painful now. This pain might discourage, or negatively reinforce, such old habits. The same is true of other things we shared. The pain I feel when I 'get the urge' to repeat these might train me not to 'get the urge.'"

Phil objected, "I think that the futility of the old habits is enough to discourage them without sorrow. Grief responses are not necessary for this adjustment. The pain might contribute as a partial cause of the adjustment, but it is not necessary. It is too kind to grief to say that it is consequentially good when it is an unnecessary evil."

Connie added, "Adjustment can be of three kinds. It can be 'accumulative,' in which new habits are added to the old. It can be 'subtractive,' in which the old habits are dropped, but are not replaced. Or it could be neither, in which comparable new habits replace the old. Obviously the first type of adjustment, accumulative, does not apply to the case of a person whose loved one has died. The old habits have to go. An example of the second kind, subtractive adjustment, is a widow who loses sexual desire, or any person who does not acquire new intimacies; for example, someone who lost a parent and resents an older person behaving in a caring, parental manner. In the case of subtractive adjustment, grief is not merely a phase. The *sorrow* pangs might be only a phase, but the *deprivation* becomes a part of that person's life. This deprivation is a form of inhibition. If the adjustment is subtractive, one cannot justify grief by claiming that it helped produce it, for the effect is bad! It is no justification of sorrow that it contributes to inhibition!"

Jeff nodded.

Phil smiled at Connie in approval, and resumed, "My other objection to Jeff's statement that grief assists in the adjustment is that grief is an *effect* which occurs during the transition; it is not a *cause* of the transition. The repeatedly frustrated old habits cause sorrow and inhibition. For example, you are about to leave work and think 'Time to call mom.' But of course, this impulse is frustrated. That frustration is the grief. This is an effect of the futility of the old habit.

"After the adjustment, the same frustration no longer exists, though there will remain memory of this frustration. Thus, if grief is an effect of frustrated habits, then the loving one *stops* grieving when the habits go, except insofar as the frustration is recalled. This seems to be a plausible account of grief and the aforementioned 'Time heals' phenomenon, which we explained differently earlier. On this account, the grief responses of sorrow and inhibition are effects. They are disturbing by-products of the futility of old habits. They do not *cause* the adjustment; the *inefficacy* of the old habits phases them out. Therefore, one cannot consider the byproducts, grief responses, to be consequentially good on the ground of aiding adjustment."

Jeff responded to Connie's point. "Grief can prevent new enjoyments, so sometimes it causes subtractive adjustment. But subtractive adjustment is better than repeated frustration."

Phil reminded, "But as I've claimed, grief responses are not necessary causes of this transition. The uselessness of the impulses is enough for them to wane."

Jeff replied, "I'm not sure that grief responses, particularly sorrow, are not helpful. I doubt that the uselessness alone of the old habits would cause them to wane so quickly. I think that sorrow can hasten the adjustment because affects are 'salient.' Affects focus a person's attention. A griever's sorrow focuses attention on the loss and therefore the need to discard the old habits. Again, pain—as in sorrow—is a *negative* reinforcement to the now obsolete habits.

"To adapt a point which Connie earlier made, grief is obsessive and so cannot last. Grief focuses attention on the change in one's life, and so motivates adjustment. Frankly, I think about my mom more often now than when she was alive. My sorrow forces me 'to come to terms' with her death, to adjust."

Connie said, "But I see a danger here. You think more often about your mom since her death. Why? Is it to remind yourself that she is dead and you must adjust to it, or is it to feign that she is still alive and that your life is not different? If it's to feign her being alive or denial of her death, then the salience of grief might delay adjustment."

Jeff said, "My obsessive thoughts concern both her life and her death. I guess I don't know whether their tendency is to retard or hasten adjustment."

Phil added, "For the possible benefit of a quicker transition you have all the suffering involved with grief. I think it should be discouraged."

Jeff said, "Perhaps I have taken the wrong approach. I have suggested that grief responses facilitate the adjustment. You have argued that grief prolongs the transition rather than expediting it, because imagining the loved one living is like feigning that the person is still alive. Maybe so, but perhaps this feigning lessens the sorrow and inhibition which one experiences during the transition."

"It 'felicitates' rather than facilitates the transition?" Phil tried to joke.

Connie said, "*Maybe* feigning has both these consequences. It prolongs the transition but makes it less intrinsically evil. However, your point that *feigning* is consequentially good is not a defense of the grief responses of sorrow or inhibition. In fact, your defense of feigning assumed that sorrow and inhibition were evils. In effect, your defense of feigning was that it limited the evils of sorrow and inhibition.

"Grief is a complex phenomenon. That is one of the main things I have learned from our discussion. Perhaps some parts of the affect are justified, whereas other aspects are not. Our main focus has been on the responses of sorrow and inhibition, mentioning others only in passing."

Jeff sighed and said, "There is much more to sorrow and inhibition than we have discussed in considering their effects on the survivor's happiness or health. Our recent discussion has made it seem that the sole cause of grief episodes is a frustrated search for a loved one. But our earlier analysis of grief emphasized the griever's evaluations. Sorrow and inhibition, justified or not, are responses to these evaluations. The dead person's continued existence is feigned, in part, because the truth is terrible."

Connie said, "I agree that these responses cannot be totally explained as effects of frustrated habits which involved the loved one. I agree that they are, in part, responses to the griever's evaluations. But you still have not offered convincing arguments that these responses are consequentially good."

Phil added, "If grief were merely an effect of frustrated habits involving that person, the only relevant comforting remark would be that the person no longer exists. And therefore, there is no point in searching for that person or responding to some stimuli as though that person still exists. And yet, no one offers that as a comforting remark because they know that it is precisely the sore point."

Jeff said, "Even if, upon the whole, the grief responses of sorrow and inhibition are intrinsically and consequentially evil, I still believe that these are justified. I think it is justified to remain in grief, even though it continues the evils we've discussed."

Connie objected, "But surely you take these evils very seriously. You take death very seriously because it is a deprivation. But inhibition is also a deprivation. Because you are justified in believing that some event is evil you think you are justified in perpetuating another evil?"

In the background, John Lennon wailed through "Cold Turkey."

Jeff reassured, "I do take the evils of these responses very seriously. However, I do not agree that the only consideration relevant to justifying a decision is the consequences of that decision. The decision to encourage further grief has as its consequences, the grief itself, which is intrinsically bad, and the grief's consequences, many of which can be bad. But not all decisions should be justified exclusively by the consequences of the decision."

Consequentialism

Phil was puzzled. "Jeff, from our many previous philosophical discussions I've gotten the impression that you are a 'consequentialist,' meaning a proponent of the idea that the only relevant considerations for a decision were the value of the consequences of that decision, whether that value is intrinsic to the decided upon action itself —in this case, the grief responses—, or that action's consequences—in this case, the grief responses' effects on character and happiness.

"Let me explain consequentialism a little more. According to consequentialism, the 'bottom line' in making a decision is the value of the decision's consequences, whether it will benefit those affected, and other considerations are important only as they are relevant to the value of the decision's consequences. Consequentialism allows that it is often important to the justification of some decision to consider truths about the past. But the only reason it is important to consider these is that they can affect the consequences of one's action. Facts about the past alter the consequences of our decisions. For example, the consequences of my transferring money to someone are quite different depending upon whether or not that person has performed some service for me. If the person has performed some service for me, the consequences of my payment include avoiding legal or financial penalties. If the person has not performed some service, my 'payment' has no such consequences, but is a gift. Another example is that the consequences of my 'making nice' to Pam depend upon whether I have angered her. So, even someone looking 'forward,' that is, making decisions on the basis of consequences only, needs to be mindful of the past."

Jeff said, "I'm not surprised that you think that I am a consequentialist. For I have strong reservations about many of the most familiar arguments against it. For instance, a well-known alleged counterexample to consequentialism is that the decision to keep a promise is justified by more than merely the comparative values of the consequences of the decisions to keep or break it. The anti-consequentialist, or 'antecedentialist' view is that a validly made—whatever that is—promise creates a *prima facie* obligation to keep it, independently of consideration of the comparative consequences of breaking or keeping it. In other words, people making promises 'bind' themselves and can't later 'unbind' themselves, because they think that keeping the promise has bad consequences. Of course, some proponents of this view would allow that bad consequences of keeping the promise can 'override' the *prima facie* obligation created merely by the promise.

"In contrast, consequentialism maintains that a person who makes a promise to do something incurs the obligation to do that thing only insofar as the value of its performance has better consequences than its non-performance, given that the promise has been made. I admit that I incline to the latter view of promises, that a broken promise is wrong only insofar as it is harmful, either to the promise maker, 'promisee,' or a third person."

Jeff presented a second example.[8] "Others have supplied the following alleged counterexample to consequentialism. Suppose that a series of terrible crimes have been committed in the same city, and there is widespread increase in fear. In fact, the notoriety of these crimes adversely affects tourism, which in turn decreases the prosperity of the citizens as well as the city's tax base. Some social program will have to be cut and thereby some lives will be endangered. The district attorney knows that some deadbeat can be framed for the crimes. He also knows that there is very little chance that his innocence will eventually be believed beyond the tabloid circuit, which is already surfeit with allegations of frame-ups. Further suppose, however unrealistically, that the district attorney knows that the real criminal will neither be caught nor strike again.

"Given all these suppositions, realistic and unrealistic, it is reasonable to conclude that the decision to frame the deadbeat would be consequentially better than any alternative, such as leaving the case open. Therefore, consequentialism would likely recommend the frame-up. On the other hand, opponents of consequentialism claim that the theory must be defective to have such a result. They argue that the action would be wrong despite its good consequences because the person is innocent."

Jeff continued, "Phil, I no longer believe that consequentialism applies to all our decisions. Some decisions have a value independent of their consequences. I still reluctantly side with the consequentialist view of promise keeping. The decision to keep a promise or not should be based solely on the consequences of that decision. But I do not any longer agree with the consequentialist view concerning the accusation of the innocent. I do think that there are considerations besides the value of the consequences of the action which are relevant, although they might be overridden by the consideration of consequences. In my view, the major difference between the promise breaking and framing cases is that the latter necessarily involves the assertion of false statements, or at least deliberately misleading statements.

"One can break a promise, and perhaps even without repercussions, without denying that one has made the promise or denying any other truth. Perhaps *some* promise breaking requires falsehoods, such as breaking a promise to tell the truth, but not all. Further, although some promises are insincere, which *is* one way to mislead, an eventually broken promise need not have been insincere at the time it was made. Therefore, promise breaking does not necessarily and always entail lying or deliberate deception. In contrast, you cannot frame a person without at least being deliberately misleading.

"Like the case of framing, I believe that falsehoods are involved in not responding with sorrow or inhibition to the death of a loved one. And I think that, in addition to the value of the consequences of a decision, one should consider whether that decision requires falsehoods. It is this modification of consequentialism which I would make, and I believe this modification is relevant to whether grief is justified."

Now Connie was puzzled. "What do you mean that falsehoods are involved in not being sorrowful or inhibited by the death of a loved one? Are you referring to the fact that 'denial' is often a part of grief?[9] It's true that people often feign that the loved one is alive. And people sometimes falsely deny the griever's evaluations. And in part, people do either of these to avoid sorrow or inhibition. Perhaps some sorrow and inhibition is inevitable, if a survivor is truthful. However, while falsehood might be psychologically necessary to avoid any sorrow and inhibition whatsoever, falsehood is not psychologically necessary to discourage these beyond their inevitable extent. We don't need to lie or deceive ourselves to avoid encouraging grief."

Jeff said, "Indeed, I mean more than that falsehoods are psychologically necessary to avoid sorrow and inhibition. I think there is something false about not feeling sorrow or inhibition at a loved one's death. The absence of these affects themselves is a falsehood. Not feeling these things is 'dishonest.' It's not just that denial involves a falsehood or that one might falsely deny the grievers' evaluations; sorrow and inhibition are 'true' responses to death and the absence of these responses would be 'false.'"

Connie said, "Well, now I know what you do not mean; I still do not understand what you do mean."

Phil said, "Jeff has made two claims which we need to examine. One which puzzles Connie and me is that the absence of sorrow and inhibition is a kind of falsehood. The other is that consequentialism must be modified to allow for an obligation to truthfulness or veracity which is independent of the value of its consequences. Let's focus on the second point for now. Why do you think that truthfulness is justifiable independently of its consequences?"

Jeff paused, so Phil continued. "I presume that veracity, which includes believing truths and even espousing truths, usually has good consequences. We wouldn't be able to function unless *most* of our beliefs were true, so veracity is usually wise. So, why do you think that there must be a justification of veracity independent of the value of its consequences?"

Connie interrupted, "In the particular case before us, Jeff's mom's death, I doubt that *complete* veracity would have as good consequences as only partial veracity."

Phil said, "Really? It's true that pretending she were alive would ease some of the sorrow and inhibition, but such a departure from reality, especially if one also pretended that the dead person was still available for visits and so on, would have consequences for one's enjoyment of one's real environment. Yes, it would be better were these terrible things not true, but it does not follow that it is better to not believe them."

Connie said, "I agree that there are more harmful consequences than good in believing that she never died. *Partial* veracity is necessary. But I think that one or two falsehoods thrown in with the truth would have better consequences than complete veracity. For example, believing that there will be a blissful reunion in the afterlife *might* ease the grief responses."

Phil objected, "That could have the consequence of suicide."

Connie replied, "Then one must also believe that suicide is wrong."

Phil said, "It is difficult to reconcile the belief that suicide is wrong with a belief in a blissful reunion."

Connie said, "It could be done. Perhaps some other falsehoods would have to be believed, such as that the reunion will be more blissful if you wait."

Phil said, "Maybe you're right. Maybe consequentialism could not justify *complete* veracity in a case like this, but there are *dangers*, even in every particular case, in *devising* beliefs in order to obtain the best consequences from them, regardless of truth. This sort of self-deception seems difficult to 'pull off.' At some level you might know that you're deceiving yourself and a conflict might result. But I know that I'm just speculating about this—I don't want to deceive myself! Anyway, I suspect that consequentialism can justify forming beliefs based upon the evidence, rather than upon a consideration of the value of the consequences of the beliefs. So a consequentialist would, at least usually, form beliefs based on the evidence, but this policy would be justified because of its consequences."

Jeff asked, "You both still agree that the griever's evaluations are true?"

They nodded. Gerry and the Pacemakers advised "Don't Let the Sun Catch You Crying" and the Flying Machine requested "Smile a Little Smile for Me."

Jeff asked, "Then what advice should a consequentialist give to me? Which part of the affect of grief should I discourage? Should I disbelieve these evaluations which you admit are true? Is this that part of the affect which I should change? Or should I believe them but not respond to them with sorrow or inhibition?"

Connie said, "A comforter cannot admit that the griever's evaluations are true and then recommend that they be disbelieved by the person to whom the admission was made. So, even if this were a good recommendation, it is no longer available to us, for we have admitted them.

"Therefore, our only remaining recommendation can be that, though you believe the griever's evaluations, you do not encourage responding to them with sorrow or inhibition."

Jeff said, "I think that it is not merely too late to recommend disbelieving these evaluations which are true. I believe that such a recommendation would be unjustified, even if it were practical, and even if it would have good consequences, because the decision to believe that which is true has a justification distinct from the value of the consequences of believing that which is true.

"It's important to understand why we should believe the griever's evaluations regardless whether these beliefs have good consequences; *these* reasons will *also* show why it's wrong to discourage sorrow and inhibition. We must be justified in believing things simply because the evidence indicates they're true, independent of whether the belief has good consequences."

Arguments that the Obligation of Veracity Is Independent of Consequences

Phil asked, "Why do you think that believing something can have justification independent of the value of the consequences of that belief?

Jeff began, "The *evidence* for a belief, or more precisely, for the truth of some statement, is independent of the value of the consequences of the belief. Sometimes people seem to confuse the two. They're eager to believe something because they think the belief will have good consequences. For example, thinking that a scandal involving a politician whom one dislikes might have good consequences is different from the evidence of wrongdoing. Monica Lewinsky's dress stain was the evidence of her affair with Clinton; the consequences of the nation's belief in Clinton's infidelity might please a Republican, but the consequences were not evidence to support the belief.

"Often, in politics and in widely publicized trials, people seem to eagerly accept or adamantly reject allegations depending on whether the allegation would support or harm a social cause which they value. The evidence seems to be treated like just a means or worse, an obstacle, to the desired conclusion."

Phil replied, "There is a sense in which a belief is 'justified,' called 'epistemic justification,' which means that the belief can be shown to be *true*. A belief can be shown to be true independently of the value of its consequences. But, there is a sense in which a belief is 'justified,' called 'moral justification,' which means that one *should* believe it. This latter sense is the one we are presently discussing: whether the moral justification for a belief—whether we should hold that belief—is partly independent of the value of its consequences. And it does not follow that because a belief is epistemically justified independently of the value of its consequences that it is morally justified independently of the value of its consequences. Do not confuse the consequentialist independence of epistemic justification of a belief with consequentialist independence of moral justification of a belief.

Connie added, "Perhaps Jeff's examples show that bad consequences ensue when people adopt beliefs based on their consequences rather than on the evidence. The integrity of public discourse suffers terribly from such cases."

Phil stated, "Yes. There are usually bad consequences when beliefs are adopted because of the belief that they'll have good consequences. To the question 'Should one believe a statement because supported by the evidence?' consequentialism can answer 'Yes, because the consequences are good.' *Hopefully*, it would be true in the case of death and grief also, that the belief with the best consequences is also true, though I realize that this has not been proven.

Connie said, "Just let me make sure I follow. Jeff thinks there is a moral justification for believing truly which cannot be derived from consequentialism. And he thinks that this justification will also apply to being sorrowful and inhibited by a loved one's death. Therefore, to some extent, one would be justified in encouraging sorrow and inhibition despite the bad consequences of such a decision."

Jeff said, "You got it. I have several arguments to show that the consequences of a belief are not the only decisive criterion for adopting a belief. *First*, the reason that consequences should be considered is because of their intrinsic value. Consequences are important because some things are intrinsically good and some things are intrinsically bad. Now, if some *future* thing is intrinsically *bad* that thing is still intrinsically bad after it is past, assuming a point made in an earlier discussion, that temporality does not alter a thing's intrinsic value. Furthermore, we can conceive of cases such that it is consequentially good to believe that some future thing is intrinsically *bad*, for example, in an effort to try to prevent it, but that it is consequentially good to believe that the thing was intrinsically *good* once it is past, for example, in order to restore public calm or individual peace of mind.

"In fact, that might be exactly the way some consolers think. Death is to be avoided, but once it's come they highlight the good side of it. Or to take the 'sour grapes'-type case, in which people think that something is *good* in prospect, but are unable to obtain it, and then comfort themselves by telling themselves that the thing was *bad*. There might be good consequences—such as peace of mind—to limited 'sour grapes' thinking or 'cognitive dissonance,' as psychologists call it. Therefore, it is conceivable, regardless whether realistic, that as long as consequentialism is the only criterion for the justification of holding a belief, that it would be justified to believe a contradiction.

For it is a contradiction to state that a thing is intrinsically good at one time and the very *same* thing intrinsically bad at another time."

Phil said, "It furthermore follows that it is conceivable that consequentialism would justify holding a false belief since contradictions are false. But so what? All you have shown is that a criterion for the justification of adopting a belief which is independent of the evidence for a belief conceivably justifies a false belief. But *of course*! The question becomes whether there is an obligation to avoid false beliefs, or contradictions specifically, which is independent of the bad consequences of believing false statements, or believing contradictions specifically. You have not shown that there is any such independent obligation. Nor have you shown that consequentialism is itself contradictory because it conceivably justifies believing contradictions."

Jeff said, "All right, in my second and third arguments I will show that the consideration of the value of consequences—and consequently, consequentialism—'depends' upon a belief formed independently of the belief's consequences, in the sense of 'depends' that one thing cannot be performed without the other. In other words, one cannot put consequentialism into practice unless one forms beliefs independently of consideration of the value of their consequences.

"My *second* argument is that the knowledge of consequences depends upon evidence of the truth of particular statements, and that prior to applying consequentialism to a particular decision one must have *already* determined, on the basis of the evidence alone, that one should believe that a proposed action would have such and such consequences.

"Let me explain with the following example. Suppose a particular person kills a stranger for pocket change. Now a consequentialist must decide whether to believe that he did it. It might be easier to disbelieve his guilt, or even that the crime occurred. For if it is believed, then it must be investigated, *et cetera*. And all this can be very expensive and tiring. Sometimes it's easier to 'hide one's head in the sand,' as when, according to the tabloids, police departments label suspicious deaths as suicides. But a consequentialist would also observe that *worse* consequences would follow from disbelieving that the crime occurred or that he did it. For example, the killer would probably continue to show disregard for human life. Therefore, a consequentialist would usually recommend that it be believed that a crime was committed, and by the person who in fact committed it whenever this can be ascertained. But this recommendation, based upon the probable consequences of the beliefs, depends also upon the belief that the crime was committed, *et cetera*. That is, if no crime were already believed to have been committed, one could not argue that disbelief in it would have bad consequences. Therefore, the consideration of consequences cannot work unless one already regards the evidence as obliging one to believe certain things.

"It is not merely the case that it must be *true* that the crime was committed for the belief that it was committed to have good consequences; it must be *believed* that the crime was committed in order to believe that there would be good consequences to believing that the crime occurred. You cannot decide that a belief will have good consequences unless you already have other beliefs which are not based on a belief about their consequences. Therefore, at least in such cases, there must be some basis other than its consequences upon which to decide whether one should believe. Presumably that basis would be the evidence that the belief is true."

Connie said with a smile, "I'm not sure I get that!"

Jeff responded, "Let me make my point in another way using an example in which a person deliberately adopts a belief believing that this adoption would have good consequences. People who reluctantly marry try to convince themselves that they're making the right choice. They suspect that as long as they doubt the wisdom of their choice, they'll be less happy with it. So, they adopt the belief 'My fiancée's the one for me,' hoping that the belief will have good consequences. So, there's a belief 'My fiancée's the one' and *another* belief about that belief—let's call it a 'second-order belief' which holds that the first belief will have good consequences. I want to make two points: first, unless the second-order belief is itself based on the evidence our reluctant groom is building on a 'house of cards' with a very good chance of *bad* consequences! So, we cannot wisely apply consequentialism to beliefs unless some belief is accepted on the basis of the evidence alone.

"Using the same example in another way we can show that some beliefs must be based on the evidence alone. We start with 'She's the one for me.' Then there's the second-order statement 'The belief that she's the one for me will have good consequences.' If the second-order statement should not be believed on the basis of the evidence alone, but on the basis of a *third* order statement 'The belief that the belief that she's the one for me will have good consequences will have good consequences,' we see that we have begun an infinite regress. The only way to avoid this regress is for some statement to be accepted on some other basis than the consequences of the belief, presumably the evidence."

Phil laughed. "I knew we couldn't go the night without an 'infinite regress' argument at sometime!"

Jeff continued, "In sum, one cannot apply consequentialism to some particular decision unless one has already formed beliefs independently of consideration of the value of the consequences of those beliefs.

"My *third* argument is that, in addition to the *application* of consequentialism being dependent upon an independent justification of belief, the belief in consequentialism *itself* depends upon an independent justification of belief. It is possible that a belief in consequentialism has good consequences. Nevertheless, even if it were true that such a belief had good consequences, this alone could not prove consequentialism. For such an argument would already assume that the person to be persuaded thinks that statements should be believed ultimately solely for the value of the consequences. In other words, one cannot *adopt* consequentialism on the ground that such a belief would have good consequences because that would be begging the question.

"In general, whatever evidence on behalf of consequentialism which one might present, regardless whether it be the consequences of the belief, the evidence must be judged to be acceptable prior to the adoption of consequentialism. Therefore, the person must use some criteria other than that provided by consequentialism for determining whether to believe the evidence. Again, presumably that basis would be the evidence itself. Not already a consequentialist, what reason could one have? Not the consequences of such a belief. The evidence would not merely be the epistemic justification, it would be the moral justification, as well.

"Therefore, while it might be consequentially good for people to be consequentialists, making the world as good as we can make it, we cannot justify to anyone the belief in consequentialism except on non-consequentialist criteria for adopting beliefs.

"By the way, my arguments against consequentialism do not assume that a consequentialist actually checks on the consequences before adopting any belief. I know that that would be impossible. Rather, my arguments assume only that a consistent, thoroughgoing unmodified consequentialist must regard the consequences as the ultimate moral justification for beliefs, even though these are not actually consulted at every turn. But the ultimate justification of belief cannot be belief's consequences. Therefore, we must modify or limit consequentialism when the issue is what one should believe."

"Whew!" Connie said.

Phil commented, "Right now I cannot point out any error in your argument. Provisionally, I'm convinced. However, I do want to emphasize something which you indicated three times with the word 'presumably.' Although you have more or less convinced me that the consequences of a belief cannot be the sole ultimate criterion for the justification of adopting the belief, you have not proven that the *evidence* is the additional criterion. Nevertheless, I agree that it is, though some, such as authoritarians, might not. Some would say that it is not the evidence for or against a statement which obliges belief or disbelief, but that this obligation comes from some authority, such as revelation or the sovereign or other source of power."

Connie leaned over and whispered, "People who say that are at the *next* table, not ours." Connie smiled at her little joke.

Jeff smiled, but addressed Phil's comment. "Actually, I think that my arguments modifying consequentialism when it comes to beliefs apply against authoritarians. Since authoritarians recommend beliefs without evidence the only *reason* they give to accept a belief is that such acceptance will have good consequences, such as eternal salvation or political stability or avoidance of persecution. Unfortunately, there's even *less* evidence in their case that the required belief will have good consequences than in the case of our jittery groom."

Connie said, "Strictly speaking I think that the most that you've shown against consequentialism is that *some* beliefs must be accepted on the basis of the evidence alone; you haven't shown that all beliefs must be so accepted. In effect, you've argued that belief can't get *started* unless some beliefs are based on the evidence alone. But once 'the ball gets rolling' on the basis of evidence alone other beliefs could be accepted on the basis of the evidence of their consequences. If so, you haven't proven that grief responses shouldn't be discouraged for their consequences, even if they are like beliefs."

Connie added, "Even if there is a factor obliging belief which is independent of the consequences of belief, and were it to follow that a survivor was obliged to believe the griever's *evaluations*, even if these beliefs had bad consequences, it does not follow that the decision to encourage particular *responses* is not determined solely by the value of the consequences of that decision. Therefore, while one might be obliged to believe the griever's evaluations, one is not obliged to encourage a loving one's sorrow or inhibition; as such a decision would have bad consequences."

Jeff said, "Except that I think that affective response is similar to belief; that at least some affective responses are an integral part of knowing. Thus, it is plausible that if our beliefs are obliged by factors additional to their consequences, then at least some of our affective responses are obliged by factors additional to their consequences."

Connie said, "I think you are all wrong about this. Let's discuss it."

Jeff said, "Good! But I guess it will have to be our last topic this evening before they throw us out!"

Phil said, "There's a solution to that. Jeff, order dessert."

A few patrons remained in the restaurant as the Beatles' melancholy "For No One" played.

Summary of the Conversation

Grief, or the responses of sorrow and inhibition are intrinsically evil, the first diametric, the second as a deprivation. Grief can also harm our health and our character. However, it is not certain that a loving one has a better alternative. Grief might be bad but better than any alternative for an indefinite period of time following the loss. Many evaluation consolations are dreary and potentially harmful to our character. "Suppression" can harm our health while only postponing the evils of grief. However, it is not clear whether persuasive consolation would have the same effects as "suppression." Perhaps persuasive response consolation would, but persuasive evaluation consolation would not. Failed consolations of either kind might cause suppression. This is merely speculation on difficult empirical matters.

Assuming that (at some time following the loved one's death) we can find better alternatives to grief, does it follow that the loving one's grief (beyond that time) should be discouraged? Assuming that (after some time) the decision to discourage grief has better consequences than the decision to encourage it, does it follow that we should discourage grief (after that time)?

Even if at some point grief has more bad consequences than good, one *might* argue that grief should be maintained because it is "true." Acceptance of truth is partially independent of the consequences of acceptance. Some beliefs are "appropriate" because true. Perhaps likewise, grief is "appropriate" to a loss. I will discuss this topic in Chapter Fifteen.

The rational practice of consequentialism *conceptually* requires that we adopt some beliefs (at minimum in part) on the basis of their evidence, independent of the consequences of those beliefs. We should not adopt consequentialism except on the basis of evidence alone; and it cannot be applied to a particular situation without beliefs about that situation formed on the basis of the evidence alone. Therefore, we have an obligation to adopt some beliefs and *perhaps* an obligation to encourage some emotional responses independent of the value of their consequences.

Incidentally, the Norse myth about the death of the beloved god, Balder, combines themes prevalent in the discussion of response consolations. Balder was the son of Odin and Frigga. Frigga, in an attempt to make her son immortal, extracted promises of protection from everything, except that she neglected to ask for protection from the mistletoe, thinking it too insignificant; all the while, Odin knew that Balder would die. Overconfident about his invulnerability, the gods played a game in which Balder was the target of their projectiles. He was killed by a branch of mistletoe. Balder's wife then died from grief. Next, the queen of the underworld agreed to return Balder on the condition that every living thing mourn for him. One Giantess refused to weep, and so Balder was not returned.[10] This single myth illustrates the following response consolation themes: *first*, grief is harmful; *second*, grief is futile; *third*, death is inevitable (though its inevitability does not prevent denial of mortality); and *fourth*, grief is partial, an aspect of which is the fact that not everyone mourns for the same person.

Study Questions

(1) Give examples of additive and subtractive adjustment.

(2) Should the consequences of a belief be one factor in deciding to accept or reject the belief?
   - Give examples of situations in which people do appear to accept or reject a belief based on the consequences they believe will ensue.

(3) Do we have moral obligations regarding beliefs? Explain.

(4) Jeff argued that we are (at minimum partly) obliged to base beliefs on evidence, but the example of the district attorney raises an additional question. The district attorney who is framing the "deadbeat" forms his *own* beliefs on the basis of the evidence, but misleads *others*. Do Jeff's arguments that we are obliged to base beliefs on the evidence also show that we are obliged not to mislead others?

Fifteen

GRIEF AS A WAY OF KNOWING

"Ain't No Sunshine" by Bill Withers began playing as Phil requested, "I recall you telling us that you won't have cheesecake and a beer anymore because it reminds you of your mom. As a symbol of the progress we've already made with response consolations and of confidence in us, your consolers, to make further progress, why not order a beer and cheesecake?"

Jeff smiled, "I'll order it on condition that, if we do not make further progress, then you two have to consume them!"

Phil groaned, "Not after the brownie sundaes we had!"

Connie said, "How much confidence can we ask him to show in us if we have so little confidence in ourselves that we are afraid of cheesecake?"

Phil complied, "All right, but the beer would be Connie's since I'm driving. I'm just afraid that the cheesecake will give Connie an incentive to abandon further response consolation!"

And so Jeff ordered dessert.

Epistemic Thesis

Jeff began, "I shall defend the view that feelings, such as sorrow and other affective states, such as inhibition, are a kind of knowledge of states or events, and therefore should be maintained even though unpleasant. Specifically, feelings and other affective states can be the knowledge of the *values* of things or events. More precisely, my 'epistemic thesis' is that feelings and other affective states can be that *through which* a person knows or apprehends values, and that feelings and other affective states can be either true or false, or veridical or illusory cognitions of value. At the moment I shall state my view simplistically. Intrinsically good feelings can be a true awareness of good events or things; intrinsically bad feelings can be a true awareness of bad events or states.[1]

"Another way of putting it, with respect to the present case, is that the relation between a loved one's death and the emotion of grief is like the relation between evidence and belief, or even like the relation between a state of affairs and sense-perception. Through the sorrow and inhibition we know the evils involved in death. If I was emotionally indifferent to my mom's death, it would be like falsely denying these evils. It would be dishonest."

Phil said, "As we realize, grief is a complex phenomenon. For example, it involves various objects and different responses. Clearly, insofar as this complex phenomenon *includes* beliefs, grief can be said to be true or false, and rational or irrational, that is, derived in accordance with, or contrary to the evidence. However, I do not think it makes sense to say that any of the *responses* to these beliefs, such as the feeling, or 'tone' of sorrow, or inhibition can be said to be *in themselves* true or false, or derived in accordance with, or contrary to the evidence. These responses are *prompted* by beliefs which can be true or false, rational or irrational, but the responses themselves can be none of these things. The responses themselves can be rational or irrational only in the sense that they have good or bad consequences. Indeed, I have several arguments against your 'epistemic thesis.' On this point, I am more confident than on any other which I have offered in the hopes of comforting you."

Connie concurred. "I don't think that feelings, apart from the beliefs which prompt them, can be true or false."

Jeff said, "Before you offer me these arguments, I would like to argue that most of the consolations you have offered have presupposed the very point which you now confidently deny!"

"No!" Connie protested.

"Go on!" Phil urged, with a little laugh of surprise that faded into a smile of skepticism.

Jeff said, "If the strategy of evaluation consolation does not assume some sort of cognitive relationship between the griever's evaluations and the griever's responses, then why attack the evaluations in order to discourage the responses? Why not criticize the responses directly, ignoring the evaluation consolation strategy entirely?"

Connie said, "Yes, a consoler is interested in more than simply overturning the griever's evaluations. Indeed, the consoler's primary interest in overturning these evaluations is to alleviate the griever's distress, the sorrow and the inhibition. However, the attempt to use the evaluation consolation strategy as a means to alleviate grief need not assume some cognitive or epistemic connection between the griever's evaluations and the grief responses. The strategy need not be: if the griever's evaluations are false, then the grief responses are false. You seem to think that the griever's evaluations *justify* the grief responses. But I doubt that they justify these responses. Instead, there might be some psychological connection between the evaluations and the responses. The evaluations might cause the sorrow and inhibition rather than justify them. And if the connection is something 'we just do' without justification, then the evaluation consoler need not argue against the responses after having supposedly disproved the evaluations. If the evaluations were disproved, the responses will 'disappear' on their own, after some time. If the responses persist for awhile thereafter that would be due to either emotional inertia or continued frustration of old habits."

Phil added, "Let me remind you, Jeff, that you said that even more than wanting to rid yourself of grief responses you wanted to disbelieve the griever's evaluations. That's another reason to try evaluation consolations."

Jeff admitted, "You have satisfied me that the evaluation consolation strategy does not require the epistemic view of feelings or inhibition."

As the cheesecake and beer arrived for Jeff, Phil raised another point. "Concerning emotions or affects, there are so *many* factors, some useful for justifying, some useful for criticizing an affect, and so many of uncertain application, that I am beginning to wonder whether there can be a theory of *appropriate* affect. It follows that grief responses cannot be justified because the issue is so muddy as to allow no justified position."

"I'm beginning to wonder about that too! The factors influencing emotional response include, among others, the extent of the value prompting the response, degree of intimacy between the affected persons, degree of temporal proximity, and the intrinsic and consequential values of the emotion," Connie enumerated.

Jeff pleaded, "Don't give up on me now, guys. Are you going to settle for the thesis that no view of affect is justified? That grieving is as well justified as not? Or even that grief over *good* news is just as justified as grief over bad news?"

Then Jeff threatened them with their wager, "Have you two got room for this cheesecake?"

Then Jeff reasoned, "Affects are complex, that's for sure. They have a direct bearing on one's own well-being and only a slightly less direct bearing on others' well-being. This makes them subject to ethical criteria. But I also maintain that emotions are cognitive or a way of knowing. . . ."

Connie said, "Yet another factor, according to you, thus making their appraisal even more complex!"

Standard Cases of Knowledge

Phil said, "We've been warming up to this issue for quite awhile. Let's get at it!"

Connie suggested, "Jeff, provide us with an overview as to how you intend to use the epistemic thesis to defend the responses of sorrow and inhibition."

Phil said, "Yes, how is the epistemic thesis supposed to be used to defend these responses? Even if we know values through feelings, we know values in other ways. An example of knowing values by reasoning rather than by feelings is our previous discussion of the griever's evaluations! These were justified independently of the grief responses. Indeed, if the griever's evaluations were justifiable only through the grief responses, then the griever's evaluations could not be used to justify the grief responses. And in large part, you are trying to justify sorrow and inhibition as responses to these evaluations."

Jeff said, "Yes, without these feelings one can justify the griever's evaluations. However, the grief responses can motivate a clarification of these evaluations, as they have in our discussion. The responses are not part of the evidence which we used for these evaluations, but they have contributed to this knowledge, as motivation. The salience of these responses is one of their main epistemic advantages."[2]

Phil objected, "Why is it good that we have been motivated to clarify the griever's evaluations? If the only reason for clarifying them is to see whether one can get rid of the grief responses, as in our discussion, then the grief responses cannot get credit for this motivation! That is, if the only value of clarifying the evaluations is conditional upon the responses, especially to alleviate them, then we would not be losing out on some good by not clarifying them, were we spared the responses altogether."

Connie interjected, "Another smokers fallacy!"

Jeff replied, "Yes, except that the clarification of the griever's evaluations, especially the sympathy evaluation, does have a value which is not conditional upon seeking to alleviate the grief responses. Besides the value of clarification itself, clarification of the sympathy evaluation reminds us of the value of life, and clarification of the ego evaluation reminds us of the value of loved ones."[3]

Connie objected, "Clarification of the sympathy evaluation *reminds* us of the value of life, it does not teach it in the first place. Let us not overvalue this clarification by confusing these two points. Just as death does not teach us the value of life, as you earlier pointed out, the sympathy evaluation does not teach us life's value."

Jeff concluded, "All right, but in the epistemic defense of grief responses I want to point out that they have epistemic *advantages*, such as salience, that is, the power of focusing attention. Therefore, they are not epistemically *dispensable*, although they are not *necessary* to apprehend the truth of the griever's evaluations. The responses are helpful without being absolutely necessary."[4]

Phil began, "First, feelings might be *responses* to the values of things, but they are not *representations* of the values of things. A picture can represent something or a sentence can represent something, and so these can be true or false or accurate or inaccurate. But I think that feelings are not themselves cognitions (or, that through which a person knows or cognizes) because there is nothing *representational* in them.[5] Feelings are not themselves pictures or descriptions of anything. That is, supposing one examines a feeling, either as behavior or as an introspectible state of consciousness, one will uncover no characteristic which 'refers' to something outside itself, let alone some particular state of affairs or event. *Emotions* do refer to states or events, have objects, but only because they are complex phenomena which include beliefs. The feelings themselves do not refer to an object."

Jeff replied with a surprised, even disappointed, tone. "Phil, it's true that you cannot observe or introspect, or 'read off' from a feeling itself the cognized object, the apprehended value. You can't 'read off' from a sorrow attack that it is about my mom's death. But it *is* about her death. The same is true of all standard examples of knowing. A review of standard cases will bear this out. You can't tell from the look or sound of a word what it stands for. Yes, feelings do not hold up little signs naming their object. But even if they did, how would we know the referent of the little sign? By its fine print?"

Pretending to have been chastised, Phil said, "All right. Let us review standard cases of knowing, understanding for each type what it means to say that a person knows something by it, and see whether this can be used for or against an epistemic account of feelings, and further, for or against an epistemic defense of grief responses."

Jeff said, "People know—or cognize—by using symbols; by sense-perception; and by images, as in memory and expectation. For example, we know or think about cats by learning the use of the word 'cat,' by seeing cats and by having memory images of cats."

Connie asked, "Beginning with the first you mentioned, what does it mean to say that a set of symbols thought, spoken, or written by a person is cognition by that person?"

Jeff said, "To make a very long story very short, a person knows or thinks something through a set of symbols when they are used in certain ways. The only point that I want to bring out is that knowing something through symbols means using them in a certain way. A word refers to a thing or event by the way it is used."

Jeff continued, "The point is that one cannot tell the object, the thing or event, from the symbols themselves. Referring to an object depends, in part, upon the use of the symbol. For example, you cannot tell from the look or the sound of the word 'cat' that it refers to cats. You only know this by learning the way the word is used. Thus, it is not necessary for feelings to be cognitions that one can tell their object from an inspection of them."

Phil said, "Largely, I agree. But there is another point, as well. If you are going to compare feelings with the use of symbols, then you would have to admit that feelings are cognitions only through custom or conventions. For the use of symbols is determined only through conventions. I suppose that the epistemic thesis would then be something like this: through training we learn to express our awareness of values through particular affects or emotions. For example, we learn from others to react to death with certain feelings. We learn from others to feel sorrow about bad things and feel joy about good things.

"Now Jeff, I'll concede to you even more: not only do we learn to *express* our awareness of values through affects, but we also learn to become aware of values through affects. Perhaps, in some manner, a result of this training that we get from others in expressing values through feelings is that we react to values with certain affects even *prior* to any *other* conscious awareness of these values. An example is feeling uneasy that there will be a quarrel when you meet your romantic partner, even before you *notice* the telltale expressions or tones. You might already know from the feeling you get that there is going to be a quarrel or a rough time. This uneasy feeling one might have learned to have in some relevantly similar situation. If that is the case, then feelings might make some epistemic contribution. . . ."

Connie warned, "Please Phil, don't concede anything you'll regret."

Phil continued, "But the point is that Jeff seems to take the view that emotional responses are learned just as we learn language or the use of symbols, and that he's learned from others to grieve in response to death. Just as we learn the use of symbols from others we learn how to react from others. One learns a convention to have a certain feeling in a certain situation. Having learned this convention sometimes we're aware of the feeling before we're aware of whatever it was in the situation which prompted the feeling. So, the feeling can 'put us onto something,' such as the surly mood of a romantic partner. But if conventions are crucial to the status of sorrow and inhibition as cognitions, that is, as awareness of evil, then I think that *new, better* conventions should be adopted, rather than justifying grief by this convention. Because of the intrinsic and consequential evils of these responses, the custom is difficult to defend, let alone lend justification to something else. If these grief responses are cognitions of the evils involved in death because of a convention that a loving one expresses the griever's evaluations in that way, then find yourself a different custom!"

Jeff replied, "First, I haven't yet agreed that the best model for understanding an epistemic account of affective states is supplied by cognition through the use of symbols.

"Second, it remains to be seen whether there could be a *better* convention for either expressing the griever's evaluations or knowing the griever's evaluations than the custom of expressing or knowing them through these grief responses. It's true that these responses are intrinsic evils, and are also somewhat evil consequentially, but they might have some advantages over any other convention for knowing or expressing the griever's evaluations.

"My third reply is that, even if better conventions were conceivable, it would not follow that I should not follow the prevailing conventions. After all, it is not up to the individual to adopt conventions. Just as I can't use words anyway I want, I can't react anyway I want. I *could try* to grieve in my own way, but it remains to be seen that the same functions would be fulfilled."

Connie suggested, "Let's consider other standard cases of knowing. I doubt that the cases of sense-perception or imagining will serve as a better model for your epistemic thesis."

Jeff said, "In these cases too, the object of the cognitions cannot be determined simply from an inspection of the image or the sense-perception itself. So again, I do not see that this sets them apart from feelings."

Connie objected, "But we *can* determine the object of an image or sense-perception simply by inspecting the image or sense-perception. The characteristics of an image or a sense-perception show us its object. For example, close your eyes and picture a fish; isn't the thought image of a fish a cognition of a fish? We know from the image itself that it refers to a fish."

Jeff asked, "Does a fish image refer to one fish? All fish? Blurrily-outlined fish? My 'fish images' more closely resemble fish images than fish.

Thus, if one could determine the object simply from the characteristics of the image itself, the object of the 'fish image' would be a fish image, rather than a fish!"

Connie replied, "What about my image of my dad? Your image of your mom? Surely, these are not just as easily cognitions of something other than those particular persons, such as parenthood or American citizens."

Jeff said, "I agree up to a point. There is a non-conventional element to some cognition. In particular, resemblance is a factor in imagining. Your image of your dad resembles your dad."

Connie added, "An image of a fish more suitably represents a fish or all fishes than these are represented by the image of a cat! And the images of our parents represent our parents much better than these images represent something more general."

Phil said, "Convention does not determine the object of a sense-perception. Instead, a sense-perception is related to its object by resemblance and causality. The details of this relation differ from theory to theory."

"Please explain," Connie requested.

Phil resumed, "I can't explain it fully tonight, but there are different theories concerning the relation between a sense-perception and its object, that is, the thing sensed. One way in which these theories vary is in the extent of the resemblance between a sense-perception and the sensed object. For example, according to some theories, the sensed object has the same colors as the sense-perception. The object, such as the glass I'm holding, is blue and the visual sensation I have of that object is blue. So, the blue object causes my blue sensation. To put it differently, I'm aware of the blue object through my blue sensation which was produced by the blue object. According to other theories, we can't say that the sensed object and the sensation are alike in colors, but they are alike in other ways. According to each theory there is *some* resemblance between sensation and sensed object. Although spatial relations between physical objects are not the same as spatial relations between visual or tactile sensations, at least there is some analogy in the spatial order of physical objects and that of sense-perceptions. For example, perception Y is between perceptions X and Z, as object Y is between physical objects X and Z, although the relation of 'between' is only analogous, not identical in the two cases."

Connie said, "I won't worry about why it is merely analogous. I understand that there is a kind of resemblance in the relation."

Phil summarized, "Besides resemblance between the sensed object and the sensation itself there is a causal relation between them; the sensed object causes the sense perception."

Connie reviewed the standard cases of cognition, "Symbols, such as words and sentences, refer to objects only through conventions about how the symbols are used. That is, a symbol comes to represent things by being used to represent them. Causality and resemblance determine the object of a sense-perception. A sense-perception represents that object which caused it and to which it—in some ways—resembles. That which determines the object of an image is partly resemblance, partly the way it used; the extent of the role played by each varying from example to example.

"And our questions are 'Can any of these standard cases be used to defend the epistemic thesis, and if so, could it be developed into a defense of your grief responses?'"

Grief Responses Compared with Standard Cases of Cognition

Jeff said, "I admit that convention *partly* determines how we emotionally respond to a thing or event. It cannot be denied that social conventions largely, though not entirely, determine how feelings are to be expressed. For example, one might express approval of a performance by clapping or stomping or cheering or whistling. This differs culturally. And the way grief is expressed varies somewhat culturally. In some cultures pulling on one's hair is an expression of grief. And it is further true that the expression of a feeling partly characterizes the details of the feeling itself. There are *slight* differences to feeling in whether one cheers or applauds. As these are different physical actions they affect feeling differently. Therefore, convention *partly* determines the feeling we have in response to a particular object, and in particular, the details of grief responses. Conventions also partly determine the frequency and intensity of a feeling. In some societies, people exhibit more restrained responses than others; some demonstrate longer grieving than others, and so on.

"However, I believe that there is *also* resemblance and causality between some objects and affects, and particularly between the griever's evaluations and sorrow and inhibition. And when I say that the evils involved in a loved one's death cause these responses, I mean more than that we have learned from others to respond with such an affect to such evils. I mean that the evils involved in a loved one's death cause the affect, though not in all its details, in a manner similar to that by which a sense-perception is produced by its object."

Connie said, "I agree that a feeling of sorrow can resemble another feeling of sorrow and one instance of joy resembles another instance of joy. But I think it is implausible to say that feelings or affective states could resemble the values of things or events and by that we thereby apprehend outside values."

"I agree," said Phil. He added, "The first version of the annihilation consolation pointed out that the dead have no sorrow. Therefore, a griever cannot justify sorrow by claiming that it resembles the evil death entails for the loved one. Furthermore, you cannot justify further sorrow because it resembles the sorrow you've already experienced, even if this past sorrow had been inevitable. *I won't let you* do it! If past inevitable sorrow were sufficient to justify further sorrow on the grounds that the latter constituted knowledge of the former, then a person would be justified in feeling further sorrow for having needlessly afflicted oneself with sorrow, and that's ridiculous!

"In sum, sorrow's resemblance to sorrow could not be used to justify sorrow as a cognition or awareness of the griever's evaluations."

Jeff said, "All right, I won't try to justify it in exactly that manner. Connie, do you think that a feeling of joy can resemble anything besides another feeling of joy?"

Connie answered, "If by 'resembles' you mean 'feels like,' I think the feeling of joy *slightly* resembles the feeling of hope, and perhaps other feelings as well."

"Would you say that there is a specific resemblance, that is, more specific than that of being a feeling, between all intrinsically good feelings, and also a specific resemblance between all intrinsically bad feelings?" Jeff asked.

He repeated, "Do all intrinsically good feelings have some resemblance to each other which 'goes beyond' the fact that they are all feelings? Likewise for intrinsically evil feelings?"

Connie hesitated. "I suppose so, although I am uncertain. Frankly, I'm puzzled by my uncertainty since I know my own feelings so well."

Jeff ignored both the uncertainty and the puzzlement over it.

"And is that resemblance between all bad feelings that they are bad, and that resemblance between all good feelings that they are good?"

"I suppose," said Connie, without conviction.

Jeff stated, "We agree that sorrow is intrinsically evil. We also agree that there are intrinsic evils besides intrinsically evil feelings. Because some emotions are intrinsically bad they resemble, and so represent, bad states of affairs. Thus, the intrinsic evil of grief, which counts so much against it, is crucial to the epistemic defense of grief."

Phil objected, "Sorrow and death's evils are alike in that they are worth avoiding as intrinsic evils, but sorrow does not 'feel like' death's evils. So, I object to stating that sorrow 'resembles' death's evils. Sorrow is a feeling, so it only resembles things it feels like."

"I agree," Connie stated emphatically.

Phil continued, "Although some theories of sense-perception minimize the resemblance between sensation and its object, there is always *some* resemblance. In some sense, the spatial order of my sense-perceptions resembles the spatial order of the objects. But I see no resemblance between death and the bereaved one's sorrow.

"And another point: earlier, when considering the objection against the ego evaluation that it is conceivable that a loved one's death could benefit the loving one more than it has harmed the loving one, you stated that, nevertheless, some goods are irreplaceable. You said that it was not the case that any intrinsic good could replace any other intrinsic good because they are of different kinds. I assume also that different intrinsic evils would be of different kinds. But now you claim that all intrinsic evils have the same property, and I assume that all intrinsic goods have the same property. These views seem contradictory. If all goods have the same property, why can't any good, of whatever kind, be replaced by a good of any other kind?"

Jeff replied, "Partly, it is as I said before, that a good of one kind cannot satisfy a desire for a good of another kind. Water can't satiate hunger. But the selectivity of affects, which we have since discussed, can also help us understand why survivors who have been more benefited than harmed by a loved one's death should nevertheless grieve, not only for the loved one's loss, but for their own as well.

"Thus far I have only claimed that grief responses resemble the evils involved in death only in the very general though important respect that they are intrinsically evil too. But I am proposing an epistemic defense of two responses, one of which is a diametric evil, the other of which is a deprivation evil. These categories are more specific than 'intrinsic evil.' Therefore, there might be a more specific resemblance between either of these responses and the apprehended values than that entailed by their both being intrinsic evils."

"Even so, the resemblance, or whatever it is, is very general," Phil reminded them.

Connie examined Jeff's suggestion. "The apprehended evils of death are both diametric and deprivation. However, they are predominantly deprivations. We agree that death entails deprivations for the dead. We also think that the prospect of death causes diametric evils, such as fear, and deprivations due to that fear. As for the loving ones, death is mostly a deprivation evil, though it causes diametric evils. It deprives the loving one of some organic goods. These evils are mostly deprivations."

Jeff said, "Yes. They are mostly deprivations especially if we add that the deprivation for the dead is infinite. You and Connie deny this, although I still believe it. But not even I claim that death entails or produces infinite diametric evils."

Phil concluded, "Since the apprehended evils are mostly deprivations, and inhibition rather than sorrow is a deprivation, then it would seem that you would have a 'stronger' epistemic defense of inhibition than sorrow. Inhibition more specifically resembles more of the apprehended evils than sorrow. Mind you, I am not endorsing the epistemic defense of inhibition; I'm only saying that in this one respect the epistemic defense is stronger for inhibition rather than sorrow."

Connie interjected, "I find this to be a most disturbing result! Jeff, I've been hoping to convince you to decrease both your sorrow and your inhibition. But frankly, I am more concerned about the inhibition. If you could enjoy yourself again, it wouldn't be so bad to have bouts of sorrow. Therefore, I'm upset to hear an argument which might 'favor' inhibition."

Jeff confessed, "I also am more concerned about remaining inhibited than I am about continued sorrow attacks, even as agonizing as these are. I have asked both of you to try to convince me that I should discourage both sorrow and inhibition, but inhibition frightens me more. Nevertheless, I do not want to discourage either of these affects, unless it is the right thing to do."

Jeff said, "At least one reason why inhibition concerns me more than sorrow is that I think it is easier for there to be more of it. It takes energy to have a sorrow attack, whereas it might demand energy to overcome inhibition. If I could enjoy life again, intermittent attacks of sorrow would be tolerable, and they would at least reassure me that my lost loved one is still part of my life."

Connie sighed, "Find a less painful way to reassure yourself of this. Put together a photo album."

Phil said, "I was wrong when I suggested that an epistemic defense of inhibition was 'stronger' than an epistemic defense of sorrow. I had thought that inhibition was a better representation of the apprehended evils because, like them, it is a deprivation. If grief responses were in part justified as resembling the apprehended evils, then to some extent inhibition is better justified.

"However, whereas a feeling, such as sorrow, *is* a state of awareness, inhibition is a *limit* upon awareness. Inhibition is in part the absence of response, and it is not representational, unless it is given that significance. Analogous to inhibition, blindness is a limit of one's awareness. And a blind person in a dark room is *not* cognizing the darkness. Similarly, a person deprived of good feelings in response to some evil is not cognizing deprivation, unless the inhibition is construed in that manner, using it as some sort of symbol."

Jeff said, "I think I understand your point. However, you make too much of it. The epistemic thesis concerning sorrow must be different from the epistemic thesis concerning inhibition. That is, they both represent outside evils, but they do so differently. Therefore, the epistemic defense of these will probably differ from each other. However, it does not follow that the epistemic defense of inhibition must fail. The epistemic theses in the two cases must be different because, not being a state of awareness, inhibition can represent only conventionally. However, it might be a convention with epistemic advantages. One advantage might be that inhibition is a deprivation, like the represented evils."

Jeff returned to an earlier point in order to emphasize it. "I claim that grief responses, by being bad, resemble in a very general way the bad things about a loved one's death. We've discussed that. But I also claim that the evils involved in death *cause* the affects of sorrow and inhibition. And I think that bad things cause bad feelings, and good things cause good feelings, not merely as the result of training, but also analogous to the manner in which a sensed object causes a sense-perception. Red objects cause one to see red. Bad events cause one to feel bad. For these reasons I think that affective states can be knowledge of outside values just as sense-perceptions are knowledge of objects. Affects can resemble their objects, and they can be caused by them, without the response being trained.

"My argument is that sorrow and inhibition are caused by death's evils and therefore these responses are ways of knowing those evils. At first, these responses are hardly controllable, as one would expect of a sense-perception; and since grief is an awareness of the evils involved in death, it has a value as knowledge, and is therefore good even when it is no longer inevitable."

Phil objected, "I know that you are not claiming that the relation between object and affect is *exactly* like that between object and sense-perception, but the analogy is much further away than I believe you imagine. I agree that good news tends to produce good feelings and that bad news tends to produce bad feelings. And I agree that this is not merely the result of training; although the *details* of the feelings are the result of training. It is not merely conventional that one reacts with affects of the same intrinsic value as the state of affairs which prompted them. But I deny that the relation is closely analogous to sense-perception.

"You say that person P is aware of some object X through cognition C because X causes C and X and C resemble each other. But there is much more than this which occurs in sense-perception. In the case of sense-perception, the cognition has the characteristics it has because the object has these same characteristics. Simply put, in sense-perception, the cause, which is the object, and the cognition do not 'just happen' to resemble each other. But this is not the case with affects and their causes. Let me explain. As I stated earlier, different theories claim more or less extensive resemblance between a sense-perception and its object. To illustrate my point, I'll first take a theory which asserts an extensive resemblance between the two. Just for purposes of illustration, I will take the theory that visual sensations resemble their objects—and causes—with respect to color. For example, a veridical sense-perception of a red object is red. The object and the sensation are both red. In this example, P is aware of a red object through a sensation because that object causes that sensation, and the sensation is red because the cause of the sensation is red. P has a red sensation, that is, C is red, because X is red. The state of awareness has a particular characteristic *because* its object has that characteristic. It is not the case merely that one causes the other and they resemble; one causes the other to have—some of—the characteristics it has. It is not a coincidence that the sensation and its object are both red. The redness of the object causes the sensation to be red.

"I shall also illustrate with an example having to do with spatial relations just so you do not think that my point is only true of theories claiming extensive resemblance between a sense-perception and its object. P knows three objects X, Y and Z and the fact that Y is between X and Z through the cognition C. In that case, the sensation of Y is between the sensations of X and Z. X causes C, and X and C resemble each other, and C has the characteristics it has, for example, the order of the sensations, because X has the resembling characteristic. The spatial order of the objects causes the spatial order of the sensations.

"Putting it very simply, on the first illustration, the redness of the sensation evinces awareness of the red object, and on the second illustration, the order of the sensations evinces awareness of the order of the objects. But this is not the case with affective response. The intrinsic value of the affect, though resembling the object, is not an awareness of the value of the object. I agree that, even apart from the way we learn to respond, bad things generally cause bad feelings and good things generally cause good feelings. But it is not the case that the goodness of the object caused the feeling to be good or that the evil of an object caused the feeling to be bad.

"For example, the prospect of a bad thing sometimes makes me fearful. And fear is an intrinsically bad feeling. But why does the prospect of a bad thing give me this bad feeling of fear? Fear does not feel bad *because* it has an object which is bad. Instead, prospects of evil increase my heart rate, shorten my breath, tighten my muscles, and increase stomach acidity and dryness in my throat. And *these* things feel bad. They don't feel bad because the prospects are bad. That's just the way these physiological responses feel. Certain autonomic *et al* responses feel good, others feel bad. Bad things cause the former, good things cause the latter. But the former do not feel bad because they are caused by bad things, and the latter do not feel good because they are caused by good things.

"In sum, a feeling is an awareness of a certain condition of one's own body. Therefore, the value of that feeling is an awareness of a certain condition of one's own body. It is not the awareness of an 'outside' value. In particular, sorrow is the awareness of a certain condition of one's body."

Connie began the litany, "Such as tightness in the throat, in the chest, burning in the eyes . . ."

Jeff replied, "You make a very good point. Sorrow feels bad because tightness in the throat is bad, not because the object of sorrow is bad. However, I am not convinced that feelings, sorrow in particular, are nothing more than an awareness of certain conditions of one's own body. To some extent, a feeling, though like every state of awareness caused by neurophysiological states, is not solely the awareness of a neurophysiological state."

Connie said, "Maybe to the extent that feelings are something more they are just vivid recollections of certain physiological conditions. You can feel sorrow even when your throat isn't tight because you vividly recall the feeling when your throat is tight."

Phil said, "All right Jeff, suppose there is more to a feeling than the awareness of one's body, either its present state, or a recollection of a former state. Even so, it's not an awareness of outside values on the model of sense-perception. The claim that a feeling is an awareness of outside values in a manner similar to sense-perception makes feelings seem like 'spider sense.'"

Connie laughed, "What is 'spider sense?' Another philosophical term?"

Phil explained, "No, spider sense is one of the amazing Spider-Man's super powers."

Connie laughed again, "An air traffic controller who reads comics!"

Phil said, "Sure, what do you think we do in the control tower all day?"

Jeff added, "Come to think of it, it scares me that an air traffic controller would offer as a consolation the inevitability of death!"

Phil joked, "Why do you think I read comic books?"

Phil continued his explanation. "Through his spider sense Spider-Man is able to sense danger. Spider sense is more than a keen awareness of perceptual clues that something or someone might be amiss; it is more than being prone to the affect of suspicion. It is supposed to be like sense-perception. He can perceive danger the way we perceive colors or sounds. But such a thing is impossible, and so is the claim that feelings are an awareness of outside values in a manner similar to sense-perception."

Jeff commented, "Of course spider sense makes no sense! Spider-Man supposedly senses danger, as we see colors, hear sounds, feel heat, and so on. But danger is not a sensible property. More technically, danger is neither a specific form of energy emitted from an object, such as light or sound, nor is it a specific type of particle, such as scents. We can only *infer* danger, we can't sense it. But values *are* sensible properties. We see, taste, and touch the goodness and badness of things. We feel pain, hear noise and smell putrid odors, taste bitter things, and so on. We don't merely infer them. Therefore, the reason that spider sense is nonsense does not apply to my view that affects can apprehend outside values, similarly to sense-perception."

Phil said, "Once again, there is an important difference between diametric and deprivation evils. Even if I agree that we sense diametric evil, I cannot agree that we sense deprivations. We do not, strictly speaking, *sense* the *absence* of something. Rather, deprivations are inferred from what we do sense. To this extent, our awareness of deprivations is like our awareness of danger. Furthermore, we agree that you grieve mostly over deprivations. Therefore, little can your grief responses be construed as awareness, in a manner very like sense-perception, of outside values.

"A new wrinkle has been added to the *modified* annihilation consolation that there is no *diametric* evil for the dead. It is an obstacle to the epistemic defense of grief.

"Maybe sorrow and inhibition are a *kind* of cognition of evils. There might be some slight similarity with sense-perception, but there are important dissimilarities, as well."

Jeff took a sip of beer and a bite of cheesecake.

Phil continued, "There are further dissimilarities between affect and sense-perception. Affects are not veridical cognitions of an external state of affairs because affects violate the principle that a veridical awareness of a thing varies only as the object varies. But affects vary when the outside values do not. Feelings change even when the thing has not.[6] Therefore, affects are not a veridical awareness of an external value. An example of the principle is that my sense-perception of you, in order to be veridical, must vary only when you vary. The sound I hear should become louder only when you raise your voice. I should see you put a sliver of cheesecake in your mouth only when you do, and so on. If your voice suddenly sounded louder to me, even though you didn't really start speaking louder my sense-perception would be to that extent non-veridical or inaccurate. If the color of your hair didn't change, but it suddenly looked green or brown to me, then my perception would be non-veridical."

Jeff said, "I understand what you are getting at, but you've oversimplified the principle...."

Jeff interrupted himself with a bite, so Connie said, "How does the principle show that sorrow and inhibition are not veridical cognitions of external objects?"

Factors Affecting Grief Responses

Phil explained, "Grief responses vary in several ways, although the object, which is the facts of some person's death, does not. Grief responses vary according to the *relation* of persons to the dead person; they vary according to the *nature* of the relationship; they vary with respect to *temporal* relations to the death; and they vary according to whether the person expects, or is otherwise prepared for the death. Let's discuss each of these."

Skeeter Davis' recording of "The End of the World" played as Phil continued. "As already discussed, whether or not one grieves over another's death depends upon the relation between the dead person and the person who believes the griever's evaluations. Connie and I believe these concerning your mom, but neither one of us grieve for her...."

"Nor would I want you to grieve for her," Jeff said.

"That is, two people who are aware of a third's death, both believing that death is a terrible evil for the third person and for that person's loving ones will have different affects according to differences in their relation to the third person. Specifically, the loving ones will feel a great deal of sorrow and be inhibited, but not anyone else. Now, we have already discussed the relativity of grief, that grief is not a response based upon equal concern for everyone; that it depends upon one's relation to the affected persons. We discussed whether grief was morally objectionable because of this prominent feature. But now I am proposing that grief's relativity, even if morally unobjectionable, shows that the affective states are not in themselves an awareness of death's evils.

"And now we have a further version of the consolation that death is universal. Everyone dies. But every griever grieves only for a few individuals. The object is basically the same in every case—at least for death ending decent, pleasant lives of the same length; yet people respond quite differently depending upon their relationship to the dead. Therefore, grief responses are not like sense-perception of evils of death."

Jeff said, "Certainly, the reactions vary according to the relation, but the very predictability of the variation suggests that there is something objective in the reactions."

Phil replied, "The predictability can be explained otherwise than by supposing that the response is like sense-perception. It could be due to different circumstances placing different consequential values on the responses in those different circumstances. It could be due to the laws of human psychology operating in different circumstances. It could be due to social conventions about who should grieve."

Connie said, "And the affect varies according to the nature of the relation. For example, not only do intimates grieve much more than others, but grief varies according to the nature of the intimacy. For instance, people usually grieve less insofar as the relation was a good one, when the relation had little conflict. And people usually grieve less the less dependent they were on the dead person."[7]

Phil said, "And, as in several ways already observed, grief varies with respect to time. In fact, there are two temporal factors in accordance with which grief varies. First, loving ones usually grieve more *after* a loved one's death, even though it was inevitable that that person would die at some time. Second, loving ones usually grieve in *proximity* to the death. When they do grieve in advance, it is generally when death is imminent. And, as we know from 'Time heals,' grief fades as the time of death becomes more remote. In sum, people usually grieve more when the death is past, and people usually grieve more when the death is proximate."[8]

Connie added, "The variability is so complicated that one must be careful when stating that intimates grieve less as time goes by. For sometimes people experience 'delayed grief.' This especially happens to people who had a conflicted relationship with the dead, or who suppress their grief.[9] Still, I agree that proximity is one factor which determines grief. And one must also be careful when stating that people generally grieve only after a loved one's death, or else when it is imminent. When a loved one's death is expected well in advance, and within a predictable period of time, loving ones often grieve in advance. There might even be some feeling of relief when the waiting is over. But again, people usually grieve only after a loved one's death, though it is inevitable that everyone dies."

Phil responded, "Yes, that is another respect in which grief varies though its object does not. It varies according to expectation and even preparation.

"And this is a further version of the consolation that death is inevitable. That a loved one will die is a fact known long beforehand. Yet people usually grieve only after the fact, or when it is imminent. There is no change in the fact that a loved one must die, but the response to that fact is very different. Therefore, grief cannot be justified as something like a sense-perception of the evil of death."

The Beatles' "I Should Have Known Better" played as Jeff said, "Before I reply, let me be clear about the consolation you are offering, and what you are not offering. You do not mean to argue that since I did not grieve much beforehand, or that, as you assure me, my grief will fade, that therefore I should not grieve now. That is, you are not arguing that consistency requires me to have now the attitude I had before her death and the attitude I will have sometime in the future.

"Nor are you arguing that if I had been better prepared, I would now be grieving less. I should have been better prepared, therefore, I should now be grieving less."

Connie said, "I would not offer either argument. The second argument is particularly bad. It would be like arguing that if you had saved your money earlier, you wouldn't need to save it now. You should have saved it earlier, therefore you should not save it now, even though you did not save it earlier!

"Nor would I argue that, since you grieved little before the event, you should grieve little afterwards. For by now I know very well that you would reply that perhaps you should have grieved more earlier! True, it is too late for you to change that, but unless consistency *alone* was the criterion, your lack of earlier grief would not be enough reason for less grief now.

"Also, as a thing's consequences depend upon its circumstances and circumstances change, something can be consequentially good at one time and consequentially bad at another. Therefore, one cannot argue that a thing was consequentially bad at one time and so must be consequentially bad at another time, unless one argues that the circumstances are relevantly similar. So, even if it was right that you grieved little before, that would not prove that it is still right."

"Besides," Jeff added, "the argument that I should grieve less now because I grieved little before makes an unfavorable impression on me because I am concerned that I made many errors earlier, one of which might have been insufficient grief."

"You do afflict yourself with such thoughts," acknowledged Connie. "I think that it is partly because you believe that you earlier made mistakes that you fear that it would be wrong to let grief go now."

Phil resumed, "I am not offering you arguments that consistency requires you to grieve little now. Instead, I am arguing that these variations in grief responses show that they are not veridical cognitions of the truth conditions of the griever's evaluations. For instance, these responses are not like sense-perception. Death is the same, regardless of the relation, regardless of the details of that relation, regardless of whether it is past or proximate, and regardless of whether it is expected. The object is the same, but the responses are very different depending upon these relations. But the veridical awareness of an object varies only according as the object varies."

Jeff said, "Your observations about the factors which determine whether, and to what extent, a person grieves are true. But as I started to say a minute ago, your principle about veridical awareness is oversimplified. Grief violates only the oversimplified version, not the accurate version.

"First, it is true that grief varies according to the relation between the person aware of the truth conditions of the griever's evaluations and those truth conditions. However, sense-perception also varies according to *relations* between the perceiver and the object. For example, perception varies according to the *spatial* relation between the object and perceiver. Using your example, my voice might sound louder if you come closer, even though I'm speaking with the same volume. This fact does not make the sense-perception illusory. In general, a veridical sense-perception can vary when the object does not."

Phil replied, "Yes, my principle was too simple. But a more accurate version which holds for veridical sense-perception is violated by grief. The new version is that a veridical awareness does not vary according to the *person* who perceives it. But intimates react differently from others. And the dependent and those in conflict react differently from others. And the prepared act differently. And so on."

Jeff objected, "But sense-perception does vary in similar ways. As an example, take the decrease of grief through expectation and preparation. This is similar to the sense-perception phenomenon of adaptation. Adaptation occurs when a person ceases to sense some object because of its routine familiarity. For example, a long time bakery employee usually does not smell the bread, unless the task requires it. This does not mean that the customer, whose nostrils thrill to the aroma, is not having a veridical awareness of the bread.

"In general, people have different sense-perceptions of the same object according to different degrees of familiarity with that object. Persons unfamiliar with an object observe details different from those familiar with it."

Connie said, "Yes, such phenomena are common, but Phil's principle does not deny their occurrence. His principle only entails that these perceptions are illusory or non-veridical."

Jeff replied, "But neither the baker nor the customer is having illusory experiences. The baker's awareness of the bread does not include the aroma; perhaps the customer's awareness lacks something which the baker has. In that case, neither of them is having *complete* experiences of the object. But it is a little misleading to characterize either's sense-perception as 'illusory.'[10] But I do not wish to wrangle over the proper use of the words 'illusory' and 'veridical.' The only points I need to make are first, that such sense-perceptions are not epistemically worthless, even if incomplete. That is, they do contribute to knowledge. Therefore, my affective states might have epistemic value even though others do not share my grief. Second, you have not demonstrated to me that sense-perception is disanalogous to affect insofar as the affect differs from person to person because sense-perception can also differ according to the person.

"But furthermore, it is not quite true to say that the object to which an intimate responds is the same as the object to which others do not respond. Yes, the facts of a person's death are the same, regardless of who is aware of that death. But intimates have more knowledge of a particular person's life and therefore greater knowledge of deprivation caused by the death than others. Therefore, intimates are not responding to exactly the same object as others. Therefore, the variation in their responses is in accordance with a variation in the object, construing the object as the person's *knowledge* of the state of affairs.

"In addition, although death is inevitable, the length of a person's life is seldom known beforehand. That is, the extent of the deprivation entailed by death is usually known only after the person's death. Therefore, a person responding to a past death usually has additional information. In other words, the objects differ in the two cases."

"What about the differences in response based on whether the relation includes conflict and dependence?" Connie asked.

Jeff said, "As already noted, the griever's evaluations are not the only objects of grief. Guilt, which can be caused by conflict, is also commonly a part of grief. In sum, grief compounded by guilt can explain why people who had a conflicted relationship to the dead respond with greater sorrow or inhibition. Therefore, it is not accurate to claim that the same object, the griever's evaluations, is met with different responses depending upon whether the relation was conflicted.

"As for dependence, a dependent survivor grieves more than an independent survivor because the evil of a loved one's death is greater for a dependent survivor than an independent one. And the dependent survivor is both more aware of, and more concerned with, the greater evil in his or her own case. So, the differing response is partly explained by the greater concern which a person has for him or herself.

"In addition, another component of grief is fear, even *after* a loved one's death. And a dependent survivor has more reason to fear than an independent survivor.

"I have never maintained that sorrow and inhibition are *only* responses to the griever's evaluations, or that they are only responses to external values. Therefore, insofar as sorrow and inhibition are determined by other things, they will vary. But this does not entail that these affective states are not in any way apprehensions of external values."

Phil objected, "This alone shows how very different are sense-perception and affective response. Sense-perception is much more specific. That is, hallucinations aside, we have visual perceptions only in response to phenomena of light, aural sensations only in response to phenomena of sound, and so on. However, our affects are a response to a *host* of different kinds of things."

Jeff closed his eyes as he savored the last sliver of cheesecake.

Epistemic Advantages and Disadvantages of Grief Responses

Then Jeff said, "All right, affective response is less like sense-perception than I had thought. Deprivations are inferred rather than sensed; though bad feelings are prompted by bad things, they don't feel bad because their cause is bad; and feelings vary according to more factors than those controlling sense-perception. Nevertheless, through affects we can increase our knowledge of external values. Through their resemblance intrinsically evil affects are representations of evils which *remind* us that their object is evil. Also, since bad news naturally tends to produce bad affects, these affects are very convenient representations.

"I have already mentioned that affects have the epistemic advantage of motivating inquiry. In particular, my grief has motivated our clarification of the griever's evaluations and grief itself."

Connie said, "All right, and it might be good for us that we were motivated to clarify these. But now they are clarified. Therefore, the justification of your grief responses as motivators of clarification of the griever's evaluations does not justify further grief. As I said before as a criticism of a possible consolation, a thing can be consequentially good at one time, but consequentially bad at another."

Jeff nodded.

Phil added, "I am clearer and more certain of the griever's evaluations now than before our conversation. And I suppose the cause of this was your suffering. So, your suffering has benefited me. But now I am clear and certain about these evaluations. And you are too. These evaluations are now far more *articulate* than any feeling which you will ever have![11] Therefore, your sorrow and inhibition have made themselves obsolete! Let's toast them and bid them good riddance!"[12]

Jeff said, "I know that evaluations based solely on emotions are often unreliable. They can distort, as well as direct the inquiry.[13] But I also know that articulated evaluations which are 'contrary' to one's automatic emotional responses or 'gut feelings' have also been unreliable. Unreliable reassurances that all is well are opposed by feelings of sorrow. And automatic gut feelings can be controlled with difficulty. This presents epistemic problems as well as advantages. On the one hand, affects can resist good reasons, but they also resist manipulation by poor reasons, on the other hand. But in the present case, our articulated evaluations concerning a loved one's death are 'consistent' with my sorrow and inhibition. Perhaps therefore, I no longer need these responses for epistemic purposes. I am confident that these evaluations are true and perhaps don't need the reminders of intrinsically bad affective states."

Barbara brought the bill.

Phil said, "Furthermore, I think that inhibition has an epistemic disadvantage for any epistemic advantage that sorrow might have had. The inhibition from which grievers suffer is of two kinds. *First*, inhibition is a lack of positive affect, such as joy, when made aware of good things. *Second*, inhibition is a reluctance to experience good things.

"Now, if it is true, as you claim, that there are epistemic advantages in responding to an external value with an affect of the same value, then inhibition of the first kind is an epistemic disadvantage.

"Furthermore, inhibition of the second kind has the epistemic disadvantage of 'closing off' a part of reality from the inhibited person. Any inference about life which such a person made would have to be even more suspect than the usually 'iffy' impressions which people form. At the opposite extreme of inhibition, I suspect lack of breadth and depth in the knowledge of life from people who are always cheerful. I think that inhibited people are equally epistemically impoverished, and unhappy to boot.

"Inhibition *could* motivate inquiry into its cause, which in this case is the griever's evaluations, if only because of a desire to put an end to inhibition, but it discourages inquiry into anything else. While the value of a person's death for that person and her loving ones is important, it is not the *only* important value in the world, and is not even the only important value for the loved and loving ones. For example, other important values were the good times you had. Therefore, upon the whole inhibition discourages knowing.

"Therefore, I think that sorrow is at least epistemically preferable to inhibition. Of course, we must not be naive and ignore the fact that one tends to produce the other."

"So, is the epistemic thesis true?" Connie asked.

Jeff said, "Now I think that affective states are not related to their objects in a manner closely resembling sense-perception. To some extent, we learn to respond with particular affective states to particular evaluations, but it is largely not learned."

"But is the epistemic thesis true? Are affective states cognitions or not? This issue was crucial to your defense of these responses against the consolation that these responses are bad," Connie insisted.

Jeff said, "I do not think that there is a 'cut and dry' answer to the question 'Are the affective responses of sorrow and inhibition cognitions?' The facts are simply the similarities and dissimilarities between these and standard cases of cognition, and the epistemic advantages and disadvantages of these responses."

Phil added, "These grief responses are not a substitute for articulated beliefs, but they have motivated this articulation. But if this was their only epistemic advantage, then they would be justified only as a phase."

Jeff added, "After the articulation, these responses are at least automatic reminders of the articulated truths, and can prevent facile neglect of these truths."

Connie cautioned, "Yes, these responses might retain some use, but if the strength of an affect is justified only as a reminder, it should only be strong enough to be a reminder. And I think that less strength is necessary to remind a person of lessons learned than is necessary to motivate inquiry."[14]

Jeff nodded and began to cry.
Connie and Phil looked at each other with some relief.
Connie rubbed Jeff's back as he dried his face.
The Beatles harmonized in the a cappella version of "Because":

Because the world is round it turns me on.
Because the world is round.
Because the wind is high it blows my mind.
Because the wind is high.
Love is old, love is new.
Love is all, love is you.
Because the sky is blue it makes me cry.
Because the sky is blue.

The bill was paid, pleasantries were exchanged with Barbara, and the three descended the stairs from the mezzanine. As they left the restaurant, the Mamas and the Papas sang, "And the darkest hour is just before dawn," from "Dedicated to the One I Love."

Summary of the Conversation

According to the epistemic thesis, a person knows the evils involved in a loved one's death through sorrow and inhibition.

Inhibition is not itself a state of awareness, although the inhibited person might use the inhibition to symbolize deprivation evils. While sorrow and inhibition can motivate and facilitate an awareness of the griever's evaluations, inhibition discourages the awareness of other values. Thus, inhibition is of limited epistemic value.

Even veridical sense-perception of the same object varies somewhat from person to person. The variation of response to the griever's evaluations can be partly explained because knowledge about an individual person's death differs from person to person. Much of the variation is due to the difference in the amount of knowledge, not to a difference in the responses to the same knowledge. Still, affective response is unlike sense-perception, as it varies according to more factors and because a feeling's properties are not due to the objects properties. The feeling cannot be defended as though it were a veridical sense-perception.

Two further dissimilarities between feelings and sense-perception might be first, the lack of a distinction between objective perception and illusion in the case of feelings and second, the inertia of feelings.[15]

In addition, feelings are not entirely like beliefs. For example, because emotions, such as fear, are most useful when directed toward immediate situations, we do not usually require that people have the same emotional response to the same situation regardless whether it is proximate or remote.

However, consistency requires similar *beliefs* for similar situations, regardless of proximity.[16]

Perhaps a phase of intense sorrow can be justified for its initial epistemic function of motivating inquiry, but afterwards, its only epistemic function appears to be a reminder of the griever's evaluations. For this function, intensity might be unnecessary.

Perhaps additional meaning has been given to the paradoxical idea that the only firm foundation for human happiness is despair.[17] Intense unpleasant affect looses its epistemic function when we have articulated the evil and the great goodness of the world.

Study Questions

(1) Continuing the discussion of this chapter, what are the epistemic benefits and harms of emotions?

(2) Why do you suppose that Jeff insists on such an "honest" discussion of death? Is that wise?

(3) This book *barely* touches on grief as manifested in different cultures.
  - Are there universal features of grief? If not, why not? Explain.

(4) Would a cultural study of grief lead to the conclusion that grief responses are merely conventional?

(5) In the last two chapters, it was suggested that grief has "jobs" to perform. In the previous chapter, grief's task was to assist the bereaved to adjust to the loss of the loved one. In this chapter, Jeff maintained that grief's task was to help the bereaved understand their loss. Can you suggest other ways in which grief could be useful?

(6) News which is contrary to our interests ("bad news") usually gives us an emotion which feels bad. News about some benefit to ourselves ("good news") usually gives us an emotion which feels good. Explain why good news evokes good feelings and bad news evokes bad feelings.

Sixteen

CONCLUSION

The three friends walked "stiff-legged" out onto the sidewalk.

"The fresh air feels good!" Jeff sighed.

The others agreed.

"I love a summer evening in midtown when almost everyone has already gone home," Connie added.

Phil said, "My car is in the municipal garage a couple of blocks away. Why don't I give you both a ride to Grand Central Station? Besides, we can't leave our conversation dangling."

Jeff and Connie accepted the offer.

Summary of Main Points and Final Thoughts

They walked further west on 57th Street, and Connie asked, "What conclusions have we reached? What have we accomplished? And what remains to be done?"

Phil turned to Jeff and said, "You're the one we've been trying to help. What do you think?"

Jeff hesitated, "Yes, I'm the one you've been trying to help. But Connie has already been through this, and unfortunately, we all go through it. So, it's not enough to say what I think."

They agreed, but Jeff commenced the review anyway.

"Grief is a set of responses to various objects, including the loved one's death and its value for the loving ones. The responses include belief in the griever's evaluations, and sorrow and inhibition. In passing, we also discussed the responses of obsession and mimicry. Consolation is one of several strategies to alleviate the distress of grief. Of course, if this distress should not be alleviated, no comfort strategy is right. In this respect, *all* comfort strategies presuppose at least some claims which might be part of consolation.

"Continuing the review: one form of consolation criticizes the griever's evaluations. But if properly understood, the griever's evaluations are true."

Connie added, "The intrinsic sympathy evaluation is true, although death is not a diametric evil for the dead, because it is a deprivation evil for the dead. However, we have been unable to convince you that this deprivation, though great, is finite."

Jeff said, "We do agree that it is better for one to have a long, good life than a short, good life."

Phil said, "The prospect of death has both good and bad consequences, and I agree that probably more are bad. However, I think that there are more good consequences than you allow, Jeff. Several of our discussions involved speculation into complicated empirical subjects. We were always careful to acknowledge the limits of our ability to settle such issues. Of course, the question of the consequences of the prospect of death is one of those complicated empirical questions."

Jeff continued, "Phil, you and I still disagree about whether death entails greater evil than good for the organic value of a person's life as a whole. However, we all agreed, in the end, that the organic value of a person's life was a value *for* that person only if that person was aware of that value, or in some other manner that organic value benefited the person."

Connie continued, "Death entails and causes evils for the loving ones. However, it is possible and in some cases real that the benefits of a loved one's death for a loving one surpasses the harm."

Jeff interjected, "Nevertheless, in such a case, grief could still be justified, because it is consequentially good that affects are selective. Besides, grief is partly a response to the sympathy evaluation which is unaltered by benefits to the loving one."

Phil continued the review, "The evils for the loving one decrease as the loving one changes. And change one must."

"But this change is itself an evil for the loving one as it limits the mutual understanding one can have with one's future self," Jeff said. "Such drastic changes make us strangers or indifferent to our own histories."

"There were more loose ends in our discussion of response consolations, partly because it involved a greater number of complicated empirical questions," Phil said.

"But one comparatively straightforward empirical claim is that sorrow and inhibition are intrinsically bad."

Jeff said, "Although grief can harm one's health, suppression of grief can also be harmful. Sometimes there is nothing which one can do which has more good consequences than bad."

Phil reminded, "But it remains to be seen whether consolation, as we have defined and employed it, has the consequences of suppression."

Jeff continued, "You both argued strongly against mimicry of the dead, although you allow that it, along with obsession, might play some role in helping a survivor adjust to the new situation."

Phil added, "Hopefully, the adjustment will be more than just an acceptance of one's inhibitions. Hopefully, new habits, providing enjoyments of their own, will replace the obsolete habits."

Jeff resumed, "If 'taken to heart,' many evaluation consolations could lead to further sorrow and harmful actions. Consolations which entail that life is not good can be both depressing and productive of apathy or worse."

Connie said, "But grief can also be bad for one's character. Certainly in the short term it can be very bad, making a person either very self-absorbed or focused on a person who can no longer be helped."

Jeff said, "Yes, but grief's long term effects probably depend upon the character which the person had before losing the loved one. One interesting thing about grief is that it is a response to an evil for both oneself *and* another. Thus, it is a stinging reminder that one's interests often coincide with others. This can be ethologically good."

Phil objected, "Yes, but the interests of oneself and one's loved one can conflict with the overall interest for everyone. Sometimes it is better overall that a person die, even a decent, reasonably happy person. In such a case grief can be ethologically bad."

Connie said, "The long term effects of grief on one's character do indeed depend upon one's prior character. The griever need not be a merely 'passive' vehicle, but can be to some extent an active contributor toward grief's consequences."

Jeff said, "I do not believe that the only decisive considerations as to whether grief should be discouraged are its consequences for our happiness or character. A further consideration is whether sorrow and inhibition offer epistemic advantages unavailable without them."

Connie remarked, "Affects can motivate inquiry into an important issue. But they can also motivate the 'direction' of an inquiry not only in the sense of prompting it, but also in the sense of determining its conclusions. Like the ethological effects of emotions, their epistemic effects depend upon one's prior character."

Phil kidded, "Warning! Children, do not attempt this at home! We are trained professionals!"

Connie concluded, "But besides inhibition having an epistemic disadvantage of closing off a part of the world, the epistemic advantage of even sorrow is largely only temporary. Once the prompted intellectual work is completed the emotion serves only as a reminder."

Phil stated, "The work which was prompted by *your* grief was largely an examination of the griever's evaluations. It was necessary to offer you evaluation consolations, if for no other reason, in order to complete that work. Even the weakest evaluation consolations served a purpose."

Connie teased, "That lets *us* off the hook, Phil! Our weak consolations were therapeutic!"

Jeff teasingly accused Phil and Connie. "You got the better of me, at last, in the final part of our discussion. But I think it was only because my mind was dulled by that beer which you tricked me into drinking!"

Phil said, "It's no coincidence that we only got the better of you at the end. For the whole purpose of our discussion was to get the better of you! Naturally, it concluded when we did!"

Jeff said, "There is no 'recipe' for grief. One cannot say how intense, how frequent or how prolonged must be sorrow or inhibition. The most which philosophical analysis allows is to distinguish the relevant factors, and try to determine the application of each. Grief is good in this respect, bad in another. Grief is good at this time, bad at another. And so on."

Having arrived at the garage, the three got into Phil's car. Jeff sat in the front passenger seat.

The car radio was tuned to the classical station. It was playing Grieg's "Morning" from *Peer Gynt*.

Jeff resumed the review. "One recurring *theme* of our discussion was that many evaluation consolations were dreary."

Phil said, "One problem which came up over and over again concerned the meaning of 'x is a value for person P.' As we already mentioned in connection with the organic value of a person's life as a whole, the value of a person's life is not necessarily a value for that person. Another illustration of this is when a person's death is consequentially good for others. That good does not benefit the dead person."

"Furthermore, in order for something to be an intrinsic value for a person it need not be a state of that person, let alone a state of awareness of that person. However, it must concern a state of awareness of that person. For example, death is not a state of a person but it does concern a state of awareness of that person. The person concerned in the sympathy evaluation is an imaginary extension of the life of the dead person. Nevertheless, the evil is real as the deprivation is real. The sympathy evaluation is about an absence from the world of good experiences which would have been part of the continued existence of the dead person," Jeff added.

The three paused and another piece began playing on the radio which got their attention.

"That's by Liszt. But I can't remember the title. It's not one of his most famous compositions," Connie said.

"I can't think of the title," Jeff said. But his mind was wandering.

Connie asked, "How do you feel, Jeff?"

"Tired. It's late. I'm too beat for more sorrow attacks tonight. But I still feel uneasy. And I expect that tomorrow I'll have more sorrow attacks. But I will *not* coddle my inhibitions; at least, I'll try to overcome them."

Phil said, "You know we've been trying to alleviate your distress by arguing that it is irrational. Connie and I have suggested that, though the evaluation consolations failed, our understanding of their failure has made grief obsolete; at least we don't need it to know the griever's evaluations. We've articulated the evil; the affects' epistemic purpose has been achieved, and they no longer have an outstanding epistemic purpose. Maybe they will go. If you find them going, *let them go*.

"Now it occurs to me that perhaps our discussion can end your distress in another way. . . ."

"Besides by making it obsolete?" Connie asked.

"And besides being a distraction from the grief attacks?" Jeff asked.

Phil said, "Sometimes affects last only when they remain spontaneous. And a lengthy discussion of whether one should do something kills spontaneity. Maybe a result of our discussion will be that it will be more difficult to grieve. Perhaps we have eliminated a psychological condition for grieving."

Jeff retorted, "Maybe, but lengthy discussion can strengthen an emotional disposition as well. Reflection on a woman's charms is a good example!"

Connie said, "Supposing that our discussion does make grief more difficult—that might not be a good result. If grief is needed for adjustment or for health's sake, then it is better not to put up psychological obstacles."

Phil commented, "We agree that 'suppression' can be harmful. But we also agree that the concept of 'suppression,' as it applies to the alleviation of grief, requires further analysis. In particular, I am not sure that making grief more difficult by making it less spontaneous counts as 'suppression,' in the sense in which it is harmful."

"Keep your eyes on the road!" Connie said half-teasing.

Connie leaned forward and asked, "Besides further clarification of issues already discussed, what needs to be discussed to alleviate your distress?"

Jeff suggested, "Next time maybe we can discuss guilt. At least our present discussion has convinced me that I should try to enjoy the rest of my life. My inhibition does not benefit anyone. And I think that I see that it doesn't expiate anything either."

Phil said, "Our discussion tonight might make it easier to discuss guilt the next time. For example, the evaluation/response distinction is also prominent in arguments to dissuade a person from feeling guilty. And I think we have outlined, though not fully discussed, *nearly* all the main themes of arguments against particular emotions. But I'd have to think harder about this concept of 'expiation' which seems unique to guilt."

Partings

The car pulled up to Grand Central Station. Phil and Connie said good night.

"We tried, pal!" Connie said.

"We made some progress!" Phil assured.

Jeff and Phil said goodnight.

Phil said, "I busted a gut tonight!"

Jeff laughed, "I love you, too!"

As Phil drove away Jeff and Connie entered the now quiet terminal. Connie glanced above at the vast mural depicting the constellations of the zodiac. "It's the only place in New York where you can see stars," she mused. Jeff did not respond.

They walked together in silence until they had to part, Connie for the suburban train and Jeff for the subway.

"I wonder how the Yanks did tonight," Jeff said half-heartedly.

Connie had something else on her mind.

"Although it is terrible that your mom died, in one respect your position is enviable. You have no commitments now. You can do what you want, live where you want. You can start all over. I've thought of moving to San Francisco," Connie said.

"It's ironic that you should say that. For instead of starting something new, I've decided to finish old business. I have decided to go back to school, write my dissertation, and get my degree," Jeff revealed.

"That's great!" Connie said.

"Actually, that decision was not the result of my mom's death, for I made the decision before she died," Jeff clarified.

"Oh! But this is the first you ever told me. Did your mom know?" Connie asked.

"No. I was waiting to hear from the school before telling her. I didn't want to get her hopes up, just in case it didn't come off. So no, I never told her," Jeff said.

"Oh," muttered Connie.

It was almost time for Connie's train to leave.

Connie tried to distract Jeff.

"'In twenty-five words or less' what did you learn tonight?" Connie asked her final question.

"That I can't say anything in twenty-five words or less! But if I tried: life can be good, though it isn't always. Therefore, death is bad. Grief is a response to the fact that a discontinued life might have been good. But grief is not, by and large, a part of the good which life offers."

"Way over the limit!" Connie observed.

"And what have you learned?" Jeff asked.

Connie smiled tiredly. "That it's about time that grievers and consolers were 'on the same page.'"

Jeff nodded, and they hugged.

"Don't miss your train," Jeff cautioned.

"Yes, I've got to go!" Connie agreed.

"Thanks. Thanks for everything," Jeff said.

"Goodnight," Connie said as she kissed Jeff's cheek and squeezed his arm.

"Call me," she said, and Jeff nodded again. She hurried onto her train.

Jeff turned away. He was now too exhausted to think clearly; his thoughts were spontaneous and jumbled, his feelings subdued. The familiar silent grandeur of the terminal followed him as he slowly walked to the subway. Far below the immense ceiling his footsteps felt almost weightless.

Study Questions

(1) Apply some of the ideas in the appraisal of grief to the appraisal of guilt.
- Give examples of an evaluation consolation and a response consolation as applied to guilt.

(2) This book does not address all motives or reasons for grieving in part because some motives or reasons do not require extensive philosophical analysis. What are some motives or reasons for grief *not* mentioned in the dialogue?
   - Evaluate these other motives.

(3) What does it mean to be "comforted to know that one is inconsolable?"
   - Does Jeff receive such comfort?

(4) Unlike Phil and Connie, many people have afterlife consolations available to them.
   - If an afterlife exists, would such a consolation based on the promise of it be adequate to dispel grief?

(5) In addition to afterlife consolations, does religion offer other consolations (as the term is defined in this book) unavailable to an agnostic?
   - If so, are these adequate consolations?
   - Explain your reasons.

NOTES

Introduction

1. Seneca, *Moral Essays*, vol. 2, trans. John William Basore (Cambridge, Mass.: Harvard University Press, 1932), pp. 7–9.
2. Elizabeth Kübler-Ross, *On Death and Dying* (New York: Collier Books, 1969), pp. 7–10.
3. Colin Murray Parkes, *Bereavement* (New York: International Universities Press, 1972), p. 44.
4. Ibid., p. 58.
5. Ibid., p. 40; Colin Murray Parkes and Robert Stuart Weiss, *Recovery from Bereavement* (New York: Basic Books, 1983), pp. 70–71.
6. Parkes, *Bereavement*. p. 46.
7. Ibid., p. 75.
8. Parkes and Weiss, *Recovery from Bereavement*, pp. 70–71.

Chapter Two

1. Colin Murray Parkes, *Bereavement* (New York: International Universities Press, 1972), p. 163.

Chapter Four

1. Ray Coleman, *Lennon* (New York: McGraw Hill, 1984), pp. ix, 159, 162; Peter Brown and Steven Gaines, *The Love You Make* (New York: McGraw Hill, 1983), pp. 60, 397, 399.
2. Clive Staples Lewis, *A Grief Observed* (New York: Bantam Books, 1963), p. 1.
3. Clarence Irving Lewis, *An Analysis of Knowledge and Valuation* (La Salle, Ill.: Open Court, 1946), p. 491.

Chapter Five

1. Tacitus, Cornelius. *The Complete Works of Tacitus*, eds. Alfred John Church, Moses Hadas, and others (New York: Random House, 1942), p. 695.

Chapter Seven

1. Derek Parfit, *Reasons and Persons* (Oxford: Oxford University Press, 1984), pp. 303–306); "Personal Identity," in John Perry, ed., *Personal Identity* (Berkeley: University of California Press, 1975), pp. 217–219.
2. Amélie Oksenberg Rorty, *Mind in Action* (Boston: Beacon Press, 1988), pp. 124–127.
3. Thomas Nagel, *Mortal Questions* (Cambridge: Cambridge University Press, 1979), pp. 13–21.

Chapter Nine

1. Harriott Sarnoff Schiff, *The Bereaved Parent* (New York: Penguin Books 1978), p. 23.
2. Savine Gross Weizman and Phyllis Kamm, *About Mourning* (New York: Human Sciences Press 1985), pp. 99–100; Colin Murray Parkes, *Bereavement* (New York: International Universities Press, 1972), pp. 122–124; Colin Murray Parkes and Robert Stuart Weiss, *Recovery from Bereavement* (New York: Basic Books, 1983), pp. 47–48, 52, 131–138, 164.
3. Parkes and Weiss, *Recovery from Bereavement*, p. 122.
4. Augustine of Hippo, *The Enchiridion on Faith, Hope, and Love* (Chicago: Gateway Editions, 1961), pp. 81, 82; Brian Sayers, "Death As a Loss," *Faith and Philosophy* 4 (1987), p. 157.
5. Friedrich Wilhelm Nietzsche, "Twilight of the Idols," in *The Portable Nietzsche*, trans. Walter Arnold Kaufman (Viking Press: New York, 1954), p. 467.
6. Colin Murray Parkes, *Bereavement* (New York: International Universities Press, 1972), pp. 158–159.

Chapter Ten

1. Bertrand Russell, *Why I Am Not A Christian* (New York: Simon and Schuster, 1957), p. 114; Russell, *Portraits from Memory and Other Essays* (New York: Simon and Shuster, 1951), p. 52.
2. Richard Wollheim, *The Thread of Life* (Harvard: Harvard University Press, 1984), pp. 107–109.
3. Jonathan Glover, *I: The Philosophy and Psychology of Personal Identity* (New York: Penguin Books, 1988), p. 145.
4. Ronald de Sousa, *The Rationality of Emotion* (Cambridge, Mass.: MIT Press, 1988), pp. 178, 180.
5. Terence, *The Comedies*, trans. Betty Radice (New York: Penguin Books, 1976), p. 120.

Chapter Eleven

1. Richard M. Gale, *The Language of Time* (London: Routledge and Kegan Paul, 1968) pp. 8–9, 15–22, 24–30, 91; John Leslie, "The Value of Time," *American Philosophical Quarterly* 13 (1976), pp. 110–111.
2. Bertrand Russell, *Why I Am Not A Christian* (New York: Simon and Schuster, 1957), p. 99.
3. Ibid., p. 96.

Chapter Twelve

1. Jeffrie G. Murphy, "Rationality and the Fear of Death," *Monist* 59 (1976), p. 189.
2. Ibid., p. 188.

Chapter Thirteen

1. Patricia S. Greenspan, *Emotions and Reasons: An Inquiry into Emotional Justification* (London: Routledge and Kegan Paul, 1988), p. 120.

2. Ronald de Sousa, *The Rationality of Emotion* (Cambridge, Mass.: MIT Press, 1988), pp. 196–197.
3. Martha Nussbaum, *The Fragility of Goodness: Luck and Ethics in Greek Tragedy and Philosophy* (Cambridge: Cambridge University Press, 1986), p. 49; Greenspan, *Emotions and Reasons*, pp. 120, 127; Patricia S. Greenspan, "A Case of Mixed Emotions: Ambivalence and the Logic of Emotion," in Amélie Oksenberg Rorty, ed., *Explaining Emotions* (Berkeley: University of California Press, 1980), pp. 232–234; 238–241.

Chapter Fourteen

1. Savine Gross Weizman and Phyllis Kamm, *About Mourning* (New York: Human Sciences Press 1985), p.63; Colin Murray Parkes and Robert Stuart Weiss, *Recovery from Bereavement* (New York: Basic Books, 1983), pp. 7, 39, 294; Colin Murray Parkes, *Bereavement* (New York: International Universities Press, 1972), pp. 15–21, 29–33.
2. Thomas Nagel, The View from Nowhere (Oxford: Oxford University Press, 1986), pp. 221–222.
3. Ronald de Sousa, *The Rationality of Emotion* (Cambridge, Mass.: MIT Press, 1988), p. 153; Amélie Oksenberg Rorty, "Explaining Emotions," in *Explaining Emotions*, (Berkeley: University of California Press, 1980), p.103; Michel de Montaigne, *Complete Essays,* trans. Donald M. Frame (Stanford, Calif.: Stanford University Press, 1958), pp. 14–15.
4. Rorty, "Explaining Emotions," p.106.
5. Benedict (Baruch) Spinoza, *Spinoza Selections*, ed. John Daniel Wild (New York: Scribners, 1930), pp. 333–334; Seneca, *Moral Essays*, vol. 2, trans. John W. Basore (Cambridge, Mass.: Harvard University Press, 1932), p. 15.
6. Colin Murray Parkes, *Bereavement* (New York: International Universities Press, 1972), pp. 110, 139, 159; Weizman, and Kamm, *About Mourning*, pp. 81–82.
7. Weizman and Kamm, *About Mourning*, p. 41; Colin Murray Parkes and Robert Stuart Weiss, *Recovery from Bereavement* (New York: Basic Books, 1983), pp. 12, 17; and Colin Murray Parkes, *Bereavement* (New York: International Universities Press, 1972), p. 159.
8. James Rachels, *The Elements of Moral Philosophy* (New York: Random House 1986) pp. 96–97.
9. Elizabeth Kübler-Ross, *On Death and Dying* (New York: Collier Books, 1969), pp. 38–49; *Living with Death and Dying* (New York: Collier Books, 1981), p.25; Weizman and Kamm, *About Mourning*, p.44.
10. Edith Hamilton, *Mythology* (Boston: Little, Brown and Co., 1942), pp. 456–458.

Chapter Fifteen

1. Ronald de Sousa, *The Rationality of Emotion* (Cambridge, Mass.: MIT Press, 1988), p. 178; Robert Gordon, *The Structure of Emotions* (Cambridge: Cambridge University Press, 1987), p. 29; Martha Nussbaum, *The Fragility of Goodness: Luck and Ethics in Greek Tragedy and Philosophy* (Cambridge: Cambridge University Press, 1986), p. 15.

2. Nussbaum, *The Fragility of Goodness*, p. 15; Patricia S. Greenspan, *Emotions and Reasons: An Inquiry into Emotional Justification* (London: Routledge and Kegan Paul, 1988), p. 87; Patricia S. Greenspan "A Case of Mixed Emotions: Ambivalence and the Logic of Emotion," in Amélie Oksenberg Rorty, *Explaining Emotions* (Berkeley: University of California Press, 1980), p. 241; Amélie Oksenberg Rorty, *Mind in Action* (Boston: Beacon Press, 1988), pp. 203–204; de Sousa, *The Rationality of Emotion*, pp. 196–197; Charles Dunbar Broad, *Critical Essays in Moral Theory* (London: Allen and Unwin, 1971), pp. 288–290.
3. Warren A. Shibles, *Death: An Interdisciplinary Analysis* (Whitewater, Wisc.: The Language Press, 1974), p. 1; Greenspan, *Emotions and Reasons*, p. 169.
4. Greenspan, *Emotions and Reasons*, pp. 9, 147–150, 170–171.
5. David Hume, *A Treatise of Human Nature*, ed. P. H. Nidditch (Oxford: Oxford University Press, 1978), p. 415.
6. de Sousa, *The Rationality of Emotion*, pp. 150–152, 206, 225–231.
7. Colin Murray Parkes and Robert Stuart Weiss, *Recovery from Bereavement* (New York: Basic Books, 1983), pp. 52, 131–138, 164.
8. de Sousa, *The Rationality of Emotion*, pp. 227, 231.
9. Parkes and Weiss, *Recovery from Bereavement*, pp. 123–127, 131.
10. de Sousa, *The Rationality of Emotion*, p. 150.
11. Greenspan, *Emotions and Reasons*, p. 87; Greenspan "A Case of Mixed Emotions," pp. 230–233.
12. François duc de La Rochefoucauld, *Maxims*, trans. Leonard Tancock (New York: Penguin Books, 1959), p. 28; Greenspan, *Emotions and Reasons*, p. 138.
13. de Sousa, *The Rationality of Emotion*, p. 197.
14. Greenspan, *Emotions and Reasons*, pp. 104–105.
15. de Sousa, *The Rationality of Emotion*, p. 153; Ronald de Sousa, in Rorty, "The Rationality of Emotions," in Rorty, *Explaining Emotions*, p. 133.
16. Greenspan, *Emotions and Reasons*, p.150.
17. Bertrand Russell, *On Ethics, Sex and Marriage* (Buffalo, N.Y.: Promotheus Books, 1987), pp. 313–314.

BIBLIOGRAPHY

Augustine of Hippo. *The Enchiridion on Faith, Hope, and Love*. Chicago: Gateway Editions, 1961.
Broad, Charles Dunbar. *Critical Essays in Moral Theory*. London: Allen and Unwin, 1971.
Brown, Peter, and Steven Gaines. *The Love You Make*. New York: McGraw Hill, 1983.
Coleman, Ray. *Lennon*. New York: McGraw Hill, 1984.
de Sousa, Ronald. *The Rationality of Emotion*. Cambridge, Mass.: MIT Press, 1988.
———. "The Rationality of Emotions." In Rorty, *Explaining Emotions*, pp. 127–152.
Gale, Richard M. *The Language of Time*. London: Routledge and Kegan Paul, 1968.
Glover, Jonathan. *I:The Philosophy and Psychology of Personal Identity*. New York: Penguin Books, 1988.
Gordon, Robert. *The Structure of Emotions*. Cambridge: Cambridge University Press, 1987.
Greenspan, Patricia S. *Emotions and Reasons: An Inquiry into Emotional Justification*. London: Routledge and Kegan Paul, 1988.
———. "A Case of Mixed Emotions: Ambivalence and the Logic of Emotion." In Rorty, *Explaining Emotions*, pp. 223–250.
Hume, David. *A Treatise of Human Nature*. Edited by P. H. Nidditch. Oxford: Oxford University Press, 1978.
Kübler-Ross, Elizabeth. *On Death and Dying*. New York: Collier Books, 1969.
———. *Living with Death and Dying*. New York: Collier Books, 1981.
La Rochefoucauld, François duc de. *Maxims*. Translated by Leonard Tancock. New York: Penguin Books, 1959.
Leslie, John. "The Value of Time," *American Philosophical Quarterly*, 13 (1976), pp. 109–119.
Lewis, Clarence Irving. *An Analysis of Knowledge and Valuation*. La Salle, Ill.: Open Court, 1946.
Lewis, Clive Staples. *A Grief Observed*. New York: Bantam Books, 1963.
Montaigne, Michel de. *Complete Essays*. Translated by Donald M. Frame. Stanford, Calif.: Stanford University Press, 1958.
Murphy, Jeffrie G. "Rationality and the Fear of Death," *Monist*, 59 (1976), pp. 187–203.
Nagel, Thomas. *Mortal Questions*. Cambridge: Cambridge University Press, 1979.
———. *The View from Nowhere*. Oxford: Oxford University Press, 1986.
Nietzsche, Friedrich Wilhelm. "Twilight of the Idols." In *The Portable Nietzsche*. Translated by Walter Arnold Kaufman. Viking Press: New York, 1954.
Nussbaum, Martha. *The Fragility of Goodness: Luck and Ethics in Greek Tragedy and Philosophy*. Cambridge: Cambridge University Press, 1986.
Parfit, Derek. *Reasons and Persons*. Oxford: Oxford University Press, 1984.
———. "Personal Identity." In Perry, John, ed. *Personal Identity*. Berkeley: University of California Press, 1975, pp. 199–226.
Parkes, Colin Murray. *Bereavement*. New York: International Universities Press, 1972.
———, and Robert Stuart Weiss. *Recovery from Bereavement*. New York: Basic Books, 1983.

Rachels, James. *The Elements of Moral Philosophy*. New York: Random House 1986.
Rorty, Amélie Oksenberg. *Mind in Action*. Boston: Beacon Press, 1988.
———. "Explaining Emotions." In *Explaining Emotions*, pp. 103–126.
———, ed. *Explaining Emotions*. Berkeley: University of California Press, 1980.
Russell, Bertrand. *Portraits from Memory and Other Essays*. New York: Simon and Shuster, 1951.
———. *Why I Am Not A Christian*. New York: Simon and Schuster, 1957.
———. *On Ethics, Sex, and Marriage*. Buffalo, N.Y.: Prometheus Books, 1987.
Schiff, Harriott Sarnoff. *The Bereaved Parent*. New York: Penguin Books 1978.
Sayers, Brian, "Death As a Loss," *Faith and Philosophy*, 4 (1987), pp. 149–158.
Seneca, Lucius Anneus. *Moral Essays*. Volume 2. Translated by John William Basore. Cambridge, Mass.: Harvard University Press, 1932.
Shibles, Warren A. *Death: An Interdisciplinary Analysis*. Whitewater, Wisc.: The Language Press, 1974.
Spinoza, Benedict (Baruch). *Spinoza Selections*. Edited by John Daniel Wild. New York: Scribners, 1930.
Tacitus, Cornelius. *The Complete Works of Tacitus*. Edited by Alfred John Church, Moses Hadas, and others. New York: Random House, 1942.
Terence, *The Comedies*. Translated by Betty Radice. New York: Penguin Books, 1976.
Weizman, Savine Gross, and Phyllis Kamm. *About Mourning*. New York: Human Sciences Press 1985.
Wollheim, Richard. *The Thread of Life*. Harvard: Harvard University Press, 1984.

FOR FURTHER READING

Abrams, Meyer Howard, ed. *The Norton Anthology of English Literature.* Edited by M. H. Abrams. New York: W. W. Norton and Company, 1974: Lord George Gordon Byron, "Childe Harold's Pilgrimage," and "Don Juan"; Edward Fitzgerald, "*The Rubayait* of Omar Khayyam"; Elizabeth Jennings, "In Memory of Anyone Unknown to Me"; Alfred Lord Tennyson, "In Memoriam A. H. H."; and V. William Wordsworth. "The Ruined Cottage."
 Tennyson and Wordsworth's poems provide insights on grief. That life becomes tedious even in youth is illustrated most famously in Byron's protagonists. Jennings grieves over a stranger whose death left none bereaved. Fitzgerald recommends inebriation in response to death's prospect.

Augustine. *The Confessions.* Translated by John K. Ryan. Garden City, N.Y.: Image Books, 1960.
 His autobiography includes his reactions to the loss of loved ones and so presents for study an interesting case of grief.

Birch, Cyril, and Donald Keene, eds. *Anthology of Chinese Literature.* New York: Grove Press, 1965.
 Includes selections from Chuang Tzu's consolations. Han Yu's letter to his dead nephew is moving. The predominant theme of Chinese poets is loss: of love, of youth, of life, and of imperial favor. I approve of the attitude of Yu-an Mei, who entertains no false consolation but is comforted by companionship (including that of long dead authors).

Boethius. *The Consolation of Philosophy.* Translated by Richard Green. Indianapolis: Bobbs-Merrill, 1962.
 Boethius consoles himself while imprisoned by arguing, among other things, that anything less than the eternal is indifferent, that perseverance requires evils, and that we should not desire exceptions to universal mortality.

Boswell, James. *The Life of Samuel Johnson.* New York: Penguin Books, 1979.
 When Boswell reported that the notorious infidel David Hume, while terminally ill, calmly compared death to prenatal non-existence, Johnson retorted that death is the loss of everything. I agree with Johnson over Hume. Later Johnson stated that grief must be "digested" with the remainder dissipated by distraction.

Broad, Charles Dunbar. "Emotion and Sentiment." In *Broad's Critical Essays in Moral Theory.* Edited by David Ross Cheney. London: Allen and Unwin, 1971.
 An early contribution to the topic of the epistemic value of emotions and includes perceptive comments on grief.

Bruecher, A., and Fischer, J. "Why is Death Bad?" *Philosophical Studies* 50 (1986), pp. 213–214.
 These authors discuss the consolation based on our supposed indifference to prenatal non-existence.

Choron, Jacques. "Death and Immortality." In *Dictionary of the History of Ideas: Studies of Selected Pivotal Ideas*. Edited by Philip P. Wiener. New York: Scribners, 1968.
    Survey of thoughts on the topic of grief and consolation.

Cicero. "On Friendship"; "On Old Age." *Offices*. New York: E. P. Dutton and Co., 1909.
    "On Friendship" is a dialogue centered on the death of Scipio Africanus, an exemplary Roman. Although the dead are as if they were never born, the memory of Scipio's virtue consoles, according to Cicero. "On Old Age" adds further consolations.

———. *Tusculan Disputations*. Translation by John Edward King. Cambridge, Mass.: Harvard University Press, 1927.
    This readable dialogue emphasizes the theme that reason should control emotion and has a good discussion on consolations drawn from death's inevitability and universality.

———. *De Re Publica De Legibus*. Translated by Clinton Walker Keyes. Cambridge, Mass., Harvard University Press, 1928.
    Cicero's twist to the comparison between death and prenatal non-existence unwittingly shows the weakness of the comparison. Arguing that posthumous fame is unimportant, he points out that it is not important that no one spoke of you before your birth!

Confucius. The Analects (Lun yü). Edited and translated by Dim Cheuk Lau. New York: Penguin, 1979.
    When a disciple complains that prolonged inhibition causes skills (such as musical skills) to deteriorate Confucius (Kung Fu-Tzu) defends the conventional three year mourning period for a parent's death by implying the following rule: mourning should be long enough to requite the love received.

de Sousa, Ronald. *The Rationality of Emotion*, Cambridge, Mass.: MIT Press, 1988.
    De Sousa presents an excellent discussion of the epistemic role of emotions. He considers both death and immortality as evils.

Diogenes Laertius. Solon; Xenophon. In *Lives of Eminent Philosophers*. Edited and translated by Robert Drew Hicks. Cambridge, Mass.: Harvard University Press, 1925.
    The biographies of Solon and Xenophon include sharp contrasts to the death of a son, Solon weeping because his tears cannot undo the loss and Xenophon stalwart because of death's inevitability.

Donnelly, John . ed. *Language, Metaphysics, and Death*. New York: Fordham University Press, 1994.
    Donnelly's article is a must for readers to decide whether there is more to the annihilation consolations than my criticisms allow. Grace M. Jantzen argues that death's prospect benefits and that it is enough to have a "fulfilled" life. Fred Feldman defends the view that death is evil as a deprivation.

Edwards, Paul. "My Death"; Robert Owens. "Death." In *The Encyclopedia of Philosophy*. Edited by Edwards. New York: Macmillan Publishing, 1967.
Edwards' contribution, "My Death," provides an overview on the difficulty of conceiving or believing in one's own mortality. Robert Olson's "Death" surveys ideas about how best to live with the knowledge of one's own mortality.

Epictetus. *The Discourses of Epictetus*. Edited by Christopher Gill. Translation revised by Robin Hard. London: Dent, 1995.
Epictetus' consolations include the partiality of grief and the central stoic tenet that things beyond one's control are indifferent.

Euripides. "Alcestis." Translated by Richmond Lattimore. In *The Complete Greek Tragedies*, vol. 3. Chicago: University of Chicago Press, 1942.
Deals primarily with grief.

Feldman, Fred. *Confrontations with the Reaper:* A Philosophical Study of the Nature and Value of Death. New York: Oxford University Press, 1992.
As in my case, Feldman was motivated to articulate his objections to the annihilation consolation by the death of a loved one (his daughter).

Gale, Richard M. *The Language of Time*. London: Routledge and Kegan Paul, 1968.
Gale provides the clearest exposition of the A- and B-theories of time.

Gaskin, John C. A., ed. *The Epicurean Philosophers*. Translated by C. Bailey, R. D. Hicks, and Gaskin. London: Everyman, 1995.
Epicurus offers the most famous statement of the annihilation consolation. As part of his masterful exposition of Epicureanism, Lucretius offers several versions of the annihilation consolation and the point that death is required that others might live.

Greenspan, Patricia S. *Emotions and Reasons: An Inquiry into Emotional Justification*. London: Routledge and Kegan Paul, 1988.
In an excellent discussion of the epistemic role of emotions, she makes the salient point that emotions need only be as strong as to direct attention. By that measure grief is certainly not an economic emotion.

Homer. *The Iliad*. Edited by Bernard Knox. Translated by Robert Fagles. New York: Penguin Books, 1990.
Achilles' grief prompts one of the greatest, most explicit bloodbaths in literature. Not until the special effects of the television program *CSI* were the details of violence so graphically depicted.

Hume, David. "The Sceptic." In *Essays, Moral, Political, and Literary*. Edited by Eugene E. Miller. Indianapolis: Liberty Classics, 1985.
Though brief, "The Sceptic" is the closest thing to a comprehensive critique of consolation prior to my effort.

Isenberg, Arnold. "Natural Pride and Natural Shame." In *Explaining Emotions*. Edited by Amélie Oksenberg Rorty. *Explaining Emotions*. Berkeley: University of California Press, 1980.
> Rorty does another great job as editor with fine contributions from Ronald de Sousa and Patricia Greenspan. Arnold Isenberg's article includes a brief criticism of Hume's "The Sceptic."

James, William. *The Principles of Psychology*. New York: Dover Publications, 1950.
> James masterfully places proprioception in the forefront of the analyses of emotions and personal identity in his classic examination of consciousness.

Jerome. "A Letter of Consolation." In *Select Letters of St. Jerome*. Translated by Frederick Adam Wright. Cambridge, Massachusetts: Harvard University Press, 1933.
> Borrows consolations that we should rejoice for the good we had, not grieve its loss; once finished, no difference remains between short and long lives. In other letters, Jerome admits to lengthy and incessant mourning for lost friends.

Johnson, Samuel. *Rasselas, Poems, and Selected Prose*. Edited by Bertrand H. Bronson. New York: Holt, Rinehart, and Winston, 1952.
> Johnson argues, contrary to the stoics, that patience requires real evils. He also shares insight on grief brought on by his mother's death.

Kamm, Frances Myrna. "Why Is Death Bad and Worse than Prenatal Non-Existence?" Pacific Philosophical Quarterly 69 (1988), pp. 161–164.
> Kamm's answer is that death is a decline.

Kübler-Ross, Elizabeth. *On Death and Dying*. New York: Collier Books, 1969.
> The best known presentation of the stages of grief.

———. *Living with Death and Dying*. New York: Collier Books, 1981.
> Despite her thesis that grief must complete its stages, she unfortunately offers several problematic evaluation consolations.

La Rochefoucauld, François, duc de. *Maxims*. Translated by Leonard Tancock. New York: Penguin Books, 1959.
> La Rochefoucauld's refreshingly cynical aphorisms include the sensible distinction between stalwartness and indifference toward evils. Against the consolation that suffering provides opportunity for virtue's exercise he rejoins that good fortune is a greater test of virtue than ill fortune!

Legge, James, trans. *The Texts of Taoism*. New York: Dover Publications, 1962.
> Chuang Tzu's ethics and consolations make an interesting comparison to stoicism. This work, the product of several hands, argues for impersonal indifference to death, but also advertises Taoism as an aid to longevity.

Le Shan, Eda J., and Paul Giovanopoulos. *Learning to Say Good-by: When a Parent Dies*. New York: Macmillan, 1976.
> Thoughtfully considers grief over a parent's death.

Leslie, John. "The Value of Time," *American Philosophical Quarterly* 13 (1976), pp. 109–121.
    Discusses the B-theory consolation that the past is as "real" as the present.

Lewis, Clarence Irving. *An Analysis of Knowledge and Valuation*, La Salle, Ill.: Open Court, 1946.
    One source of the concept of organic value.

Lewis, Clive Staples. *A Grief Observed*. New York: Bantam Books, 1963.
    In this little book on his reaction to his beloved wife's death, Lewis goes abruptly and inexplicably from inconsolable to accepting the loss.

Marcus Aurelius. *Meditations*. Translated by Martin Hammond. London: Penguin, 2006.
    Offers a host of consolations, advising that we "live in the present," and argues that the past, regardless how long, feels like a moment. Minimizes the difference between life and death by arguing that nothing persists through life.

Montaigne, Michel de. *Complete Essays*. Translated by Donald M. Frame. Stanford, Calif.: Stanford University Press, 1958.
    Montaigne borrows many consolations, including those from death's affinity to prenatal non-existence, and that life degenerates into mere repetition, and yet he also objects to grief that it is inadequate to represent death's immensity.

Moore, George Edward. *Principia Ethica*. Cambridge: Cambridge University Press, 1971.
    Moore emphasizes the concept of organic value.

More, Thomas. *A Dialogue of Comfort against Tribulation: Edited for Modern Readers with a Critical Introduction and Notes*. Edited by Leland Miles. Bloomington: Indiana University Press, 1965.
    God was More's source of comfort as he awaited execution in the Tower of London. Recommended as a supplement to the non-theistic consolations discussed in my dialogue.

Murphy, Jeffrie G. "Rationality and the Fear of Death," *Monist* 59 (1976), pp. 187–203.
    Although bad, death should not be feared for it is inevitable, Murphy argues.

Nagel, Thomas. "Death." In *Mortal Questions*. Cambridge: University Press, 1979.
    Fascinating essays include "Death" in which he opposes consolations based on annihilation, prenatal non-existence and death's inevitability.

Nussbaum, Martha. *The Fragility of Goodness: Luck and Ethics in Greek Tragedy and Philosophy*. Cambridge: Cambridge University Press, 1986.
    Nussbaum discusses the epistemic importance of emotions.

Ovid. *Metamorphoses*. Translated by Mary M. Innes. New York: Penguin Books, 1955.
    Aching for Rome during his interminable exile, Ovid recounts several stories in which immortality is a curse and grief has terrible consequences.

Parfit, Derek. *Reasons and Persons*. Oxford: Oxford University Press, 1984.
> Parfit provides first rate analyses of personal identity and temporal bias, and rejects the annihilation and prenatal non-existence consolations.

Parkes, Colin Murray. *Bereavement: Studies of Grief in Adult Life*. New York: International Universities Press, 1972.
> In my reading Parkes (with Weiss, next) offers the clearest, most thorough psychological analysis of grief.

———., and Robert Stuart Weiss. *Recovery from Bereavement*. New York: Basic Books, 1983.
> Provide poignant testimony by the bereaved on missing loved ones.

Perry, John, ed. *Personal Identity*. Berkeley: University of California Press, 1975.
> Topnotch collection of essays on reductionist analyses of personal identity.

Plato. "Axiochus"; "The Apology"; "The Republic." In *Complete Works*. Edited by John Madison Cooper and D. S. Hutchinson. Ind.: Hackett Publishing, 1997.
> Socrates compares annihilation favorably to life in "The Apology." "The Republic" criticizes theatrical tragedy as disposing us to grieve at real losses. The pseudo-Platonic "Axiochus" offers the annihilation consolation.

Plutarch. *Plutarch's Lives*. Edited by Arthur Hugh Clough. Translated by John Dryden. New York: Random House, 2001.
> Plutarch reports the laws on grieving established by the Spartan Lycurgus and the Roman Numa, and relates that Pyrrho and Alexander assuaged their grief with slaughter.

———. "A Letter of Condolence to Apollonius." In *Plutarch's Moralia*. Vol. 2. Translated by Frank Cole Babbitt. Cambridge, Mass.: Harvard University Press, 1928.
> A work spuriously attributed to Plutarch, the unknown author offers a wide variety of ancient consolations.

———. "On Tranquility of Mind." Translated by W.C. Helmbold. In *Plutarch's Moralia* 6:439–523B. Cambridge, Mass.: Harvard University Press, 1939.
> In this essay, negative emotions are discouraged.

———. *Plutarch's Moralia*. 7, 523c–612b. Translated by Phillip H. de Lacy and Benedict Einarson. Cambridge, Mass.: Harvard University Press, 1959.
> Plutarch coldly consoles his wife on their daughter's death. The conceptual difficulties of "deprivation evil" were never better illustrated than by his consolation that as the brevity of their daughter's life prevented her from conceiving of many of life's goods her deprivation could not be considered as great as those who died after attaining maturity.

———. *Plutarch's Moralia*. 13. Part 2 : 1033a–1086b. Translated by Harold Fredrik Cherniss. Cambridge, Massachusetts: Harvard University Press, 1976.
> Plutarch's criticisms of Stoicism extend to some of their consolations.

———. *Plutarch's Moralia*. 14. 1086c–1147a. Translated by Benedict Einarson and Phillip H. de Lacy. Cambridge, Mass.: Harvard University Press, 1967.
In this volume Plutarch criticizes Epicurean consolations.

Rorty, Amélie Oksenberg. "Fear of Death." In *Mind in Action*, Boston: Beacon Press, 1988.
Rorty discusses the annihilation consolation and the various uses of emotions, and three other insightful essays explore the concept of personal identity.

———, ed. *The Identities of Persons*. Berkeley: University of California Press, 1976.
Excellent articles on personal identity by David Lewis, Georges Rey, John Perry, Derek Parfit, Bernard Williams, and Terence Penelhum.

Rosenberg, Jay Frank. *Thinking Clearly about Death*. Englewood Cliffs, N.J.: Prentice Hall, 1983.
Rosenberg argues that annihilation is not dreadful and makes the prenatal non-existence comparison. He also argues that an immortal's character would be fixed and presents an interesting defense of bodily continuity as the criterion of personal identity.

Ruben, David-Hillel. "A Puzzle about Posthumous Predication," *The Philosophical Review* 97 (1988), pp. 211–236.
Ruben offers a good discussion on posthumous predication.

Russell, Bertrand. "A Free Man's Worship" "Seems Madam? Nay It Is" In *Why I Am Not a Christian*. New York: Simon and Schuster, 1957.
Russell finds comfort in the inevitability of universal extinction; argues that, through theatrical tragedy, human beings "triumph" over death by finding its aesthetic value. Argues persuasively that belief in a timeless immortality comforts only by equivocation with belief in temporal survival of death.

———."How to Grow Old." In *Portraits From Memory and Other Essays*, New York: Simon and Shuster, 1951.
In "How to Grow Old" (and many other writings) he states that death is less terrible to those with interests concerning things which will survive them.

Sayers, Brian. "Death As a Loss," *Faith and Philosophy* 4 (1987), pp. 149–159.
Sayers argues, contrary to one version of the annihilation consolation, that awareness of a loss is not necessary for a deprivation to be an evil.

Schopenhauer, Arthur. *The World as Will and Representation*. Translated by E. F. J. Payne. New York: Dover Publications, 1969.
Schopenhauer's fascinating but implausible philosophy borrows a host of ancient consolations ranging from annihilation to pessimism about life to the tedium of immortality. He adds to the comparison between death and dreamless sleep that just as one should not dread sleeping thousands of years one should not dread infinite sleep, that is, death!

———. *Essays and Aphorisms*. Selected and translated by R. J. Hollingdale. London: Penguin Books, 1970.
> Schopenhauer borrows the ancient argument that as others' deaths were necessary for our own existence we should accept our own mortality.

Seneca, Lucius Annaeus. *Ad Lucilium Epistulae Morales*, vol. 1. Translated by Richard Mott Gummere Cambridge, Mass.: Harvard University Press, 1917.
> Consolation was Seneca's most frequent literary concern and he offers most of the ancient consolations.

———. *Moral Essays*, vol. 2. Translated by John W. Basore. Cambridge, Mass.: Harvard University Press, 1932.
> Seneca argues that it is haughty to wish that oneself and loved ones were exempt from universal mortality.

———. *The Stoic Philosophy of Seneca: Essays and Letters of Seneca*. Edited by Moses Hadas. New York: Norton, 1958.
> More consolations. Most intriguing is the idea that life is of adequate length to those who do not plan on immortality. He means that we should not waste time hoarding goods we will never use, but the idea could be applied to wasteful "insurance policies" of an afterlife.

———. *Letters from a Stoic. Epistulae morales ad Lucilium*. Translated by Robin Campbell. Harmondsworth: Penguin Books, 1969.
> Letters 77, 78 and 91 continue Seneca's efforts to console.

———. *Naturales Quaestiones*. (Two Volumes) Translated by Thomas H. Corcoran. Cambridge, Mass., Harvard University Press, 1971.
> Primarily a physics book, Seneca, ever the moralizer, emphasizes death's universality and inevitability; offers the intriguing (but unsatisfactory) consolation that the passage of time deprives us of goods, so death is not an evil.

Shibles, Warren A. *Death: An Interdisciplinary Analysis*. Whitewater, Wisc.: The Language Press, 1974.
> Shibles astutely criticizes several consolations including those that death benefits us by "giving life meaning" and creating urgency.

Sophocles. "Electra"; "Oedipus at Colonus." In *The Complete Plays of Sophocles*. Edited by Moses Hadas. New York: Bantam Books, 1982.
> These plays include familiar themes regarding grief.

Voltaire. "Micromegas." In *The Portable Voltaire*. Edited by Ben Ray Redman. New York: Penguin Books, 1949.
> Voltaire uses science fiction to nicely state both sides of the consolation that immortality would be tedious. He imagines a creature with seventy-two senses and the same number of emotions who would nevertheless become bored; yet death would be dreadful even after living 15, 000 years.

Williams, Bernard Arthur Owen. *Problems of the Self: Philosophical Papers 1956–1972*. Cambridge: Cambridge University Press, 1973.
> Consoles that immortals' character would be fixed or change so drastically as to make them "different persons." Against consolers, argues that awareness of it is not necessary to have the loss; criticizes the view that death's prospect creates urgency. Includes interesting discussion regarding "categorical desires." Though I cannot completely agree, Williams brilliantly defends the view that bodily continuity is the basis of personal identity.

Wollheim, Richard. *The Thread of Life*. Cambridge, Mass.: Harvard University Press, 1984.
> This work is critical of some consolations.

Xenophon. *Conversations of Socrates*. Edited by Robin Waterfield. Translated by Robin Waterfield and Hugh Tredennick. New York: Penguin Books, 1990.
> On the day of his execution Socrates admonishes his friends for their weeping on the ground that they knew all along that he was mortal.

ABOUT THE AUTHOR

TERENCE O'CONNELL was born and raised in New York City. As an adolescent, O'Connell lost interest in his formal education and later enrolled in college only because his parents expected it of him despite his being the first in his family ever to attend. In his first college class, he learned the principle of logical form—that the validity of an argument depended on its formal structure—which spurred his longest held passion—philosophy.

He received his PhD in philosophy from the State University of New York at Buffalo. He taught a wide variety of philosophy courses before becoming an employee of the federal government.

Because of its relationship to other disciplines, O'Connell's interest in philosophy led to interests in many other fields, such as psychology and comparative religion. His research into Western and Eastern literature, and Western ancient, medieval, and modern philosophy prepared him to compose *Dialogue on Grief and Consolation* in response to his mother's death.

O'Connell left New York City for the beauty of northern California, where he has remained for love of the climate. He and his wife, Barbara, are raising their daughter, Sara Beth, who recently turned six.

Photography by Barbara Hollander

INDEX

To a great extent, this is an index of concepts instead of specific terms. The index refers the reader to the principal discussions of these concepts, but the listed term may not be found on every referenced page.

acceptance/resignation, 11
Annie Hall, 71
annihilation consolation, 41, 42, 44, 63, 135, 138, 140, 240, 246. *See also* consol(ation)(er)(s)
    a. c. criticized, 49, 64, 65, 260

Balder (Norse god), 230
bargaining, 11, 70
The Beatles, 41, 254
Buddhism, 160

cognitive dissonance, 225
comfort(ing) strategies, 30, 32, 33, 257
    sounds c., 45, 46, 165
concerns, personal, impersonal, and non-personal, 146–148
conditional value, 52–54, 65–66
consequentialism, 220–230
consol(ation)(er)(s), 1, 30. *See also* emotions
    annihilation c., 41, 42, 44, 63, 135, 138, 140, 246
    arbitrary c., 13, 15, 22
    death, c. over premature, 67–69, 89
    "Death prevented greater suffering," 17
    dreary c., 15, 16, 22, 71, 114, 121, 145, 155, 185, 186, 197, 213, 214, 260
    harmful, c. as, 213, 214
    "He didn't suffer," 21
    grievers, c. and, 13–15, 18–20, 22, 225, 262
    "It could be/have been worse," 14, 17
    response c., 28, 34, 36, 191
        evaluation c., r. c. compared with, 102, 103, 143, 149, 167
    "She had a full life," 24–28
    "She had a long life," 67, 69
    "She's no longer suffering," 13–18, 20, 21
    "She wouldn't want you to grieve," 156

    "There are greater evils," 14, 15, 21, 110
    "Think of the good things," 20, 24–27, 253
    "Time heals," 156, 218, 248, 249
    "Why me?" 187–190

dead, imagining being, 42, 45, 46, 183
death. *See also* life
    beneficial to others, d. as, 142, 143, 192–195
    continued existence, d. compared with, 144–152, 159
    cycle of life, d. and the, 195–197, 209
    deprivation, d. as, 11, 13, 17, 49, 65
    disbelief in eventual d., 1, 183
    egalitarian, d. as, 96, 186, 187
    inevitable, d. as 180, 182–185, 190, 248, 249, 251
    infinite or finite loss, d. as, 26, 67, 69, 70, 158
    loss of the past, d. as, 51
    parent, d. of a, 8, 78, 88, 110, 115
    part of nature, d. as, 98, 198, 202
    prenatal non-existence, d. contrasted with, 56–61, 66, 68, 69, 81, 95, 96, 108, 168
    rest or peace, d. as, 45, 46, 72
    universal, d. as, 185–190, 247
    urgency, d. and, 81–83, 85, 89
deliberation, based on death's inevitability, 180–182
denial, 9, 11, 219, 222
depression, 11
deprivation,
    awareness of d., 55, 65
    diametric evils, d. contrasted with, 49, 50, 65, 70
    good, d. of a conceivable, 25, 80, 89, 145, 146, 174, 182, 183
    whether survivors increase d., 112, 113
disembodied observer, 45, 46
disinterestedness, 106, 107

distraction, 20, 21, 32, 33

ego evaluation, 34, 78, 109–125
   e. e. and consolation drawn from personal identity, 152–156, 159
emotions
   dispositions, e. as magnetizing, 214, 215
   obligations, e. and fulfillment of, 200–202
   performance, e. and, 202–209
   physiology, e. and, 245
   salient, e. as, 218, 235, 236, 252, 255
   sense-perception, e. compared with, 202, 204–206, 240, 241, 243–252
   suppression, e. and, 3, 215–217, 229, 261
   e. inertia, 214, 234, 254
eternity, 173, 177
evaluation consolations, 28, 34, 35. *See also* consol(ation)(ers)
evaluating contrasted with deliberating, 18, 19
evil as privation, 203

grie(f)(ving), 30–32, 191
   adjustment, g. and, 4, 5, 154, 155, 217–219, 230, 258
   anger, g. and, 10, 11, 212, 213
   character, g. and, 212–214, 217, 258, 259
   conflicted g., 248
   conventional, g. as, 237, 238, 240, 248, 255
   delayed g., 248
   dependence, g. and, 114, 248, 251
   dreams, g. and, 161–163
   envy, g. and, 186, 189
   expectation, g. and, 187, 248, 249
   fear, g. and, 10, 251
   guilt, g. and, 10, 11, 34, 249, 251, 261, 262
   harmful/beneficial, g. as, 184, 185, 212–217, 258, 259
   inevitable, g. as, 5, 109
   knowledge, g. compared with, 222, 229, 233–255, 259
   reasoning, g. and, 1–5, 20, 21
   objects of g., 33, 34
   partial, g. as, 14, 15, 102, 103, 192, 197–210, 247–251
   phases of g., 10, 11
   selective, g. as, 24, 98, 99, 108, 115, 116, 125, 199, 205–207, 242, 258
   useless, g. as, 184, 209, 258
goods, irreplaceable, 115–117, 241, 242

ideas, under-described, 78, 206
immortality, 72–81, 83–89, 92, 101, 106, 111, 151. *See also* cycle of life *under* death
   fixity, i. and, 73–81, 89
The Incredible Shrinking Man, 169
inhibition, 31, 111–113, 124, 211, 242, 243, 253, 254

Kübler–Ross, Elizabeth, 3, 4

Lennon, John, 29, 30
Lewis, Clarence Irving, 38
life. *See also* death
   death makes l. possible, 96, 97, 99
   death makes l. unfinished, 24, 106, 107
   stages of l., interrelatedness of, 110–112, 155
      milestones, stages of l. and, 110–112, 124
   l.-story, death wrests control of ones, 107
   narrative structure, l. and, 100, 101
"Life is short, days long," 71, 72, 90

The Mamas and the Papas, 254
mimicking, 156, 157, 191

Nietzsche, Friedrich, 117

obsession, 41, 219

Parkes and Weiss, 3, 4
Paths of Glory, 212
Paul McCartney and Wings, 109
perseverance, 118–123, 125
   faith and p., 119
personal identity, 25, 28, 98, 127–134, 160. *See also* ego evaluation
   consolations, p. i. as a basis for presenting, 135–137, 144–147
   discussion of these consolations, 137–143, 147–152, 157–159
philosophizing as therapy, 5, 21, 38, 259, 261

Plato, 145
posthumous predicates, 62, 65

regret, 8
revisionism, 18–20
Russell, Bertrand, 162, 163

Saturday Night Live, 19
self–deception, 222, 223
The Self-Tormentor (Terence), 156
Seneca, 2
Simon and Garfunkel, 11
smokers fallacy, 87, 90, 117, 118, 121, 122, 215, 216, 236
sorrow, 31, 211, 242, 243, 255
suicide, 54, 56, 63, 104, 223
sympathy, 32, 152
   s.evaluation, 34

Tacitus, 45
temporal bias, 26, 27, 58, 59, 61, 88, 89, 93
   A–theory, t. b. and, 170, 171, 176
Terence, 156
   The Self-Tormentor, 156

Three Dog Night, 127
theatrical tragedy, 108
time, A-/B-/M-theor(ies)(y) of, 163, 164, 172, 174–176
   B-t. consolations, 164–169, 176

uniqueness, individual, 95, 99, 108, 193

value
   consequential/intrinsic v., 36, 37, 39, 102, 117
      consequential and intrinsic v. confused, 102, 103
   v. direction, 92–95, 108
   v. of/ for, 99, 100, 102–107
   organic v., 37, 38, 91
   v. for a person, 43, 44, 46, 57, 62–65, 105, 123, 124, 141, 143, 258, 260
virtue. *See also* perseverance
   death, v. tested by, 117, 125
   heroic death, v. of, 102–104
   magnitude of v., 103, 104

VIBS

The **Value Inquiry Book Series** is co-sponsored by:

Adler School of Professional Psychology
American Indian Philosophy Association
American Maritain Association
American Society for Value Inquiry
Association for Process Philosophy of Education
Canadian Society for Philosophical Practice
Center for Bioethics, University of Turku
Center for Professional and Applied Ethics, University of North Carolina at Charlotte
Central European Pragmatist Forum
Centre for Applied Ethics, Hong Kong Baptist University
Centre for Cultural Research, Aarhus University
Centre for Professional Ethics, University of Central Lancashire
Centre for the Study of Philosophy and Religion, University College of Cape Breton
Centro de Estudos em Filosofia Americana, Brazil
College of Education and Allied Professions, Bowling Green State University
College of Liberal Arts, Rochester Institute of Technology
Concerned Philosophers for Peace
Conference of Philosophical Societies
Department of Moral and Social Philosophy, University of Helsinki
Gannon University
Gilson Society
Haitian Studies Association
Ikeda University
Institute of Philosophy of the High Council of Scientific Research, Spain
International Academy of Philosophy of the Principality of Liechtenstein
International Association of Bioethics
International Center for the Arts, Humanities, and Value Inquiry
International Society for Universal Dialogue
Natural Law Society
Philosophical Society of Finland
Philosophy Born of Struggle Association
Philosophy Seminar, University of Mainz
Pragmatism Archive at The Oklahoma State University
R.S. Hartman Institute for Formal and Applied Axiology
Research Institute, Lakeridge Health Corporation
Russian Philosophical Society
Society for Existential Analysis
Society for Iberian and Latin-American Thought
Society for the Philosophic Study of Genocide and the Holocaust
Unit for Research in Cognitive Neuroscience, Autonomous University of Barcelona
Whitehead Research Project
Yves R. Simon Institute

Titles Published

Volumes 1 - 171 see www.rodopi.nl

172. Charles C. Hinkley II, *Moral Conflicts of Organ Retrieval: A Case for Constructive Pluralism.* A volume in **Values in Bioethics**

173. Gábor Forrai and George Kampis, Editors, *Intentionality: Past and Future.* A volume in **Cognitive Science**

174. Dixie Lee Harris, *Encounters in My Travels: Thoughts Along the Way.* A volume in **Lived Values:Valued Lives**

175. Lynda Burns, Editor, *Feminist Alliances.* A volume in **Philosophy and Women**

176. George Allan and Malcolm D. Evans, *A Different Three Rs for Education.* A volume in **Philosophy of Education**

177. Robert A. Delfino, Editor, *What are We to Understand Gracia to Mean?: Realist Challenges to Metaphysical Neutralism.* A volume in **Gilson Studies**

178. Constantin V. Ponomareff and Kenneth A. Bryson, *The Curve of the Sacred: An Exploration of Human Spirituality.* A volume in **Philosophy and Religion**

179. John Ryder, Gert Rüdiger Wegmarshaus, Editors, *Education for a Democratic Society: Central European Pragmatist Forum, Volume Three.* A volume in **Studies in Pragmatism and Values**

180. Florencia Luna, *Bioethics and Vulnerability: A Latin American View.* A volume in **Values in Bioethics**

181. John Kultgen and Mary Lenzi, Editors, *Problems for Democracy.* A volume in **Philosophy of Peace**

182. David Boersema and Katy Gray Brown, Editors, *Spiritual and Political Dimensions of Nonviolence and Peace.* A volume in **Philosophy of Peace**

183. Daniel P. Thero, *Understanding Moral Weakness.* A volume in **Studies in the History of Western Philosophy**

184. Scott Gelfand and John R. Shook, Editors, *Ectogenesis: Artificial Womb Technology and the Future of Human Reproduction.* A volume in **Values in Bioethics**

185. Piotr Jaroszyński, *Science in Culture.* A volume in **Gilson Studies**

186. Matti Häyry, Tuija Takala, Peter Herissone-Kelly, Editors, *Ethics in Biomedical Research: International Perspectives.* A volume in **Values in Bioethics**

187. Michael Krausz, *Interpretation and Transformation: Explorations in Art and the Self.* A volume in **Interpretation and Translation**

188. Gail M. Presbey, Editor, *Philosophical Perspectives on the "War on Terrorism."* A volume in **Philosophy of Peace**

189. María Luisa Femenías, Amy A. Oliver, Editors, *Feminist Philosophy in Latin America and Spain.* A volume in **Philosophy in Latin America**

190. Oscar Vilarroya and Francesc Forn I Argimon, Editors, *Social Brain Matters: Stances on the Neurobiology of Social Cognition.* A volume in **Cognitive Science**

191. Eugenio Garin, *History of Italian Philosophy.* Translated from Italian and Edited by Giorgio Pinton. A volume in **Values in Italian Philosophy**

192. Michael Taylor, Helmut Schreier, and Paulo Ghiraldelli, Jr., Editors, *Pragmatism, Education, and Children: International Philosophical Perspectives.* A volume in **Pragmatism and Values**

193. Brendan Sweetman, *The Vision of Gabriel Marcel: Epistemology, Human Person, the Transcendent.* A volume in **Philosophy and Religion**

194. Danielle Poe and Eddy Souffrant, Editors, *Parceling the Globe: Philosophical Explorations in Globalization, Global Behavior, and Peace.* A volume in **Philosophy of Peace**

195. Josef Šmajs, *Evolutionary Ontology: Reclaiming the Value of Nature by Transforming Culture.* A volume in **Central-European Value Studies**

196. Giuseppe Vicari, *Beyond Conceptual Dualism: Ontology of Consciousness, Mental Causation, and Holism in John R. Searle's Philosophy of Mind.* A volume in **Cognitive Science**

197. Avi Sagi, *Tradition vs. Traditionalism: Contemporary Perspectives in Jewish Thought*. Translated from Hebrew by Batya Stein. A volume in **Philosophy and Religion**

198. Randall E. Osborne and Paul Kriese, Editors, *Global Community: Global Security*. A volume in **Studies in Jurisprudence**

199. Craig Clifford, *Learned Ignorance in the Medicine Bow Mountains: A Reflection on Intellectual Prejudice*. A volume in **Lived Values: Valued Lives**

200. Mark Letteri, *Heidegger and the Question of Psychology: Zollikon and Beyond*. A volume in **Philosophy and Psychology**

201. Carmen R. Lugo-Lugo and Mary K. Bloodsworth-Lugo, Editors, *A New Kind of Containment: "The War on Terror," Race, and Sexuality*. A volume in **Philosophy of Peace**

202. Amihud Gilead, *Necessity and Truthful Fictions: Panenmentalist Observations*. A volume in **Philosophy and Psychology**

203. Fernand Vial, *The Unconscious in Philosophy, and French and European Literature: Nineteenth and Early Twentieth Century*. A volume in **Philosophy and Psychology**

204. Adam C. Scarfe, Editor, *The Adventure of Education: Process Philosophers on Learning, Teaching, and Research*. A volume in **Philosophy of Education**

205. King-Tak Ip, Editor, *Environmental Ethics: Intercultural Perspectives*. A volume in **Studies in Applied Ethics**

206. Evgenia Cherkasova, *Dostoevsky and Kant: Dialogues on Ethics*. A volume in **Social Philosophy**

207. Alexander Kremer and John Ryder, Editors, *Self and Society: Central European Pragmatist Forum*, Volume Four. A volume in **Central European Value Studies**

208. Terence O'Connell, *Dialogue on Grief and Consolation*. A volume in **Lived Values, Valued Lives**

www.ingramcontent.com/pod-product-compliance
Lightning Source LLC
Chambersburg PA
CBHW030108010526
44116CB00005B/144